CROSSING BOUNDARIES IN GRAPHIC NARRATIVE

CROSSING BOUNDARIES IN GRAPHIC NARRATIVE

Essays on Forms, Series and Genres

Edited by JAKE JAKAITIS *and*
JAMES F. WURTZ

McFarland & Company, Inc., Publishers
Jefferson, North Carolina, and London

LIBRARY OF CONGRESS CATALOGUING-IN-PUBLICATION DATA

Crossing boundaries in graphic narrative : essays on forms,
series and genres / edited by Jake Jakaitis and James F. Wurtz.
p.   cm.
Includes bibliographical references and index.

ISBN 978-0-7864-6663-4
softcover : acid free paper ∞

1. Comic books, strips, etc.— History and criticism.
I. Jakaitis, Jake.   II. Wurtz, James F.
PN6710.C76 2012   741.5'9 — dc23   2012000534

BRITISH LIBRARY CATALOGUING DATA ARE AVAILABLE

Front cover: American comic strip *Krazy Cat,* created by
cartoonist George Herriman; cover design by
David K. Landis (Shake It Loose Graphics)

Manufactured in the United States of America

*McFarland & Company, Inc., Publishers
Box 611, Jefferson, North Carolina 28640
www.mcfarlandpub.com*

Table of Contents

Introduction: Reading Crossover

JAKE JAKAITIS *and* JAMES F. WURTZ

Relatively speaking, the scholarship of comics is a nascent field, and the idea that graphic narrative is an important literary form worthy of study at the highest levels is still capable of engendering debate. Recent years have seen comics scholarship emerge into wider scholarly contexts, with dedicated panels at the MLA conference, a special issue of *Modern Fiction Studies*, and essays in *PMLA*, all of which ask whether comics can be considered literature. *Time Magazine*'s inclusion of Alan Moore and David Gibbons' *Watchmen* in its list of the one hundred best English-language novels from 1923 to the present further evidences the extent of this debate. The increasing volume of scholarship, including the monographs and collections published by scholarly and commercial presses, speaks rather convincingly to an affirmative answer to the question. In this collection of essays, we go beyond this notion to consider literary approaches to graphic narrative and sequential art. In particular, we examine the politics of comic form and narrative, the ways in which graphic narrative and sequential art "cross over" into other forms and genres, and how these articulations challenge the ways that we have learned to read and interpret texts. This volume brings various types of literary theory to bear on graphic narrative and balances readings of individual texts with larger ideas about comics and comics scholarship as a whole. In that sense, it is not simply a collection of essays on individual works, nor is it an overview of graphic narrative arguing that "comics are literature," but it is a careful reading of the ways in which graphic narratives achieve political effects through their crossovers.

This collection acknowledges that the comics medium challenges the ways in which we read and questions conventional notions of genre and readership. The fundamental struggle at play in the form is revealed in one of the recurrent debates: what, exactly, to call it? In the controversy over naming, "graphic novel" emphasizes the textual; in its reference to an established literary form it foregrounds the words. "Sequential art," on the other hand, emphasizes the image and implies that, like Egyptian hieroglyphs or the Bayeux Tapestry, meaning is found primarily in the arranged order of the pictures. Various

1

writers and thinkers have been attached to these terms. For instance, Will Eisner, who is often considered the father of the graphic novel, introduces the term "sequential art" in his influential 1985 book *Comics and Sequential Art*. However, what is most interesting to us about this debate is that the name generally denotes the approach taken towards analyzing the literature. For this reason, Scott McCloud, whose *Understanding Comics* remains a touchstone text for the study of graphic narrative and sequential art, uses the term "comics" and defines it broadly. However, we cannot dissociate "comics" from its contexts, and all too often the medium suggests a juvenile readership and a black-and-white worldview. While this volume does not focus on the appropriate name for the genre, the question of whether images or words are predominant implied in the question of what to call it misses the unique synergy among the various narrative registers and the reader. Aaron Meskin's recent definition of comics as "a hybrid art form that evolved from literature and a number of other art forms and media" also evokes this synergy, once more suggesting that crossover is central to the medium (219).

The idea of "crossover" is essential to understanding this genre: graphic narrative functions most effectively precisely through many of its points of intersection. At its most basic level, the connections and disjunctions between image and word drive the text, guiding the reader's eye from panel to panel to comprehend the story. Graphic narrative, however, frequently engages in multiple acts of crossing over, between different genres, different forms, different linguistic registers, different types of art, and different storylines and character "universes." Traditionally in the comics medium, crossover has referenced a single story arc effected across multiple titles or the appearance of one character in another character's series or universe. The commercial benefits to publishers like Marvel or DC are obvious. Readers who typically purchased only a few titles through crossover story arcs would purchase additional titles to remain current with content that often effected material changes in the DC or Marvel universe. While the conventional definition of "crossover" applies exclusively to these extended story arcs, the medium has always also participated in the more complex and engaging conceptual crossovers discussed in this collection, linking the comics medium to the cinema, the literary, and the political.

Some relatively recent crossovers seem "natural" to the medium: Marvel's *Spiderman*, *X-Men*, *Hulk*, and *Iron Man* films, the company's revival of *Classics Illustrated* and its presentation of Stephen King's *Dark Tower* and *The Stand*, and Orson Scott Card's *Ender's Game*, for example. Visual crossovers also adapt films and television shows to the comics medium. Dark Horse adaptations of *Firefly*, its long-running series of *Star Wars* and *Buffy the Vampire Slayer* comics, and Boom! Studio adaptations of SyFy Channel shows like *Farscape* and *Eureka* appeal to comics readers already familiar with science fiction content and plots through their engagement with superhero comics. Graphic novel adaptations of literary works, of course, have appeared for some time although, except for the *Classics Illustrated* publications, most of these have adapted popular genres like science fiction to the graphic novel medium. DC's late 1980s adaptations of Hugo and Nebula Award winning works like Frederik Pohl's *The Merchants of Venice* (1986) and George R.R. Martin's *Sandkings* (1987), its three book adaptation of Roger Zelazny's *Nine Princes in Amber* (1996), and its presentation of Harlan Ellison's *Dream Corridor* anthology series (1995–96) are representative examples. Just as Ellison participated in adaptation of his work for

Dream Corridor, even writing and designing the interstitial framing sequences that link the stories, Ray Bradbury has authorized and written the introduction to Tim Hamilton's 2009 graphic novel of *Fahrenheit 451*.

While these and similar adaptations of popular culture literary works traditionally have effected visual crossovers by balancing image and word and adhering to the implicit industry standard of a maximum of one hundred and fifty words on any single page, others have pushed that limit, experimenting with literal transcription of novels enhanced by sequential art. The most dramatic example is Boom! Studios' in-progress twenty-four issue adaptation of Philip K. Dick's *Do Androids Dream of Electric Sheep* (June 2009).[1] Tony Parker's art, the lettering by Richard Starkings and Jimmy Betancourt, and the colors by Blond collaborate to produce a visually engaging text. However, the series, which reproduces the complete text of Philip K. Dick's novel, is more effective at validating the necessity of limiting the number of word per page in a graphic novel than it is at re-creating or enhancing the experience of Dick's work. The characters' speech is represented in the traditional dialogue balloons, while the internal monologues clutter the frames in peach or blue boxes and the narration appears against the backdrops of walls or open spaces, stealing the function of visual art. The project seems to have lost sense of the function of sequential art to convey visually what in other contexts is conveyed through language that itself provokes visuals. Boom! Studios' ambitious adaptation of *Do Androids Dream of Electric Sheep*, then, both is the logical outgrowth of developing trends in visual crossover and tests the limits of graphic narrative and sequential art. By way of contrast, Marvel's much more successful five issue adaptation of Dick's "Electric Ant" (June–August 2010) relies on a script by David Mack and art by Pascal Alixe to re-present Dick's short story, updating and altering the plot but maintaining the spirit of the original text. By relying on scriptwriter and artist collaboration to produce the visual text, Marvel acknowledges both the strengths and limits of graphic narrative while effecting a crossover coincident with traditional and recent developments in the comics industry.

These recent developments to some extent are implied in Michael Chabon's Pulitzer winning *The Adventures of Kavalier and Clay* (2000) and the author's follow-up comic series, *The Escapist* (2004). Chabon's emphasis on visual crossover and on graphic narrative as adult fare can be seen through a brief address to a few signature moments in his novel. As they prepare to present to Shelly Anapol, the owner of Empire Comics, their plan to encourage an adult audience for comics, Joe Kavalier and Sam Clay debate the status of the medium. Clay argues that "Comic books actually are inferior" (363), but Kavalier, drawing on their recent encounter with Orson Welles, declares that in "its inextricable braiding of image and narrative — *Citizen Kane* was like a comic book" (362). He further explains that comics must move beyond "somehow adapting the cinematic bag of tricks" employed by films to "the total blending of narration and image ... that was the fundamental principle of comic book storytelling" (362). For Kavalier, this was how Welles and *Citizen Kane* transcended mere cinema and achieved the "full collaboration of writer and artist" (369) available through sequential art. These moments in Chabon's novel, among many others, promote the idea of crossover central to this volume while implicitly revealing intersections of the cinematic, literary and political as historically central to graphic narrative and sequential art.

While Chabon's novel emphasizes the cinematic and literary over the political, Art Spiegelman's Pulitzer winning graphic novel, *Maus* (1986; 1991), among other works, seems to have popularized aggressively politicized graphic narrative and culture crossovers that previously appealed only to rather small audiences like the readers of Will Eisner's *New York: The Big City* (1981). Collectively, the texts discussed have generated academic interest in the politics of sequential art and graphic narrative. By looking at the "crossovers" that graphic narrative, in its many guises, participates in, this volume examines how graphic narrative challenges the way we read, how we understand the form itself, and how it engages political culture.

We demonstrate the centrality of the "crossover" to graphic narrative by reading two quite different texts: Marvel's recent *Civil War* series, which brings characters from different Marvel comics together in a story arc that clearly responds to post-9/11 American politics, and *Charley's War*, a newly reissued series that follows a boy's experiences in the British army during the first world war. Among the "crossovers" in *Charley's War* are the tension between art and words, the interrelationship of history and fiction, the reception of the narrative as a weekly strip in a British boy's comic magazine as opposed to the new, finely bound "graphic novels," and the work's relevance as an historical document vis-à-vis the timeliness of the present moment (Vietnam/Falklands war vs. Iraq/Afghanistan). Marvel's *Civil War*, though structurally a traditional crossover story arc designed to alter the Marvel Universe and generate a steady stream of new series, directly engages the politics of post-9/11 America through its Superhero Registration Act. The event that generates government regulation of superheroes parallels the terrorist attack on the Twin Towers, while the Superhero Registration Act parallels the Patriot Act and calls into question the patriotism and loyalty of Marvel's heroes. Clearly, *Civil War* critiques the landscape of post-9/11 America and crosses over into political culture.[2]

This Marvel event is an exemplary combination of the commercial interests driving traditional crossovers and the implicit political and social criticism informing comics culture at least since the original Human Torch, Jim Hammond, Prince Namor the Sub-Mariner, and Captain America joined forces to combat the Axis powers in Europe and the Pacific in comics of the 1940s. Including a few *Black Panther* issues that present related plot material but are not officially considered *Civil War* tie-ins, the Marvel event encompasses one hundred and seven individual comics spanning no fewer than twenty-three Marvel titles in addition to the *Civil War* (May 2006-Febuary 2007) and *Front Line* (August 2006-April 2007) stand-alone series.[3] While one can follow the broad crossover plot by reading *The New Avengers: Illuminati* one-shot (May 2006), the seven issues of *Civil War*, and the eleven issues of *Front Line*, each of these texts references events that can only be fully understood through an engagement with multiple additional Marvel titles. Readers invested in the crossover, then, feel compelled to purchase titles beyond those coincident with their typical reading habits. The commercial effects of the crossover extend beyond the event itself, for the civil war impacts the entire Marvel Universe, effecting changes in multiple titles and inspiring readers who have not followed the crossover to purchase the *Civil War* and *Front Line* trade paperbacks in order to remain current with events and politicized conflicts in their favorite Marvel titles.

In a Newsarama interview posted shortly after publication of *Civil War #7* (January

2007), Mark Millar acknowledged the presence of "political allegory" in *Civil War*, evoking issues central to the debate over the Patriot Act by declaring the crossover "a story where a guy wrapped in the American Flag is in chains as the people swap freedom for security." However, Millar also states that the series is really just about superheroes in conflict and that most young readers would see only that emphasis while the politically astute would read it for its implicit commentary on current events.[4] Despite this disclaimer, *Civil War*'s principal conflicts in both Millar's and Jenkins's texts and in the crossovers to other Marvel titles are more about trading freedom for security and about corporate power and a secretive and deceptive government than about superhero conflict. An overview of the event, focusing principally on *The Road to Civil War*[5] trade paperback and the *Civil War* and *Front Line* series, reveals how Millar's and Jenkins's overtly political content crosses over to commentary on political culture and current events.

Marvel's Civil War event begins in *The New Avengers: Illuminati* one-shot when Iron Man calls a meeting of superheroes in Wakanda, Africa, to discuss tensions building in Washington, D.C., following a devastating war fought between two alien races, the Kree and the Skrull. Since members of the superhero community knew of the presence of one or the other of the alien races but failed to share information or collaborate to stop the war, Washington and the public are becoming impatient with the freedoms afforded vigilantes, and forces interested in superhero registration legislation are gaining power. Iron Man calls for a single organization encompassing "The X-Men, The Avengers, The Inhumans, The Fantastic Four, everyone else." He suggests that "Instead of these little factions of heroes and mutants ... running around doing the best they can," they could "pool all of [their] resources and all of [their] information and do it right" (Grünwald 3). Prince Namor, the Sub-Mariner, is the first to object, followed by King T'Challa, the Black Panther. Both see the difficulty of managing so large a group of previously independent superheroes; both also understand that Iron Man has implicitly identified himself as the probable leader of the proposed group. When Iron Man argues that by banding together, superheroes could protect and improve the world, Namor's reply provokes associations with post-9/11 America, associations enhanced by the text's bold print: "How many convicted **criminals** and supposed ex-mutant **terrorists** do you have on the Avengers **right now**?" (Grünwald 5). However, even Namor concedes to form the group once they agree to psychic surveillance by Charles Xavier, leader of the mutants, to prevent any member from revealing the secrets of any of the others. Only T'Challa questions the ethics of their declaring themselves the planet's protectors, refuses to make the vote unanimous, and asks them to leave his country. The meeting establishes the tensions over leadership, security, and privacy that will lead to civil war and extend the crossover to more than one hundred comics encompassing the entire Marvel Universe.

These tensions accelerate when Bruce Banner loses control as the Hulk and destroys Las Vegas, leading Tony Stark and Reed Richards to devise a plan to lure Banner to a failing satellite and blast him into space, presumably exiling him forever. Stark and Richards justify their plan through Professor Xavier's probing of Banner's mind to discovery that Banner would have killed himself long ago if he could have done so. Sacrificing privacy — even at the level of the individual mind — for security becomes a motif in Marvel's Civil War, echoing the surveillance of American citizens justified by The Patriot Act.

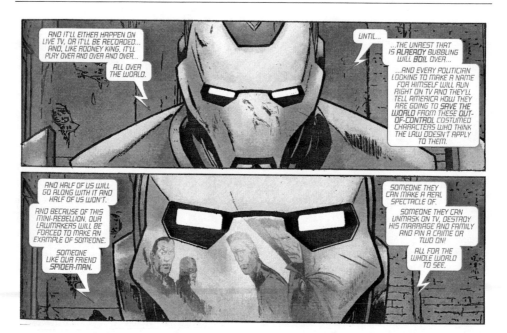

Iron Man's comments recall the televised images of airliners destroying the World Trade Center (*The Road to Civil War* 33).

Essentially, the Civil War begins here when Namor refuses to comply and battles Stark as Iron Man in an attempt to prevent the Hulk's exile. Doctor Strange uses his mystical powers to separate the combatants and Namor ultimately exiles himself to Atlantis after Iron Man urges the New Avengers and all superheroes to "voluntarily support and obey" (Grünwald 27) the impending superhero registration legislation. Iron Man's rationale, depicted in two consecutive panels, again firmly situates this Marvel crossover in Post-9/11 America, implicitly critiques the motivations of politicians in response to national crises, and establishes the conditions for superhero allegiances that subvert the expectations of regular Marvel readers.

Despite Iron Man's specific reference to Rodney King, we cannot help but recall the image of airliners destroying the World Trade Center when the superhero notes that an anticipated tragic event will be televised "over and over … all over the world." His comments on politicians and on the likely conflicting allegiances of superheroes lay the groundwork for the extended crossover, and his reference to Spider-Man prepares us for that rebellious character's manipulation by Iron Man and initial compliance with the Superhero Registration Act, just as the Hulk's exile prepared us for Reed Richards and Tony Stark's inter-dimensional superhero prison, the crossover's Guantanamo substitute. As the *New Avengers: Illuminati* episode of *The Road to Civil War* ends, Doctor Strange rejects Iron Man's plea, calling it "giving in to other people's ignorance and fears" (Grünwald 31), Namor returns to Atlantis, T'Challa remains isolationist in Wakanda, and the New Avengers have disbanded, leaving Iron Man and Reed Richards to devise a response to the impending legislation.

The Amazing Spider-Man #529–531, comprising the final three episodes of *The Road to Civil War*, validates manipulation of Congress and the public as crucial to the nation's best interest. Called to Washington to testify before the Senate Metahuman Investigations Committee (SMIT), Tony Stark recruits Peter Parker as his protégé, appealing to his patriotism and trust and insisting that Parker reveal none of Stark's activities to other superheroes, including Steve Rodgers. Ironically, Stark lures Parker to the SMIT hearings as part of an elaborate plot to delay passing of a Superhero Registration Act, thereby betraying Parker's trust. Unknown to Parker (and to the reader) Stark has hired the Titanium Man for a fake assassination attempt on himself as Parker and Stark exit the hearings. As Spider-Man, Parker intercedes, battling the Titanium Man against the backdrop of national monuments on the Mall. He pauses before the Gettysburg Address and is moved by Lincoln's words. Once the Titanium Man flees, Stark and Parker return to the Lincoln Memorial where Stark expresses his admiration for Lincoln and his belief that Lincoln adopted a stance that he knew would lead to civil war because that fight was necessary to maintain the republic and restore the nation (Grünwald 45–46). While Stark's motives seem pure, his actions justify the concerns expressed by Namor early in *The Road to Civil War*, for he unilaterally decides what is best for the country and his fellow superheroes and betrays both the public trust and that of his young protégé, whom he will ultimately convince to unmask before the nation, by hiring a Russian assassin to fake an attempt on his life, then denies his complicity in the event while standing before the Lincoln Memorial. Stark's efforts fail, however, once Speedball and the New Warriors precipitate the televised event anticipated in Iron Man's appeal to the New Avengers by provoking Nitro, a villain capable of generating an atomic blast, into destroying a Stamford, Connecticut, neighborhood and elementary school, an event revealed to Parker as he watches the evening news in the final moment of the volume. *The Road to Civil War* establishes the conflict between personal freedom and security, between the public's right to know and the relation of privileged information to national security, and between democratically elected leadership and corporate power as functioning oppositions in post-9/11 America.

While the political critique of *The Road to Civil War* is largely implicit, enacted through indirect reference and events parallel but not identical to the 9/11 attack on the World Trade Center and its aftermath, Paul Jenkins's *Front Line* overtly states the crossover between contemporary political issues and the Marvel event through the interaction of two reporters, Ben Urich, who works for Jonah Jameson's conservative, if not reactionary *The Daily Bugle*, and Sally Floyd, employed by *The Alternative*, a progressive publication. *Front Line* is actually an anthology series, each of the eleven issues containing chapters developing "The Embedded," following Urich and Floyd; "The Accused," covering Speedball, the only New Warrior to survive the Stamford, Connecticut, event; and, in issues three through nine, "Sleeper Cell," depicting covert operations by Atlanteans posing as humans. Except for the final two issues, each *Front Line* installment ends with a postscript depicting an historical moment of civil strife. Unlike *The Road to Civil War* and *Civil War*, which conform to Millar's Newsarama comments and focus primarily on superhero conflict while only indirectly effecting political critique, Jenkins's script overtly historicizes and critiques political and cultural inducements to civil strife while drawing parallels to post-9/11 stressors. It is no accident, for example, that Jenkins ends *Front Line #1* with a poem written by a Japanese internee at the Poston War Relocation Camp, juxtaposing

Poston images with those of Spider-Man telephoning Mary Jane as he tries to come to a decision about the Superhero Registration Act. The postscript ends with a Japanese-American father and family entering the camp and explaining that they must do so "Because it is our **duty**. Because we are Americans," while Spider-Man stares up at the Statue of Liberty saying, "with great power, huh?" (32). Other issues juxtapose images of World War I Doughboys unsuccessfully attempting to revive a comrade with contemporary firefighters failing to revive a citizen injured during a superhero conflict, or Billy Joel's "Goodnight Saigon" asking who was wrong and who was right with images of marines invading a Vietnam village and S.H.I.E.L.D. agents capturing resistant superheroes (*Front Line #4* 28–32). Although these and other postscripts to *Front Line* issues question the imprisoning of citizens or critique military solutions to civil strife, they also tend to promote ambiguity rather than sustain any clearly defined positions.

Millar refers to the ambiguity governing the entire crossover in his Newsarama interview when he responds to arguments by some that the pro-registration group is undermined and to those presented by others that the anti-registration group is unfavorably depicted by saying that Stark's group "gets the better rep" in *Civil War* and "the tie-in books demonized them a little." On the surface, this is an accurate assessment, but the ambiguity can be resolved through a look at the trajectories of Ben Urich and Sally Floyd in the *Front Line* "tie-in" and of Iron Man and Captain America in *Civil War*. *Front Line #1* begins with the funeral of John Fernandez, a journalist killed in Stamford, followed by a barroom conversation between Sally Floyd and Ben Urich about the Superhero Registration Act and their respective assignments. *The Alternative* has assigned Floyd to cover "the erosion of civil liberties in America" linked "to the wiretapping thing," while Jameson has charged Urich to "shove [Stamford] so far up the liberals' keisters they think the Wednesday sports page is the Sunday edition" (4). Echoing the concerns of *The Road to Civil War*, but referencing them through post-9/11 tensions, Floyd thinks, "This was civil liberty versus civil comfort; wiretapping versus terrorism; Fox versus CNN" as she drives home from the bar (5).

While Floyd's and Urich's views are not governed entirely by the perspectives of their respective publications, they do represent opposing political positions early in the series. Their coming together by the end of the series, when they join forces to produce frontline.com, enacts a choice that resolves the apparent ambiguity governing the crossover. As Sally sits in their tiny office, working at her computer, her back to Urich, he contemplates how she has changed and views with "pride" the liberal's "newfound objectivity" (20). Urich's views, although not as reactionary as Jonah Jameson's, become clear when Jameson fires him for insisting on writing a story exposing Iron Man's use of criminals like the Green Goblin as S.H.I.E.L.D. agents. Urich replies, "What's next, we refuse to publish an editorial cartoon in case we offend a terrorist?" (*Front Line #5* 9). Urich, neither far right nor far left, ultimately disabuses Floyd of her liberal notions, but he needs help.

When Urich is fired in *Front Line #5*, Floyd and her editor, Neil Crawford are arrested for "conspiracy to commit terrorist acts and harboring the identity of an unregistered combatant" (12). Incarcerated at a Guantanamo-like facility, Floyd is interrogated by the arresting agent, Eric Marshall, whom she had previously met when he tried to hit on her at a press corps Christmas party. He, of course, does not remember her. None of this serves to disabuse Floyd of her liberal values. In *Front Line #7,* her civil rights denied, Floyd blames the Superhero Registration Act and "the seeding of paranoia and the fostering of mistrust that only a police state like the Soviet Union could perfect" for the ongoing civil strife (6). At her lowest point, she puts her head down and cries, thinking that she needs a drink. The recovering alcoholic becomes a recovering liberal through the intervention of Congressman Sykes, sponsor of the Registration Act.

Sykes visits Floyd in her cell, hands her an envelope that she may open only when he gives her the OK, and attempts to convince her that the Registration Act is fair and that he is a patriot. When he tells her that he spent three tours of duty in Vietnam, was wounded and captured, spending two years in a POW camp, and has vowed to protect the freedom of speech that he was denied as a POW, she accuses him of trying to trick her. At that point, Sykes tells her to open the envelope, which contains a piece of paper saying, "You will accuse me of trying to trick you" (10). Converted by this moment, Floyd later secretly meets with Captain America in *Front Line #9.* She cuts her meeting with him short after lecturing him on being "duty bound to defend the rule of law, even if it means defending something you don't personally agree with.... Because the alternative means civil war" (2). Floyd's conversion is complete, and we are urged to take the establishment side in the civil war, shedding any residual liberalism and trading some of our freedoms for security. Floyd's newfound disdain for Captain America's defense of constitutional rights when threatened by terrorist activity lays bare the commercially driven political critique sustaining Marvel's crossover event. While the pro- and anti-registration elements are said by Millar to be given relatively equal representation across multiple titles, moderate political values appealing to a broad readership are finally validated by the events that close both *Civil War* and *Front Line.* This is apparent in the disparity between Floyd's and Tony Stark's positions on constitutional rights and civil war. While Congressman Sykes has converted Floyd to the establishment side, seemingly aligning her with Starks, her comments to Captain America urge him to sacrifice his principles in order to avoid civil strife. Stark before the Lincoln Memorial urged Peter Parker to understand that civil war is sometimes necessary to preserve the republic. Throughout Marvel's *Civil War* crossover, individual moments appeal to politically diverse audiences, but collectively they cancel each other, carefully effecting a moderate political perspective. While this moderation seems to reject the politics of either the extreme left or right, however, Floyd and Urich's final *Front Line* interviews with Steve Rogers and Tony Stark and the resolution of *Civil War* enact revisionist definitions of patriotism that justify the reader concerns ineffectively glossed over by Millar in his Newsarama interview.

Floyd's critique of Captain America and his resistance movement continues in *Front Line #11,* when she and Urich interview the imprisoned Steve Rogers — Captain America in uniform but unmasked — after his surrender during the final battle between Iron Man and his S.H.I.E.L.D. agents and Captain America and the superheroes resistant to the Superhero Registration Act. When asked to explain his actions, Rogers expresses his belief "in the fundamental freedoms accorded us by our constitution," calls upon our "right to bear arms," and invokes his "oath to defend America from external forces, and from within" even if doing so requires "standing against [his] own government, rejecting a bogus law passed by [his] own superiors" (12). Responding to this conventional expression of American values evocative of the U.S. Constitution and The Declaration of Independence, Sally Floyd asks Rogers if he knows "What MySpace is," or who won the last episode of *American Idol*, or if he has ever "attended a NASCAR race ... watched *The Simpsons* ... or logged onto YouTube." In response to Rogers's initial silence and claim that he was doing what he thought was right, Floyd explains his problem as a belief in "an ideal," in America as "mom and apple pie." However, for Floyd, America is now about "high cholesterol and Paris Hilton and scheming your way to the top." For her, America "treats its

The firefighter and EMTs grappling with Captain America further evoke 9/11 (*Civil War* #7 24).

The image of America's greatest patriot in handcuffs completes the transition to Iron Man as the people's choice (*Civil War* #7 25).

celebrities like royalty and its teachers like dirt," but at least it is the country that she loves and she "know[s] what it **is**" (14). Floyd and Urich leave a dejected Steve Rogers, seated, hunched over, head down and hands clasped between his thighs. In his Newsarama interview, Mark Millar suggests that tie-ins like *Front Line* present alternatives to the perspectives of Iron Man and the pro-registration superheroes. However, as *Front Line* ends the Captain America subplot, there seems to be no place in modern America for the outmoded superhero's ideals and values, which are replaced by the peculiar construction of a people's democracy voiced through NASCAR, YouTube, *The Simpsons*, and *American Idol*.

Rather than providing alternatives to the pro-registration emphasis of *Civil War*, then, *Front Line* sustains that emphasis. In the final chapter of *Civil War*, Captain America's forces, supported by the Black Panther and the superhero prisoners that he has freed from their Negative Zone prison, as well as by Prince Namor and his Atlantean army, are winning the day and Captain America has defeated Iron Man in single combat. As the helpless Iron Man says, "What are you waiting for, Steve? Finish it." (#7: 20), Captain America is attacked by the crowd. The composition of this image is central to the implicit message of the crossover event. The fireman in the foreground wrapping his arms around Captain America's chest and the two emergency medical technicians attacking from the left and the background evoke images of 9/11. The African American woman, blond man, and dark-haired Asian American civilians restraining Captain America evidence Iron Man, prone and barely conscious in the foreground, as the people's choice. Realizing that his troops are "not fighting for the people anymore," but are "just fighting," Captain America drops his shield, removes his mask, and surrenders, declaring that "They're not arresting Captain America…. They're arresting Steve Rogers. That's a very different thing" (25). This moment and the image that follows of the Marvel hero typically identified as America's greatest patriot being led away in handcuffs by local police, his uniform a tattered American flag, parallels and sustains the critique of Captain America and his values stated by Sally Floyd in *Front Line*.

While he cannot possibly anticipate Sally Floyd's particular critique, here a dejected Captain America knows that he has lost the American people. As noted, Sally Floyd associates this disconnect with his outmoded idealism, an indictment that dissociates him from the interests of America's youth. However, *Civil War*, *Front Line*, and the Marvel crossover end not with the story of Captain America's fall, but with Tony Stark as the new American patriot, a concept implicit in a panel from *Civil War #6*. Framed by the American flag, Iron Man explains to Reed Richards that their Negative Zone incarceration of resistant superheroes without specific charges or trials and their incorporation of reclaimed super-villains into the S.H.I.E.L.D. forces are producing a crime free and safe society. In *Civil War*, neither Iron Man nor Richards, who has lost Sue Richards and Johnny Storm to the resistance, seems concerned about the costs inherent in the construction of this new society. The series ends with Richards's appeal to his estranged wife, who returns to him after receiving his letter explaining that he and Stark had done what was necessary to re-create America as "a superpower for the twenty-first century" (*Civil War #7* 31), a phrase oddly reminiscent of Paul Wolfowitz's call for a new American century in what has come to be called the Wolfowitz Doctrine. Of course, when Marvel's crossover officially ends, America's conflicts with Namor and the Black Panther continue as Tony Stark's S.H.I.E.L.D. forces and the American military blockade Wakanda and invade Atlantis, attempting to prevent either culture from achieving superpower status. These post-crossover events, also reminiscent of the Wolfowitz Doctrine's call for military intervention to maintain the United States as the planet's only superpower, both continue the political analogies sustaining the *Civil War* crossover and extend its commercial effect by inspiring readers of *Civil War* to follow continuing subplots in *The Black Panther* and *Sub-Mariner* comics.

The political implications of *Civil War* are most forcefully presented, however, in the final panels of *Civil War #7* and *Front Line #11*. Both events end with Tony Stark. In *Civil War #7*, as the newly appointed director of S.H.I.E.L.D., Stark hosts the mother of one of the schoolchildren killed in Stamford aboard a S.H.I.E.L.D. helicarrier hovering five miles above New York City. Mrs. Sharpe had previously spit in Stark's face as he exited a memorial service for the Stamford victims because she blamed him and all superheroes for the deaths. Now, guided by Stark, she realizes that a brave new America has been created from the tragedy at Stamford and embraces Stark's vision: "You're a good man, Tony Stark. You risked **everything** to get us to this place, but I truly believe you've given people heroes we can **believe** in again." Sharpe utters these words as she and Stark stand on the helicarrier's observation deck, surrounded by a glass geodesic bubble and bathed in the light of a brilliant sunrise. Stark replies, "The best is yet to come, sweetheart…. That's a promise" (36). The final image and final word of *Civil War*, then, validate Reed Richards and Tony Stark's plan and the sacrificing of personal freedoms for security as they promote hope in a newly defined America.

As Mark Millar suggested in the Newsarama interview, the *Front Line* tie-in does modify the favorable treatment of the pro-registration forces and the hopeful conclusion of *Civil War*, but it ultimately does not counter the crossover's substitution of Iron Man for Captain America as the image of the new American patriot. As Sally Floyd and Ben Urich interview Tony Stark at the end of *Front Line #11*, they reveal the results of their investigation into his role in the civil war. They now know that Stark provoked conflict among superheroes in part to justify building of the Negative Zone prison so that the facility would later be available to support his "superpower for the twenty-first century"; that he controlled nanites in the Green Goblin's bloodstream, causing the Goblin to attack an Atlantean delegation; that the impending war with Atlantis both increased the voluntarily registered superheroes by thirty-eight percent and allowed Stark to manipulate the stock market, earning a profit of more than $90 million; and that Stark channeled most of that profit through a Swiss bank account to a charity funding pensions for firefighters, police, their families and registered superheroes. The no longer liberal Sally Floyd ends their summary by applauding Stark and saying, "You **knew** this would happen all along. You sacrificed your status as a friend, colleague and hero for the greater good of this country. You alone understood the ramifications of such an action" (29). Floyd and Urich exit, promising never to publish their exposé, and Stark is left angry and in tears, our last view of him hunched over and on his knees, his left hand covering his eyes. The final four panels of the crossover mimic a camera dollying back, out the window of Stark's office and up to a helicopter shot of the Stark Industries tower.

Iron Man, the new American patriot, and Reed Richards willingly sacrifice civil rights to control crime (*Civil War #6* 6).

While our final view of Tony Stark parallels that of Steve Rogers, evoking our sympathy if not our pity, Sally Floyd's rejection of Captain America and his outmoded definition of American values still resonates here. Stark's actions are validated, Rogers's condemned, civil rights and personal freedoms are sacrificed for security, and Stark becomes the image of the new patriot, the self-sacrificing corporate leader who feels guilt over his deception but is presented as an object of sympathy, for we implicitly understand that what he has sacrificed for us is necessary to our security. As Travis Langley suggests while paraphrasing the Newsarama interview in "Freedom versus Security: The Basic Human Dilemma from 9/11 to Marvel's *Civil War*," Millar intended the crossover to be "read first and foremost as a super-hero story," but he "acknowledged undercurrents of allegory to add depth and resonance and some degree of political commentary regarding political and social realities of the post-9/11 world, such as privacy issues, controversial wiretapping, and civil liberties compromises rising out of the Patriot Act." While Marvel's crossover is primarily a superhero event driven both by the desire to tell a compelling story and by commercial interests, it also crosses over into political commentary enacted by a diverse collection of writers across a wide range of texts. These diverse influences certainly do not self-consciously sustain a singular political viewpoint, but by provoking associations with political culture, they implicitly challenge definitions of patriotism and engage tensions over secrecy and security that open a space for political critique.

The phenomenon of crossover does not restrict itself to the superhero genre, however. As we have argued, the crossover drives the graphic narrative, both at the level of story and (sometimes literally) in the margins. Beyond the obvious interpolation of images and words, or competing layers of visual and literary allusiveness, graphic narrative crosses generic boundaries in ways that challenge its reader and belie the stereotypical identification of comics as "kids' stuff." For example, Pat Mills' and Joe Colquhoun's serial *Charley's War*, while ostensibly for a juvenile or pre-teen audience, presents a multi-layered narrative reliant on allusions to a wide range of First World War literature, in-depth research, and traditional British boys' comics. At every instance, *Charley's War* works to undermine itself, creating a critical distance that forces the reader to question both the violence of battle and the validity of the social structures that give rise to the wholesale slaughter of the war.

In 1979, the first issue of *Charley's War* ran in *Battle Picture Weekly*, and immediately brought a new sensibility to the British war comic.[6] Mills imbued his scripts with a subversive quality that belied the age demographic for the comic, while Colquhoun's heavy inking and unflinchingly explicit depictions of the carnage of First World War battlefields played with the conventions of the genre, both complicating and complementing the narrative. In stark contrast to the heroic paragons of "muscular Christianity" that were so popular in British comics, the titular character Charley Bourne was an underage, undereducated, and decidedly unexceptional Tommy who enlisted and was sent to the front just before the Battle of the Somme. Carefully researched, his story maintained a firm grounding in the reality of daily life in the trenches while presenting its anti-war message in terms that readers could both understand and enjoy reading. With *Charley's War*, the crossover between boys' war comic and mature scripts and situations enabled the narrative to occupy a political space.

Crossover allows *Charley's War* to be thematically subversive, but the graphic narrative's self-conscious use of the limitations and advantages of comic form also made it possible to stake a clear position against the capitalist and imperialist impulses of its historical context. *Charley's War* came into existence shortly after the "Winter of Discontent," a series of general strikes over pay issues which culminated in the fall of the Labour party and the election of Margaret Thatcher to prime minister. Early strips had Charley writing home and asking for money, on account of pay shortages. Shortly after the Falklands War, *Charley's War* ran a storyline on the Battle of the Falklands (where the SMS Nürnberg was sunk in 1914). Although it was a historically based comic, *Charley's War* clearly reflected the fears and concerns of the time which produced it. From a formal perspective, *Charley's War* consistently works against linearity. Its art was highly detailed and did not confine itself to a simple paneled format. Images would consistently break through the divides of the panels, lending a further sense of urgency to the dramatics of the narrative. Frequently, panels would not be employed at all; with only a series of pictures on the page, the sequence had to be determined by the reader. The dialogue and the captions are clearly aimed at a younger audience, but the complexities of the art and the relationship between the pictures and the words undermine the idea that this was children's literature. While other visual media, such as film or television, incorporate a concrete sense of time on a structural level, graphic narrative relies on its reader to interpret time presented spatially. The space between panels, the dialogue in the word bubbles or captions, and the composition of the pictures themselves all need to be considered in decoding the sequence of the narrative. The comic form brings together verbal and visual, as it collapses the planes of space and time, existing both immemorially and within finite boundaries of page and ink.

The crossover between image and word is a familiar topic in critical discussions of comic form. In what is perhaps the most substantial critical work on *Charley's War*, Esther MacCallum-Stewart comments on the ways in which Mills and Colquhoun explore this divide between verbal and visual, noting that "multiple narratives on each page deliberately divorced the art from the writing" (14). Building off of MacCallum-Stewart's analysis, we contend that in its simultaneous deployment of competing narrative structures, *Charley's War* demonstrates how the crossover operates at the narrative level to both advance and politicize the story. For instance, the captions to the beginning of each strip resound with the type of hyperbolic language familiar to comics. To take one early strip as an example: "The Battle of the Somme, 1916! 'Lonely,' one of Charley Bourne's comrades, is hiding a terrible, un-named secret, the knowledge of which is driving him to the verge of madness. Suddenly, he rushes into No Man's Land and Charley and 'Ginger,' Charley's Friend, run off in pursuit of him" (Mills and Colquhoun). The caption encourages one interpretation of the events, meant to push the narrative forward and keep the reader identifying with Charley and remain invested in his story. It describes the events that are unfolding with exaggerated language and misuses exclamation points and ellipses to create a sense of action and suspense.[7]

But this caption doesn't quite fit the actions it describes. For one thing, Lonely's madness, which causes him to rush into no-man's land, is not martial fervor but rather

The panel's caption provides one narrative framework for interpreting the action of the comic (*Charley's War 2 June...* n. pag.).

Charley's letters home provide a competing narrative framework, asking the reader to negotiate between divergent words and images (*Charley's War 2 June... n. pag.*).

indicative of a death wish: "Shoot me, Jerries! I deserve to die — for the sake of the Lost Platoon!" The Germans, for their part, are looting bodies and not seeking any conflict with the enemy. The action on the page, such as it is, consists of Charley and Ginger tripping Lonely, and then hiding in a watery shell hole. They escape by throwing a bucket of stew at their hunters, but end up wandering into a German trench, where they are taken prisoner. The story moves immediately to the next scene, which begins the story of their escape from the German trench. The Titan reprints further reinforce this by having each volume end on a "cliff-hanger," in the middle of a narrative arc. This is not a linear narrative; it never ends, but simply begins again. Perhaps like the war itself, *Charley's War* is a comic of infinite beginnings and the only ending for the characters is death. There is a disconnection between the caption and the story itself that, although subtle, carries a powerful political message. For Charley and the other enlisted men, the war is a series of mind-numbing and physically taxing jobs, juxtaposed with moments of sheer terror. Officers like Charley's C.O. Snell, however, enjoy picnic baskets and live in relatively leisurely safety behind the front lines, organizing cricket matches and placing their own comfort above the lives of their men. This reinforces the class commentary that cuts through the series and strengthens the anti-war message of the comic.

On top of the caption and the "action," we can see the phenomenon of crossover operating in another layer of narrative that frequently weaves itself in and out of the early issues of *Charley's War*: Charley's letters to and from his family back in "Blighty." These letters serve multiple purposes, allowing Charley to represent himself and comment on the situation he finds himself in as well as playing up the distance between civilian and combatant that has become a cliché for war literature. This signals not only the shift in narrative consciousness from interpreting the image and caption to interpreting Charley's correspondence, but also the deep connections between *Charley's War* and the literary tradition of British World War I writing. The divide between home and front echoes Robert Graves or Siegfried Sassoon, as Charley's family writes to ask what he'd like for his birthday. Colquhoun juxtaposes this question with the image of Charley and Ginger cowering in a muddy shell hole as the Germans approach, pointing out the absurdity both of the question and of the situation that confronts Charley.

By far the greater effect of the epistolary narrative is to undercut any sense of narrative integrity. The letters highlight the fact that this is not the "Great" War, but it is in fact Charley's War. There is no pretension here that this is a representative view of the conflict, and so the focus of the narrative shifts from the war to the character. His letters home barely mention the war, except by indirect suggestion; in the example discussed here, he wants a "hot bath a cuppa coco and a good nights sleep between *cleen sheets*." The consistent misspelling of simple words makes clear that Charley's lack of intelligence limits his ability to think about the war or to discuss it in any depth.[8] They de-center *Charley's War* by challenging his capability to represent his experience, in this way linking him to other recorders of the war. First World War memoirs had to "recreate horror and to describe [the writer's] awakening to the fact that the individual holds no special place in an indifferent universe where the breakdown of the sense of self parallels the fragmentation and defilement of the body" (Kaplan 15). Given the horrors that Charley sees (and that Colquhoun draws), the narrative is necessarily unstable. Charley as witness is charged with representing the unrepresentable, and the letters make clear that the language available to him is not up to the task.

The complexities of the narrative technique, coupled with the advantages of a form that relies on its reader's interpretation of images, words, and the blank space on the page, allow *Charley's War* to critique both class and war. Because the narrative is so often at odds with itself, it foregrounds the act of reading and forces its reader to grapple with the issues raised by the war in unexpected ways. As with other postmodern forms, understanding the comic "no longer simply involves construction on the one hand or reading on the other, but what is called 'browsing around' in a given narrative environment. We can 'fill narrative in,' both visually and aurally, choosing and adding to what is seen and heard in a given narrative space" (Gibson 11). Reading becomes active and engages the reader. Further, the text also engages in the act of crossover between graphic narrative and more conventional literary forms. In its range of literary allusion, *Charley's War* links itself to its literary forbears and situates itself within the tradition of Great War literature through its intertextual relationship with two of the most prominent British accounts of the war from 1929, Robert Graves' *Good-Bye to All That* and Frederic Manning's *The Middle Parts of Fortune: Somme and Ancre 1916* (also published as *Her Privates We*).

The eponymous Charley Bourne takes his surname from the primary character in Manning's novel, whose experiences are based on Manning's own service on the Somme (Manning does not give Bourne a first name). Unlike Charley, Manning's Bourne is clever and resourceful, at times serving as a company translator and at other times with the signaling section, and one element that drives the plot is the question of whether Bourne will be promoted and receive a commission. The character in *The Middle Parts of Fortune* who most resembles Charley is the young Martlow, who is repeatedly described as "little Martlow" and who is not yet seventeen (28). Like Charley, Martlow speaks in dialect (in this case Cockney), and when in action reveals a hidden strength of character that springs in part from his working-class background: "Bourne had seen the boy blubbering like the child he really was, as they went over the top a couple of days earlier, but unaware that he was blubbering, and possessed at the same time by a more primitive fury than filled the souls of grown men…. Probably life to him had always been a kind of warfare" (38). Charley's immediate superior in *Charley's War* is Sergeant Tozer; likewise, Bourne's sergeant is Sgt. Tozer. One of Charley's friends in the comic is "Weeper" Watkins, named for the effects of poison gas on his tear ducts as well as for his sense of humor. Bourne is good friends with "Weeper" Smart, named for his pessimism and hangdog demeanor. Perhaps coincidentally, there is a character named Watkins in *The Middle Parts of Fortune* who is killed in action on the first day of the battle: "Mr. Watkins had been killed outright, and there was no more to be said on that point, except that he was one of many good fellows" (22). In *Charley's War*, characters die regularly, reflecting the uncertain and random nature of life in the trenches. Manning kills off his characters as well, their deaths brief and arbitrary, another instance of crossover with *Charley's War*.

Although the characters in *The Middle Parts of Fortune* are fictitious, Manning is careful to note in his preface that the book is "a record of experience on the Somme and Ancre fronts, with an interval behind the lines, during the latter half of the year 1916; and the events described in it actually happened" (Manning n. pag.). Robert Graves, on the other hand, presents his war experience as a memoir (the Anchor Books subtitle is "An Autobiography"), yet he does not hesitate to point out that memoirs "are not truthful if they do not contain a high proportion of falsities" (vi). Written in just eleven weeks, when Graves found himself in need of "a lump of money," *Good-Bye to All That* "deliberately mixed in all the ingredients that [he knew] are mixed into other popular books" (viii). Manning's fiction, in a similar manner, relies heavily on Manning's memories of serving at the Somme. The coexistence of attention to historical accuracy and invention of seemingly implausible situations in *Charley's War* reflects Manning's and Graves' struggles to balance the memory of lived experience with the pleasing artifices of fiction. When challenged on this point, Mills has responded by referencing further accounts of the war:

> [T]he serial has been criticised for showing such supposedly "unlikely" scenes. However, it is taken from a number of sources, including some upbeat and dramatic accounts of life in the trenches written and published during the Great War … it's unlikely such books would be reprinted today, because the accepted wisdom for our generation is that the conflict was unrelentingly boring, grim, and nightmarish [Mills commentary to book III, n. pag.].

Graves also contributes to *Charley's War* in a more direct way, however, as Mills names Charley's kind and protective Lieutenant after Graves' friend David Thomas, who "came from South Wales: simple, gentle, fond of reading. He, Siegfried Sassoon, and I always went about together" (178).[9] Charley's Lt. Thomas orders his men to fall back when the British guns fall short and shell their own lines, thereby saving the lives of

Charley's comrades. He is arrested, court-martialed for cowardice in the face of the enemy, and sentenced to death by a firing squad comprised of his own men. Although he does not appear in many strips in the series, Lt. Thomas is an important figure in *Charley's War*, for he comes to represent a moral standard for Charley and his case typifies the shortcomings of the British Army, setting up the primary conflict in the comic not between Germans and British, but between upper and lower classes behind the British lines. By way of contrast, Charley's enemy, Mr. Snell, takes his name from a character in David Jones' *In Parenthesis*, widely considered to be one of the greatest experimental accounts of the First World War, and a text that is about as far from the commercial friendliness of Robert Graves' memoir as is possible.

By now, it should be relatively apparent that the crossover operates along a variety of registers in order to challenge the way that we read a text and to open a space for political critique of existing systems of cognition and interpretation. The essays in this collection investigate the various ways that graphic narrative engages in the practice of crossover, and in so doing they demonstrate that the political contexts of these works emerge most fully in their moments of crossover.

Locating political elements of graphic narrative in moments of crossover, we observe how graphic narrative is uniquely positioned, as a visual literature, to deal with issues of race, gender, sexuality, and ethnic prejudice. We argue that one has to "read" these cultural markers of difference using visual and verbal clues, and books like *Stuck Rubber Baby* or *Persepolis* offer strategies for doing so. Graphic narrative forces us to read actively. Although we have become so accustomed to reading comics that we largely do it automatically, we are actually processing information very quickly, just as we evaluate a person's gender, ethnicity, or even sexuality on first impression.

The chapters in this volume deploy literary theory and close readings of individual authors, artists and works to examine the "crossovers" of graphic narrative. The chapters in the first section focus specifically on how the "crossovers" of graphic narrative work to challenge and change the way we read. Examining the links between literary fiction and graphic narrative, John Joseph Hess looks at Michael Chabon's *The Amazing Adventures of Kavalier & Clay* and analyzes how the centrality of the comic book to Chabon's work redefines the relationship between literary and popular art. Daniel Stein argues that George Herriman's early twentieth-century comic *Krazy Kat* bridges the gap between mass readership and literary "high modernism," and in so doing, endows the comic medium with an explicitly political sensibility. Julia Round's chapter, "Fantastic Alterities and *The Sandman*," by contrast, contends that in its creation of multiple worlds and its denial of mimesis, graphic narrative, like the Fantastic, destabilizes any notion of reality by exposing it as a constructed referent. These first three chapters specifically engage the crossovers between literature and comic form, but the final chapter of this section examines the nature of the crossover outside of the framework of literary connections to graphic narrative. In her chapter, Rikke Platz Cortsen provides an architectural reading of Alan Moore's "How Things Work Out" to show how, by working with a house as the literal frame for the graphic narrative, the comic form disrupts the way that we read time and space. The surprising crossover from architecture to literature forces the reader to read in multiple directions simultaneously in order to construct meaning.

The crossovers of graphic narrative not only ask us to confront the ways that we understand literature, they also require us to reassess how we read human qualities like ethnicity and sexuality. The second section of the volume, then, examines how this challenge to the practice of reading works through issues of race and gender. David Bordelon's chapter analyzes the role of books and reading in Howard Cruse's *Stuck Rubber Baby*. Bordelon identifies the act of reading as something of a double-edged sword, as it serves to both challenge and reinforce the racial and sexual prejudices of the characters. In doing so, he highlights the simultaneous connections and disjunctions between graphic narratives and their literary and visual counterparts. Pamela J. Rader examines self-representation in Marjane Satrapi's *Persepolis* books, with particular attention to the way that graphic narrative foregrounds the storytelling process and thus reveals the constructed nature of gender and ethnicity in Satrapi's visual autobiography. In a similar manner, Luminita Dragulescu turns her attention to issues of representation in *Maus* and shows how Art Spiegelman questions how we read racial, national, and ethnic difference in the wake of the Holocaust. Finally, Ellen M. Gil-Gómez reads the crossovers between history, literature, and art in *Latino USA* as an entry point for a subversive political commentary on the imposition of an "official" history of American Hispanics and the erasure of "other" histories.

The third and final section in the collection takes up, with one exception, that most stereotypical of comics figures, the superhero, and analyzes the role that the superhero plays in visual and cultural crossovers. This final section unifies the ideas discussed in the previous sections. Martyn Pedler explores how superhero comics structure and present action and dynamic movement in static form, and reads this against cinematic presentations of action. By looking in particular at the Flash, Spider-Man, and Superman, he demonstrates how the temporal and spatial qualities of graphic narrative operate and how superheroes can violate those boundaries in ways that other media, including prose fiction and cinema, cannot emulate. In so doing, he echoes and builds on the addresses to ways of reading presented in the first section of the volume. Andrew J. Friedenthal's chapter on the critical reception of Wonder Woman by feminist groups relates ideas discussed in the second section of the volume to a discussion of gendered politics and the appropriation of the superheroine. Friedenthal investigates the importance of Wonder Woman to second wave feminism, and to Gloria Steinem and *Ms.* magazine in particular, while also exploring how commercial interests driving transformations of corporately owned characters sometimes conflict with the appropriation of those characters' iconic imagery by readers and special interest groups. As a result, his analysis investigates both how audience response can cross over to influence and reshape a character's iconic status and the extent to which that influence is limited by commercial interests. In the volume's final chapter, Michael P. Millington explores how converting an extended comics series, Brian K. Vaughan's sixty-issue *Y: The Last Man*, to a trade paperback impacts reader reception. While his discussion of Vaughan's Yorick does not address a traditional superhero, Millington's re-examination of the comics hero through literary allusion, psychoanalytic and gender issues, and the effects of publication format on the reader's experience of a graphic narrative establishes links among the three sections of the volume.

The aim of this collection is to bring together the multiplicity of visual and cultural intersections often discussed in the critical landscape of comics scholarship through the concept of crossover. Moving beyond the debate over the idea of "comics as literature," the following chapters focus on presenting theoretically informed analyses of individual authors, artists, and works in order to raise larger questions and make wider observations about the capabilities and distinctiveness of comic form. In particular, and in keeping with Aaron Meskin's argument, this book concentrates on the notion of graphic narrative as hybrid form, not simply in identifying the tension between images and words, but in emphasizing its engagement with other genres and cultural forms. Comics, we argue, work through these crossovers, and the political dimensions of graphic narrative are exposed precisely in those moments of crossover. Although the chapters stand as discrete arguments in their own right, together they work to advance this position. Collectively and individually, then, the chapters in this volume shed light on the purpose and functionality of graphic narrative while providing points for further discussion that we hope will be taken up by future scholars and enthusiasts.

Notes

1. The series began in June 2009 and produced 13 issues as of July 2010. While Boom! does produce its own line of original comics under the direction of its editor in chief, Mark Waid, it has also aggressively promoted the idea of visual crossover through its adaptations and creation of original stories based on popular science fiction television series like *Farscape* and *Eureka* and its publication of *Cold Space*, an original series written by the actor Samuel L. Jackson and Eric Calderon.

2. In *Uncle Sam and the Freedom Fighters*, an eight-issue miniseries published between July 2006 and February 2007, DC Comics produced its own response to 911 and the Patriot Act. However, Jimmy Palmiotti and Justin Gray's script is less sophisticated than Mark Millar's *Civil War*, Paul Jenkins's *Front-line*, and the extended plots and subplots that crossover the entire Marvel Universe. *Uncle Sam*, in our view, is not worthy of extended analysis. In the DC series, a robot double for Senator Frank Knight replaces the senator, ascends to the presidency, and, directed by Father Time, uses the Patriot Act to establish a secret agency, S.H.A.D.E., that combats criminals and terrorists by assassinations and violations of civil rights allowed by the new legislation. The robot president, Gonzo the Mechanical Bastard, and Father Time conspire to implant chips in all U.S. citizens, putting an end to personal freedoms and civil rights. Uncle Sam rises from the dead and convinces the Freedom Fighters, initially S.H.A.D.E. operatives, to join him in the fight against Gonzo and Father Time and in favor of constitutional rights and freedoms. There are no ambiguities in this rather straightforward series, and the political commentary is painfully obvious.

3. Throughout, we use the publication dates printed in the individual volume or referenced trade paperback or graphic novel. Of course, most comics are distributed as much as two months prior to the printed publication dates; however, tracking actual release dates and documenting accordingly becomes confusing and messy. Some *Civil War* event comics, for example, were delayed and not distributed for a month or more after the publication date printed in the issue. In the interest of standardization, we opt for adherence to the date printed in the comics themselves. When actual distribution date is central to a developing argument, that information is presented in a note.

4. Millar's comments appeared in "Mark Millar's *Civil War Post-Game Show,*" a Newsarama interview no longer available at newsarama.com. However, Travis Langley cites Millar's comments in "Freedom versus Security: The Basic Human Dilemma from 9/11 to Marvel's *Civil War*," while J. Richard Stevens incorporates Millar's views in his "On the Front Line: Portrayals of War Correspondents in Marvel Comics' *Civil War: Front Line.*"

5. The *Road to Civil War* introduces tensions within the Marvel universe building toward enactment of the Superhero Registration Act through events in *The Amazing Spiderman #529-531*, *The New Avengers: Illuminati*, and *The Fantastic Four #536-537*. While *The Amazing Spider-Man #529* was released first in February 2006 and followed in March by *The New Avengers: Illuminati* and *Fantastic Four #536*, the trade paperback reverses the order, presenting *Illuminati*, *Fantastic Four #536 & 537*, and *The Amazing Spider-Man #529, 530, & 531*. Since the trade paperback establishes an "official" reading sequence, our discussion of plot details conforms to that order. It should be noted, however, that conversion of the

single issues to a trade paperback significantly alters readers' experience of the events, a developing issue in graphic narrative explored in more detail by Michael P. Millington's examination of Brian K. Vaughan's *Y: The Last Man* in the chapter that closes this volume.

6. Elements of this discussion are adapted from portions of an article by James F. Wurtz published in *Pacific Coast Philology* no. 45 (2010) entitled "Representing the Great War: Violence, Memory, and Comic Form."

7. Thank you to Egmont UK Ltd. and Titan Books for the permission to reprint images from *Charley's War*. Full copyright information may be found in the Works Cited.

8. MacCallum-Stewart discusses this in relation to a later scene; her reading focuses on the positioning of *Charley's War* in a wider canon of British War Comics and sees Charley as "a liar who is deliberately misleading his parents" (14).

9. Sassoon refers to Thomas in his memoirs as his friend "Dick"; his death in 1916 caused Sassoon great distress.

Works Cited

Chabon, Michael. *The Amazing Adventures of Kavalier & Clay.* New York: Picador, 2000. Print.

Currie, Mark. *Postmodern Narrative Theory.* New York: St. Martin's, 1998. Print.

Gibson, Andrew. *Towards a Postmodern Theory of Narrative.* Edinburgh: Edinburgh University Press, 1996. Print.

Graves, Robert. *Good-Bye to All That.* 1929. New York: Anchor, 1998. Print.

Grünwald, Jennifer, ed. *The Road to Civil War.* New York: Marvel, 2007.

Jenkins, Paul, writer. *Front Line #1.* Art by Kei Kobayashi. Colors by Christina Strain. Letters by Randy Gentile. New York: Marvel, August 2006. Print.

_____. *Front Line #4.* Art by Ramon Bachs. Inks by John Lucas. Colors by Laura Martin. Letters by Randy Gentile. New York: Marvel, September 2006. Print.

_____. *Front Line #5.* Art by Ramon Bachs. Inks by John Lucas. Colors by Laura Martin. Letters by Randy Gentile. New York: Marvel, October 2006. Print.

_____. *Front Line #7.* Art by Ramon Bachs. Inks by John Lucas. Colors by Laura Martin. Letters by Joe Caramanga. New York: Marvel, November 2006. Print.

_____. *Front Line #9.* Art by Ramon Bachs. Inks by John Lucas. Colors by Laura Martin. Letters by Randy Gentile. New York: Marvel, December 2006. Print.

_____. *Front Line #11.* Art by Ramon Bachs. Inks by John Lucas. Colors by Larry Molinar. Letters by Randy Gentile. New York: Marvel, April 2007. Print.

Kaplan, Laurie. "Over the Top in the Aftermath of the Great War: Two Novels, Too Graphic." *The Graphic Novel.* Ed. Jan Baetens. Leuven: University of Leuven Press, 2001. 13–22. Print.

Langley, Travis. "Freedom versus Security: The Basic Human Dilemma from 9/11 to Marvel's *Civil War*." N.p. n.d. Web. 8 August 2010.

MacCallum-Stewart, Esther. "The First World War and British Comics." *University of Sussex Journal of Contemporary History* 6 (August 2003): 1–18. Web. 30 March 2008.

Manning, Frederic. *The Middle Parts of Fortune: Somme and Ancre, 1916.* 1929. New York: St. Martin's, 1977. Print.

Meskin, Aaron. "Comics as Literature." *British Journal of Aesthetics* 49:3 (July 2009): 219–239. Print

Millar, Mark, writer. *Civil War #6.* Art by Steve McNiven. Inks by Dexter Vines. Colors by Morry Hollowell. Letters by Chris Eliopoulis. New York: Marvel, December 2006. Print.

_____. *Civil War #7.* Art by Steve McNiven. Inks by Dexter Vines, John Dell, and Tim Townsend. Colors by Morry Hollowell. Letters by Chris Eliopoulis. New York: Marvel, January 2007. Print.

Mills, Pat. and Joe Colquhoun, *Charley's War: 2 June 1916–1 August 1916* (London: Titan, 2004, compiled from Battle Picture Weekly, by arrangement with Egmont UK Ltd. Charley's War and Battle Picture Weekly © Egmont UK Ltd.) Print.

_____. *Charley's War: 17 October 1916–21 February 1917* (London: Titan, 2006, compiled from Battle Picture Weekly, by arrangement with Egmont UK Ltd. Charley's War and Battle Picture Weekly © Egmont UK Ltd.) Print.

Newsarama. "Mark Millar's Civil War Post-Game Show." N.p. n.d. Web. 20 June 2007.

Stevens, J. Richard. "On the Front Line: Portrayals of War Correspondents in Marvel Comics' *Civil War: Front Line*." *The Image of the Journalist in Popular Culture Journal* 1 (Fall 2009): 37–69. Web. 8 August 2010.

PART I

WAYS OF READING

1

Michael Chabon's Amazing Adventures with Dark Horse Comics

JOHN JOSEPH HESS

When Michael Chabon released *The Amazing Adventures of Kavalier & Clay* in 2000, *Publishers Weekly* greeted it with a starred notice and an author interview. The anonymous reviewer proclaimed the book to be "an epic novel about the glory years of the American comic book (1939–1954)," a book that "fulfills all the promise of Chabon's two earlier novels ... and two short story collections ... and nearly equals them all together in number of pages" (44). The reviewer concluded with a prediction quickly proven true: "well researched and deeply felt, this rich, expansive, and hugely satisfying novel will delight a wide range of readers" (*Publishers Weekly* 44). The novel must have delighted a range of readers since a "Behind the Best Sellers" feature less than two months later reported that the book already had "60,000 copies in print" (Maryles 22). *The Amazing Adventures of Kavalier & Clay* was a blockbuster comic book novel for the new millennium.

In the ten years since *The Amazing Adventures of Kavalier & Clay* won the Pulitzer Prize for fiction in 2001, a number of other high profile comic book novels have appeared. Jonathan Lethem's characters obsess over Marvel Comics in 1970s Brooklyn in his acclaimed *The Fortress of Solitude*. Junot Díaz's own Pulitzer-winning novel *The Brief Wondrous Life of Oscar Wao* (2007) focuses on a protagonist who "had always been a young nerd ... who loved comic books" (20). Díaz foregrounds the importance of comics within the novel with an epigraph taken from issue 49 of *Fantastic Four*. This proliferation of literary novels rooted in comics traditions has led literary critics like Marc Singer to begin to theorize the emerging genre of the "Comic-Book Novel" (273).[1]

The emerging "Comic-Book" genre of literary fiction would appear to fit nicely with the rise in prestige of the comics medium over the last two decades, as Gerard Jones has convincingly argued in *Men of Tomorrow: Geeks, Gangsters, and the Birth of the Comic Book* (2004). Thanks to the lessons of postmodern hybridity, the rise of cultural studies as a disciplinary approach, the success of works like Jay Cantor's *Krazy Kat* (1987), Art

Spiegelman's *Maus* (1991), Chabon's *The Amazing Adventures of Kavalier & Clay*, and Díaz's *The Brief Wondrous Life of Oscar Wao*, comics have infiltrated the academy, finding their way into edited volumes and university curricula. Hillary Chute's article on "the changing profession" in *PMLA*, the *Publication of the Modern Language Association of America*, one of the top American journals of literary studies, aptly summarizes the new approach to comics in her title: "Comics as Literature? Reading Graphic Narrative" (2008). Critics in a variety of disciplines are increasingly comfortable with the idea that comic books might be literature, quality art, or good cinema.

Nevertheless, that set of comics culture that most concerns Chabon — superhero comics — has remained somewhat outside of the increasing academic interest in comics studies. In her account of "the changing profession," a discussion of how comic books can be situated within literary studies and literature education, Chute largely ignores the seven decade legacy of superhero comics. In fact, she explicitly states that she "offer[s] a context for American work but do[es] not emphasize the development of the commercial comic-book industry, which is dominated by two superhero-focused publishers, Marvel and DC" (455). Chute avoids even such classic graphic novels as Frank Miller's Batman book, *The Dark Knight Returns* (1986), focusing instead on the development of the comics medium primarily with respect to avant-garde and independent publishing aesthetics. Chute's literary history of comics effectively writes out their best known form. Nor is she alone in the dismissal of superhero comic books. It is no coincidence that the superhero comics afforded the most significant critical attention are precisely those comics such as Miller's *The Dark Knight Returns* and Alan Moore's *Watchmen* (1986–1987) that effectively deconstruct the superhero genre.

While Chabon's *The Amazing Adventures of Kavalier & Clay* prominently features superhero comic books, critics of the novel have been reluctant to discuss the significance of Chabon's use of comics. In her analysis of the novel, "*Ragtime, Kavalier & Clay* and the Framing of Comics," for example, Chute eschews consideration of the cultural elements of superhero comic books. Instead Chute examines the similarity of Chabon's novel to E.L. Doctorow's *Ragtime* in its consideration of how popular art, history, and the artistic avant-garde intersect. Lee Behlman skeptically considers Chabon's use of comics in Behlman's discussions of the relationship between superhero comics and Jewish-American identity. For Behlman, comics are an "escapist" reaction to the horrors of the Holocaust ("Michael Chabon" and "The Escapist: Fantasy, Folklore, and the Pleasures of the Comic Book in Recent Jewish American Holocaust Fiction"). In Behlman's view, Art Spiegelman's classic second-generation Holocaust narrative *Maus* offers a more favorable attempt to represent the Holocaust aesthetically through the comics medium ("The Escapist").

With the notable exception of Marc Singer, literary critics have found a way to marginalize what *Publishers Weekly* recognized as central to Michael Chabon's *The Amazing Adventures of Kavalier & Clay*, its enthusiastic celebration of mainstream, mass-market superhero comic books. In spite of Chabon's evident interest in superhero comics culture inside and outside of the pages of *The Amazing Adventures of Kavalier & Clay* in his own novel and in its seldom discussed after-market life in two Dark Horse Comics titles (*Michael Chabon Presents the Amazing Adventures of the Escapist* and *The Escapists*), this interest has remained largely unexamined. This is especially unusual given Chabon's investment throughout *The Amazing Adventures of Kavalier & Clay* in displaying his strong grasp of actual comics history. In fact, the most obvious feature of Chabon's novel — its embrace of superhero comics traditions — is actually its most radical. Not only has Chabon inaugurated new developments in the comic book novel, but his emphasis on the cultural hybridity and market potential of superhero comics, coupled with his own active cross-promotion of his novel with Dark Horse Comics, has indeed "delight[ed] a wide range of readers" while altering the established relationships between literary fiction and comic books and suggesting new directions for contemporary literary producers.

Chabon's non-ironic emphasis on superhero comics marks his most significant contribution to the set of texts that might be designated "comic book novels." The use of the superhero genre differs markedly from such earlier comic book novels as Jay Cantor's *Krazy Kat*. Cantor appropriates George Herriman's early twentieth-century newspaper strip *Krazy Kat* and recontextualizes its main characters, Krazy Kat and Ignatz Maus, in contemporary situations like Freudian analysis. Miles Orvell has argued that this approach, as well as Art Spiegelman's aesthetic in his quite different *Maus*, appeals to a "wide audience." According to Orvell, "in appropriating cartoon culture Cantor and Spiegelman ... have projected the mentality of the cartoon world with the complexity of high art, aiming at a broader based audience, a middle space between high and popular culture" (111). Orvell supports this contention admirably, noting for example, that Spiegelman attempted to actively distance himself from traditional comics culture by ensuring that *Raw* magazine, in which *Maus* originally appeared, "was printed on oversize paper and in high quality color, making it more marketable in bookstores and newsstands than in comic book stores" (122–3). *Maus* and *Krazy Kat* are indeed remarkable achievements, but they are achievements that also have the potential to alienate wider audiences through their aesthetic styles, through Cantor's playfully self-reflexive take on a largely forgotten comic strip and through Spiegelman's stripped down indie aesthetic. If, as Orvell argues, Cantor and Spiegelman are attempting to "create high art" for a "broad based audience," they have (explicitly) *not* tried to do so in the most immediately accessible comics traditions.

In electing to focus on the comics tradition with the broadest appeal of all, Chabon's *The Amazing Adventures of Kavalier & Clay* gains a different, and immediate, measure of cultural recognition. This recognition ultimately enables its far wider appeal both inside the novel and in its cross-market afterlife as an actual comic book. As Gerard Jones argues in *Men of Tomorrow*, "comic books have become reference points in the most popular and the most esoteric fiction and art. Everyone understands a Superman allusion or a Batman joke" (339). As Jones implies, not everyone understands Superman or Batman from their comics incarnations. Thanks to Adam West, Tim Burton, and Jerry Seinfeld, most Americans are reasonably familiar with the contours of Batman's story or with the concept of Bizarro and his world.

Cantor begins *Krazy Kat* with a cast of characters titled "Our Town." This section explains for readers what they could have expected of Harriman's original characters, setting them up for Cantor's subsequent manipulations. Nothing of the sort is required for Chabon's novel since "everyone understands a Superman allusion or a Batman joke." When Clay explains Batman's origin in the moment that his parents are shot by a robber, the well-read comics fan presumably imagines a version of the robber, small-time crook

Joe Chill, as originally drawn by Lou Schwartz and Batman co-creator Bob Kane.[2] Another of Chabon's readers might imagine a scene from Christopher Nolan's film *Batman Begins* (2005). Still another might remember the scene from Tim Burton's *Batman* (1989). The reader's essential understanding of Chabon's scene will remain the same, even if they have never read a Batman comic. No introduction is necessary because, as Jones suggests, readers know Batman through his various incarnations in multiple media markets. Chabon's direct engagement with the superhero comics tradition automatically enables the widest possible audience for a comic book novel.

Chabon's use of superhero comics is, however, far from shallow. In fact, his investment in superhero comics history is so heavy that, with comparatively little effort, a reader undoubtedly could quickly and effectively produce an annotated edition of *The Amazing Adventures of Kavalier & Clay* that highlights Chabon's manipulations of comic book history. Indeed, Chabon concludes the novel with an "Author's Note" that details his sources, including personal interviews with legendary comic book creators like Will Eisner, Stan Lee, and Gil Kane. Chabon also mentions his debt to books like Mike Benton's *The Comic Book in America: an Illustrated History* (637–8).[3] In a subsequent comics history, *Men of Tomorrow*, Gerard Jones relates the early history of the superhero comic, periodically noting the similarities between the work of Chabon (whom he interviewed) and actual comics history. Of particular interest for Chabon's ideal, historically minded superhero comics annotator, is Jones's description of "a weekend that captured an era" (139). Following one of Chabon's acknowledged sources, Jules Feiffer's *The Great Comic Book Heroes*, Jones describes how several young comics creators assembled the premier of *Daredevil*. Jones concludes that this weekend became, with some alteration, the "two day" blur in which Chabon's own Joe Kavalier and Sam Clay create the Escapist (Jones 189; *Kavalier & Clay* 144–151).[4] Comparison between Chabon's novel and Jones's history emphasizes the historical realities behind Chabon's plot details: like early Jewish-American comic book creators Bob Kahn (Bob Kane), Jake Kurtzberg (Jack Kirby), and Stan Lieber (Stan Lee), Sam Klayman and Josef Kavalier change their names to what they believe to be the less explicitly Jewish sounding Sam Clay and Joe Kavalier (Jones 369–371; *Kavalier & Clay* 71).[5]

Chabon's incorporation of these historical elements clearly enhances the detail of his novel. It also enables narrative and character development. Late in *The Amazing Adventures of Kavalier & Clay* Chabon includes a chapter that provides the transcript of Sam Clay's testimony before the Subcommittee to Investigate Juvenile Delinquency of the Senate Judiciary Committee on April 22, 1954 (613). The narrator notes that these hearings were inspired by Dr. Frederic Wertham's unfavorable 1954 analysis of comics, *Seduction of the Innocent*. The narrator calls this book "a motive force behind the entire controversy over the pernicious effects of comic books" (*Kavalier & Clay* 613). Benton's *The Comic Book in America* sketches the importance of this controversy to the evolution of the superhero comic:

> Three significant things happened in 1954. Dr. Frederic Wertham, a long-time vociferous critic of the comic-book industry, published *Seduction of the Innocent*, a book which detailed the allegedly ill effects upon children of reading comic books containing crime, sex, and violence.

Next, the U.S. Senate Subcommittee to Investigate Juvenile Delinquency in the United States held primary hearings on the deleterious effects of comic books on children.

Finally, in October 1954, comic-book publishers established the self-regulatory Comics Code Authority which imposed a strict set of industry standards upon comic books. All these events would change comic books forever, and not necessarily for the better [51–2].

Chabon uses these details to publicly shame the homosexual Sam Clay, a move that ultimately leads to Clay's own self-discovery and self-imposed exile at the novel's conclusion. Inspired by Wertham's "theory ... that the relationship between Batman and his ward [Robin] is actually a thinly veiled allegory of pedophilic inversion," the Subcommittee questions Clay at length about the frequent recurrence in his work of similar teams of older male superheroes and their youthful sidekicks — "the Rectifier and Little Mack the Boy Enforcer. The Lumberjack and Timber Lad. The Argonaut and Jason. The Lone Wolf and Cubby" (615).[6]

In creating his convincingly detailed comic book world, Chabon repeatedly emphasizes the hybrid origin of such real comic book heroes as Superman. Chabon's emphasis on these origins further enhances the historical detail of his comic book novel. The narrator repeatedly describes superheroes as "amalgamation[s]" (587). Chabon illustrates this hybridity in his creation of the Escapist and in his construction of a novel that equally emphasizes its influence by both superhero comics and classic novels. Late in the novel, the narrator claims that

> as Sammy had always argued, the character of Superman itself represented the amalgamation of "a bunch of ideas those guys stole from somebody else," in particular from Philip Wylie, whose Hugo Danner was the bulletproof superhuman hero of his novel *Gladiator*; from Edgar Rice Burroughs, whose orphaned hero, young Lord Greystoke, grew up to become Tarzan, noble protector of a world of inferior beings; and from Lee Falk's newspaper comic strip *The Phantom*, whose eponymous hero had pioneered the fashion for colorful union suits among implacable foes of crime [587–8].

Clay's analysis of Superman's amalgamation sounds convincing for anyone familiar with the basic contours of the stories and images of Superman, Tarzan, or the Phantom and, again, it echoes the history of superhero comics. Jones explains that Batman creators Bob Kane and Bill Finger put their superhero together out of elements taken from "*The Mark of Zorro* ... Superman ... Doc Savage ... the Green Hornet ... the Shadow ... and the original Phantom" (150). The amalgamations of "ideas those guys stole from somebody else" that became Superman and Batman in turn influence Kavalier and Clay as they invent the Escapist, a superhero amalgamation that is equal parts personal experience, Harry Houdini, Batman, and Captain America.

Within the novel, it is significant that these amalgamations, made of "a bunch of ideas those guys stole from somebody else," are, rather than copies, their own unique syntheses. When Kavalier escapes Europe and moves in with Clay's family, Clay helps him to obtain a job with the New York creators of "midget radios ... and joy buzzers," Empire Novelty Company, Inc. (80).[7] Having quickly convinced their boss that he should "try to come up with a Superman" the pair walk around New York considering what sort of hero they could create (88). Inspired by the examples of Superman and Batman, Clay decides that their superhero should also blend approaches. Noting that "Superman flies,"

Clay thinks that "to be original" the Escapist should not. In Clay's words the Escapist should have "no flying, no strength of a hundred men, no bulletproof skin" (92). He should not be a straight copy. Instead, Clay decides that their character requires a convincing story because "that's what makes Batman good, and not dull at all, even though he's just a guy who dresses up like a bat and beats people up ... his parents were killed ... right in front of his eyes" (95).[8] Kavalier and Clay soon develop Chabon's original amalgamation.

Chabon presents the creation of the Escapist in a stand alone chapter depicting various details familiar to comics readers (123–134).[9] Like Superman and Batman before him, Chabon's Escapist is an "amalgamation" of ideas. Like Batman, and later Marvel's 1960s Spider-Man, the Escapist finds his calling to fight crime when a member of his family, his uncle Max, is murdered. The Escapist, a vaudeville escape artist by day, combines Clay's knowledge of his father's past as a vaudeville performer with Clay's own acknowledged interest in Harry Houdini as well as Kavalier's own training as an escape artist in Prague (98, 3, 120, 111).[10] The Escapist fights "the evil forces of the Iron Chain" and, like the super solider Captain America, also combats Nazis (134). He even receives a call to just action that anachronistically recalls Spider-Man's as Chabon writes "that freedom was a debt that could only be repaid by purchasing the freedom of others" (*Kavalier & Clay* 131), in echo of Stan Lee's concluding words in *Amazing Fantasy* #15 (1962) that remind Spider-Man's readers that "in this world with great power there must also come — great responsibility!" (Lee 13). Kavalier and Clay finish Chabon's synthesized vision of the Escapist with a comic book cover illustration that shows the Escapist punching Hitler in the face, a move nicked from the cover of the first issue of *Captain America* (130).[11]

Chabon the comics fan, like Jones the comics historian, sees that the comics marketplace has nearly always been one of cross-market promotion. Chabon emphasizes this merchandising when introducing the chapter of *The Amazing Adventures of Kavalier & Clay* that presents the Escapist's transition into radio drama. This chapter serves the narrative function of introducing Clay's sometime lover Tracy Bacon, enabling Chabon to set into motion the situations leading to Clay's eventual public exposure and gradual self-revelation. As with many of the novel's comics details, it also heightens the verisimilitude of Chabon's comics world. The narrator catalogues numerous non-comics Escapist promotions as key elements in the character's overall performance in the comics market:

> In 1941, its best year ever, the partnership of Kavalier & Clay earned $59,832.27. Total revenues generated that year for Empire Comics, Inc.— from sales of all comic books featuring characters created either in whole or in part by Kavalier & Clay, sales of two hundred thousand copies apiece for each of two Whitman's Big Little Books featuring the Escapist, sales of Keys of Freedom, of key rings, pocket flashlight, coin banks, board games, rubber figurines, windup toys, and diverse other items of Escapism, as well as the proceeds from the licensing of the Escapist's dauntless puss to Chaffee Cereals for their Frosted Chaff-Os, and from the Escapist radio program that began broadcasting on NBC in April — though harder to calculate, came to something in the neighborhood of $12 to $15 million [291].

Thanks to merchandising, the Escapist, like Superman and Batman, is everywhere. This passage represents more than a simple portfolio of assets suggesting the character's success, however. It also presents more than a simple plot motivating device that introduces the Escapist radio program. By including this program, Chabon briefly considers the aesthetic concerns of transferring material from one medium to another. When Kavalier and Clay are invited to "run-throughs for the debut" of the new radio drama *The Amazing Adventures of the Escapist* (297), Clay finds the performance "depressing." Although the narrator emphasizes that the radio script is adapted from one of Clay's comics, Clay is unsettled by "his first experience ... with having one of his creations appropriated and made to serve the purposes of another writer ... It was pretty much the same stuff ... and yet somehow it was all totally different. It seemed to have a lighter, more playful tone than in the comic books" (301).

What most distinguishes *The Amazing Adventures of Kavalier & Clay* from the Escapist radio program and from other novels is that its non-literary market afterlife is not characterized by adaptation. *Michael Chabon Presents The Amazing Adventures of the Escapist* as published by Dark Horse Comics is not "pretty much the same stuff." Instead, Michael Chabon, Pulitzer Prize-winning novelist, became Michael Chabon, Eisner Award-winning superhero comics collaborator. In offering a variety of new material, Chabon's adventures with Dark Horse Comics differ radically from previous comics based on novels, comics Chabon flags by including *Classics Illustrated* and *Picture Stories from the Bible* among Kavalier's boxes of comics (574). The Dark Horse *Escapist* books also differ from previous graphic novel adaptations of literary fiction such as Paul Karasik's and David Mazzucchelli's graphic novel version of Paul Auster's *City of Glass* (1985).[12] Dark Horse Comics issues of *The Amazing Adventures of the Escapist* primarily feature original stories, rather than straight adaptation from Chabon's work.

The *Escapist* collections continue to advance the ruse developed in *The Amazing Adventures of Kavalier & Clay*, namely that Kavalier and Clay were real comics creators and the Escapist an actual comics superhero. The back cover of the first *Escapist* anthology purports that it contains "over sixty years' worth" of "the original **Amazing Adventures of the Escapist**, the legendary yet seldom-seen comic book feature that ... served as the ... inspiration for Michael Chabon's Pulitzer-Prize winning *The Amazing Adventures of Kavalier and* [sic] *Clay*" (back cover, emphasis theirs). To further the illusion that the stories are original, they are presented in a variety of styles that range from pieces designed to replicate the visual aesthetics of 1940s or 1960s comics, to newspaper comic strips, comics with painted frames, and cartoons with art apparently indebted to such recent non-superhero comics artists as Chris Ware. The stories are not original in the stated sense of having chronologically preceded, and inspired, Chabon's prize-winning fiction, but they are largely original takes on Chabon's comics creations.

Only the first anthologized *Escapist* story, "The Passing of the Key" presents straight adaptation as Eric Wight, Michelle Madsen and Randy Gentile visually adapt a "Story" by Michael Chabon directly from *The Amazing Adventures of Kavalier & Clay*. The writing remains identical down to the Spider-Man inspired charge that "freedom is a debt which can only be repaid by purchasing the freedom of others!" The artists memorably illustrate Chabon's claim with a pointing finger for emphasis (20). After this initial adaptation, the several volumes of *The Amazing Adventures of the Escapist* and the subsequent *The Escapists*, feature entirely new, non–Chabon stories, art, and commentary by such current and legendary comics figures as Brian Bolland, Howard Chaykin, Gene Colan, Will Eisner, and Frank Miller.[13] Not every *Amazing Adventure of the Escapist* even features Kavalier and Clay's primary character. The first *Escapist* anthology features two different stories "The Mechanist" (by Kevin McCarthy and Bill Sienkiewicz) and "Reckonings (by Jim Starlin, Christie Scheele, and Krista Ward) that focus on Luna Moth, a "Kavalier and Clay" creation presented only briefly in Chabon's novel (95–102, 103–111). The same issue also includes "Divine Wind," a story in which Kevin McCarthy, Tony Leonard Tamai, and Tom Orzechowski update the Escapist with a *manga* aesthetic as the spirit of escape finds its way into a Japanese kamikaze pilot (81–91). The *Amazing Adventures of the Escapist* anthologies offer amalgamations of classic and contemporary comics styles inspired by Chabon's own interests in *The Amazing Adventures of Kavalier & Clay* in celebrating the hybridity of superhero comics and in drawing on the history of superhero traditions.

Chabon inaugurates the first *Escapist* anthology with an "Introduction" that serves several functions: it replicates standard comics practice and it highlights his character's escape from the world of print fiction. Chabon's "Introduction" is similar to those that often precede comics anthologies and reprints. Chabon claims that:

> I still remember the first *Escapist* comic I ever came across. It appears to have been one of the later Fab Comics issues, from 1968, though I did not discover it until four or five years later, at the bottom of a box of old comics passed along to me by my cousin.... It contained a story in which the Escapist fell prey to a villain named the Junkman, who employed an "atom spike" to administer a dose of "superjunk" that first plunged the Escapist into a deep coma and then subjected him to an endless string of nightmares. All I can really remember about the story — but I have never forgotten it — is a single, stunning panel (possibly drawn by Neal Adams). It depicted the Escapist, in his simple blue costume, in the disturbing, inspiring, and surrealistic act of *escaping from his own head* [4, emphasis Chabon's].

Chabon's "memories" of the Escapist convincingly mimic standard comics introductions. His introduction captures the same sense of non-specific, but "never forgotten" wonder as Frank Miller's introduction to the Tenth Anniversary Edition of his landmark *Batman: The Dark Knight Returns*, in which Miller remembers "1963. (Or is it '64? The exact year is uncertain. But the memory is vivid.) A department store in Vermont. I'm 6 (or 7) years old. I come across an 80-page Giant comic starring Batman. I open it. I look it over. I fall in" (5). Chabon's earliest Escapist memory, the "stunning panel (possibly drawn by Neal Adams)" also perfectly sets the tone for the Escapist anthology since the anthology itself represents the character's escape from Chabon's own head into the words and pencils of Howard Chaykin, Jim Starlin, Gene Colan, and others.

The image of the Escapist "*escaping from his own head*" also signals his transfer to a new artistic medium. Although Chabon largely relinquishes creative control to comics professionals, he remains an active presence in the *Escapist* anthologies as Michael Chabon, as the anagrammatic comics critic Malachi B. Cohen, and perhaps the enigmatic comics historian Bubbles La Tour. In the paragraph after the Escapist's "surrealistic act" of cranial escape, Chabon states his enthusiasm for escape:

> That single panel, it seems to me, perfectly expresses the appeal not only of the Escapist, Master of Elusion, but of the entire genre of comic books from which, as from a great dreaming forehead, he sprang. Escape and escapism, in art and literature, have received

a bad name. It was given to them, I believe, by the very people who forged the locks and barred the windows in the first place [4].

Chabon later exploits the Escapist's move to the comics medium to consider the character's post–*Kavalier & Clay* fortunes, and changes in the comics medium itself, in Cohen's "Escapism 101: The tangled and glorious history of one of the comics' greatest characters."[14] Building on and quoting his own *Kavalier & Clay* material, Chabon presents the history of the Escapist from the 1940s through the present, claiming that examining the character's "legal fortunes" demonstrates the way that "the character has changed, evolved, at times regressed, along with the medium of comics itself" (Cohen 25). Chabon concludes with the evolution of the Escapist from the "Sunshine Comics Years *1972–1976*" in which the character was updated to become "'relevant' and expressive of the 'nitty gritty'" to the "Escapist Comics Era *1984-Present*" in which "with the birth of the independent comics scene ... [the] *New Adventures of the Escapist* update[d] the character and his cohorts, rais[ed] the quality of the writing and the level of realism" (30). Chabon presents a textual history of the contortions the Escapist might undergo in the hands of the various writers and artists of the Dark Horse project.

Chabon has differed most radically from previous novelists turned comic book progenitors, like Paul Auster, in his enthusiastic collaboration with professional comics artists, colorists, letterers, and editors. Chabon's active participation in extending, rather than simply adapting, his novels, has in turn inspired other contemporary novelists like Jonathan Lethem to explore the comics medium outside of their own fiction. Chabon presents his own "nitty gritty" tale as the writer of *Michael Chabon Presents The Amazing Adventures of the Escapist* No. 7, an issue whose cover promises "80 PERVERSELY PERSPICACIOUS PAGES! Featuring an original issue-length story written by Michael Chabon!" Rather than adapting his own material or trying his hand at creating another Escapist narrative, Chabon elects to create an entirely new character, the tortured killing machine Mr. Machine Gun. The cover's title *Michael Chabon Presents The Amazing Adventures of the Escapist* is boldly written over in large black letters renaming the issue *The Amazing Adventures of Mr. Machine Gun*. Mr. Machine Gun, presented in Brian Bolland's cover art as a man in a tuxedo and top hat with a machine gun in place of his right hand, is a character briefly mentioned in *The Amazing Adventures of Kavalier & Clay* (368). He is, according to an editorial note in *Escapist #7*, a character created "by Kavalier & Clay" (3, 31). One character in the issue also describes a picked lock as "worthy of the Escapist himself" (39). Apart from these references designed to further the illusion of Kavalier and Clay's reality, the 80 pages of the comic otherwise yield Chabon's efforts to develop an entirely new character for the comics medium.

Chabon gives his story the Vergilian title "Arms and the Man I Sing" in reference to the right arm of protagonist Ben Vanderslice, who has had his hand replaced with a mechanical device capable of becoming both a hand and the weapon that will make him into the conflicted hero Mr. Machine Gun (1). The main action of Chabon's Mr. Machine Gun adventure takes place in Nixon-era Washington D.C. where Vanderslice attempts to pass gun control legislation in the face of opposition from and machinations by his father, owner of Vanderslice Gun and Rifle, and a lobbyist named Fowler from the National Rifle Association (3, 7, 17). As in many politically-themed superhero comic book subplots — Marvel Comics's *The Uncanny X-Men* or, more absurdly the first issue of *Squadron Supreme*, in which Nighthawk (Kyle Richmond) has been elected president of the United States — the political plot serves as a commentary on and motivation for the main superhero action. Vanderslice's political problems are soon compounded by his wife's suicide, naturally by self-inflicted gunshot wound, and by *Washington World* reporter Sarah Schwartz's interest in the unexpected return of Vanderslice's alter-ego, the World War II hero Mr. Machine Gun. Like the Escapist and Captain America, Mr. Machine Gun had once "laid waste to entire Nazi divisions" (and later "Commies") but he seems to have returned to the nation's capital a changed man (55). In the screaming words of one of Schwartz's headlines, he is a "'HERO' ON A RAMPAGE," murdering the small-time robbers he finds on the streets of early 1970s Washington (26–7).

Chabon's "Arms and the Man I Sing" synthesizes narrative and visual styles, using editorial interjection and graphic art to illustrate the transitions between the story's various comics worlds. At the end of the first page, next to a panel depicting Vanderslice's conversation with his father about his proposed "Saturday Night Special bill," someone, either Chabon or series editor Diana Schutz, has inserted "Editor's Note: With the exception of the origin chapter by Kavalier & Clay, this story was first published in *Heavy Heroes* #1, Sunshine Media Group, July 1974" (3). This brief note links a number of Chabon's own Escapist incarnations, connecting Mr. Machine Gun's brief reference in *The Amazing Adventures of Kavalier & Clay* to Malachi B. Cohen's consideration of the "Sunshine Comics Years *1972–1976*" in "Escapism 101." The Sunshine Media publication date furthers the illusion that the comic's "original" publication came in the contemporary moment of the 1970s it describes. The game is continued in the story's second chapter, in which Bernard Schwartz narrates Mr. Machine Gun's 1940s origin in a story attributed to "Kavalier & Clay" (31). Eduardo Barreto's art and M.K. Perker's and Paul Hornschemeier's colors enhance this interplay between narrative periods, shifting between the bold lines, bright colors, and dynamic but anatomically limited action of 1940s comics and the realism, darker colors, and blackened alleys of 1970s comics artists like Neal Adams. Chabon's writing similarly shifts from the gothic castles, global plots, and unquestionably heroic heroes of the comic book "golden age" to the more realistically conflicted heroes of the "nitty gritty" 1970s.

The insider references, famous creators, and cultural interplay of the Dark Horse comics *Escapist* anthologies proved successful within the comic book industry. *Michael Chabon Presents the Amazing Adventures of the Escapist* won an Eisner Award, one of the industry's highest honors, for "Best Anthology" at the 2005 San Diego Comic Con (Comicbooks). As with such real superhero franchises as Batman, Superman, Spider-Man and the X-Men, the success of Chabon's comic book hero was soon rewarded with an additional title, *The Escapists* (2006), a six part mini-series created by writer Brian K. Vaughn and artists Jason S. Alexander, Steve Rolston, and Chabon's own Mr. Machine Gun collaborator Eduardo Barreto. This mini-series focuses on the revival of the Escapist for the new millennium by a team of young comics artists from Cleveland, which, fictional writer Max Roth notes is "Superman's ... hometown" (*Escapists* #1 1). Along the way, they create the comic, consider how to "create demand for ... [the] book with carefully staged [Escapist] appearances," and struggle with an evil media conglomerate (22). Editor Diana

Schutz has noted that this storyline "echoes the source novel ... in its focus on the real world of creating comic books" (*Escapists* #5 27). Like Chabon's Mr. Machine Gun adventure and the earlier Dark Horse line, one of the strategies employed by the creators of the new title is to visually differentiate between narrative worlds by employing the radically varied styles of several artists.

Each issue of *The Escapists* concludes with a letter section called "Chain Mail." These letters demonstrate the success that Chabon and Dark Horse Comics have had in bringing together in unprecedented ways comic book and fiction readers and creators with *The Amazing Adventures of Kavalier & Clay*, *The Amazing Adventures of the Escapist*, and *The Escapists*. Some readers, like Kenny Coble, comment that "this is the highest quality 'inspired by' comic I have ever read. This comic fits perfectly into the *Amazing Adventures of Kavalier & Clay* world" (*Escapists* #5 27). Others wish for further development of Chabon's novel. M. Jacob Alvarez reports that "when I first read Michael Chabon's book, it was not the description of the Escapist comics that grabbed my attention so wholly that I wished I could run out and buy them, but Josef Kavalier's Golem project" (*Escapists* #1 25). Adam White enclosed a review of *The Escapists* that he claimed to have already posted on ComicsCritique.com; this review concludes that "*The Escapists* serves up a unique comic book experience that takes place firmly in Chabon's world, Vaughn's world, and the real world all at once" (*Escapists* #3 25).

A letter printed in the fourth issue of *The Escapists* illustrates the market synthesis that Chabon and Dark Horse have exploited. Long time Chabon fan Frank Plowright suggests the complexity of the Chabon/Dark Horse nexus. Plowright writes:

> This is an impulse letter after reading *The Escapists* with my lunch just now. The whole *Escapist* thing puzzles me to an extent. Despite the top-of-the-line creators you've had working on the comic, the issues I've tried have done nothing for me. I first suspected the reason is that the novel stands alone saying everything that needs to be said, and there's the whiff of tawdriness about a spinoff dealing with what was largely incidental to the story being told (it could have been any old superhero, really, although the name obviously sparked parallels) ... I've come to the conclusion that the reason the main *Escapist* [*Michael Chabon Presents the Amazing Adventures of the Escapist*] leaves me cold is that it's spun off from something that was deeply personal, and no matter the quality of the creators used on the comic, it's not something personal to them and doesn't inspire them in the manner that the superheroes of their childhood can elsewhere.... Still, all this brings me to [the new comic project] *The Escapists*, which does have the heady aroma of personal involvement, and I thoroughly enjoyed an issue I might never have tried had it not been for the $1.00 price.... It's always a treat to see Phil Bond's art as well. A long time ago Tundra U.K. were going to finance a football comic in the U.K., and on my notice board in front of me I still have a great little cartoon self-portrait Phil did in marker when submitting some artwork.... As you're mining Kavalier & Clay [sic] for the Escapist, have you considered introducing elements from Michael Chabon's other novels? I first read *The Mysteries of Pittsburgh* around twenty years ago now, and themes from that would make groundbreaking comics [*Escapists* #4 27–8].

Plowright's letter is illuminating since his critique of *Michael Chabon Presents the Amazing Adventures of the Escapist* is *not* grounded in a traditional "highbrow" literary aversion to comics. What initially reads as a criticism of literary adaptation becomes a critique grounded within the comics medium. Indeed, Plowright emphasizes his familiarity with the artists involved in the project based on his own employment in the field as a former editor for Tundra U.K. Instead, his criticism of the "main *Escapist*" line is grounded by a reasoned comparison of the strengths of the novel against the perceived weaknesses of that particular comic line, weaknesses he feels minimized by the newer title. Plowright credentials himself not only as a comics industry insider, but also as an avid reader of Chabon's fiction, noting that he had "read *The Mysteries of Pittsburgh* around twenty years ago," or, at the start of the novelist's career, right when recent MFA recipient Michael Chabon published his first novel in 1987. Seldom has the border between the worlds of comic books and of literary fiction seemed as small as it does in Plowright's letter.

In the conclusion to his own Eisner-winning *Men of Tomorrow*, Gerard Jones briefly gestures towards Dark Horse's *Escapist* titles, using them as evidence of the increasing acceptance of comic book culture within other markets.[15] Jones sketches the history of Michael Chabon's Escapist:

> In 2001 Michael Chabon's novel about the "golden age" of the superheroes, animated with references to Will Eisner and Jack Kirby and Jerry Siegel and Joe Shuster, won the Pulitzer Prize. A few years later he turned Kavalier and Clay's creation, *The Escapist*, into a comic book. So the superheroes loop from junk to literature and back to junk again. Nothing has tested or proven or forced the fluidity of contemporary arts like comic book superheroes [339].

Jones describes Chabon's project as nearly a reverse of Miller's *Dark Knight Returns*, which he notes was "a sensation among comics fans, a best seller in the general book trade, and a litmus test of pop-cult hip among twenty-five-year-olds nationwide" (330). Although Jones doesn't quite trace out all of these connections, his book suggests that this "pop-cult hip" finds its culmination in the contemporary moment of Chabon's Escapist, a moment in which, "once the field of first entrance and last resort for men who wished they could do something better, superhero comics now possess a mystique all their own" (Jones 338). Jones supports this claim by noting two other high-profile media entrepreneurs who crossed over to comic book culture around the same time as Chabon's Dark Horse *Escapist* titles: "Kevin Smith, after making his name as a filmmaker with *Clerks* and *Chasing Amy*, took time away from the movies to write *Daredevil* for Marvel. When Joss Whedon retired from producing *Buffy the Vampire Slayer* he started writing *X-Men*" (338). Chabon, in Jones's comics history is following a developing trend, differing from Smith and Whedon in working on his own project rather than existing hero lines, perhaps, but representing a new development in the evolving "mystique" of the often-neglected superhero comic book.

Jones is, almost, exactly right. "Comics" is no longer a dirty word for literature and superhero comics do seem to be "test[ing] … the fluidity of contemporary arts." Superhero comics are, however, still testing that fluidity, precisely because they have been left out of the contemporary academic conversation of comics arts for so long. Michael Chabon has inaugurated a new development in the culture of contemporary literary fiction, one that demands the reconsideration of the relationship between literary fiction and mainstream, commercial superhero comic books. Chabon's evident enthusiasm for superhero comics and mainstream markets contrasts sharply with the irony of earlier comic book novels like Jay Cantor's *Krazy Kat*. Chabon's active participation in Dark Horse Comics's *Escapists* projects differ markedly from the graphic novel adaptation of *City of Glass*. That adaption had, after all, included an introduction by comics artist Art Spiegelman (rather than *City of Glass* novelist Paul Auster). Spiegelman's introduction had emphasized Auster's reluctance to "collaborate with a cartoonist," preferring instead that comics creators "adapt one of his already published works" (i, ii). The explosion of Singer's "Comic Book Novels" over the last decade, coupled with Jonathan Lethem's turn writing *Omega the Unknown* (2008), a new interpretation of the 1970s Marvel comic that made cameo appearances in Lethem's own *The Fortress of Solitude*, suggests both the extent to which old boundaries are continuing to merge and Michael Chabon's significance in that process. The lesson of Chabon's various *Kavalier & Clay* enterprises is that together literature, superhero comics, and their audiences might be able to have amazing adventures.

Notes

1. I follow Hillary Chute in referring to the medium as "comics." In "Comics as Literature? Reading Graphic Narrative," Chute claims that "*Comics*, like the term for any medium, requires a singular verb. Treating *comics* as a singular has become standard; McCloud ... [and] numerous other scholars support this usage" (462 emphasis hers).

2. For Kane and Schwartz's version refer to "The Origin of Batman" in *Batman* 47 (1948), reprinted in *The Greatest Batman Stories Ever Told* (66–78). The plot to this episode is neatly resolved with a narrative box: "And so, at last, the case is closed — the case without which there would never have been a Batman!" The image accompanying the text is of Batman writing the word "closed" on a case file titled "Murder of Thomas Wayne" (78).

3. Chabon's list of sources also suggests the variety of his influences, ranging from the Jewish mystical texts discussed by Lee Behlman ('The Escapist'), to works by novelist Richard Wright and comics legend Jack Kirby. Chabon concludes the "Author's Note" with the frank claim, "Finally, I want to acknowledge the deep debt I owe in this and everything else I've ever written to the work of the late Jack Kirby, the King of Comics" (639). Chabon has discussed his interview with Will Eisner in a *Publishers Weekly* interview conducted by David Walton and at greater length in the chapter "Thoughts on the Death of Will Eisner" in his own book of essays *Maps and Legends* (141–4).

4. I am indebted to Scott Smith of Pennsylvania State University for directing me to this book and passage.

5. Chabon discusses the relationship between Jewish-American identity and comic book creation in the interview with Walton. For more on Chabon's examination of Jewish-American identity and his use of the traditions of Jewish mysticism, please refer to Behlman. Additional discussion of the relationship between Jewish-American culture and the history of early comics may be found throughout Jones's *Men of Tomorrow*.

6. Benton does not provide a specific date for the hearings. Jones does not clearly present this sequence, but he appears to date the events to "three days in May 1954" (274).

7. The same sort of items were commonly found for sale in the pages of seemingly every D.C. or Marvel superhero comic book through the 1960s, 1970s, and 1980s, prior to the move towards glossier, more prestigious, comics in the 1990s.

8. Chabon again builds on real comics history as Clay tells Kavalier "How ... is not the question. What? is not the question ... the question is *why* ... why is he [the superhero] doing it" (94). Jones claims that writer Bill Finger's greatest contribution to the creation of Batman was that he was "the first to bring a novelist's questions to bear on a superhero. Why would a man choose such a life ... he ... turned just another Superman knockoff into a character with soul" (155). Benton describes Batman as "the perfect complement to the almost bright and cheery Superman" (24).

9. Behlman calls this an "origin story" and notes that Chabon "inserts a full chapter in which the origin tale of the Escapist is told as a short story, in prose that manages to combine sophisticated narrative and descriptive material with the gee-whiz dialogue of Sam Clay's comic book. The comic book story, then, is transmuted in the narrator's hands into a kind of literary hybrid ... yet is also clearly a comic book story, with all the trappings of its fantasy world" ("The Escapist" 65).

10. Hillary Chute discusses the importance of Houdini for both Escapist creators. She positions Houdini as a middle ground between the high culture represented by Kavalier and the low represented by

Clay (283). The anonymous *Publishers Weekly* reviewer notes that "Sammy's contribution to the super-hero's alter ego, Tom Mayflower, is his own stick legs, a legacy of childhood polio" (44).

11. I am indebted to Scott Smith for this observation. Chute notes the similarity of the two covers in her analysis of the novel, linking the covers to Chabon's "debt to Jack Kirby, who drew, in 1941, the cover of *Captain America Comics* 1, which depicts the titular superhero punching Hitler in the jaw" (296). Behlman does not note the similarity of covers but does remark that "'The Escapist' … like Captain America and the Human Torch, can fight whole divisions of Nazi soldiers single-handedly" ("The Escapist" 65, 63). A rendering of the cover Chabon describes was subsequently included as an illustration to Malachi B. Cohen's article "Escapism 101," itself an adaptation of sections of Chabon's novel, in the Dark Horse Comic *Michael Chabon Presents the Amazing Adventures of the Escapist*, Volume 1 (25). This version of the cover oddly fails to conform to many of the details as described by Chabon in *The Amazing Adventures of Kavalier & Clay*.

12. In *Classics Illustrated: A Cultural History with Illustrations* (2002), William B. Jones Jr. contends that "*Classics Illustrated* may be the most misunderstood comic books in the history of sequential art" having been "dismissed … as vulgar corruptions of the literary masterpieces on which they were based" or "condemned … because they were not superhero comics" by "certain comics champions" (vii).

13. Chute describes the dark Horse Comics series as "a far-reaching commercial enterprise," but mis-leadingly states that Chabon "now publishes an ongoing actual comic book series, which he scripts" (281).

14. Malachi B. Cohen is an anagram for Michael Chabon. Cohen also contributed the brief essay "Independent Comic Book Publishers of the Pre–Independent Era," an account of Chabon's childhood efforts to create comic book heroes with his friends, to *McSweeney's Quarterly Concern* 13 (127–8). The cover of *Michael Chabon Presents the Amazing Adventures of the Escapist, Volume 2* includes a drawing of "The Puppet Master … Malachi B. Cohen … a premier 'comic book' historian"; the image is a drawing of Chabon. Subsequent commentary on Dark Hose *Escapist* titles has been provided by the more enigmatic presence of "Bubbles La Tour." One of LaTour's articles concludes with the byline "Bubbles LaTour is resident comics historian at Dark Horse. She would like to extend her utmost gratitude to Ms. Ayelet Waldman for her help in preparation of this article" (*Escapists* #4 25). Waldman is Chabon's real-life wife.

15. Jones won an Eisner award for "Best Comics-Related Book" at the 2005 Eisner Awards, the same ceremony for which *The Amazing Adventures of the Escapist* won "Best Anthology" (Comicbooks).

Works Cited

"*The Amazing Adventures of Kavalier & Clay*" [review]. *Publishers Weekly*, August 21, 2000, 44.

Auster, Paul. *City of Glass* [graphic novel]. Adapted by Paul Karasik and David Mazzucchelli. Introduction by Art Spiegelman. New York: Picador, 1994, 2004.

Behlman, Lee. "The Escapist: Fantasy, Folklore, and the Pleasures of the Comic Book in Recent Jewish American Holocaust Fiction." *Shofar: An Interdisciplinary Journal of Jewish Studies* 22.3 (2004): 56–71.

_____. "Michael Chabon." *Holocaust Literature: An Encyclopedia of Writers and Their Work*. New York: Routledge, 2003. 224–230.

Benton, Mike. *The Comic Book in America: An Illustrated History*. Dallas: Taylor, 1989.

Burton, Tim, Dir. *Batman*. Perf. Jack Nicholson, Michael Keaton. VHS. Warner Home Video, 1989.

Cantor, Jay. *Krazy Kat*. New York: Vintage, 1987.

Chabon, Michael. *The Amazing Adventures of Kavalier & Clay*. New York: Picador, 2000.

_____. "Arms and the Man I Sing." Art Eduardo Barreto, M.K. Perker, et al., in *The Amazing Adventures of the Escapist* 7. Ed. Diana Schutz. Milwaukie, OR: Dark Horse, 2005.

_____. *Maps and Legends: Reading and Writing Along the Borderlands*. San Francisco: McSweeney's, 2008.

Chute, Hillary. "Comics as Literature? Reading Graphic Narrative." *PMLA* 123.2 (2008): 452–466.

_____. "*Ragtime, Kavalier and Clay*, and the Framing of Comics." *MFS Modern Fiction Studies*. 54.2 (2008): 268–301.

Cohen, Malachi B. "Independent Comic Book Publishers of the Pre–Independent Era." In *McSweeney's Quarterly Concern* 13. Ed. Chris Ware. San Francisco: McSweeney's, 2004. 127–128.

Comicbooks. http://comicbooks.about.com/od/conventionsandevents/a/eisner05.htm. Accessed 7/17/08.

Díaz, Junot. *The Brief Wondrous Life of Oscar Wao*. New York: Riverhead, 2007.

Jones, Gerard. *Men of Tomorrow: Geeks, Gangsters, and the Birth of the Comic Book*. New York: Basic, 2004.

Jones, William B., Jr. *Classics Illustrated: A Cultural History with Illustrations.* Jefferson, NC: McFarland, 2002.

Lee, Stan, and Steve Ditko. "Spider-Man!" *Amazing Fantasy* 15. August 1962. Reprinted in *Marvel Masterworks Presents: The Amazing Spider-Man, Volume 1 Collection The Amazing Spider-Man Nos. 1–10 and Amazing Fantasy No. 15.* New York: Marvel, 2003. 1–13.

Lethem, Jonathan. *The Fortress of Solitude.* New York: Doubleday, 2003.

Maryles, Daisy. "Behind the Bestsellers." *Publishers Weekly,* October 9, 2000, 22.

Miller, Frank, Klaus Janson and Lynn Varley. *Batman: The Dark Knight Returns,* Tenth Anniversary Edition. New York: DC, 1996.

Nolan, Christopher, Dir. *Batman Begins.* Perf. Christian Bale, Morgan Freeman, Liam Neeson. DVD. Warner, 2005.

"The Origin of the Batman." Art by Bob Kane and Lou Schwartz, coloring by Adrienne Roy. *Batman* 47 (1948). Reprinted in *The Greatest Batman Stories Ever Told.* New York: DC, 1988. 66–78.

Orvell, Miles. "Writing Posthistorically: *Krazy Kat, Maus,* and the Contemporary American Fiction Cartoon." *American Literary History* 4.1 (1992): 110–128.

Schutz, Diana, ed. *Michael Chabon Presents the Amazing Adventures of the Escapist,* Vol. 2. Milwaukie, OR: Dark Horse, 2004.

Schutz, Diana, and Dave Land, eds. *Michael Chabon Presents the Amazing Adventures of the Escapist,* Vol. 1. Milwaukie, OR: Dark Horse, 2004.

Singer, Marc. "Embodiments of the Real: The Counterlinguistic Turn in the Comic-Book Novel." *Critique* 49.3 (2008): 273–289.

Smith, Scott. Conversation. April 25, 2005.

Spiegelman, Art. *Maus I.* New York: Pantheon, 1980.

_____. *Maus II.* New York: Pantheon, 1992.

Vaughan, Brian K. *The Escapists* 1. Art Philip Bond, Eduardo Barreto, et al. Milwaukie, OR: Dark Horse, 2006.

_____. *The Escapists* 2. Art Jason S. Alexander, Steve Rolston, et al. Milwaukie, OR: Dark Horse, 2006.

_____. *The Escapists* 3. Art Steve Rolston, Jason S. Alexander, et al. Milwaukie, OR: Dark Horse, 2006.

_____. *The Escapists* 4. Art Jason S. Alexander, Steve Rolston, et al. Milwaukie, OR: Dark Horse, 2006.

_____. *The Escapists* 5. Art Jason S. Alexander Steve Rolston, et al. Milwaukie, OR: Dark Horse, 2006.

_____. *The Escapists* 6. Art Jason S. Alexander, Eduardo Barreto, Steve Rolston, et al. Milwaukie, OR: Dark Horse, 2006.

Walton, David. "PW Talks with Michael Chabon." *Publishers Weekly,* August 21, 2000, 45.

2

The Comic Modernism
of George Herriman

Daniel Stein

Introduction

When Virginia Woolf wrote in *Mr. Bennett and Mrs. Brown* that "[o]n or about December 1910, human character changed" (4), she provided literary critics with a convenient birth date for the modernist period. For students of the American newspaper comic, however, she was off by a few months. It was in the summer of that year, July 26, to be precise, that a New Orleans-born cartoonist named George Herriman decided to add a second layer of action at the bottom of his successful strip *The Family Upstairs*: a tiny mouse hurling a little pebble at the head of an oblivious cat. In the weeks and months to follow, Herriman continued the sideshow scenario, spinning a series of humorous variations on a basic theme: the queer feud between the ingenious mouse and the simple-minded cat. The readers of William Randolph Hearst's *New York Evening Journal*, in which the strip appeared, delighted in the doings of these funny animals, and Herriman soon separated the action into two strips running side by side: *The Dingbat Family* and *Krazy Kat and Ignatz*. Beginning in October 1913, *Krazy Kat* finally appeared as an independent daily strip, and on April 23, 1916, Herriman started a large-sized weekly Sunday page. Quite amazingly, he continued to draw both daily strip and Sunday page until his death on April 25, 1944, creating what comic scholar Bill Blackbeard recently dubbed an "opus giganticus" ("Pilfering" 6).

To argue that the history of modernism should be rewritten because of the work of a newspaper cartoonist like George Herriman may be considered an act of intellectual heresy. Yet I believe that it makes sense to investigate the relationship between modernist cultural production, especially literature and the visual arts, and the unique phenomenon of *Krazy Kat*. After all, Herriman's life span fits the modernist period to a T (1880–1944), and *Krazy Kat* was readily embraced by luminaries such as Gertrude Stein — who showed newspaper clippings to Pablo Picasso in Paris and read them over the telephone to James

Joyce — as well as T.S. Eliot and e.e. cummings.[1] What is more, for avid readers of *Krazy Kat*, the modernist implications of the strip have long been apparent. Following Gilbert Seldes's celebration of Herriman in *The Seven Lively Arts* (1924), critics have characterized *Krazy Kat* as "one of the wonders of modern literature" (Amiran 57) that "combined the aesthetics of modernism with a jazzy American voice" (Heer 8).

The question remains whether such nods toward the modernism of Herriman's comic strip can withstand analytical scrutiny and, if they do, where we should place it in "the space of modernist practice" (Gendron 4–5). Adam Gopnik's view of *Krazy Kat* as an "uncannily modern" work "bearing deep affinities to the spirit and form of crucial styles in vanguard art" ("Genius") provides a useful working thesis. This view is intriguing for two reasons. First, it does not assign *Krazy Kat* a place in the modernist canon of "high" art by naively suggesting that Herriman's strip pursued goals and applied representational techniques identical with those of modernist writers and painters — Gopnik wisely speaks of "deep affinities" rather than a shared aesthetic program. Since newspaper comic strips were published in daily and weekly installments as entertainment for a mass audience of urban dwellers, they were subject to commercial considerations and emerged from creative processes much different from the more self-determined aesthetic practices of modernist poetry, fiction, and painting. They must be understood as "another kind of modern art" (Gopnik, "Comics" 153), as "an outcome of the process of modernization" and "a humor-based response to the problems of representation faced by a society in transition" (Gordon 6). Second, *Krazy Kat*'s modernism points to the status of the comic strip as "a despised medium" (Seldes 231) that began as a culturally marginal phenomenon — as a means of increasing the readership of tabloid newspapers — and only slowly and imperfectly made its way into the cultural center.

Initially created "to fill up the waste space" (Herriman quoted in McDonnell 52), Krazy and Ignatz tiptoed their way into the consciousness of an intellectual readership by traveling "across the cultural divide" between "low brow" culture and the modernist avant-garde.[2] I suggest that we map Herriman's modernist aesthetics and the affinities between his comic strip and the modernist literature and visual arts of the early twentieth century by asking a series of questions about *Krazy Kat*'s place in what Daniel Singal calls modernist culture: the "constellation of related ideas, beliefs, values, and modes of perception […] that came into existence during the mid to late nineteenth century […] and that has had a powerful influence on art and thought on both sides of the Atlantic since roughly 1900" (2). These questions are: What are the strip's cultural origins? How does it stage racial and gender identities? What languages does it speak? What is its relation to the visual culture of modernism? And how does it work through, and comment on, its own mediality? It is important to note at the outset that the task of unraveling Herriman's comic modernism is complicated by the silences surrounding the cartoonist's influences and intensions. As Thomas Inge notes, "we hardly know what he thought about society and politics" (*Comics* 44). Bill Blackbeard, too, has a point when he concludes that "Herriman's intellectuality remains still unplumbed" ("Man" 11).[3] The aim of this essay, then, is to make sense of Herriman's participation in American modernism by plumbing the literary and visual intellectuality of the strip: "I ain't a Kat … and I ain't Krazy," we are told, "it's wot's behind me that I am" (quoted in Seldes 234–35).

"So Ginteel, so Riffime, so Soba": The Genteel Tradition

Newspaper comic strips emerged in the 1890s, when cartoonists like Richard Felton Outcault (*Yellow Kid*) and Rudolph Dirks (*Katzenjammer Kids*) developed a style of graphic humor different from the more serious and high-minded tradition of the political caricature printed in the weekly magazines *Puck*, *Life*, *Judge*, and *Punch*.[4] The purpose of these strips, which were offered as colored supplements to the Sunday editions of newspapers such as Hearst's *New York Journal* and Joseph Pulitzer's *New York World*, was to provide an easily accessible type of graphic humor with which a mass of readers — workers, immigrants, and their children — could identify. In order to appeal to such a heterogeneous audience, cartoonists drew on existing popular entertainment, for instance the slapstick routines of vaudeville theater. Frederick Burr Opper's *Happy Hooligan* is a fitting example here, as is *Krazy Kat*, whose basic punch line (delivered in almost every strip) is the comic essence of vaudeville: Ignatz's successful "beaning of the kat's bonnet" or "creasing of the kat's noodle with a brick."[5]

If modernism is understood in very general terms as a conscious rejection of the genteel Victorian values and traditions that had shaped American life and the arts in the nineteenth century, the appearance of a new medium like the comic strip shared in modernism's project of cultural change. In 1846, about half a century before the inception of the first strips, William Wordsworth composed a sonnet in which he objected to the rise of "Illustrated Books and Newspapers." Speaking of "this vile abuse of pictured page" and associating this new "dumb Art" with a regression "back to childhood," Wordsworth appealed to the heavens to "keep us from a lower stage" of visual culture (16). Read in this context, comic strips like *Krazy Kat* are part of a visual turn in the course of which a graphic form of mass entertainment — the movies being another form — took precedence over the more traditional literary genres of prose and verse.

Herriman repeatedly punned on the genteel tradition which George Santayana had associated with American intellectual parochialism in his lecture on "The Genteel Tradition in American Philosophy" (1911).[6] As Mrs. Henn tells Krazy on August 19, 1928: "You are indeed genteel." A few years later, Krazy enjoys "a dellightfil poddy [party]" because it is "so ginteel, so riffime, so soba" (so genteel, so refined, so sober; September 29, 1935), and Offissa Pupp declares in yet another episode that "the good the genteel the gracious" and "the sinful — the shameful the seditious — they shall *not* meet" (March 21, 1937). Singal speaks of the Victorian wish for "a radical standard of innocence" and of the attendant struggle against everything evil and corrupted (5). Recalling Matthew Arnold's ideal of a symphonic world of "harmonious perfection" (11), Offissa Pupp battles the "symphony of sin" (November 16, 1941), while Krazy dreams of a world in "poifick hominy" (perfect harmony; October 15, 1939) and refers to Herriman as the strip's "conductor" (*Panoramic* 33).

Herriman's world of harmonious perfection is depicted most vividly in a Sunday page of 1936 (December 13). The episode begins with Krazy's lonely singing and commences with Offissa Pupp, Mrs. Kwakk Kwakk, and even Ignatz joining in to sing in harmony. Krazy insists on the comic page as a poetic space in which the ravages of modernity cannot intrude: "Then, terry a while with me, for I am this day dwellink in peace," he muses elsewhere, and "[i]n these blissful hours my soul will know no strife / In my kosmis there will be no feeva of discord / All my immotions will function in hominy, and kind feelings" (quoted in Blackmore 19).[7] It is important to realize that this world of harmonious perfection is never fully attained; there is always the brick which simultaneously signifies love (for Krazy), rejection (for Ignatz), and sinful transgression (for Offissa Pupp). Offissa Pupp's inability to root out Ignatz's "evil" doings constitutes Herriman's challenge to the Victorian standard of innocence, even though the wish for innocence is central to the comic strip. Herriman should thus be understood as a "post–Victorian" who "did not at heart desire to overthrow nineteenth-century moralism, but rather to temper or emend it [...]" (Singal 6).[8]

The climax of the strip (Ignatz's brick throw and Krazy's reaction) builds on the works of classical antiquity, especially Roman mythology. As such, it combines a comic critique of nineteenth-century neo-classicism with both the irreverence of popular culture and the more serious modernist practice of intertextual reference to canonized literature. As a symbol of love — a "missil of affection" — the brick replaces Cupid's arrow, and Ignatz becomes Krazy's "l'il Cupid" (June 28, 1925). Like Cupid, Ignatz is a "l'il anjil" with the power to instill instant love in those he hits with his arrow/brick. Visually, this is expressed by the simultaneity of the brick's impact on Krazy's head ("Pow") and the Kat's love (an iconic heart), both of which are always rendered in the same picture. Moreover, in one of Herriman's first *Krazy Kat* strips (1911), Ignatz gazes at a painting that depicts Cupid looking at his reflection in the water of a pond. Inspired by this image, which combines Robert Anning Bell's painting *Cupid's Mirror* with the story of Narcissus, Ignatz runs to a nearby lake to watch his own reflection. While he succeeds at first, a dumb-looking Krazy appears from the depths of the lake, his face supplanting Ignatz's reflection. Angered by this displacement of self-love with the kat's unnatural love, Ignatz hurls a boulder at Krazy and a brick at the painting: "Krazy Kupid," he rants (*Panoramic* 16), mocking genteel aspirations toward classical refinement by using it as the basis for a vaudevillian shtick.[9]

"Rigid Vogna in Beer Fleet": Modernist Minstrelsy

The deep affinities between Herriman's comic modernism and modernist culture lie partly in a shared investment with minstrelsy and vaudeville entertainment, which allowed Herriman to construct humorous allusions to "high" culture and motivated a poet like T.S. Eliot to insert snippets of "low" culture onto his work.[10] A comparative reading of selected works by Eliot and various episodes from *Krazy Kat* may illustrate this point. Michael North and David Chinitz have argued that Eliot's and Ezra Pound's epistolary blackface posturing (Eliot as "Possum," Pound as "Brer Rabbit" and "Tar Baby"); the subtitle of *Sweeney Agonistes* ("Fragment of a Comic Minstrelsy"); and quotations of Rosamond Johnson, Bob Cole, and James Weldon Johnson's "coon" song "Under the Bamboo Tree" (1902) reveal the minstrel show as "an unexpected prototype for Eliot's experiments" (North, *Dialect* 85). Associating minstrelsy's "art of mélange" (the combination of mock speeches, sentimental singing, melodramatic plots, and slapstick humor) with Eliot's eclectic intertextuality, North finds an essentially modernist practice of "slumming in slang"

(82) that makes use of a wide range of popular sources. What critics have not recognized, however, is the connection between Eliot's minstrel elements and Herriman's comic involvement with minstrelsy. While this connection does not seem to be a direct one — Eliot knew *Krazy Kat* (cf. Aiken 21), but we find neither clearly marked intertextual references to the strip in Eliot nor obvious allusions to Eliot in *Krazy Kat* — it provides insight into the "unkenna" (Krazy's version of uncanny) relationship between high modernism and modern popular culture.

Among the most fascinating elements of this connection are Eliot's self-identification as a banjo-player as well as several references to minstrelsy in *The Waste Land* (1922) and *Sweeney Agonistes* (1932), all of which are either preceded or echoed by *Krazy Kat*. In a letter to Mary Hutchinson (1920), Eliot identified himself as an American minstrel figure in contradistinction to a bard of European suasion: "it is a jazz-banjorine that I should bring, not a lute" (*Letters* 357). As Chinitz notes, "Eliot's comment effectively cast him as a blackface comic" since the banjo was the most readily recognizable visual and sonic emblem of the minstrel show (22). In *The Waste Land*, references to "that Shakespeherian Rag" (l. 128) and "[t]he rattle of the bones, and chuckle spread from ear to ear" (l. 186) conjure up minstrel parodies of Shakespeare's plays, the musical productions of the endmen Tambo (tambourine) and Bones (bone castanets), as well as their exaggerated blackface grin (represented through the synaesthetic "chuckle spread from ear to ear").[11] Equally intriguing are two lines Eliot used in a draft version of *The Waste Land*: "Meet me in the shadow of the watermelon vine / Eva Iva Uva Emmaline" (quoted in North, *Dialect* 85).[12] These lines cite the "coon" song "By the Watermelon Vine" (Thomas S. Allen 1904) and the vaudeville number "My Evaline" (Mae Anwerde Sloane, 1901). Eliot's revised lyrics of "Under the Bamboo Tree" complete the minstrel continuum. They include the phrases "Under the bamboo tree / Two live as one / One live as two / Two live as three" sung to the musical rattle of SWARTS AS TAMBO, SNOW AS BONES (*Complete* 81).

The very concept of Herriman's strip — funny anthropomorphic animals seeking to outsmart each other — feeds off the minstrel show's investment in costume and disguise. In an early daily strip (August 29, 1918), Krazy and Ignatz appear on stage as Tambo and Bones (the color scheme corresponds with Eliot's Swarts and Snow), and Ignatz opens the show with the familiar "Gentlemen — Be Seated!!"[13] Herriman further makes a series of intertextual references to the many minstrel versions of Harriet Beecher Stowe's *Uncle Tom's Cabin* (1851/52) which had dominated American theatrical entertainment since the early 1850s. Krazy repeatedly calls Ignatz "Ole Topsy" (a member "of the well known 'Turvy' femly"), misquotes the names of central characters ("Simon Degree"), parodies Uncle Tom's evangelism ("You may beat this pore ole black body, but my soul belongs to 'Sitting Bull'!!!"), argues that Uncle Tom is better off than Uncle Sam because "he at least had a 'cabin,'" and finally introduces his own disgruntled "Unkil 'Tom Ket'" (*Panoramic*, March 10, March 31, June 16, June 24, July 28, October 21, 1920).[14] Add to this Krazy's love of the stereotypical "darky" food, the "watta-melon," his spirited banjo playing (the depiction of which is indebted to "coon" imagery), and his singing of popular tunes (including Stephen Foster's minstrel evergreen "My Old Kentucky Home" on March 1, 1936), and you have a minstrel presence that is both substantial and richly suggestive.[15]

Apart from the resonances between *Krazy Kat* and Eliot's minstrelsy already mentioned—Tambo and Bones, the banjo—three additional and to date unacknowledged concurrences exist. First, Eliot's lines "Under the bamboo tree / Two live as one / One live as two / Two live as three" perfectly capture the basic plot of *Krazy Kat*: the two who live as one are, at least to the Kat's romantic delusions, Krazy and Ignatz, yet this unusual couple cannot enact its mating dance without a third essential party: Offissa Pupp, who continually seeks to foil Ignatz's assaults on Krazy and who is secretly in love with the Kat. The comic duo, the endmen Krazy and Ignatz, cannot live without the minstrel show's master of ceremonies, the interlocutor: the two therefore must live as three. Second, Eliot's blackface references to the lovers' shaded locus of affection—"under the bamboo tree"; "meet me in the shadow of the watermelon vine"—are mirrored by Herriman's use of the watermelon as a comic prop and by a recurrent plot development: Ignatz's attempts to lure Krazy to nightly meetings "at the 'blue bean bush'" (October 26, 1941), "under the old smoke tree by the hot rock" (May 22, 1927), and similar clandestine places, where the rambunctious mouse plans to thwart Krazy's love by tossing the ubiquitous brick. In Eliot's draft of *The Waste Land*, this minstrel parody of the melodramatic love scene resurfaces in the quotation of "My Evaline" as "Eva Iva Uva Emmaline"; in *Krazy Kat*, it shapes the Kat's declaration of eternal affection for Ignatz: "To he, I am for evva true" (quoted in Crocker, "Gender" n. pag.).

The third element of Eliot's modernist indebtedness to minstrelsy and Herriman's comic use of minstrel entertainment are the many references to Shakespearian drama that litter the authors' intertextual and intermedial universes. For Eliot, quotations of Shakespeare work in two ways: (primarily) as evidence of an exhausted literary tradition and (occasionally) as allusions to American popular culture (cf. *The Waste Land* ll. 128–30: "O O O O that Shakespeherian Rag—/ It's so elegant / So intelligent"). Eliot's reference to "That Shakespearian Rag" must thus be understood as a self-conscious dip into the lower strata of popularized Shakespearian drama. For Herriman, who worked in a "low" medium, a tune like "That Shakespearian Rag" was only one of the countless comic Shakespeare adaptations that could serve as an inspiration for his comic strip.

Shakespearian parodies had long captivated American audiences by the time Herriman included them in *Krazy Kat*. As Lawrence Levine notes, "[e]verywhere in the nation burlesques and parodies of Shakespeare constituted a prominent form of entertainment" (13), and most often, references and skits from Shakespearian drama were "inserted into other modes of entertainment" (15).[16] Herriman's allusions to "Mr. Shakespear" (*Panoramic* October 8, 1920) are examples of such burlesque insertions; they translate nineteenth-century entertainment practices into the medium of the comic strip while not necessarily being interested in any serious engagement with Elizabethan theater. Thus, Ignatz's announcement "A brick—My kingdom for a brick!" (January 25, 1942) provides little intertextual commentary about *Richard III* (1592/93) but says much about Herriman's knowledge of American minstrelsy, as part of which Richard III was routinely staged.[17] Most often, Herriman used Krazy's idiosyncratic wit to pun on plays such as *Merry Wives of Windsor* (1597), *Much Ado About Nothing* (1598), *Othello* (1603), and *Macbeth* (1606). In a panoramic daily from March 24, 1921, Krazy wonders, "[d]un't you think if a fella had a lotta wives they'd be awfil unheppy," only to recall a fellow named Mr. Windsor in the next panel "who had a lotta wives and yet they was all heppy." In later episodes, Mrs.

Kwakk Kwakk calls Ignatz's fruitless attempts to hit Krazy "much adoing, nothing done" (March 3, 1940); Offissa Pupp signs a pledge to "try the milk of kindness, the unction of gentleness" (November 3, 1935); Krazy rejects Ignatz's brick because the mouse is spotting a heavy suntan and Krazy wants to be "no 'Desdamonia' you Otello" (July 26, 1921; reprinted in Heer 12).

On rare occasions, Herriman devoted a whole Sunday page to Shakespearian play. In the episode from January 10, 1926, Krazy is standing on a balcony and compares himself to "'Joliet' awaiting her 'Rummio.'" According to Ignatz's decidedly non-romantic analysis of the situation, however, Krazy is "perched up on that balcony like a pickle on a pole." Ignatz's words are a verbal version of the brick; they express impatience with high sentiments and provide a vaudevillian cure. Rounding off the vaudevillian presentations of Shakespeare are two skits about *Hamlet* (1600). The protagonist of this tragedy, if we believe Krazy, is not a great king but "a small 'ham'" (*Dailies* February 14, 1919), and while Krazy sees himself as "a tragedian 'Ket'" with "dremetic telents," he concedes: "I could do 52 weeks in Hemlet only I don't like little willages'" (quoted in Schmitz 141). The double pun — hamlet as a term for a small village and the notion that the struggle for political influence in the play is the result of an overblown will to power ("little willages") — illustrates the subdued nature of Herriman's political critique.

If the similarities between Eliot's and Herriman's minstrel roots are intriguing, the differences are equally fascinating because they foreground the discrepancies between modernist literature and popular comic modernism. These differences are captured in Eliot's citations of Richard Wagner's *Tristan und Isolde* (1859) in *The Waste Land* (ll. 31–34: "Frisch weht der Wind / Der Heimat zu / Mein Irisch Kind / Wo weilest du?") and Krazy's more cryptic, yet ultimately more comic, exclamation about a snippet of music that "sounds like the envil choritz by Rigid Vogna in beer fleet" (quoted in Forrest 251). Here, Wagner's bombastic music in b-flat (a chorus massive like an anvil penned by a rigid composer) is placed where many Americans would have actually encountered it: in the beer halls and vaudeville theaters that succeeded the minstrel shows of the nineteenth century.

"We Call Him 'Cat,' We Call Him 'Crazy' Yet He Is Neither": Staging Identity

Ever since Asa Berger discovered that Herriman's birth certificate listed him as "colored" and that his parents were labeled "mulatto" in the census of 1880, a debate has taken place about the cartoonist's racial origins and the potential "black aesthetic" of *Krazy Kat* (cf. Heer 8–9).[18] Rather than trying to settle the debate, I want to turn to Herriman's comic representations of race — but also of gender — as quintessentially modernist engagements with questions of identity that suggest a shift from an essentialist conception of racial, sexual, and social belonging to a modern understanding of identity as something contextual and performative.[19] My investigation is based on four assumptions. First, it is vital that we approach the issue with a firm understanding of *Krazy Kat*'s allegiance with blackface minstrelsy and ethnic comedy in mind — after all, Herriman placed the names of his characters in quotation marks, thus presenting them as actors playing a variety of roles. Second, we should search for a "black aesthetic" in *Krazy Kat*. Third, we should consider the practice of racial passing. Rather than conceive of passing as an endeavor steeped in self-hatred and racial betrayal, it makes more sense to view Herriman "as a figure who values individualism," "self-determination, and free choice," as Kathleen Pfeiffer proposes in her reading of passing novels (2). Fourth, Herriman's representation of race is deeply invested with questions of gender.[20]

Herriman's interest in visual indicators of race is unmistakable, even though it is often masked by comedy. On December 12, 1926, a Dalmatian prompts Krazy's exclamation: "I hate 'freckils'[...]. But, 'tan,' ah-h-h — 'tan,' that's wot I love — ooy — if only 'Ignatz' had a tan — instead of being a pale, pink, pellid l'il 'mice.'" When Ignatz finally arrives with a sun tan, Krazy croons: "Ooy-yooy-yooy wot a goldish oak finish — like a swell mihoginny piyenna — l'il dusky dahlink!!!" This is an intriguing comment about the beauties of light-black skin — Ignatz is no longer adored as a "pale, pink, pellid l'il 'mice,'" but as a "goldish," "mihoginny," and "dusky dahlink" — and it expresses Herriman's critique of American racism. On the one hand, the semantic field from which Krazy takes his formulations is that of furniture ("oak finish"; "mihoginny"), which insinuates that romantic views of racial affection often turn black people into objects of attraction (to be used for comfort like furniture). On the other hand, Krazy's remarks indicate the complexity of color codes in a country in which one drop of African blood makes one "legally black yet visibly white" (Pfeiffer 2). Instead of juxtaposing whiteness with blackness, Krazy distinguishes among various hues of skin color: pale, pink, and pallid versus goldish oak, mahogany, and dusky. From a Sunday strip of the mid–1920s (January 16, 1927) readers would have known that Krazy's own fur is "chocolate colored."

Such references to racial codes attain additional substance through a strip about scientific racism from the 1910s. This episode is devoted to the controversy between Darwinism and polygeneric theory. Reading a book titled "Darwin Theory," Krazy maintains: "It say's [sic] here that we *all* sprang from the same source." Ignatz objects by citing from another publication: "Darwin's theory — Fooey — This book, 'Kat,' is my old pal 'Rinaldo's' polygeneric theory. *He* says that Darwin is a rhummy and that you kats were always kats, and we mouses always mouses, so you see we're *not* related" (reprinted in Heer 8).[21] One may argue that Ignatz's refutation of Darwinism undermines Herriman's plea for racial integration, but such an argument would have to ignore Krazy's genuine love for Ignatz and the mouse's willingness to date the kat for several decades.[22] It would also have to ignore a daily strip from June 9, 1921, in which Krazy sows two seeds from which a black and a white tree grow. Once the trees have matured, one of them spots a wedding band, and soon after a host of black and white trees gather around their parents (reprinted in Heer 11). This "horticulturish romence" clearly rejects American miscegenation laws.

I have already discussed selected examples of Herriman's minstrel and vaudeville roots, but there is more to be unearthed about this theatrical connection. In a Sunday page from June 22, 1935, Ignatz seeks shelter from Offissa Pupp in a stove pipe and emerges covered in soot. Dreaming of Ignatz as a "l'il blondish beautifil — so pink — so fair — so like a primp rose," Krazy is startled by the appearance of the blackened mouse:

Krazy's thoughts on the color of beauty express Herriman's critique of American racism (December 12, 1926).

"Haa — a l'il eetiopium mice, bleck like a month from midnights — fuwi." With unusual verve, Krazy kicks the black mouse into a lake and insists on the social separation of the races: "I got a great care who I issociate wit' — y-y-y' sun boint koffa kake —. This will titch soitin pippils to keep in their own social spears." This illustrates Herriman's veiled commentary on American race relations. Krazy speaks a theatrical language, combining sentimental diction ("so pink — so fair — so like a primp rose") with the vocabulary of minstrelsy's Ethiopian Delineators ("l'il eetiopium mice, bleck like a month from midnights"). In the guise of a theatrical stock figure, the kat makes an important statement: Americans are intoxicated by blackface comedy ("eetiopium" as "eat the opium"), but they are quick to enforce the policy of racial segregation violently: with "social spears."[23]

Herriman's Unkil Tom Katt is a combination of the minstrel uncle with which the figure was associated through Stephen Foster's "The Old Folks at Home" (1851) and an African-American musical storyteller, who sings in his shaky voice of "bugs is in the taties — weevils in the kottin — weasels in the hen koop — honey, times is rottin'" (August 23, 1932; quoted in Heer 15).[24] Yet while the old Unkil's singing ultimately remains tied to the minstrel tradition, Herriman also used more genuinely African-American sources. As Judith O'Sullivan has noted, Krazy's singing on occasion recalls a toast called "the dozens" (cf. 42). On June 24, 1936, Krazy gets drunk on "Tiger Tea," a beverage with unknown ingredients, and boasts: "I'm a ten-toed tiger — / I'm a polo bear in a skwoil cage [squirrel cage?] / Tunda in a tea-potz / Wah — wooooooo — / Boom — / Krazy Ket / The Kannon Krecka / Wah — Wah / Boom Boom / I'm a poiminint / Tidal wave in a / Notion of dynamite / Pow — WOW" (*George Herriman's Krazy + Ignatz in "Tiger Tea"* 57). Here, Krazy reveals his "real" self; intoxicated by the drink, he throws off his social inhibitions and shows what usually remains behind doors: his intimate knowledge of African-American folk idioms.[25]

While it may be tempting to construe Herriman's forays into African-American culture as indicators of a "black aesthetic," one should not overlook equally prominent depictions of Krazy's gender-bending and racial passing. One of Herriman's most well known Sunday pages shows Krazy entering a beauty salon as a male black kat and exiting it a while later as a female white kat (October 6, 1935). Ignatz witnesses the scene but mistakes the white Krazy for an enchanting damsel who loses her handkerchief so that her pursuant can pick it up and establish romantic contact. The initials on the handkerchief ("K.K.") give Krazy away, and as Ignatz reaches for his brick, Krazy wonders: "L'il tutsi-wutsi thinks because I change my kimplection I should change my name."[26] Applied to Herriman himself, this would suggest that he may have changed his complexion (pretending to be Greek rather than African-American) in order to pass as white but that he kept his name, probably because it signified a German, and thus socially acceptable, heritage despite the anti–German sentiment during the first World War.

This reading is supported by Herriman's depiction of "Kamille Kameleon" and his way to the land of "No Color" (January 1, 1928). Like all chameleons, Kamille is "by nature compelled to assume the hue of [his] surroundings," and traveling through the Southwestern "Krazy Kwilt Kountry," he underwent "one violent change of color after another." Reposing on Krazy's couch, Kamille recalls how he was forced to change from yellow to green to black to blue and how "the last straw to bend my back was crossing 'Red Lake' in a purple boat with pink sails. — Oh, for a land without 'colors.'" The message of this episode, it seems safe to argue, is that Herriman wished for a color-blind society in which people were no longer forced to change their color (i.e., pass as white) in order to meet the expectations of others. This prefigures Jean Toomer's plea for a raceless America in "The Blue Meridian" (1936), where the author dreams of "the harmoniously developed,

Using a theatrical stock figure, Krazy makes an important statement: Americans are intoxicated by blackface comedy but they are quick to enforce the policy of racial segregation violently (June 22, 1935).

Krazy's ability to appear as male and/or female adds to the comic strip's engagement with issues of identity (October 6, 1935).

universal man, free of definition and classification that restrict or confine the vitality of his being" (Bell 343).

Krazy's ability to appear as male and/or female adds to the comic strip's engagement with issues of identity. Krazy's androgyny has always startled critics. Gilbert Seldes, for instance, referred to the kat as "androgynous, but [...] willing to be either" (235), and the strip encourages such considerations by oscillating between Krazy's yearning for nineteenth-century romance and Ignatz's immediate destruction of romantic possibilities. Here, Herriman is in line with those modernist female poets who rejected the notion of "conventional romance" and instead "offer[ed] up the illusory dramas of gender" (Nelson 80).[27] Krazy's stylish red necktie and his frequent dancing in a ballet skirt suggest such a gender drama, as does her love for Ignatz, whom the kat kisses (cf. December 24, 1917; reprinted in McDonnell 56) and whom she ultimately seeks to marry (cf. *Panoramic* 34; *A Kat A'Lilt with Song* 123) despite the fact that Ignatz is already married and the father of three children. Krazy even admits that his/her real name is "Wilhelmina" (*Panoramic* 42). The kat's queer love for the mouse is thematized again when Krazy apologizes to Ignatz's wife "for loving your husbind" (*Dailies* May 22, 1919) and when Ignatz's missile is described as a "love letter in brick" (May 1, 1927). Herriman thus proposed a flexible understanding of gender; nobody really knows whether Krazy is "a old bachelor" or an "olds [sic] maid" (reprinted in Blackbeard, "Kidding" 16), a "momma or a poppa" (*Panoramic* March 9, 1920), Uncle Krazy or Aunt Krazy (cf. various strips reprinted in Blackbeard, "Kidding" 16–17).

Krazy seems to have no concept of gender, and this is where the kat's freedom lies. "I realized Krazy was something like a sprite, an elf. They have no sex. So that Kat can't be a he or a she. The Kat's a spirit — a pixie — free to butt into anything," Herriman explained to a confused Frank Capra (quoted in McDonnell 54). What we find here is the creative synthesis of the "cross-dressing" routines readers would have known from minstrelsy and vaudeville with a modernist rejection of Victorian gender roles and sexual codes: think of Gertrude Stein playing the "husband" to Alice B. Toklas, for instance, of Virginia Woolf's exploration of androgyny in *Orlando* (1928), or of Djuna Barnes's explorations of transvestitism in *Nightwood* (1937).[28] Herriman expressed his wish for a "freedom to butt into anything" on the comic page. He questioned Victorian epistemology and its attendant "dichotomous reasoning" (human/animal, black/white, male/female) (Sanders 130) and thereby sought "to heal the sharp divisions that the nineteenth century had established in areas such as class, race, and gender" (Singal quoted in Sanders 132).

As Eyal Amiran suggests, Herriman's conception of identity cannot be separated from the poetics of his comic strip.[29] An art critic visiting Cococino County realizes that the doings of kat and mouse represent "a study in black & white" (quoted in Heer 13). Krazy makes this connection between the comic strip's color scheme and its racial implications explicit when he decides to trick the art critic by engaging in a bit of a racechange (Susan Gubar's term), saying to Ignatz: "He means us — me black. You white. [Let's] fool him. You be black and I'll be white." The animals thus change their color, the point of this symbolic switching from blackness to whiteness and vice versa being that the medium of the comic strip allows Herriman to depict something that was much more complicated in his real life: to be "neither black nor white yet both," as Werner Sollors titles his study of interracial literature.[30] Being continually forced to suppress parts of one's origins, Herriman implies in another Sunday strip, leads to the "mentil ettitude of the 'egg'—[an] interiority komplexion" (November 2, 1930). White on the outside, the egg contains a creature of color on the inside, while the creature's hidden racial identity (an *interior complexion*) is the result of a socially enforced *inferiority complex*.[31]

One of Herriman's most ingenious depictions of Krazy's racial status can be found in the Sunday page from June 29, 1919, in which the black kat stands in front of a black sheet and is therefore invisible (reprinted in Amiran 69). When Krazy is told to "open them eyes" by the dog who presents this phenomenon to a group of "ladies & gents," these eyes become visible because they shine white in front of the black background. Ignatz, however, decides to end the game by offering Krazy a bottle of milk. In a sequence of three panels, Krazy drinks the milk and becomes more and more visible as it fills his physical form. Irked by having his presentation sabotaged by the mouse, the dog then orders Krazy to drink from an ink pot until he is all black and thus invisible again. The argument behind these tent show shenanigans is that the meaning of one's skin color depends on specific contexts: You are black only if people see you in a black setting, and people should look beyond the surface to discover "wot's behind me," as Krazy says in another strip" (quoted in Seldes 235). *Krazy Kat* thus stages identity as ambiguous and performative: blackface as a comedic and strategic device, passing as a way to personal freedom, and "blackness" as social condition determined by the perception others.

"The Tower of Babble": Linguistic Modernism

Herriman's performative approach to Krazy's race and gender also characterizes his experiments with language. While the action of *Krazy Kat* is set in the small-townish environment of Yorba Linda, the inhabitants of this Southwestern enclave are immigrants or "happy exiles from the city" (Gopnik, "Genius") who speak a mixture of urban slang and regional dialects, the polyglot patois of the modern metropolis.[32] This melting pot of cultures and languages represents a world characterized by a "mix of multiple voices" and a fascination with "riveting imagery and layered allusiveness" that also guided "the literary response to modernity" (Nelson 77). The specifically modernist implications of Herriman's language emerge most forcefully from the narrator's "alliterative hyperbole" ("O'Sullivan" 39), from Krazy's "mongrelized" language as well as the kat's tendency to "place [...] words, phrases, and concepts under philosophical and cultural pressure" (Nelson on modernist poetry; 85), and from the "great diwersity of lenguage" spoken by the strip's multicultural cast (*Panoramic*, May 25, 1920).[33]

Herriman's narrator frequently diverges from the established paths of nineteenth-century diction and indulges in what Cary Nelson describes as an "almost palimpsestic thickness of image" in his discussion of Wallace Stevens (71).[34] While he merely mocks the narrative style of sentimentalism in a November 17, 1929, strip ("Dishonesty!!! Ooh, we blush, that our pen should fashion so fell a deed"), he suggests a more modern understanding of language in a Sunday page from March 7, 1926: "What cares the world for the pultaceous wisdom of a word weevil, or the dolsome dynamics of an etymological vermicule??" Here, alliterated speech is connected with a meta-linguistic statement about Herriman's poetic process: he worms ("etymological vermicule") his way through a language that is considered "dynamic" and arrives at a state of "wisdom."[35] Moreover, Herriman likens his narrator to the boll weevil, the bug that killed the cotton industry in the American South and caused millions of African Americans to move "not only from countryside to city, but from medieval America to modern" (6), as Alain Locke wrote in his introduction to the *New Negro* (1925). This is significant in terms of Herriman's life, which led him from South to North via Los Angeles and enabled him to undergo a personal metamorphosis from "colored" (according to his birth certificate) to Caucasian (according to his death certificate).[36] As Herriman's narrator insinuates, this metamorphosis is enabled by the power of artistic creation, by a linguistic inventiveness that is voracious in its tendency to devour older forms of culture and productive in its ability to spit out new forms of expression: "Again, within the konfines of Kokonino an act of arrant wickedness has been konsumated — in other words — to use a sapient 'runyonic' komment — a kat's kabeza has been kompletedly 'ka baamed'" (January 17, 1932).[37] The comically divergent spelling announced by the name of the strip and its protagonist is picked up on the level of narrative voice: the "c" is converted to a "k" at the beginning of various words; popular comedy deviates from conventional forms of representation through aberrant spelling.[38]

Krazy's idiosyncratic language is difficult to describe. In most simple terms, Krazy speaks "'ket'" (*Panoramic*, August 18, 1920), but this language is actually a melting pot of idioms and registers of speech.[39] Thomas Inge characterizes it as "bastardized" (*Comics* 49), which is an apt metaphor because it suggests a linguistic melting that connects with Ralph Ellison's understanding of American popular culture as a "melting pot [that] did indeed really melt" ("What" 580).[40] The characters in *Krazy Kat* combine literary and theatrical language with a liberal dose of ethnic and racial dialects (often in stereotypical form), as can be seen in Krazy's flexibly Yiddish/African-American pronunciation of specific terms. Sometimes he calls Ignatz "dahlink," thus suggesting a Yiddish accent (the hard k at the end of the word), sometimes "dollin," which implies a black idiom. While this flexibility can be used randomly, it frequently carries an underlying message. In a scene in which Krazy speaks of his "[m]ovink pitcher ectink" and boasts of "menegers runnink efter me" (quoted in Schmitz 141), the accent evokes the prominence of Jewish Hollywood actors like Al Jolson and the influence of Jewish-owned studios like Warner Brothers.[41] But Herriman's characters can also be African-American, as dialectal inflections and blues references such as "Oh, Loddy me" (Ignatz; February 13, 1938), "mo kines of games" (Krazy; February 19, 1939), and "rocks is my pillow to-night" (Krazy; January 28, 1940) illustrate. This may be described as an example of metaphorical blackface as well as a form of linguistic racechange in the course of which the speaker develops a chameleon-like identity.

In theoretical terms, Krazy is continually baffled by the relation between signifier and signified which Ferdinand de Saussure examined in his *Course in General Linguistics* (1916). According to Saussure, the basic unit in language is the sign, made up of signifier (spoken sound) and signified (the idea or concept associated with this sound). Krazy's tendency to take everything literally and his inability to decode homonyms (i.e., to stumble over the relation between signifier and signified; McDonnell, O'Connell, and de Havenon speak of an "illiterate-literate Joycean patois"; 27) lead to countless confusions, many of which are merely comical but some of which express a modernist suspicion toward language as a stable system of communication.[42] In a comical vein, Krazy has never seen a horse-fly because he knows that "a horse aint got wings" (*Dailies* August 30, 1918), and he is unable to distinguish between a "kettle" and "cattle" (*Dailies* February 18, 1919). In a more serious vein, Krazy refers to the new invention of the telephone as "Mrs. Telefoam," thus re-introducing a personal dimension to a medium that substitutes face-to-face communication with a less personal mode of exchange, sonic transmission (tele*phone*) giving way to a loss of sound (tele*foam*).[43] This is further exemplified by Krazy's realization that the "marvillainous" (i.e., simultaneously "marvelous" and "villainous") invention of electricity makes it possible for him "turn off the light and turn on the dark" (quoted in Crocker, "'Some Say'"). A modernist distrust of linguistic signification is combined here with a perception of modern communication as a mediated process which "altered perceptions of time and place and thereby changed consciousness itself" (Barnard 39).

Much has been written about Herriman's linguistic innovations, but a central episode about his understanding of language has remained largely unexplored. This episode was published at the beginning of the 1920s, a decade marked by "linguistic xenophobia" (North, *Dialect* 80) and anti-immigration legislation. Addressing Krazy, Ignatz explains: "[A]s long as the people who were building the tower of 'Babel' spoke one language all went well. But, as soon as they began to jabber in a lot of different languages all went wrong. And so the tower of 'Babel' was a failure." Krazy, however, is not entirely convinced by Ignatz's biblical reading. "But as the tower of 'Babble' it musta been a howling success," he answers (*Panoramic* August 17, 1920). Thus, instead of lamenting the profusion of languages in an immigration society such as the United States, Herriman identifies it as the source of popular comedy. It is exactly the funny "jabber" of cartoonists, comedians, and movie actors that revives older cultural traditions. Without this jabber, dullness reigns, as an episode from May 2, 1937, illustrates: "No skendil — no gotzip — no talk — no kon-wissation — no jebba-jebba — jess nuttin' — so dull." In more philosophical terms, Krazy's answer to his own question about the purpose of language ("Why is 'lenguage,' 'Ignatz'?") captures the productive power of linguistic confusion in modern America: "I would say, language is, that we may mis-unda-stend each udda" (January 6, 1918; reprinted in McDonnell 61).

"Limning the Moany Lizzie": Visual Modernism

Herriman not only developed a new language for his strip, he also participated in, and was aware of, "modernism's highly mediated visual culture" (Kalaidjian 8). Yet his position in this visual culture was a curious one. If he is acknowledged by art historians at all, it is as precursor of surrealism whose changing backgrounds and dreamy night sequences set in the semi-fictional space of Cococino County (the Monument Valley, located in Arizona and Utah) anticipate the work of Joan Miró and Salvador Dalí. I believe, however, that we are dealing with a very specific form of visual modernism in *Krazy Kat*, a kind of modernism that is aware of the new-ness of the medium in which it operates and that positions itself vis-à-vis contemporary developments in the visual arts. This specific type of visual modernism includes intertextual and intermedial references to modernist visual art, commentary about the comic strip as a popular medium, and the creation of a "cultural geography" (Barnard 47) that connects a Native American aesthetic with a proto-surrealist American West.

Herriman repeatedly acknowledged modernist art of the twentieth century and the avant-garde that produced it. This is revealed in a funny reference to Marcel Duchamp's *Nude Descending a Staircase*, which had been displayed at New York's Armory Show in 1913. A champion of modesty, Krazy contrasts his being "complitly clothed in a garmint of fur" with Ignatz's nakedness in a daily strip from March 7, 1919. He covers the mouse with a blanket and maintains: "And ain't you *not*, l'il 'nude,' coming down stairs what you is." Patrick McDonnell, Karen O'Connell, and Georgia Riley de Havenon write that Herriman's "comic strip explorations coincided in time and place with the revolution in the art world brought about by the famed Armory Show" (61), but I believe that we are dealing with more than coincidence. Duchamp suggested a possible affinity between modernist visual arts and the comic strip when he called his readymade urinal *Fountain by R. Mutt* (1917), recalling Bud Fisher's *Mutt and Jeff*, and when he drew a mustache on a reproduction of Leonardo da Vinci's *Mona Lisa*, calling the "new" painting *L.H.O.O.Q.*: "She's got hot pants" (cf. Short 162). Something quite similar happens in a strip in which Offissa Pupp has "limned a masterpiece" and displays it in a humungous gilt frame with Victorian picture lamp. Krazy, who is initially nonplussed by the artwork, finally suggests a fitting title: "the 'Moany Lizzie'" (May 24, 1936). This comic re-christening of the *Mona Lisa* evokes a continuum from blues aesthetic to modernist slumming in slang and thereby introduces a central principle of modern American popular culture: the ability to simultaneously use and abuse, cite and smite, refined art.[44]

Herriman's awareness of his complicity in the creation of a modern visual aesthetic becomes apparent in a Sunday page from September 4, 1927. Here, Herriman presents his readers with comic adaptations of elaborately framed paintings by "three 'old masters,'" each of which features one of his protagonists dressed in period clothing. The next two panels are offered as "an 'interlude'"; the gilt frames are replaced by comic panels, and the action takes its usual course. The page ends with a large rectangular frame that is presented as "something modern" and combines the aesthetics of the old masters with the new American popular culture. The image of Ignatz in jail is set in front of a Western landscape (an open plain, mesas, and cacti), and it is surrounded by a frame covered with Native American designs. Signifiers of the strip's modern mélange of ethnic comedy are Krazy's banjo playing and the Spanish lyrics intoned by the Kat. Carrying the nineteenth-century institutions of the dime museum (cheaply framed visual spectacles) into the era of modernist culture, this strip suggest the prominence of a particularly American form of entertainment that emerges from the juxtaposition of a genteel frame and a very ungenteel, vaudevillian and multicultural subject matter.

Herriman's commentary on contemporary developments in art climaxes in his depiction of Cococino County. His views of the Arizona desert as a scenery in constant flux

KRAZY KAT ❖ By Herriman

The juxtaposition of a genteel frame and a very un-genteel, vaudevillian and multicultural subject matter indicate Herriman's awareness of his complicity in the creation of a modern visual aesthetic (September 4, 1927).

anticipate surrealism while establishing a visual word set apart from other comic strips of the time. Gopnik wisely argues that "Herriman's style was fully evolved before Surrealism existed" and that surrealist painters like Miró actually "employed some of Herriman's devices," even though we are dealing again with aesthetic affinities rather than with a direct influence ("Comics" 172, cf. 175).[45] In other words, while "Herriman respond[ed] to the same mixture of places, myths and ambitions that would move Surrealism" (172),

it would be difficult to miss the uncanny resonances between André Breton's yearning for the naïveté of the insane and Herriman's naïve protagonist or between the way in which Breton's statement that "only the marvelous is beautiful" in the first *Manifesto of Surrealism* (1924) can be associated with Krazy's longing for the beautiful and the "movillis" (July 25, 1936).

Herriman's "surrealism of the funny page" (Gopnik, "Genius" n. pag.) emerges from representations of shape-shifting moons and a dreamy night sky, constantly shifting backgrounds, and an increasingly colorful scenery (from 1935 onwards, the Sunday pages appeared in color). In the Sunday pages from the 1920s, the moon changes from conventional half moon first to a barge in the morning sky (April 18, 1926) and then a piece of furniture on which an exhausted Ignatz rests his limbs (August 1, 1926). But Herriman's most daring experiments announce themselves in the 1930s, when the moon is depicted in different colors (it is red and green on January 23, 1938) and upside down (August 27, 1939); they culminate in a truly remarkable episode in 1941 (February 23). Here, a yellow full moon is surrounded by various geometrical shapes, first a circle, then a triangle and a square, and finally all three forms plus another circle. The whole focus of this Sunday page lies on these different appearances of the moon and the reactions to the changes by Cococino County's inhabitants, who wonder about the magic of the shifting night sky. The effect is a visual and metaphysical one. The shape surrounding the moon depends on the onlooker; it may be a circle for Offissa Pupp, but for Krazy it is a triangle and for Ignatz a square. The solution at the end, when all of them look into the sky, is that everybody has seen the moon correctly. All of the shapes are visible; visual pleasure is something personal and subjective, and the consciousness of Herriman's characters is defined by a "theatre of simultaneous possibilities" (288), as William James had observed in *Principles of Psychology* (1890).[46]

The depiction of a changing moon is connected with a scenery in constant motion. Participating in the modernist project of remapping notions of space, time, and distance (cf. Kalaidjian 1), Herriman offers seemingly random background patterns reminiscent of dreamy doodlings (January 23, 1927; April 28, 1929), elaborate ornamentations of what would otherwise have been open space (August 19, 1928; June 2, 1929), and countless scenes from the mid–1930s onwards in which the continuous action in the foreground is set against a scenery that changes from panel to panel: trees, mesas, the soil, the sky, and flowerpots constantly metamorphose from one shape and color into another (cf. Sunday pages from July 14 to September 1, 1940).[47] The effect is a playful engagement with the surrealist potential of dreams — note especially the fantastic coloring and shape of stone formations in the pages from August 27, 1939, and July 14, 1940 — but also with a modernist sense of discontinuity and flux.

One of Herriman's major achievements was the liberation of the "sublime landscape" of the American West "from the tradition of high seriousness" (Gopnik, "Genius" n. pag.), the substitution of the modernist city with a poetic vision of a modern space apart from the challenges of modernization.[48] Far from being an urban wasteland reminiscent

Opposite: Herriman's views of the Arizona desert as a scenery in constant flux anticipate surrealism while establishing a visual world set apart from other comic strips of the time (February 23, 1941).

of Eliot or a valley of ashes a la F. Scott Fitzgerald, the locus of the action — the city of Yorba Linda, located in Cococino County and surrounded by the Kaibito desert — is both a mythical space and a real place.[49] When Herriman visited the Monument Valley in the early 1910s, he found a place for his characters that was neither bound by the genteel tradition nor yet overcome by the forces of modernity: "a granulate world awash — from horizon to horizon" and "a heap of territory" (April 10, 1927).[50] In visual terms, it is both the vanishing Native-American culture and popular representations of the region that enable Herriman to develop his own form of visual modernism. When Krazy recites the lyrics to "Home on the Range" in a strip from July 26, 1942, he not only gives a verbal rendition of a romantic nineteenth-century view of the frontier — "buffalo roamin' in it"; "deer an' a entelope is playin'" — but he also conveys a sense of yearning for a culture that had been largely destroyed and displaced by the middle of the twentieth century: that of Native-American tribes of the American plains and the Southwest (Zuni, Hopi, Navajo).[51]

That Herriman's humor may have derived in part from his interest in Native-American philosophy is implied in a panoramic strip from April 8, 1920. Here, Ignatz maintains that "'Indians' [...] have no sense of humor," to which Krazy replies: "Some of them has. Them as comes from 'Yuma' has. Because if they come from 'Yuma,' they must be 'yumarists.'" Indeed, Krazy goes Native when he smokes a peace pipe and enjoys his loneliness on the vast desert plain: "peace, sweed peace — sood me, sood me" (October 4, 1931). Further signifiers of a Native-American presence include smoke signals (June 19, 1932), and references to mythological creatures like the "wind witches on wunanji" (December 17, 1939), the "'crimson cobra' of the clouds" (November 19, 1939), and the "enchanted mesa" (August 29, 1926).[52]

The Sunday page from July 6, 1930, is perhaps most revealing of Herriman's subtle critique of American policy toward its Native-American population. Appearing only two days after Independence Day, the strip tells the story of various Cococino inhabitants as they flee their hometown because a French poodle named Mr. Kiskidee Kuku has gripped Krazy's attentions. The first panel shows Ignatz as he follows a street sign to "Navajo," while a later panel refers to the biblical story of "EXODUS" as the rest of the Krazy Kat cast (minus Krazy) leave their hometown. In order to foreground the discrepancy between the biblical wandering through the desert in search for a new land — the land of milk and honey which the Puritans sought in the New World — and the bleak fate of the Navajo and other Indian tribes, Herriman included not only examples of Native pottery in this strip but also inscribed two of his panels with Native design patterns. The effect of this cultural mélange is a curious one, an accusation of the American policy of Indian removal that stays within the confines of Sunday entertainment and gentle comedy.[53]

As Krazy Kat progressed, Native-American designs informed Herriman's visual choices more and more. If these patterns performed a predominantly ornamental function in the late 1920s and early 1930s (September 30, 1928; May 18, 1930; June 1, 1930), they took on a more central function toward the end of the 30s, as Herriman's use of Native-American geometry for his logo for the strip (November 27, 1938) and an episode in which Krazy weaves a gigantic Indian carpet (December 11, 1938;) indicate. These visual signifiers are connected with a philosophical indebtedness to Native-American culture.

Evoking lines from the Navajo Night Chant, Offissa Pupp frequently enjoys a world of peace and serenity: "Today, the world walks in beauty," he muses (March 27, September 11, and November 6, 1938; July 14, September 8, 1940).[54] Yet he does so in a place in which Native Americans are no longer present and in which their culture now serves mainly as a source of creative inspiration. This, then, corresponds with Nico Israel's conclusion about the reaction of modernists to the spread of colonialism, especially the inner-American colonialism that reached its formal end with the closing of the frontier discussed by Frederick Jackson Turner in 1893. As Nico writes, "modernist expression responds to modern colonialism with creative ambivalence" (125).[55]

"Why, Gosh Goodniss!! There's Me in This Paper": Self-reflexivity and Meta-mediality

Herriman's contributions to the development of a popular visual modernism are accompanied by a self-reflexive engagement with the mediality of the comic strip. Herriman frequently drew "meta-comics" (Shannon 213; Blackmore 36), and it is in the comics themselves, not in manifestos published in little magazines, that we can locate Herriman's theory of graphic comedy. In order to systematize Herriman's self-referentiality, we may distinguish between references to the material medium in which the strips were printed (newspapers), to the actual material out of which comic strips were made (ink), to visual art as a form of representation, and to the serial and sequential principles of comic storytelling.

The most intriguing reference to *Krazy Kat*'s placement in tabloid newspapers appeared on April 16, 1922. In this Sunday page, Krazy peruses the comic section and is shocked by the following recognition: "Why, gosh, goodniss!! There's *me* in this paper!! And likewise, 'Ignatz' also — Jee-wizzil" (reprinted in McDonnell 169). Pondering being a character in a comic strip who reads about himself in a comic strip, Krazy asks, "if I are here, and you is here, *how* come I are in the paper, and you also," to which a dead-pan Ignatz, unwilling to engage in a philosophical debate, answers matter-of-factly: "Because, fool, how could it be aught were it not thus."[56] A less complex but equally revealing remark concludes a daily episode of 1914. After having been pelted by Ignatz's rocks in the four preceding panels, Krazy exclaims in the final panel: "Thenk goodness this is *not* a full page Sunday supplements" (*Panoramic* 40). This self-reflexive strain was a prominent element of the newspaper comic strip from the very outset, but in *Krazy Kat*, it is elevated from advertising gimmick to an extended consideration of the strip's mediality.

While the comic section of tabloid papers provided the space in which Herriman's strip was printed, ink was the actual medium through which the cartoonist realized his ideas. "Ink is a wonderful medium," Ignatz observes in a panoramic daily (March 23, 1920), to which Krazy responds: "Ink is most wundafil Ignatz because you is made from it." Amiran sees the blackness of ink "as a representational condition" (70), and while this condition has racial implications, it also enables the cartoonist to theorize his graphic comedy. With ink, "poets have written great poems — great songs — great lyrics," as Ignatz points out, but ink also produces the vaudevillian brick-toss: "thank goodness this brick is made out of *ink*." In this and in several other installments, Herriman included an ink bottle as a prominent prop. The purpose may have been to inform readers of the creative process involved in the making of the strip, which preceded the mechanical reproduction of the artwork and thus the "destruction" of the aura of the original artwork through mass printing (as Walter Benjamin argued a few years later).[57] This process is visualized again in a daily strip in which Krazy and Ignatz heed their master's call to return "home" by jumping back into the ink pot (March 7, 1919; reprinted in McDonnell 89) and a self-portrait for *Judge* magazine (October 21, 1922) in which depicts several characters from *Krazy Kat* as they crowd around a cartoonish Herriman (reprinted in McDonnell 24).

These self-referential excursions are connected with philosophical considerations about the nature of representational art.[58] Krazy may believe that he is a kat, but Ignatz knows better: "You're only an idea, expressed in ink on paper," to which a sobbing Krazy replies: "Ooy and all this time I had a ida I was in love with a real 'mice'" (*Dailies* April 1, 1919).[59] It is important to note that Herriman's statement about the ontology of the comic strip appears about a decade before René Francois Magritte painted *The Treachery of Images* (*La Trahision des Images*; 1928–29), the famous depiction of a pipe under which he wrote "Ceci n'est pas une pipe." Visual art, Herriman seems to argue, never presents more than a fictional image of reality. Especially in a region like Cococino County, where mirages and other sensual illusions are common, the visual senses have seized to be trustworthy gateways to an experiential truth. While Ignatz initially encounters an "optical illusion" (November 6., 1927), Offissa Pupp refers to the entertaining make-belief of the strip (an echo bouncing of the mountains and reappearing as a speech bubble) as "an optical delusion" (May 17, 1936).

The optical delusions with which Herriman provided the readers of *Krazy Kat* are amplified by repeated references to the serial and sequential principles of comic storytelling. "I did my wishing in the first picture," Ignatz tells Offissa Pupp on May 29, 1927; "Just a wee bit further my dear 'Krazy'—outside of the 'picture,'" Ignatz appeals to Krazy on April 17, 1932, and even Krazy once wonders about the fact that the picture of the jail, in which Ignatz usually ends up by the end of the strip, is in the first panel and not "the werra lest pitcha" (September 25, 1938).[60] Here, the sequential principle of the comic strip, which distinguishes the medium from other forms of visual art, participates in the serial construction of the plot: "Day, efta day—this goes on," a flabbergasted Krazy remarks in one of Herriman's late bottom panels upon seeing Offissa Pupp pursuing Ignatz on a conveyor belt that runs in circles (September 27, 1942). In this episode, a visual statement about the serial poetics of newspaper comics is connected with Krazy's words in true hybrid fashion; the structural principle behind the daily and weekly strips is not one of mere repetition, as Krazy's comment may insinuate, but one of variation. While the basic set-up and plot line of the strip never changes in the course of more than three decades, Herriman presented ever new versions of the same story. Like a conveyor belt, he was in continuous motion, yet unlike such a mechanical apparatus, he never simply reproduced yesterday's work but fashioned surprising new twists to a familiar story.

Krazy Kat "Jes' Grew": Concluding Thoughts on Herriman's Comic Modernism

Herriman was no radical modernist, no rabble-rouser who advocated the overthrow of Victorian traditions, but he was neither merely an expressionist who was run out of town by the coming tide of modernism.[61] Rather, he combined influences from nineteenth-century culture, both high and low, with a twentieth-century, modernist sensibility. While his political criticism routinely stayed within the realm of the playful, his vaudeville negotiations of Victorian values, his performative understanding of race and gender, and his presentation of language as a medium of misunderstanding that produces popular comedy expressed a desire to be more than a mere newspaper cartoonist and creator of a funny strip. Especially the yearning for a land of no color in which anybody would be free to butt into anything and in which racial, gendered, and linguistic differences could be melted down to an individual consciousness make him a central figure of American modernism. Regarding his position in the space of modernist practice, Herriman's statement that Krazy and Ignatz were penned into *The Family Upstairs* "to fill up the waste space" points to the power of popular culture and the medium of the comic strip: to create art where people would least expect it, and to do so by drawing freely on all of the sources with which his culture provided him.

Herriman once remarked that "*Krazy Kat* was not conceived, not born, it jes' grew" (quoted in McDonnell 54). Associating his comic strip with Harriet Beecher Stowe's unruly black child Topsy, Herriman implied that a marginal figure like Krazy must not be reduced to its racial, social, or cultural origins. This plea for individual freedom is further connected with James Weldon Johnson's definition of black popular music: "The earliest Ragtime songs, like Topsy, 'jes' grew,'" Johnson recalled in his *Book of American Poetry* (1922), and he, his brother J. Rosamond, and Bob Cole "appropriated about the last one of the 'jes' grew' songs. It was a song which had been sung for years all through the South." Significantly, "[t]he words were unprintable, but the tune was irresistible, and belonged to nobody. We took it, re-wrote the verses, telling an entirely different story from the original, [...] and published the song" (12–13). In other words, twentieth-century American popular culture emerges from processes of transformation, revision, and mass publication in the course of which Southern folk origins give way to a modern sense of flexibility and infectiousness. This, then, is why Robert Warshow is right when he points out that Herriman "is not to be trusted with any systems" (65) and why Franklin Rosemont concludes that *Krazy Kat* is "[e]mphatically inconclusive," not pretending to have answers but engaging in "a continual *questioning*" (126). Here, then, lies the essence of *Krazy Kat's* uncanny modernism, as T.S. Eliot must have realized. As Eliot explained about Pound's famous call to "make it new": "The perpetual task of poetry is to make all things new. Not necessarily to make new things" (quoted in Dettmar 2). No wonder the modernists appreciated *Krazy Kat*.

Notes

1. Eliot explored the comic potential of cats in *Old Possum's Book of Practical Cats* (1939); cummings credited Herriman as an influence in his essay "Foreword to Krazy" (1946).
2. I cite the phrase "across the cultural divide" from Chinitz (8).

3. While several essays and a few book chapters on *Krazy Kat* exist, McDonnell, O'Connell, and de Havenon's *Krazy Kat: The Comic Art of George Herriman* (1986) is the only book-length English-language study published to date. Daniela Kaufman's 2008 *Der intellektuelle Witz im Comic: George Herrimans Krazy Kat* is at present the only other monograph to examine *Krazy Kat* exclusively.

4. On the history of the American newspaper comic strip, see Gordon; Harvey, *Art* and *Children*; Inge, *Comics*; Marschall; O'Sullivan.

5. On the aesthetics of vaudeville, see Jenkins. The brick toss first appeared in Bud Fisher's *Mutt and Jeff*, but Herriman turned the idea into a permanent comic device: a "slapstick routine [with] a metaphysical significance" (Harvey, *Art* 180). The lack of a vaudevillian punch line was one of the reasons why Lyonel Feininger's *Kin-der-Kids* and Winsor McCay's *Little Nemo in Slumberland* were not crowned with lasting success.

6. Santayana observed: "The American Will inhabits the sky-scraper; the American Intellect inhabits the colonial mansion[...]. The one is all aggressive enterprise; the other is all genteel tradition" (188).

7. Krazy speaks a unique patois that may be as complex as any avant-garde experiment with literary language. I will discuss this patois below.

8. Herriman mocks sentimentalism (January 16, 1938), pokes fun at nineteenth-century reform movements (October 13, 1929; March 9, 1930), and jokes about old-fashioned notions of chivalry and virtue. In the Sunday page from April 8, 1934, "[t]he good dames of 'Cococino County' endow their own [Offissa Pupp] with the insignia of virtue": "a snow-white ribbon of 100% purity."

9. Krazy is also associated with Venus, who is traditionally shown with Cupid. References to Cupid and Venus are too numerous to be listed here; other mythological figures include: Atlas, Hannibal, Hercules, Jove, Spartacus, Cyclops, Jupiter, Ajax, and Cleopatra. The Bible is another source of comedy, as phrases such as "seek and ye will find" (December 5, 1926), "Solomonian wisdom" (February 2, 1930), "salt of the oit [earth]" (March 2, 1930) and the "lend of milk & honey bitznitz" (August 1, 1936) illustrate.

10. I use the terms "high" and "low" heuristically; I do not mean to suggest a cultural hierarchy between canonized art and popular culture. As Gopnik writes, "the conventional straightjacketed picture of high and low in modern art is just false" ("Genius" n. pag.). Gopnik is right, yet these terms are useful because they allow us to trace the sources and grasp the trajectories of modernist investments with popular culture and Herriman's use of modernist techniques.

11. Chinitz mentions Eliot's possible knowledge of Stephen Foster's "Ring de Banjo" (1851), which contains the phrase "de rattle ob de bones" (cf. 45). Gene Buck, Herman Ruby, and David Stamper's "That Shakespearian Rag" was a song in the 1912 version of the Ziegfeld Follies.

12. Pound was responsible for doing away with many of Eliot's "subliterary allusions" (Chinitz 41).

13. Herriman's use of stages, curtains, props, and changing scenery underscores the performative dimension of the action and expresses an understanding of the strip as an extension of minstrelsy. When Ignatz pretends to be a "komical 'kamel'" (October 20, 1940) and boasts of his abilities as a ventriloquist (July 2, 1939), he displays a familiarity with the comic routines of vaudeville theater. Herriman placed Krazy and Ignatz on a minstrel stage again on May 4, 1918 (reprinted in McDonnell 62).

14. "Unkil Tom Kat" is revived in Sunday pages from 1932 (September 11, October 9), in a daily episode from 1931 (February 10), and in a 1935 Sunday page (September 15).

15. Foster published the song in 1853. The watermelon is one of Herriman's favorite props; it is devoured (November 24, 1935), used as a disguise (July 11, 1927; October 27, 1929; January 29, 1939; April 21, 1940; September 21, 1941), and hurled in lieu of a brick (*Dailies* October 19, 1920). In a Sunday page from June 6, 1926, Krazy includes Friedrich Schiller's *Wilhelm Tell* (1804) in his world of comic minstrelsy: "If only Mr. Tell had used a watta-mellin instead of a eppil — there would be betta scores."

16. The most famous literary depiction can be found in Mark Twain's *Adventures of Huckleberry Finn* (1884/85), in which the King and Duke pass themselves off as "world renowned tragedians" and sell their lousy performance of a Shakespearian mélange — the sword fight from *Richard III*, the balcony scene from *Romeo and Juliet*, and Hamlet's soliloquy — as an offering of "sublime Shakespearian Spectacle" (140).

17. One sketch included the following dialogue: "'When was England offered for sale at a very low price?' 'When King Richard offered his kingdom for a horse'" (quoted in Levine 4).

18. Herriman claimed that his family was originally from Alsace; his colleague and friend Tad Dorgan recalled that he "didn't know what he was" and thus nicknamed Herriman "The Greek" (18). On the controversy, see Inge, "Was Krazy Kat Black?"; Amiran; Heer. Ishmael Reed dedicated his novel *Mumbo Jumbo* (1972) to "George Herriman, Afro-American, who created Krazy Kat."

19. I agree with Walter Benn Michaels, who understands modernism as an "effort [...] to work out the meaning of the commitment to identity — linguistic, national, cultural, racial[...]" (3).

20. Pfeiffer never mentions Herriman. A fifth consideration would be to place *Krazy Kat* in the context of psychoanalysis, especially Sigmund Freud's *Three Essays on the Theory of Sexuality* (1905), *Jokes and Their Relation to the Unconscious* (1905), *Psychopathology of Everyday Life* (1914), and *The Ego and the Id* (1923).

21. Ignatz is referring to Joel Rinaldo, *Polygeneric Theory: A Treatise on the Beginning and End of Life* (1910).

22. "What good is it to keep this date, 'Kat,' if you've forgotten to bring a 'brick' along," Ignatz scolds Krazy on March 1, 1931. According to the Sunday page from May 4, 1919, the beginnings of feline love for mice lie in "ancient Egypt," where "'Kleopatra Kat,' siren of the Nile enslaved the heart of a noble roman rodent — 'Marcatonni Maus'" (reprinted in McDonnell 29).

23. An earlier Sunday page reverses the color scheme; Krazy is whitened when a careless dog soaks him in "white wash," and Ignatz's perception moves from seeing Krazy as "a beautiful nymph, [...] white as a lily, pure as the driven snow" to his regular disgust of the kat (October 16, 1921; reprinted in Heer 14). For additional episodes depicting Ignatz in blackface, see the Sunday pages from November 3 and 10, 1929, and February 27, 1938. See also various daily and weekly strips from 1921 reprinted in Heer 9, 12, 13.

24. Heer (12) and Amiran (63) suggest that Unkil Tom Kat is singing the blues. The majority of musical examples in *Krazy Kat* are popular tunes such as "Sweet Adeline." Occasionally, Herriman slipped in a reference to African American music, as when the Irish brick-maker Kolin Kelly advertises his product by singing about its ability "to break the bondage of the blues" (February 22, 1931) and when Krazy thinks of the spiritual "Roll, Jordan, Roll" (1867) in the panoramic daily from August 12, 1920.

25. In the Sunday strip from May 31, 1942, Krazy sings: "I'm a grend 'kenyin' I'm a great, grend 'slem' — I'm a grend, great 'piyenna.'"

26. A panoramic daily from July 21, 1920, shows the symbolic change of race from black kat to "blondish" feline; about a decade later, Krazy enters a beauty parlor to become a blonde but runs back to become a brunette again when Ignatz ignores him (*A Kat A'Lilt with Song* 118).

27. Nelson discusses the poetry of Mina Loy and Gertrude Stein.

28. Krazy's identity as a pixie, sprite, or elf further recalls the homosexual figure of the New York "fairy," which was characterized "primarily by a cultivated feminine gender persona rather than by same-sex desire" (Lyon 227). T.S. Eliot's Tiresias, an "[o]ld man with wrinkled female breasts" (l. 219) also comes to mind, as does the indeterminate gender of the fool in Shakespeare's *King Lear* (1604/5).

29. For Amiran, "personal identity, race, and the generic requirements of narrative are logically connected in [Herriman's] work" (59); the cartoonist's "preoccupation with color" relates to "both the social marker and the comic's material, physical resources of ink" (58).

30. Sollors does not discuss Herriman.

31. The idea of an "interior complexion" recalls W.E.B. Du Bois's notion of "double-consciousness" (102). In that sense, the strip does not "transcend [...] barriers of class, sex, and species" (O'Sullivan 40) but derives its imaginative power from the struggle to overcome these barriers.

32. Offissa Pupp is no country sheriff but a (probably Irish) city cop. The major of a small town called Shonto "announces that his city [...] has this day become a 'metropolis'" because it has gained twelve new inhabitants (July 12, 1931); Herriman's narrator mocks the people of Cococino County as "kosmopolite[s] of Kayenta" (May 7, 1933). The demographic makeup of this environment is enriched by Mrs. Marihuana Pelona, Don Kiyote, Panchita Paloma, Willie Mendoza, and the stereotypical Chinese figure Mock Duck. Don Kiyote is an allusion to Miguel de Cervantes's *Don Quixote* (1605).

33. On "mongrel" modernism, see Douglas. Heer reads *Krazy Kat* as a "multicultural strip" (15).

34. In various episodes, the narrator stays within the nineteenth-century tradition of the authorial onlooker who is concerned for the fate of his protagonists and provides moral commentary about the confusions of the plot. He also speaks within the tradition of nonsense literature and can therefore be associated with authors such as Lewis Carroll and William Makepeace Thackeray. Cf. October 13, 1935: "Fall fleeing the fury of a frigid foe flaunts its florid feet upon the flora of Cococino County, and with its fiery finger fashions it into a fount of flame."

35. The invented adjectives "pultaceous" and "dolsome," which present this dynamicism and wisdom negatively, are most likely intended to be ironic.

36. Locke uses the term "metamorphosis" to distinguish between the nineteenth-century ideology of the "old Negro" and twentieth-century notions of the "new Negro" (cf. 3).

37. The phrase "runyonic komment" refers to Alfred Damon Runyon, an American writer whose stories frequently depicted the Broadway scene and the underworld culture of New York.

38. On Krazy's linguistic deviance, cf. also Schmitz 148.

39. Critics have used metaphors such as "gumbo of speech patterns" (Marschall 111), "alphabet soup" (McDonnell 63), "malapropisms and polyglossia" (Crocker, "'Some Say'" n. pag.), and "linguistic freedom and polymorphous play" (Orvell 113).

40. Considering Herriman's regional origins, the melting-pot metaphor evokes the concept of Creole languages. On Israel Zangwill's original understanding of the melting pot, see Nahshon; on the melting pot potential of popular culture, see Rogin.

41. Ignatz echoes Al Jolson's famous line from the 1927 sound film *The Jazz Singer* on August 13, 1933: "You haven't heard nothing — yet." In many instances, we are dealing with theatrical speech, as when Ignatz exclaims on December 25, 1938: "The scene is set — the props at hand — the plot put, placed, and planted — the play will now proceed." In a later episode, Ignatz proclaims over the course of several panels: "In this picture — we plot. [...] Like a bud — the plot — swells — unfolds — and flowers — into this beautiful — climax — we call it 'finale'" (January 25, 1942).

42. Berry discerns "[t]he modernist writer's emphasis on words' resistance to fixed meaning or reference" (116). Krazy's linguistic confusion emerges in dialogues which Rosemont associates with "Zen koans" (124). An example is Ignatz's suggestion that "[t]he world as it is, my dear K, is not like it was, when it used to be," to which Krazy responds: "An' wen it gets to be wot it is, will it?" (quoted in Rosemont 124). Krazy and Ignatz's Zen-like banter is different from Ezra Pound's haiku poetry, but it is a modernist engagement with Far Eastern philosophy. In the panoramic daily from October 16, 1920, Ignatz is "reading Chinese philosophy"; when he tells Krazy that the "Confucian" language "is quite simple, plain, and lucid," Krazy hears the homonym "Confusion."

43. This example is cited in Crocker, "'Some Say'" (n. pag).

44. In the panoramic daily from July 2, 1920, a Spanish-looking dog named "'Pablo Piki' the Great 'Toreador'" comes to Cococino County with a group of "stuckuppies." "Pablo Piki" and his buddies cannot fathom that Krazy may have upper-class ancestors: "L'il did they know that my Poppa was a great 'stevedore.'" Herriman associates the comic strip with working-class origins and popular music — stevedores were (mostly) black dock workers who were often featured in the tunes of Herriman's time. Moreover, Picasso becomes Pablo Piki, a character from the musical comedy *The Toreador*, which ran on Broadway in 1902 and 1904.

45. Gopnik compares Miró's *Carnival of the Harlequin* and *Dog Barking at the Moon* with Herriman's Sunday pages of the 1930s and concludes that "we sense a real, positive affinity in a shared system of form[...]" ("Genius" n. pag.).

46. Cf. North: "Objectivity, in other words, is visibly refuted in many modernist works, and with it goes the reliability of representation" ("Visual" 187). The bottom strip adds the missing humor to the episode; when Offissa Pupp muses, "Ah moon, moon — the magic of you —," Krazy thinks of honey and Ignatz of cheese. This exemplifies the modernist recognition "that vision is [...] affected by culture" (North, "Visual" 177).

47. "Metamorphosis" is a concept regularly associated with *Krazy Kat*. Cf. cummings 102; Inge, *Comics* 43; McDonnell 73. Related phrases include "mutability" (Gopnik, "Genius" n. pag.), "transmutations" (Crocker, "'Some Say'" n. pag.), "permutations" (McDonnell 57); and "flux" (Warshow 21).

48. Cococino, Neil Schmitz suggests, "dislocates its regionalism [...] and creates instead a poetic space" (26). According to Gopnik, *Krazy Kat* is a timeless "comic pastoral" and an "imaginary Eden" ("Genius" n. pag.).

49. For Krazy, it is also a "heppy lend fur fur away" as soon as Ignatz hits him with the brick (cf. October 17, 1926).

50. Arizona was one of the latest territories to join the union as a state (in 1912).

51. "Home on the Range" was composed by Brewster Higley in 1876, but a version transcribed by John Lomax in 1910 was more likely the one with which Herriman was familiar. It portrays the range as a place "[w]here the deer and the antelope play; / Where seldom is heard a discouraging word / And the skies are not cloudy all day." The second verse claims "[t]hat I would not exchange my home on the range / For all the cities so bright." The topos of the vanishing Indian appears in the third verse: "The red man was pressed from this part of the West / He's likely no more to return."

52. In a panoramic daily Ignatz sings a tune about what "was once an Indian's land" (May 24, 1920). "All this land used to belong to an Indian," he explains to Krazy, who immediately pities "the poor, poor Injin." In order to ease Krazy's anguish, Ignatz suggests: "aint we going to give it back some day as soon

as we find the Indian who used to own it." The accompanying bottom strip shows a dog wearing Indian headgear is first kicked out of a house and then given two massive books titled "deed" and "title" in exchange for his land. The teepees in the background visualize what is really going on: the dispossession of American Indians.

53. O'Sullivan finds in *Krazy Kat* "playful social statements" (47); Howe discovers "safe violations of traditional orders" (49). Herriman once explained: "We deal in 'gentle humor'—not that we are in any way spouting pin-feathers of angel-hood, all we can say that this is but the first symptom of our becoming a chronic uplifter of the 'age'—that's all—" (quoted in McDonnell 28).

54. The original chant of the Yeibichai ceremony includes the lines "[w]ith beauty may I walk [...] / With beauty all around me, may I walk" (quoted in McDonnell 75).

55. Turner proposed this argument in "The Significance of the Frontier in American History." Orvell argues that *Krazy Kat* "seems essentially modernist, the product of an imperial imagination" (112). Crocker maintains: "Herriman [...] radically combin[ed] standard representations of Old-to-New-World immigration and fulfillment of Manifest Destiny with an inversion of the rural-to-urban migration theme[...]" ("'Some Say'" n. pag.).

56. Krazy seems to have suspected something about his role as a cartoon character when he asked Ignatz in a 1914 daily: "We ain't not regular cat' and mouse' is we? [...] If we was Id eat you up wouldn't I?" (*Panoramic* 35).

57. Benjamin made this argument in "The Work of Art in the Age of Mechanical Reproduction" (1937). Examples are a puddle of ink from which two speech bubbles arise ("L'il anjil" and "Pow"; July 8, 1928); a panel in which all characters are white and accuse their "boss" of being "stingy with his '*ink*'" (February 7, 1926); and an episode in which Mrs. Kwakk Kwakk tips over an ink bottle because from it "flows sin, evil—law breakage" (November 5, 1939; the ink becomes an oil-like fluid and oozes from the upper left corner of the page to the lower right).

58. Carlin reads *Krazy Kat* as a series of "complex parables about the nature of art and representation" (46).

59. On September 5, 1938, Ignatz is "indeed an artist" who draws a brick and defends himself against Offissa Pupp by insisting that "this is only a drawing of a brick—*I can't* toss it, now, can I." The police dog replies: "You *can* erase it" (reprinted in McDonnell 93).

60. Lack of space prevents an investigation of Herriman's innovative use of panel shapes and page layouts. Cf. Schechter: "He fragmented the Sunday space in every conceivable way, organizing strips vertically, embedding frames within frames, and employing an array of nonrectangular panel designs juxtaposed in anti–Euclidean spaces that would do a deconstructivist architect proud" (554).

61. Schwartz proposes this argument (cf. 9).

Works Cited

Aiken, Conrad. "King Bolo and Others." *T.S. Eliot: A Symposium*. Ed. Richard March and Tambimuttu. Freeport, NY: Books for Libraries, 1949. 20–23. Print.

Amiran, Eyal. "George Herriman's Black Sentence: The Legibility of Race in Krazy Kat." *Mosaic* 33.3 (2000): 57–79. Print.

Arnold, Matthew. *Culture and Anarchy*. 1882. Ed. J. Dover Wilson. Cambridge: Cambridge University Press, 1971. Print.

Barnard, Rita. "Modern American Fiction." Kalaidjian 39–67.

Bell, Bernard. "Jean Toomer's 'Blue Meridian': The Poet as Prophet of a New Order of Man." *Jean Toomer: A Critical Evaluation*. Ed. Therman B. O'Daniel. Washington, D.C.: Howard University Press, 1988. 343–54. Print.

Berger, Arthur Asa. *The Comic-Stripped American: What Dick Tracy, Blondie, Daddy Warbucks, and Charlie Brown Tell Us about Ourselves*. New York: Walker, 1973. Print.

Berry, R. M. "Language." Bradshaw and Dettmar 113–22.

Blackbeard, Bill. "The Man Behind the Pupp Behind the Mouse Behind the Kat: George Herriman, 1880–1944. Herriman, *"A Mice, a Brick, a Lovely Night"* 11–13. Print.

_____. "No Kidding ... We've Run Out of Kats!" Herriman, *"Necromancy by the Blue Bean Bush"* 6–7. Print.

_____. "Pilfering Mrs. Kwak-Wak's Good Old Goods and Goodies Bag: Scoop the First." Herriman, *Complete Full Page Comic Strips 1927–1928* 6–14. Print.

Blackmore, Tim. "Krazy as a Fool: Erasmus of Rotterdam's *Praise of Folly* and Herriman of Cococino's *Krazy Kat*." *Journal of Popular Culture* 31.3 (1997): 19–46. Print.

Bradshaw, David, and Kevin J.H. Dettmar, eds. *A Companion to Modernist Literature and Culture.* Malden, MA: Blackwell, 2006. Print.

Breton, André. "First Surrealist Manifesto." 1924. Reprinted in *Surrealism.* Ed. Patrick Waldberg. New York: McGraw, 1971. 66–75. Print.

Carlin, John. "Masters of American Comics: An Art History of Twentieth-Century American Comic Strips and Books." *Masters of American Comics.* Ed. John Carlin, Paul Karasik, and Brian Walker. Hammer Museum and the Museum of Contemporary Art, Los Angeles. New Haven: Yale University Press, 2005. 24–175. Print.

Chinitz, David E. *T.S. Eliot and the Cultural Divide.* Chicago: University of Chicago Press, 2003.

Crocker, Elizabeth. "'Some Say It with a Brick': George Herriman's *Krazy Kat.*" Web. 17 January 2007.

_____. "'To He, I Am for Eva True': Krazy Kat's Indeterminate Gender." *Postmodern Culture* 4.2 (1994). n. pag. Web. 17 January 2007.

Cummings, E.E. "A Foreword to Krazy." *Sawanee Review* 1946. Reprinted in *A Miscellany.* Ed. George J. Firmage. New York: Argophile, 1958. 102–06. Print.

Dettmar, Kevin J.H. Introduction. Bradshaw and Dettmar 1–5.

Dorgan, Tad. "This Is About Garge Herriman." *Circulation Magazine,* September 1922. Reprinted in Herriman, *"A Mice, a Brick, a Lovely Night"* 18.

Douglas, Ann. *Terrible Honesty: Mongrel Manhattan in the 1920s.* New York: Farrar, 1995. Print.

Du Bois, W.E.B. *The Souls of Black Folk.* 1903. *The Oxford W.E.B. Du Bois Reader.* Ed. Eric J. Sundquist. New York: Oxford University Press, 1996. 97–240. Print.

Eliot, T.S. *Complete Poems and Plays, 1909–1950.* New York: Harcourt, 1971. Print.

_____. *The Letters of T.S. Eliot, Vol. I: 1898–1922.* Ed. Valerie Eliot. San Diego: Harcourt, 1988. Print.

Ellison, Ralph. "What America Would Be Like Without Blacks." *Time* 6 April 1970. Reprinted in *The Collected Essays of Ralph Ellison.* Ed. John F. Callahan. New York: Modern Library, 1995. 577–84. Print.

Forest, David V. "Afterword to Krazy: George Herriman's Krazy Kat Cartoon and Its Appeal to E.E. Cummings." *Journal of the American Academy of Psychoanalysis* 30.2 (2002): 249–58. Print.

Gendron, Bernard. "Jamming at Le Beouf: Jazz and the Paris Avant-Garde." *Discourse* 12.1 (1989–90): 3–27. Print.

Gopnik, Adam. "Comics." *High and Low: Modern Art and Popular Culture.* Ed. Kirk Varnedoe and Adam Gopnik. New York: Museum of Modern Art, 1990. 153–228. Print.

_____. "The Genius of George Herriman." *New York Review of Books* 33.20 (1986). Web. 10 April 2008.

Gordon, Ian. *Comic Strips and Consumer Culture 1890–1945.* Washington, D.C.: Smithsonian Institution, 1998. Print.

Gubar, Susan. *Racechanges: White Skin, Black Face in American Culture.* New York: Oxford University Press, 1997. Print.

Harvey, Robert C. *The Art of the Funnies: An Aesthetic History.* Jackson: University Press of Mississippi, 1994. Print.

_____. *Children of the Yellow Kid: The Evolution of the American Comic Strip.* Seattle: Frye Art Museum/University of Washington Press, 1998. Print.

Heer, Jeet. "The Kolors of Krazy Kat." Herriman, *The Complete Full-Page Comic Strips, 1935–1936* 8–15. Print.

Herriman, George. *"A Brick Stuffed with Moom-Bims": Krazy and Ignatz, 1939–1940.* Ed. Bill Blackbeard. Seattle: Fantagraphics, 2007.

_____. *The Family Upstairs: Introducing Krazy Kat. The Complete Strip: 1910–1912.* Westport, CT: Hyperion, 1977. Print.

_____. *George Herriman's Krazy + Ignatz in "Tiger Tea."* Ed. Craig Yoe. San Diego: Yoe/IDW, 2010

_____. *"A Kat A'Lilt with Song": Krazy and Ignatz, The Complete Full-Page Comic Strips, 1931–1932.* Ed. Bill Blackbeard and Derya Ataker. Seattle: Fantagraphics, 2004.

_____. *The Kat Who Walked in Beauty: The Panoramic Dailies of 1920.* Ed. Derya Ataker. Seattle: Fantagraphics, 2007. Print.

_____. *Krazy and Ignatz: The Complete Full-Page Comic Strips, 1935–1936.* Ed. Bill Blackbeard. Seattle: Fantagraphics, 2005.

_____. *Krazy and Ignatz Vol. 1: The Dailies 1918–1919.* Ed. Gregory J. Fink. Stinging Monkey, 2003. Print.

_____. *"Love Letters in Ancient Brick": Krazy and Ignatz, the Complete Full-Page Comic Strips, 1927–1928.* Ed. Bill Blackbeard. Seattle: Fantagraphics, 2002.

_____. "A Mice, a Brick, a Lovely Night": Krazy and Ignatz, the Complete Full-Page Comics, 1929–1930. Ed. Bill Blackbeard. Seattle: Fantagraphics, 2003.

_____. "Necromancy by the Blue Bean Bush": Krazy and Ignatz, The Complete Full Page Comic Strips, 1933–1934. Ed. Bill Blackbeard and Derya Ataker. Seattle: Fantagraphics, 2004.

_____. "A Ragout of Raspberries": Krazy and Ignatz, 1941–1942. Ed. Bill Blackbeard. Seattle: Fantagraphics, 2007.

_____. "Shifting Sands Dusts its Cheeks in Powdered Beauty": Krazy and Ignatz, 1937–1938. Ed. Bill Blackbeard. Seattle: Fantagraphics, 2006.

_____. "There Is a Heppy Lend-Fur, Fur Awa-a-ay": Krazy and Ignatz, the Complete Full-Page Comic Strips, 1925–1926. Ed. Bill Blackbeard. Seattle: Fantagraphics, 2002.

Howe, Irving. "Notes on Mass Culture." Politics 5 (Spring 1948). Reprinted in Arguing Comics: Literary Masters on a Popular Medium. Ed. Jeet Heer and Kent Worcester. Jackson: University Press of Mississippi, 2004. 43–51. Print.

Inge, M. Thomas. Comics as Culture. Jackson: University Press of Mississippi, 1990. Print.

_____. "Was Krazy Kat Black? The Radical Identity of George Herriman." Inks 3.2 (1996): 2–9. Israel, Nico. "Geography." Bradshaw and Dettmar 123–32.

James, William. Principles of Psychology. 2 vols. 1890. New York: Dover, 1950. Print.

Jenkins, Henry. What Made Pistachio Nuts? Early Sound Comedy and the Vaudeville Aesthetic. New York: Columbia University Press, 1992. Print.

Johnson, James Weldon. The Book of American Negro Poetry. Rev. ed. New York: Harcourt, 1931. Print.

Kalaidjian, Walter, ed. The Cambridge Companion to American Modernism. New York: Cambridge University Press, 2005. Print.

_____. Introduction. Kalaidjian: 1–11.

Kaufman, Daniela. Der intellektuelle Witz im Comic: George Herrimans Krazy Kat. Graz: Leykam, 2008.

Levine, Lawrence W. Highbrow/Lowbrow: The Emergence of Cultural Hierarchy in America. Cambridge: Harvard University Press, 1988. Print.

Locke, Alain. "The New Negro." The New Negro: Voices of the Harlem Renaissance. 1925. Ed. Alain Locke. New York: Touchstone/Schuster, 1997. 3–16. Print.

Lyon, Janet. "Gender and Sexuality." Kalaidjian 221–41.

Marschall, Richard. America's Great Comic-Strip Artists: From the Yellow Kid to Peanuts. New York: Abbeville, 1989. Print.

McDonnell, Patrick, Karen O'Connell, and Georgia Riley de Havenon. Krazy Kat: The Comic Art of George Herriman. New York: Abrams, 1986. Print.

Michaels, Walter Benn. Our America: Nativism, Modernism, and Pluralism. Durham: Duke University Press, 1995. Print.

Nahshon, Edna, ed. From the Ghetto to the Melting Pot: Israel Zangwill's Jewish Plays. Detroit: Wayne State University Press, 2006. Print.

Nelson, Cary. "Modern American Poetry." Kalaidjian 68–101.

North, Michael. The Dialect of Modernism: Race, Language, and Twentieth-Century Literature. New York: Oxford University Press, 1994. Print.

_____. "Visual Culture." Kalaidjian 177–94.

Orvell, Miles. "Writing Posthistorically: Krazy Kat, Maus, and the Contemporary Fiction Cartoon." American Literary History 4.1 (1992): 110–28. Print.

O'Sullivan, Judith. The Great American Comic Strip: One Hundred Years of Cartoon Art. Boston: Bullfinch, 1990. Print.

Pfeiffer, Kathleen. Race Passing and American Individualism. Amherst: University of Massachusetts Press, 2003. Print.

Reed, Ishmael. Mumbo Jumbo. 1972. New York: Scribner, 1996. Print.

Rogin, Michael. Blackface, White Noise: Jewish Immigrants and the Hollywood Melting Pot. Berkeley: University of California Press, 1996. Print.

Rosemont, Franklin. "Surrealism in the Comics I: Krazy Kat (George Herriman)." Popular Culture in America. Ed. Paul Buhle. Minneapolis: University of Minnesota Press, 1987. 119–27. Print.

Sanders, Mark A. "American Modernism and the New Negro Renaissance." Kalaidjian 129–56.

Santayana, George. "The Genteel Tradition in American Philosophy." 1911. Winds of Doctrine and Platonism and the Spiritual Life. Gloucester, MA: Smith, 1971. 186–215. Print.

Saussure, Ferdinand de. Course in General Linguistics. 1916. Trans. Wade Baskin. New York: McGraw, 1966. Print.

Schechter, Russell. "Kat and Maus." *Communication Research* 16.4 (1989): 552–66. Print.

Schmitz, Neil. *Of Huck and Alice: Humorous Writing in American Literature.* Minneapolis: University of Minnesota Press, 1983. Print.

Schwartz, Ben. "The Court Jester: Hearst, Herriman, and the Death of Nonsense." Herriman, *"A Mice, a Brick, a Lovely Night"* 8–10. Print.

Seldes, Gilbert. "The Krazy Kat That Walks by Himself." 1922. *The Seven Lively Arts.* New York: Harper, 1924. 231–45. Print.

Shannon, Edward A. "'That We May Mis-Unda-Stend Each Udda': The Rhetoric of Krazy Kat." *Journal of Popular Culture* 29.2 (1995): 209–22. Print.

Short, Robert. "Dada." Bradshaw and Dettmar 163–68.

Singal, Daniel Joseph. "Towards a Definition of American Modernism." *American Quarterly* 39.1 (1987). Reprinted in *Modernist Culture in America.* Ed. Daniel Joseph Singal. Belmont, CA: Wadsworth, 1991. 1–27. Print.

Sollors, Werner. *Neither Black Nor White Yet Both: Thematic Explorations of Interracial Literature.* New York: Oxford University Press, 1997. Print.

Twain, Mark. *Adventures of Huckleberry Finn.* 1884/85. Ed. Gerald Graff and James Phelan. 2d ed. Boston: Bedford/St. Martin's, 2004. Print.

Warshow, Robert. "Woofed with Dreams." *Partisan Review* 13 (November-December 1946). Reprinted in *The Immediate Experience: Movies, Comics, Theatre and Other Aspects of Popular Culture.* Cambridge: Harvard University Press, 2001. 19–23. Print.

Wordsworth, William. "Illustrated Books and Newspapers." 1846. *The Victorians: An Anthology of Poetry and Poetics.* Ed. Valentine Cunningham. Oxford: Blackwell, 1999. 16. Print.

Woolf, Virginia. *Mr. Bennett and Mrs. Brown.* London: Hogarth, 1924. Print.

3

Fantastic Alterities and *The Sandman*

JULIA ROUND

Introduction

This chapter explores the ways in which the comics medium enhances our understanding of literary models of the Fantastic.[1] It examines the presence and depiction of multiple worlds in Neil Gaiman's *The Sandman* and discusses the role of the comics medium and its denial of mimesis in creating such alterities. After establishing a contemporary working model of the Fantastic, it considers the ways in which the comics medium supports the creation and sustenance of both the mode and genre of the Fantastic via form and content. It then analyzes the construction of fantastic alterities in *The Sandman* using case studies drawn from *A Game of You* and *The Kindly Ones*. It concludes by identifying and summarizing the ways in which the tenets of comics narratology exemplify the criteria for construction of the Fantastic.

Defining the Fantastic

The Fantastic frequently eludes definition and resists categorization. Critics remain hesitant as to its status (as a mode or genre) and attempts at definition have focused variously upon its thematic, structural, stylistic or cultural elements. The following summary of the current critical position addresses these various approaches and establishes a working model.

As a forerunner of modern criticism, Northrop Frye's work offers a broad view of literature in identifying archetypes and modes that encompass genres. These operate as overall tendencies in literature rather than historically limited genres, although the issue is frequently confused as the modes themselves are derived from historical genre definitions. For example, Frye situates Myth and naturalism as the opposing poles of literary design, with romance (defined not as a historical genre but as a movement in literature towards the displacement of Myth into the human sphere) found between the two (*Anatomy* 136).

71

Similar models are found in the work of other critics, for example Robert Scholes's catalogue of seven modes that are derived from historical genre definitions yet encompass these ("Towards a Poetics of Fiction" 107).

Although he criticizes the non-literary nature of Frye's categories, Tzvetan Todorov's famous structuralist definition of the Fantastic mirrors Frye's work (16). Todorov situates the Fantastic between the marvelous (supernatural accepted) and the uncanny (supernatural explained), creating a similar three-part structure at the level of genre. In critiquing the ambiguities and omissions of Frye's model, Todorov exposes the distinction between historical and theoretical genres in Frye's catalogue (Todorov 13). The notion of theoretical genres goes back as far as the theories of Plato or Diomedes and defines genres that may not exist alongside those that do. Todorov then proceeds to create a similarly theoretical model of the Fantastic. His critique of Frye seems supported, for example, by Frye's own insistence in his work on the autonomy of literary criticism (*Anatomy* 6) while denying any such self-sufficiency to his literary categories, and Todorov's structuralist model remains the cornerstone definition of the Fantastic to date.

Todorov identifies three textual levels within his critical model (the verbal, the syntactical and the semantic) and proposes that the "moment of hesitation" that defines the Fantastic may be located on any of these levels (20). Whereas previously this hesitation commonly referred to perception (and therefore was most often found in the verbal area — referring to both the utterance itself and its performance, and thereby involving both the speaker/narrator and the listener/reader), Todorov proposes that language has now replaced perception as the defining factor of fantastic discourse. Consequently he concludes that hesitation is also observable both in the syntactical relations between different parts of the text, and in its semantic content (its themes, which he identifies as being either of the self or the other).

By specifically addressing the Fantastic and adding a syntactic dimension, Todorov's study breaks with previous criticism. Much of this touches on the Fantastic only as a part of a wider categorization of literary criticism (Frye) or generic theory — as Robert Scholes describes his own work: situating it between the generalizations of modal theory and the preciseness of genre study ("Towards a Poetics of Fiction" 111). Even those studies specifically directed at the Fantastic (such as John Cawelti's work on deductive genre theory, or the formalist work of Vladimir Propp) focus only on the text's semantics.

Of the preceding studies, Propp's *Morphology of the Folktale* (first published in 1928) is perhaps the most significant. It explores the text at the narrative level, focusing on its overt content and themes. Through syntagmatic analysis of individual narratives, Propp identifies thirty-one functions that he claims are common to the narrative structure of all Russian wondertales. By focusing exclusively on this limited body of work, Propp's study also includes an implicit cultural element, although this is not explicitly considered in *Morphology*. However, Propp's later book, *Theory and History of Folklore*, expands upon his earlier observations to consider the semantics of his wondertales in a cultural context: concluding that folklore reinterprets the images of the old social system in order to depict the unusual in impossible dimensions (11).

Propp also comments (somewhat more widely) that, in this way, genres may be classified according to their relationship with reality:

The character of a genre is determined by the kind of reality it reflects, the means by which reality is expressed, the relation to reality, and its assessment. Unity of form results in unity of content, if by content we understand not only the plot but also the intellectual and emotional world reflected in the work. It follows that unity of form is sustained by everything called content and that the two cannot be separated [*Theory and History of Folklore* 41].

In this way Propp gives his semantic study a syntactical dimension and, although the resulting model has been criticized (for example by Claude Lévi-Strauss), it has also been successfully defended.[2]

Subsequent criticism has built upon these previous models in various ways. Defining the Fantastic in terms of its relationship with reality is further supported by the work of Kathryn Hume, who defines fantasy as one of the overall impulses (together with mimesis) that underlie all literature (xii) and subdivides it into four different modes according to its response to reality (55). While this inclusive definition is certainly non-restrictive it is of small help in defining exactly what fantasy might be except a departure from reality.

Rosemary Jackson's *Fantasy: The Literature of Subversion* (1981) seeks "to extend Todorov's investigation from being one limited to the *poetics* of the Fantastic into one aware of the *politics* of its forms" (6) in order to consider the cultural formation of the Fantastic. Jackson also defines the Fantastic/fantasy (she uses the two terms interchangeably) as a mode that assumes different generic forms (32) and uses a linguistic metaphor (which parallels Claude Lévi-Strauss's structuralist approach to Myth) to clarify this. The mode of the Fantastic is the *langue* from which various *parole* (genres or forms) derive, according to its interpretation and the surrounding historical situation (7).

Jackson has been criticized most for her indiscriminate use of terminology (see for example Traill 6 and Cornwell 27), but her work does introduce two important terms: "alterity" and "paraxis." "Fantasy re-combines and inverts the real, but it does not escape it: it exists in a parasitical or symbiotic relation to the real" (20). Fantastic worlds are therefore alterities — "this world re-placed and dis-located" (19), and Jackson defines this process of transformation and replacement as paraxis—signifying "par-axis," being that which lies alongside the main body (or axis) (19). Jackson further notes the significance of her optical metaphor (paraxis is a technical term referring to an illusory area of perceived unity after light refraction), alerting us to the significance of perception in defining the Fantastic.

In adding a cultural dimension to Todorov's model, Jackson's criticism is largely semantic in nature, and much of her study is concerned with identifying the Fantastic's themes (such as invisibility, transformation, and dualism) and motifs (vampires, mirrors, shadows, ghosts, madness, and dreams) in her selected texts. It is again worth noting that all these revolve around difficulties of perception and the problematization of vision (45). However, she does also apply her criticism, albeit briefly, to the syntactical dimensions of the text, supporting Todorov's model in commenting that anxiety and hesitation may be found in the work's structure (28). Nonetheless, her work is not able to provide a new model for future criticism, but instead uses Todorov's model to inform a series of observations that connect a variety of works in terms of their structural characteristics and underlying semantic themes.

Subsequent criticism has continued to redefine Todorov's model in a similar manner, using stylistic and semantic deconstructions of fantastic literature to justify modifications. In *A Rhetoric of the Unreal* (1981), Christine Brooke-Rose attempts to define the Fantastic stylistically, providing an analysis of previous critical models and genre-based theories. She redefines Todorov's notion of hesitation in terms of the text's implied author and reader (as well as its narrator and narratee) and analyzes the text's related stylistic features. She concludes that the textual codes used are necessarily either over- or under-determined: we are given either too much (conflicting) information, or not enough, which sustains the Fantastic (112). Not for the first time, attention is drawn to the stylistic strategies common to the Fantastic, such as unreliable narration.

Later critics' work continues in this vein, reassessing and adapting Todorov's model in order to both refine its applicability and inform discussion of the types of strategies common to the Fantastic. A.B. Chanady's *Magical Realism and the Fantastic* (1985) attempts to clarify and distinguish between these two terms, treating them as similar modes. Commenting that "critics do not even agree whether it is a mode, a genre or an attitude towards reality" (1), Chanady goes on to draw attention to the confusions of Todorov's system, where despite naming the Fantastic as a genre, he nonetheless situates it between two modes (1). She instead adds the Fantastic to Robert Scholes's catalogue of seven modes and discusses it at this level.

Although she does not adopt Jackson's alterity terminology, Chanady also notes that fantastic literature is set in a world "very similar" (though not identical) to our own (5), in contrast to fairy tale, which takes place in the world of the outright marvelous. She defines three criteria for the presence of the Fantastic/magical realism: the co-presence of the natural and supernatural; antinomy between the two; and authorial reticence (31). The treatment of these factors is, for Chanady, the distinguishing factor between magical realism and the Fantastic: whereas the co-presence of the natural and supernatural is normalized by the presence of a realistic framework in magical realism, this is denied in the Fantastic. The antinomy of the supernatural and natural is thereby resolved in magical realism and authorial reticence leads to acceptance, whereas such contradictions are foregrounded in fantastic literature and uncertainty prevails (11).

Chanady's attempt to distinguish between the two terms is made less clear for some readers by her use of Spanish-American narratives, which are included without translation. However, her method leads to closer study of the strategies used to enable authorial reticence (such as singularization) and she concludes by suggesting further areas for research that include the character of the narrator, use of subjectivity, characteristics of enunciation, and closer analysis of structural elements such as the use of suspense, suggestion and so forth.

Neil Cornwell's study *The Literary Fantastic* (1990) seeks to link the Fantastic to both gothic and postmodern literature and in so doing offers a comprehensive literature review of many of the models examined thus far. For Cornwell's purposes, Todorov's genre theory of the Fantastic exists within the broader mode that Cornwell names as fantasy, although he notes that fantasy also exists as a sub-genre (for example Tolkien-esque fiction), and in addition defines the Fantastic as a quality that may be found in works such as the uncanny (31).

Cornwell also looks backwards to gothic fiction and aligns David Punter's definition of "paranoiac fiction" with the Fantastic (53). In this sense he again strengthens the case for consideration of the Fantastic as an overall mode rather than a historically limited genre — and goes on to criticize the narrow period from which Todorov's examples are drawn (141). Although it is clear that many of the best examples of fantastic fiction are to be found in certain eras, its applicability to the disparate periods of gothic and postmodernism refutes such a limitation. Cornwell's work therefore aligns with Jackson's in treating the Fantastic as a mode that assumes various forms according to its historical context.

As Cornwell notes, the literary Fantastic has many similarities with the postmodern, a link further supported by his identification of the current preponderance of fantastic literature. Similarly, Scholes's definition of contemporary writing as fragmented and distorted applies equally to both the Fantastic and modernist/postmodernist fiction. Some of the more general surrounding literary criticism further emphasizes this point.

This includes *Romancing the Postmodern* (1992), in which Diane Elam links the "excess characteristic" (1) of romance to postmodernism: considering romance both as a postmodern genre and as postmodernism itself (12). In so doing, she treats postmodernism not as following modernism, but as its counter-discourse (3), commenting that "postmodernism does not simply happen after modernism but is a series of problems present to modernism in its continuing infancy" (9) and hence focusing on texts that are problematized by their inclusion of romance (4). In my view, by situating romance in opposition to literary realism, defining it as "excess," commenting that its character remains "an uncertainty" (7), and focusing on its problematic tendencies, Elam's treatment of the concept may inform discussion of the Fantastic (if not outright fantasy). She also adds a gender dimension to her study in her consideration of woman "as the figure of the self-excess of romance" (17).

Bruno Latour takes a similar perspective on the coexistence of modernism and post-modernism in *We Have Never Been Modern* (1993), arguing that the historically limited genres of modernism and postmodernism are illusory and that, in fact, modernism has never existed in accordance with its own constitution. As such, he defines postmodernism not (as it presents itself) as the end of history, but instead locates it in the perpetual impasse of the avant-garde (62). In so doing, his work, like Elam's, accords with Jean-François Lyotard's definition of postmodernism, as "not modernism at its end but in the nascent state, and this state is constant" (79).

A similar revelation exists in *The Space of Literature* (1982), in which Maurice Blanchot offers an inverted way of approaching literature as a silent empty space. Blanchot argues against common literary perception in proposing that art is not the real made unreal; that we do not ascend from the real world to art, but instead emerge from art towards what appears to be a mutualized version of our world (47). Literature dwells in a silent, empty space and similarly is only able to be defined in terms of its negative attributes, such as the power to stop writing (25). As such, it is inward-looking: concerned only for its own essence (42). The illusory space accorded to the Fantastic by some of the literary models discussed above, together with the reversal of the real and fictional worlds that underpins Blanchot's framework, again seem to tie his model to the Fantastic.

The idea of literature as that which "has become concerned for its own essence" (42) also evokes the notion of metafiction: a form common to the postmodern. Patricia Waugh defines metafiction as "a term given to fictional writing which self-consciously and systematically draws attention to its status as an artifact in order to pose questions about the relationship between fiction and reality" (40). However, she also defines it as "a tendency or function inherent in *all* novels" (42) and identifies many metafictional techniques that are shared by the Fantastic, such as the defamiliarization of language, an undermining of the omniscient narrator (49), or the setting up of an opposition between the construction and breaking of illusion (52). In this way metafictional texts explore the concept of fiction and expose reality itself as a mere concept. These elements inform the mode of the Fantastic.

Cultural studies that focus on the historical genre of the Fantastic do, however, provide further information as to its function and enable semantic discussion. John Cawelti notes that, while the genre is universal, the formula behind it is cultural (*The Six-Gun Mystique* 57), and as such it may be said that studies such as Propp's *Morphology* can inform on both levels. Cawelti concludes that formula fiction has a ritualistic function: to reaffirm cultural values (100), and Jack Zipes's work on fairy tales offers a similar conclusion (*The Brothers Grimm* 143). Zipes's semantic consideration draws a distinction between the functions of the oral tradition of fairy tale and those of its written form and as such offers a syntactical element that is further enhanced by his observation that the structure of the tale is designed to facilitate recall (for example in its use of tasks as signs, or the absence of names) (Bannerman).

The various works of Marina Warner offer a similar thematic deconstruction of many of the dominant themes, motifs and symbols of fairy tale as Warner traces the historical development of this genre. She identifies changes in the depiction of certain motifs — such as the witch figure (*No Go the Bogeyman* 12) — and in this way links the semantic content of fairy tale firmly to its historical context.

As this discussion demonstrates, while cultural and semantic theories focus upon cataloguing the motifs and themes of the Fantastic, contemporary syntactic models have refined Todorov's framework to emphasize the textual structure rather than the subjective reader response. This enables consideration of the Fantastic in terms of its relationship with reality (a notion prefigured by Propp and Hume), as in the work of Nancy Traill, who uses a theory of fictional worlds (derived from possible worlds) to examine the stylistic and semantic elements of the Fantastic. Like A.B. Chanady, Traill redefines reader hesitation as the co-presence of the natural and supernatural within the text, arranged in alethic opposition (9). She identifies various modes of the Fantastic (such as the disjunctive, outright fantasy, the ambiguous, or the paranormal) and (commenting on Jackson and Todorov's definitions) defines these as being tied to a moment in history while also transcending it (20). She further reviews terms such as realism in this way, distinguishing between the historical movement (realist fiction) and the ahistorical requirement (mimesis) (43).

As such, fantastic-specific criticism has provided (and subsequently modified) a framework for analyzing fantastic texts syntactically that is enhanced by its observations of the narrative techniques common to this model. These include: narrative remove, authorial reticence, over-or under-determination, floating signifiers, the use of figurative rather than literal discourse, and irreversible temporality, to name but a few. The semantic focus of other criticism from this school similarly identifies its relevant themes (such as transformation, invisibility, and dualism) and the symbols and motifs used to emphasize these.

These critical areas seem important to a contemporary conception of the Fantastic, and will hopefully be further informed by this article's subsequent case studies. These will be performed using a model of the Fantastic derived from the critics mentioned above and which is defined as follows: The Fantastic is an overall mode or tendency in fiction that has spawned various historical genres. These genres include those named by Todorov as fantastic, uncanny, or marvelous (which last is also known as magical realism or fantasy), and also the newer genres of the paranormal, science fiction and so forth. From this point on it therefore seems appropriate to distinguish between the (ahistorical) mode of "the Fantastic" and the (historical) genre of "the fantastic," or "fantastic literature" (which is distinct from fantasy or magical realism, as noted).

As this chapter will examine the mode of the Fantastic at both a syntactical and semantic level it seems appropriate to define the conditions of the Fantastic textually. This follows later critical models in redefining Todorov's notion of hesitation as the co-presence of the natural and supernatural (while noting that this may be indicated by reader hesitation). This is the primary condition for identification of the mode of the Fantastic, which (depending on the treatment of this opposition and other textual and historical factors) may then spawn any of the genres mentioned above — such as magical realism/fantasy (if the co-presence of the natural and supernatural is normalized), or the fantastic/fantastic literature itself (where this juxtaposition is problematized).

Contemporary status

It seems important to note that the audience for fantastic literature aligns closely with that of comics. Like comics, the genre of fantasy literature is still perceived by many as children's literature. Similarly, fan conventions are events common to both comics and fantasy; and role-playing games such as *Dungeons and Dragons* link the Fantastic to the same fanboy or nerd label applied to comics. Offshoots such as live role-playing further emphasize costuming as a common factor and this is again reinforced by the existence of conventions, where costumes (such as *Star Trek* uniforms or magicians' robes) are commonplace. Finally, fantastic literature, movies and associated merchandise are often sold in comic book shops and in this way the genre literally shares a space with comics — *Forbidden Planet* (one of the largest chains of comic book stores in the United Kingdom) describes itself on its website as "the world's LARGEST and BEST-KNOWN science fiction, fantasy and cult entertainment retailer" (see www.forbiddenplanet.com).

Fantasy blockbusters such as Peter Jackson's *Lord of the Rings* movie trilogy (2001–02) or J.K. Rowling's *Harry Potter* novels (the first of which was published in 1997) may be perceived as breathing new life into the genre; however it can be argued that this is deceptive. Jackson's movies have not legitimized fantasy in a wider sense by bestowing new credibility on older fantasy movies such as *The Beastmaster* (1982) or *Krull* (1983), and Rowling's success, although paving the way for imitators, has not made it any more

acceptable for adults to read generic fantasy. In fact her books have been famously repack-
aged (using black-and-white photographs rather than character illustrations) for those
adults who wish to read them in public without embarrassment. Likewise, the credibility
that is afforded by the packaging of the glossy graphic novel and trade paperback forms
or bestowed upon independent publishers (and even the literary DC Vertigo writers) mirrors this situation — as it should be remembered that this does not yet extend to general
public perception of comics.

Case study — *The Sandman: A Game of You*

A Game of You (the fifth *Sandman* trade paperback) tells a story split between two
contrasting worlds — the dream world of its heroine, Barbie, and the "real" world of New
York.[3] The presence of these two alterities invokes the Fantastic as we struggle to decide
which world is most valid: which we should believe in. However, as Samuel Delaney
alerts us in his introduction to the trade paperback, it is a mistake to read one world as
fantasy and the other as reality. Delaney instead proposes that both worlds are fantasy,
citing as evidence the mirroring and doubling of events between worlds and the parallels
between characters such as George and Wilkinson, or Wanda and the Tantoblin.

The natural and supernatural coexist within the setting of Barbie's dream world
(which is known only as "THE LAND") — although in fact its introduction focuses entirely
on its natural elements. This is primarily achieved by showing the opening conversation
(between Luz, Prinado, Wilkinson and Martin Tenbones) without revealing the speakers
to be talking animals (*A Game of You* 1.1.1–1.3.3), and is further reinforced by the subject
of their conversation, which indicates that the laws of life and death also apply here. The
panels depict the dead body of the Tantoblin, the friend they are discussing (1.1.3).[4] In
fact our first encounter with The Land (in *The Doll's House*) emphasizes this point, as it is
introduced as: "BARBARA'S RICH DREAM-LIFE, MORE VALID AND TRUE THAN ANYTHING
SHE FEELS WHEN WAKING" (6.15.1). At least initially, the unreal seems more real than
the fiction's presentation of "reality."

Conversely, from the very first issue of this story arc, supernatural elements from
The Land invade the New York setting. Barbie's escort, Martin Tenbones (a giant dog-
like creature) crosses into this world to alert her to danger (1.15.2); ghostly cuckoos appear
and then vanish in Barbie's room (1.24.4–5); and in the final panel her neighbor, George,
reveals himself to be a servant of the Cuckoo (1.25.8). Following from my model of the
Fantastic, these may be best defined as supernatural elements that sit at odds with the
natural elements of the New York alterity and are treated as such — the police shoot down
Martin Tenbones, believing him to be an escaped animal; Barbie panics upon seeing the
cuckoos; and George is defined as abnormal as he is shown eating an entire (live) bird in
one mouthful.

Barbie's response to the presence of the supernatural in her world is pure hesitation — she repeats Martin Tenbones's name more than once in disbelief and although his
physical presence cannot be denied nonetheless continues: "BUT YOU'RE FROM MY DREAM"
(1.21.4). Similarly, the supernatural events (such as Thessaly's drawing down of the moon

so she, Hazel and Foxglove may walk its path into The Land) have natural ramifications — as George (posthumously) tells Wanda: "THESSALY WASN'T JUST DOING SOMETHING UH **SPIRITUAL**. THAT WAS UH **PHYSICAL** TOO" (4.19.7). As such, these unnatural events cannot be dismissed and therefore the New York setting may, as Delaney alerts us, also be read as a fantastic alterity.

However, there is also a third alterity present in *A Game of You*—the world of The Dreaming.[5] This too is introduced in the first issue of the story arc (1.11.1–5, 1.12.1–7), although as Morpheus's domain it is not new to us. As such we know it to be real (within the confines of the text) yet also fantasy (in accordance with the willing suspension of disbelief that is the condition of fiction). As the master shaper and storyteller who will also turn out to be the god of Barbie's dream world and whose name, Murphy, derives from Morpheus (5.31.5), Morpheus and his realm may be read as a point of reference which adds a metafictional dimension to the text.

It seems, therefore, that the mode of the Fantastic informs all of the contrasting alterities within *A Game of You* with varying effects. Whereas in The Land the co-presence of the natural and supernatural is normalized, and as such may be read as representing the magical realism/fantasy genre; the contradictions we perceive in our introduction to the New York alterity alert us to its status as a fantastic setting. The third alterity of The Dreaming further utilizes the Fantastic to create metafiction as it is revealed that Morpheus (who is often defined as a storyteller figure) is the literal creator of one of the worlds.

The opposition between the real and the unreal perceived in the worlds of The Land and New York produces a hesitation as we attempt to read this antinomy in various ways and decipher which world is real. The solution provided by the Cuckoo and reaffirmed by Barbie in the book's final pages, is that:

> EVERYBODY HAS A SECRET *WORLD* INSIDE OF THEM.
>   I MEAN *EVERYBODY*. ALL OF THE PEOPLE IN THE WHOLE WORLD—NO MATTER *HOW* DULL AND BORING THEY ARE ON THE OUTSIDE.
>   INSIDE THEM THEY'VE *ALL* GOT UNIMAGINABLE, MAGNIFICENT, WONDERFUL, STUPID, AMAZING *WORLDS* ... NOT JUST ONE WORLD. *HUNDREDS* OF THEM. *THOUSANDS*, MAYBE [6.19.2–4].

However, it may be said that by offering such a non-physical explanation this solution is problematical not magical: supporting a view of the text as fantastic literature.

Intertextual references further blur the line between fantasy/reality and fiction/metafiction in all three worlds. These include Barbie's frequent mentions of *The Wizard of Oz* (4.18.2, 6.6.2, 6.10.1, 6.23.4) and her observation that "I FELT LIKE BILBO IN MIRKWOOD, IN THAT BIT WHERE THE GIANT SPIDERS GET THEM." Her question to Wilkinson and his answering confirmation that giant spiders do indeed exist in The Land plays expertly with the medium by using the gutter (between panels 3 and 4) to mislead the reader, before subverting their expectations (both regarding the existence of giant spiders and as to their "*good*" and "*timid*" nature). In this sense both medium and content support and sustain the hesitation necessary to the Fantastic.

Aside from the co-presence of the natural and supernatural, other textual features of *A Game of You* also reveal the Fantastic. Although a third person, omniscient narrative voice is used initially to describe some of the New York setting (2.9.1–5, 3.12.1–8), this is only used to introduce the setting of "THE LAND" and Barbie's voice provides all subsequent narration for this alterity (4.1.1 onwards). Unreliable narration is also overtly used in the New York setting: for example Martin Tenbones's description of the "high stone cliffs" (1.18.2) of the city, or the voice of Barbara Wong on WRAT radio; her comment that there's "NO CHANCE" the hurricane is returning is literally shown as false by the storm tearing down New York in the surrounding pictures (5.8.1–4). By the end of the trade paperback the omniscient narrator has been completely removed and, after her return from The Land, Barbie narrates the sixth and final section.

The defamiliarization of language is another technique common to the Fantastic, and is also used here in a number of ways. It exists in Martin Tenbones's misinterpretation of the city's buildings as stone cliffs, and a slight resonance may be found in the doubling of Barbara our heroine and the ill-informed radio presenter Barbara Wong, whose full name also references a character briefly introduced in *Preludes and Nocturnes* (Gaiman 7.8.1). The main focus of this technique is upon this notion of naming.

The anonymous nature of "THE LAND" is sustained by its elements, such as the underdetermined signifiers of the mysterious "HIEROGRAM," the "PORPENTINE," and the "TANTOBLIN."[6] That unseen speakers with equally strange and unexplained names introduce these further emphasizes this effect (1.1.1–1.3.3). Explanation is not forthcoming as the text progresses; when asked what the Hierogram is, Wilkinson is only able to respond *"It's um. Well, it's um. It's sort of more like an um. Well"* (4.11.5). Similarly, the threat of "THE CUCKOO" remains unidentified until the fifth chapter — in answer to the question "WHAT IS THE CUCKOO?" George is only able to reply: "I ... DO NOT ... KNOW ... IT IS THE CUCKOO" (3.15.5). Insufficient information defamiliarizes these words so they become thingless names. Simultaneously, the visual nature of comics also enables many of these characters and figures to appear as nameless things, for example the initial depiction of the Tantoblin (1.1.3), the glowing eyes which are all that represent the opening speakers (1.3.3), or the first appearance of Martin Tenbones (1.15.2). Both the visual and verbal are under-determined.

In stark contrast, the real world suffers from an over-determination, specifically in its use of naming. Barbie's name has commercial and gender-based implications in invoking the popular children's doll, a link that her comments about her ex-husband Ken and his new girlfriend Sindy only emphasize (1.17.6).[7] Similarly, characters such as the transsexual Wanda are revealed as having multiple names and identities: as she explains, "WANDA'S MY REAL NAME, BARBIE-BABY. ALVIN'S JUST THE NAME I WAS BORN WITH" (1.17.8). Barbie's gesture at the end, amending her friend's tombstone with lipstick to read "WANDA" instead of "ALVIN" (6.21.4), further emphasizes this over-determination by demonstrating the mutability of names.

Other characters such as Thessaly, whose name refers to her origins as a Thessalian witch rather than a personal identity — Morpheus and the moon both address her as "THESSALIAN" (3.19.1, 3.19.5, 6.4.1), also emphasize the insufficiency of a name as an identity. The rat Wilkinson's speech further stresses this point:

> *I loved bein' a kid. I was one of seventeen children.*
> *We were all named Wilkinson — I suppose it was roughest on the girls, but we all got used to it in the end. [...]*

Intertextual references cross boundaries between fantasy/reality and fiction/metafiction in *A Game of You* (Gaiman 1993, 4.14.3-5).

> *I would've liked to've bin an only child. That way when someone shouts Wilkinson, you know if it's you or not.*
> *Mustn't grumble. Our parents were the salt of the earth.*
> *Lovely people. It was just when they found a name they liked, they stuck with it.* (4.13.1)

This again alerts us to the links between naming, gender and identity.

Samuel Delaney provides a Marxist reading of *A Game of You* that probes its apparent support of a dominant ideology. This hinges on his observations that the only black character (Maisie Hill) and the only transsexual (Wanda) are killed off at the end of the comic "so that we can feel sorry for them, then forget about them." He concludes that: "Making the supernatural forces in the tale the enforcers of a dominant ideology is what makes it a fantasy — and a rather nasty one at that. And it remains just a nasty fantasy unless, in our reading of it, we can find some irony, something that subverts it, something that resists that fantasy" (Delaney).

However, Delaney does find the sort of irony he deems necessary in order for this ideology to be subverted — initially in the motifs and themes that are doubled and echo throughout both of his identified alterities. He aligns the initial references to the "**CUTE FROG MUG**" (*A Game of You* 1.8.6) that Wanda uses for Barbie's coffee with the Cuckoo's question "**I'M AWFUL SWEET, AREN'T I? I'M AWFUL CUTE**" and Barbie's response "**YOU'RE ... CUTE ... AS A ... / ... BUTTON ...**" (5.6.5). This allows him to conclude that the supernatural forces' apparent support of the dominant ideology (to the reader's dismay, as Wanda is a likeable character) is actually no more than a comment on its sustenance by our natural world.

It seems to me that this parallel may in fact be taken a step further, as Barbie's observation "**YECCHY COFFEE. / CUTE MUG, THOUGH**" (1.10.6) can inform our later perceptions of the Cuckoo. Though she seems sweet and innocent on the outside; that which is inside is certainly not, as she plans to fly out of Barbie's dream world "INTO LITTLE GIRLS' MINDS AND LAY EGGS OF MY *OWN* THERE" (5.27.2), in the "SECRET WORLDS" (5.23.4) that we all have inside ourselves. It seems that Gaiman uses the Fantastic in this way to explore an ideology that focuses specifically on notions of gendering. The Cuckoo explains:

> BOYS AND GIRLS ARE DIFFERENT, YOU KNOW THAT?
>   LITTLE BOYS HAVE FANTASIES IN WHICH THEY'RE FASTER, OR SMARTER, OR ABLE TO FLY. WHERE THEY HIDE THEIR FACES IN SECRET IDENTITIES, AND LISTEN TO THE PEOPLE WHO DESPISE THEM ADMIRING THEIR REMARKABLE DEEDS.
>   PATHETIC, BESPECTACLED, REJECTED PERRY PORTER IS SECRETLY *THE AMAZING SPIDER.* GAWKY, BESPECTACLED, UNLOVED CLINT CLARKE IS REALLY *HYPERMAN. YES?* [...]
>   NOW, LITTLE *GIRLS*, ON THE OTHER HAND, HAVE DIFFERENT FANTASIES. MUCH LESS CONVOLUTED. THEIR PARENTS ARE NOT THEIR PARENTS. THEIR LIVES ARE NOT THEIR LIVES.
>   THEY ARE *PRINCESSES.*
>   LOST PRINCESSES FROM DISTANT LANDS.
>   AND ONE DAY THE KING AND QUEEN, THEIR *REAL* PARENTS, WILL TAKE THEM BACK TO THEIR LAND, AND THEN THEY'LL BE HAPPY FOR EVER AND EVER.
>   LITTLE CUCKOOS [5.4.5–5.5.2].

Gendered identity is clear at the beginning of the trade paperback, where the dominant ideology is enforced — Wanda's nightmare shows her confusion at her identity in revealing her self-image to be male while insisting she's a woman: "MY NAME ISN'T ALVIN. IT'S WANDA. / I'M A WOMAN" (2.12.6). As Wanda's nightmare continues, the visual medium further emphasizes this; as the panels depict her as increasingly muscled and masculine

Wanda's "cute" frog mug belies the bad coffee inside. Likewise, Wanda's masculine features cover her feminine identity (Gaiman 1993, 1.9.6).

(2.13.2). Similarly, Wanda's description of her adolescent fantasy of being a Weirdzo (an intertextual reference to the Bizarros)[8] is, according to the Cuckoo's rules quoted above, a masculine rather than a feminine fantasy. Both society and nature align in their support of a rigid and unalterable gender taxonomy. Just as the moon will not let Wanda walk its path, "IT'S *CHROMOSOMES* AS MUCH AS ANYTHING" (4.19.5), Wanda's Aunt Dora says: "GOD GIVES YOU A BODY, IT'S YOUR DUTY TO DO WELL BY IT. HE MAKES YOU A BOY, YOU DRESS IN BLUE, HE MAKES YOU A GIRL, YOU DRESS IN PINK. / YOU MUSTN'T GO TRYING TO *CHANGE* THINGS" (6.14.3). Events such as

Wanda's untimely death further support this, and even Morpheus says (speaking of the Cuckoo): "She acts according to her nature. / Is that evil?" (6.2.2). As Delaney notes, both the natural and supernatural elements of the comic reinforce the dominant ideology.

However, by the end of *A Game of You* the rules of identity formation have begun to shift and become less rigid. This may be seen in the focus on naming already discussed, but is made more overt as the book continues by comments such as "IDENTITY BLURS ON THE MOON'S ROAD" (5.9.1), or Barbie's regretful "I REALISE THAT I'M *ALREADY* BEGINNING TO FORGET WHAT WANDA LOOKED LIKE. / IS IDENTITY *THAT* FRAGILE?"

The transformative structure of the narrative is most clearly evidenced by Wanda's gender transformation, demonstrating how static notions are redefined as fluid and changeable (Gaiman 1993, 6.23.6).

(6.17.5). This shift in viewpoint is achieved through a motif of transformation, the treatment of which specifically relies upon consideration of the book's three alterities.

This motif of transformation most obviously invokes the Fantastic. As Marina Warner comments, tales of metamorphosis "embody the transformational power of storytelling itself, revealing stories as activators of change" (*Fantastic Metamorphoses* 210). Barbie's amendment of Wanda's tombstone with lipstick (6.21.4) is, as noted, a transforming gesture, but it should also be acknowledged that it is an impermanent one: rain will wash the lipstick away in no time. However, the dream Barbie recalls from her coach journey to Kansas provides a different vision of Wanda as "PERFECT. DROP DEAD GORGEOUS. THERE'S NOTHING CAMP ABOUT HER, NOTHING ARTIFICIAL. AND SHE LOOKS HAPPY" (6.23.4). The presence of Death (Morpheus's elder sister) as her companion validates this vision of Wanda, and other visual elements of the panel further support it. Although comics' style of art can be used to fictionalize (such as Barbie's painted-on veil which is indistinguishable from the real thing), close perusal of Wanda's depiction at the start of the comic reveals clues as to her masculine identity, whereas in this final illustration she is indeed entirely feminine.

Following from this, it may be argued that the actual structure of *A Game of You* is transformational, that two fantastic worlds have merged by the end of the comic. Textual indicators such as the continuation of Barbie's narration (rather than a return to an omniscient narrator) or the preponderance of intertextual fantasy references in the final chapter further support this — Barbie decides to take "THE DOROTHY OPTION" (6.6.2) to get her and her friends home safely from The Land; Wanda's funeral actually takes place in small-town Kansas (6.10.1); and in Barbie's dream the feminized Wanda "REMINDS ME OF GLINDA IN THE OZ MOVIE" (6.23.4). It may not even be too much to suggest that Barbie's observation of her fellow Greyhound passengers — "THE MAN IN THE SEAT IN FRONT OF ME KEEPS WHISPERING, 'MR. WIGGLY HASN'T GOT NO NOSE' TO HIMSELF, THEN BURSTING INTO TEARS" (6.23.2) — may be another of Gaiman's literary jokes and refers to Nikolai Gogol's story *The Nose* (1835).[9] This story has often been aligned with Franz Kafka's *Metamorphosis* as a problematic example of the pure fantastic.

Barbie's comment on the names of the Kansas towns she passes — "THEY SOUND LIKE THE NAMES OF MAGIC KINGDOMS" (6.18.4) — again seems to indicate that the waking world has become fantastic, that the two spheres have merged. The transformative structure is most clearly evidenced by Wanda's now-possible gender transformation, and similarly by the Cuckoo's metamorphosis into the bird she so desperately longs to be (6.7.1–3). The result is that static notions (such as identity or home) are redefined as fluid and changeable, as in Barbie's comment that "I DON'T THINK HOME'S A PLACE ANYMORE. I THINK IT'S A STATE OF MIND" (6.15.3). This in itself again calls to mind A.B. Chanady's observation that "critics do not even agree whether it [the Fantastic] is a mode, a genre or an attitude towards reality" (1). That Gaiman has also introduced alterities such as his land of Faerie — "WHICH IS A *PLACE*, BUT PERHAPS ALSO, I LIKE TO THINK, AN *ATTITUDE*" (*The Kindly Ones* 10.9.1) — in this way further supports this reading.

Finally, notions of metafiction are supported by both the structure and content of the comic. Cornwell notes that metafiction "forms a part of the general uncertainty and discontinuity of much recent fiction" (158) and Gaiman's use of Morpheus as a point of reference to contrast with the uncertainties of the other worlds in *A Game of You* further supports this. Morpheus's presence validates certain worlds (such as Barbie's final vision of Wanda) and, read in this way, his creation (and subsequent uncreation) of The Land redefines *A Game of You* as metafiction about the power of fantasy worlds (or fiction) to change real life. This view is further informed by Maurice Blanchot's treatise on the space of literature, and specifically his observations that literature/fiction leads to reality (and not vice versa) (*The Space of Literature* 47). As Mark Currie says: "the realistic novel constructs, rather than reflects, the real world, or, to put it another way, [that] the outside world is always mediated by language and narrative, however much it is naturalized by the transparency of realistic language" (*Postmodern Narrative Theory* 62). The fantasy alterities of *A Game of You* support this view of literature as the source of our construction and understanding of reality and identity.

Case study — *The Sandman: The Kindly Ones*

The Kindly Ones (the ninth *Sandman* graphic novel) tells the story of Lyta Hall's quest to find her son Daniel and revenge herself on Morpheus.[10] As such, it employs many of the same motifs and themes identified in *A Game of You*, specifically those relating to notions of gender and identity. However, the treatment of these varies wildly in places: whereas the alterities of *A Game of You* are distinct and equally valid, *The Kindly Ones* places us in doubt as to the mere existence of many of the fantastic worlds it depicts. It is hoped that the previous case study may therefore inform this discussion.

It should initially be noted that the fantastic elements of *The Kindly Ones* are, unlike those of *A Game of You*, drawn from established myths. These include the triple goddess (a pagan figure that has been thoroughly documented, for example by Robert Graves in *The White Goddess*); the Norse gods (whose names are familiar from legend); and well-known fairy-tale and literary characters such as Puss-in-Boots (*The Kindly Ones* 4.10.1) or the Puck.[11] The fantastic elements of the text are, in this sense, simultaneously validated and revealed as pure fiction.

It may not be too much to suggest that using intertextuality and legend in this way validates other elements of the text — for example the Three tell Lyta that "THERE'S A DOWNSTAIRS IN EVERYBODY. THAT'S WHERE *WE* LIVE" (2.15.2). This supports the notion (that there are multiple worlds inside everybody) previously expressed in *A Game of You*. Other observations such as Larissa's statement "NOTHING IS TOO CUTE AND SWEET TO BE DANGEROUS" (7.14.5) also refer back to this text.[12] Comments on the inevitability of acting according to one's nature are also reiterated by characters including the Corinthian and Matthew (5.11.1–2) and the Puck (10.13.2).

Similarly, the doubling of characters observed by Samuel Delaney in *A Game of You* is repeated here — for example the gorgons Stheno and Euryale (4.16.4) — are paralleled visually with "real" characters such as Chantal and Zelda who were first introduced to us in *The Doll's House* (6.2.4). Characters such as the witch Thessaly (now calling herself Larissa) also reappear, and her new identity alerts us to the importance of naming, a motif repeated in this text. Apparent in the thingless name that is the recreated Corinthian, or the snake Geryon's discourse on the etymology of Lyta's name (4.18.3), the implications of naming are however explored most deeply (and, again, tied to notions of gender and ideology) when Lyta finally encounters the Kindly Ones:

> LYTA: I AM SEEKING THE FURIES.
> MOTHER: *NOT* THE FURIES, MY LOBELIA. THAT'S SUCH A *NASTY* NAME. IT'S ONE OF THE THINGS THEY *CALL WOMEN*, TO PUT US IN OUR *PLACE*...
> THE THREE: TERMAGANT.
> SHREW.
> VIRAGO.
> VIXEN.
> WITCH.
> BITCH [7.21.5–6].

The titular Kindly Ones are also referred to as the Furies, the Erinyes, the Eumenides, the Hounds of Hades, the Dirae and the Morrigan. By using these Greek, Roman and Celtic names interchangeably, Gaiman establishes their function as primary rather than their name, and as such they may also be read as nameless things.

Notions of transience are also explicitly mentioned in the text (5.6.2) and the transformation motif appears many times — most obviously and literally in Daniel's transformation into Morpheus (13.22.1–6), but also in Loki's fight with the Corinthian, during which he changes form many times (9.12.1–6); or when Lyta sees Larissa as a white bird (7.3.3–6). These last two emphasize the role of perception within the Fantastic. Transformation also exists on a structural level, as Morpheus's humanization is shown to be the catalyst for all the events of *The Kindly Ones*. As he says: "I told Ishtar that she was wrong. That I was not changed. That I did not change. But in truth, I think I lied to her" (11.6.7), and his newfound humanity is also evidenced visually when the Furies inflict physical harm upon him (11.19.4).

Like naming, transformation is also linked to gender, for example in the revelation that the character of Vixen LaBitch is Rose Walker's old landlord Hal (12.10.1). It should also be noted that the very first panel of the trade paperback begins "THERE'S A DREAM IN WHICH HUGE FACELESS WOMEN WITH WOLVES ASTRIDE THEM ARE CHEWING AT MY ENTRAILS AND LEGS" (*The Kindly Ones* "Prologue" 1.1). Although unlinked to the rest of the book this initial image of faceless women resonates with the multiple, confused female identities that are subsequently explored in the text.

Lyta herself is doubled and multiplied in various ways: initially when she sees her reflection in a shop window and engages in debate with two identical versions of herself: "WHO *ARE* YOU?" "TAKE A MOMENT TO REFLECT" (5.21.2). She later engages in similar conversation in front of another mirror, seeing herself in a variety of forms — as the sophisticated Lyta of the first few pages of the book; as a child; as the Fury; and in her current deranged state, daubed with Larissa's protective potion (7.17.2–6). These contradictory visions of Lyta cast doubt on the existence of the various alterities she has wandered through; as these seem to coexist in the same physical space, we may conclude that Lyta's body remains in the waking world/reality.

After entering what can be perceived as either a world of myth or a hallucination, the panel where she wakes is triplicated (fig. 3). We see Lyta as she appears in the waking world, Lyta as she appears in her hallucination or "myth world," and Lyta as she appears in The Dreaming, as one of the Furies. One effect of this is to validate all three perspectives, encouraging the reader not to dismiss two of the three versions as unreal. The reader is forced to hesitate throughout *The Kindly Ones* as pictures of Lyta in her myth world are doubled with the waking world. This hesitation is frequently mirrored in the semantics of the tale: themes of perception are emphasized again and again, most overtly when Morpheus dies and we are repeatedly told that what is being mourned is no more than "A PUH-POINT OF VIEW" (44.4).

As also seen in *A Game of You*, two alterities are set up alongside The Dreaming, which remains as a fictive point of reference. Although the hallucinatory quality of Lyta's myth world, the doubling of its characters with people and objects in reality (6.19.6–8) could imply that it is entirely fictional, other events belie this. For example, a homeless man comments of Lyta: "SHE'S GOT SNAKES IN HER HAIR. AND SHE'S NOT ALONE IN HER HEAD ANY MORE" (5.17.8), which is how she does indeed appear in her myth world.

Again, the myth world seems to comment on the real-world alterity — while the Three appear in many forms, their existence may most obviously be linked to the three main characters such as Zelda (the crone), Lyta (the mother) and Rose (the maiden). All the female characters of the book fit into this sort of triple-part structure — not only do the Three appear as the Fates and the Furies but also as mortals when Rose Walker returns to the nursing home where her grandmother spent her life (*The Kindly Ones* 6.8.3). Of these three old ladies, Helena (whose last name is unpronounceable, according to the other two) may well represent Lyta's mother, Helena Kosmatos, the golden-age Fury.[13] In response to a story, Helena comments that:

ACTS OF REVENGE ARE *SANCTIFIED*. I HAVE *ALSO* DONE IT. I SPENT TWO DECADES LOOKING FOR THE MAN WHO HAD KILLED A PERSON I LOVED. I HOUNDED HIM FOR YEAR AFTER YEAR AFTER YEAR, ACROSS THE WORLD... [...] EVENTUALLY, I KILLED HIM. FIRST, THOUGH, I DESTROYED HIS LIFE [6.19.1–2].

This certainly fits with the idea and the purpose surrounding the Furies, and Helena's subsequent denial and then affirmation of her story (6.19.3) further comments on the impossibility of establishing truth with any certainty.

Similarly, notions of reality are completely denied more than once, whether this is indicated subtly (Larissa reads a book entitled "WHEN REAL THINGS HAPPEN TO IMAGINARY PEOPLE" (13.20.2) whose title signifies Harold S. Kushner's popular bestseller while replacing its notions of "bad" and "good" with these concepts) or more obviously, as when Delirium threatens Mazikeen: "IF YOU DON'T LET ME *IN* I WILL TURN YOU INTO A DEMON HALF-FACE WAITRESS NIGHT-CLUB LADY WITH A CRUSH ON HER BOSS [Lucifer], AND I'LL MAKE IT SO YOU'VE *BEEN* THAT FROM THE BEGINNING OF TIME TO NOW AND YOU'LL NEVER *EVER* KNOW IF YOU WERE ANYTHING *ELSE* AND IT WILL ITCH INSIDE YOUR HEAD WORSE THAN LITTLE BUGSES" (12.7.3). Of course, this is precisely what Mazikeen is. Such a statement refutes any notion of an objective, unalterable reality, further confirming that we should read the settings as fantastic alterities.

Perhaps this is the one of the fundamentals that underlies the medium itself: to write

The reader is forced to hesitate throughout *The Kindly Ones* as pictures of Lyta in her myth world are doubled with the waking world, encouraging the reader not to dismiss two of the three versions as unreal (Gaiman 1996, 13.7.2–4).

a comic book is not a way of telling a story with illustrations replicating the world it is set in, but a creation of that fantastic world from scratch. In this sense the medium evokes the hyperreal and supports Blanchot and Currie's view of literature as previously mentioned.

As seen from the intertextual references identified above, the irony of Lyta/Fury working with the Furies is obvious; however, Gaiman again uses the medium to emphasize this. In basing his pictures of both the Fates and the Furies on the three witches from the 1970s DC title *The Witching Hour*, Gaiman grounds his version of the Furies within his industry and within the DC universe, itself an alterity that exists in a state of the hyperreal. In this way, intertextuality is used to further emphasize the role of the Fantastic.

While the disturbing presence of multiple worlds is enhanced by the visual nature of the medium (a good example is the splash page at 4.7), its verbal elements are equally disconcerting. Underdetermined and unexplained signifiers such as Morpheus's "**reflectory**" (11.24.2) or the "NIMBIC GLIMMERING" (5.15.4) haunt the text, as do the overdetermined — words with multiple meanings are mentioned but undefined (10.19.4); as when the Puck says to the Corinthian: "I SHALL RESTRAIN MYSELF FROM ENQUIRING WHETHER YOU TAKE YOUR NAME FROM THE LETTERS, THE PILLARS, THE LEATHER, THE PLACE, OR THE MODE OF BEHAVIOUR" (10.3.1).

Other textual features such as unreliable narration (provided by Lyta) further evidence the existence of the Fantastic. In fact, this narrative strategy is taken to a new level as the narration provided by Destiny's book, which throughout *The Sandman* has prefigured the comic's narration, and, as such, emphasized its validity (11.14.3–4) is shown to be uncharacteristically uncertain by the existence of multiple Destinies (3.10.1–2; 7.11.2; 11.14.2; 11.15.1–2). Both the metafictional function of Destiny's narration and its sudden unreliability are typical of the Fantastic.

All these textual features evidence the Fantastic, which is again linked to notions of gender. Lyta's quest to find her son is semantically, if not structurally, feminized: the fairy-tale figures she encounters include a female Puss-in-Boots (contrary to the Perrault version of the tale, though present in Strapola and Basile's versions), a female Cyclops, and a maiden who is attempting to free her prince from his imprisonment in a castle (4.10.1–5; 4.9.1–4; 4.8.1–6).[14] These standardized figures support Propp's model of the wondertale (which focuses on functions rather than characters) and also enable metafictional comment on the nature of fairy tale, for example as when Puss tells Lyta:

> PUSS: I INTEND TO WAGER THE SILVER COLLAR AROUND MY NECK THAT THE OGRE
>   CANNOT CHANGE ITSELF INTO THREE THINGS THAT I SHALL NAME FOR IT.
> LYTA: WILL THE *THIRD* SHAPE BE A *MOUSE*?
> PUSS: OF COURSE
> LYTA: BUT ... DON'T THEY *EVER* LEARN?
> PUSS: THEY *CAN'T*. THEY'RE PART OF THE STORY, JUST AS I AM [4.10.4–5].

Mark Currie states that "theoretical fiction is a performative rather than a constative narratology, meaning that it does not try to state the truth about an object-narrative but rather enacts or performs what it wishes to say about narrative while itself being a narrative" (*Postmodern Narrative Theory* 52). As theoretical fiction, *The Sandman* concerns itself with the telling of stories and invokes the Fantastic in this regard, as seen from the textual features examined thus far. In both these trade paperbacks The Dreaming is contrasted with various alterities, whose fantastic elements comment on their mimetic ones. As seen in the work of Maurice Blanchot, here fiction informs fact: supporting Diane Elam's observation that "romance threatens to expose 'reality' as a constructed referent rather than a 'natural' state of existence to which we all naturally, textually, refer" (8).

A debate on nature, change and gender seems to underlie both stories, as Gaiman repeatedly questions the idea of identity and being true to one's nature. While many characters ostensibly believe that nature is fixed and unchanging this is persistently belied by many of the texts' themes and motifs, such as the focus on transformation or the presence of characters such as Loki.[15] The conclusion of *The Kindly Ones* does not provide any real answers to this debate: we are aware that Morpheus's destruction has been caused by both the changes he has made in himself as a consequence of his eighty-year imprisonment (in *The Sandman: Preludes and Nocturnes*) and his inability to change enough (*The Kindly Ones* 13.6.3–6).[16] Similarly, although we are given the impression throughout the text that Lyta is acting outside any notion of fate (as indicated by the conflicting Destinies that appear), Morpheus's death has in fact been prophesized by Cluracan and we have already seen his funeral procession (*Worlds' End* 6.18.1; 6.19.1–3). In prolonging such thematic uncertainty *The Sandman* again evokes the Fantastic.

Conclusion

In the broadest possible terms, the Fantastic is based around a notion of hesitation between reality and the marvelous (Todorov 25), achieved through the co-presence of natural and supernatural elements. It takes place in an alterity that may be defined in terms of its relationship with reality; however, Diane Elam comments further that: "Romance does not offer alternative realities, rather it underscores the fictionality of the 'real' and the unreality of culture" (Elam 49–50). As such, the fantastical coexistence of the natural and supernatural within *The Sandman* destabilizes our understanding of both reality and fantasy, leading us towards a linguistic situation where meaning cannot ever be firmly established.

Such indefinite, multiple linguistic meanings also reference postmodernism and, it therefore seems that another way of approaching this hesitation is in postmodern terms. In this sense, hesitation becomes a response to the lack of a grand narrative dictating the conventions of subject and form to establish reality. Like the Fantastic, the comics medium exposes the notion of "reality" as a constructed referent, which the text's alterities comment on. The nature of the medium allows for the construction and sustenance of multiple worlds without recourse to a stable notion of reality. This uncertainty extends to other elements of the text and, as the reader's hesitation destabilizes interpretation of reality versus fantasy, absolute meaning is denied. It therefore seems that comics offer what might be best described as a postmodern vision of the Fantastic.

Notes

1. Throughout I shall use the term "comics" to refer to the medium itself (McCloud 4). Although it takes the form of a plural noun, the common usage when referring to comics as a medium is to treat it as singular.

2. In "Structure and Form" (an essay responding to *Morphology*) Lévi-Strauss states that Propp errs in his treatment of signifier and signified; that is, by attempting to separate grammar and vocabulary (in discarding the specifics of content (vocabulary) to focus on the stages of the structure (grammar). Lévi-Strauss argues that these are inseparable in Myth since (as a metalanguage) it has no recourse to any level not created by its own rules. Therefore, everything is syntax, but simultaneously everything within is also vocabulary since the distinctive elements are words (Lévi-Strauss 1984, 188). However, Propp's response ("The Structural and Historical Study of the Wondertale") defends his approach, denying that he divides form and content since his analysis focuses on both plot and composition. His argument is that plot incorporates content and composition reflects form, so his work analyses both simultaneously (*Theory and History of Folklore* 77). He goes on to turn Lévi-Strauss's own arguments against him: saying that, if content and form are inseparable, then he who analyses one is also analyzing the other (77), and arguing that Lévi-Strauss overextends Propp's work to a generalized, abstracted level in order to critique it, when Propp's conclusions only refer to individual narratives and their specific laws (74).

3. Barbie (first introduced to us in *The Doll's House*) is troubled when her old fantasy dream world (which she has not visited in some time) starts to invade her waking life. Due to interference from agents of the Cuckoo (the Land's evil ruler) she becomes trapped in this alterity. Her friends Hazel, Foxglove and Thessaly travel to her dream world to save her, calling down the moon to do so, which causes a hurricane to hit New York. They defeat the Cuckoo and return safely, although Barbie's transsexual friend Wanda (who remained behind in reality) and the other occupants of her apartment building are all killed by its collapse during the hurricane. The book concludes with Barbie traveling to Kansas to attend Wanda/Alvin's funeral, during which she dreams of a new world where Wanda's transformation is complete.

4. In some trade paperbacks page numbering is retained from individual issues. In these instances I shall cite references as here, where 1.1.1 corresponds to part 1, page 1, panel 1. When quoting from comics I have used "/" or a new line to indicate divisions between speech balloons or narrative boxes, and imitated the use of font and style so far as is possible in order to avoid inflicting my own capitalization, punctuation and so forth on the text.

5. Home of the titular Sandman, Morpheus, one of seven deities known as The Endless and responsible for the domain of dreams.

6. Although Gaiman is aware of the meaning of at least one of these words (Bender 1999, 120), as they remain unexplained within the text I feel justified in describing them as underdetermined. However, all date from the seventeenth century and variously refer to a sacred symbol ("hierogram"); an Elizabethan word for porcupine ("porpentine"); and a cake or tart ("tantoblin"), later also to become a slang word for excrement — the origin of which meaning is perhaps also hinted at in *A Game of You* by the "*Old Wilkinson family saying*" (4.11.6).

7. Sindy was a British doll produced by Pedigree Dolls and Toys in 1963 in response to the popularity of the Barbie doll, launched by the American company Mattel in 1959.

8. A Superman spin-off series from the late 1950s. The Bizarros are flawed copies of Superman and other characters, created by Lex Luthor's imperfect duplication ray. They live on the square planet Htrae: a mad version of Earth where everything is done backwards and all words have the opposite meaning.

9. The story of Major Kovalyov's search for his mischievous missing nose, which has taken on a life of its own and run away.

10. A heavily pregnant Lyta Hall and her dead husband Hector were introduced to us in *The Dolls House*, where they lived inside the mind of Rose Walker's brother Jed for two years, having been fooled by two of Morpheus's escaped servants into believing that Hector was the Sandman himself. Upon discovering this Morpheus restored them to reality (meaning death for Hector), and told Lyta that the child she carried for so long in dreams would someday belong to him. *The Kindly Ones* begins three years later, showing us a paranoid, obsessive Lyta who has barely let her son Daniel out of her sight since his birth. When he is subsequently kidnapped a completely unhinged Lyta begins her quest to track him down and revenge herself on Morpheus. She invokes the Furies, or Kindly Ones, in this regard: an act that is only made possible by Morpheus himself (as legend has it the Furies are only empowered to hound those who spill family blood) since years back Morpheus killed his son Orpheus in an act of mercy after he was ripped apart by the Bacchae (Gaiman retells this Greek myth in *The Sandman: Fables and Reflections*). Although Lyta does not regain her son (who was initially kidnapped by the Norse god Loki and the faerie Puck for their own reasons, and whose mortality was burnt away before Morpheus could track him down), her quest for revenge is ultimately successful and the Morpheus

we know dies in #69. However, as he is one of the Endless another aspect of Morpheus instantly takes his place — the transfigured form of Daniel.

11. Although only one appears in *The Sandman*, Gaiman accords with the accepted meaning of "puck" as a generic word (Holland 35) as the character refers to himself as "A PUCK" and also speaks of "WE PUCKS" (*The Kindly Ones* 10.2.7).

12. Larissa was introduced to us as the witch Thessaly in *A Game of You* and the recurrence of this character, as well as such comments, therefore recall this text.

13. Prior to the *Crisis on Infinite Earths* retcon (a 12-issue series published 1985–86 which rewrote much of the DC universe), Lyta Trevor was Fury, daughter of the golden-age Wonder Woman and pilot Steve Trevor. Lyta and her husband Hector Hall/Silver Scarab joined the supergroup Infinity Inc. while at University. As per her history in *The Sandman*, she fell pregnant by Hector Hall, who then died. When he became the second silver-age Sandman, Lyta went to live with him in the Dream Stream (which is where Gaiman picks up the story in *The Doll's House*). Post-*Crisis* her origins were rewritten by Roy Thomas as the daughter of Helena Kosmatos, the golden-age Fury, who received her powers from the Greek Furies to avenge her husband's death and who was also created at this time to be part of *The Young All-Stars*, in a rewrite of the golden age (Niederhausen n. pag.). Lyta was adopted by Derek and Joan Trevor after her mother's mysterious disappearance and while at university took the name Fury and joined Infinity Inc. with her fiancé Hector Hall, until he was killed and Lyta herself vanished, pregnant with their child.

14. As noted above, these characters are juxtaposed with their waking world equivalents: a stray cat (4.9.6), a traffic light (4.9.5) and a stranger who gives Lyta money (4.8.7).

15. In Norse myth Loki often represents change.

16. The Furies are able to hound Morpheus because he killed his son, Orpheus, in an act of mercy that went against Morpheus's previous decision to abandon him. Morpheus is, however, unable to change enough to disregard the rules a second time (for example, he could simply kill Lyta; or remain safe in The Dreaming despite being summoned by Nuala in accordance with the boon he granted her), which causes his death.

Works Cited

Bannerman, Kenn. "A Short Interview with Jack Zipes." *Biting Dog Press*, April 2002. Web. 6 June 2002.

Bender, Hy. *The Sandman Companion*. London: Titan, 1999. Print.

Blanchot, Maurice. *The Sirens' Song*. Ed. Gabriel Josipovici. Trans. Sacha Rabinovitch. Brighton, Sussex: Harvester, 1982. Print.

_____. *The Space of Literature*. London: University of Nebraska Press, 1982. Print.

Brooke-Rose, Christine. *A Rhetoric of the Unreal*. Cambridge: Cambridge University Press, 1981. Print.

Campbell, Joseph. *The Hero with a Thousand Faces*. London: Fontana, 1993. Print.

Carden, P. "Fairy Tale, Myth, and Literature: Russian Structuralist Approaches." Strelka. 179–197.

Cawelti, John G. *Adventure, Mystery and Romance: Formula Stories as Art and Popular Culture*. London: University of Chicago Press, 1976. Print.

_____. *The Six-Gun Mystique*. 2d ed. Bowling Green, OH: Bowling Green State University Popular Press, 1984. Print.

Chanady, A.B. *Magical Realism and the Fantastic*. London: Garland, 1985. Print.

Cornwell, Neil. *The Literary Fantastic: From Gothic to Postmodernism*. London: Harvester Wheatsheaf, 1990. Print.

Coyle, William, ed. *Aspects of Fantasy: Selected Essays from the Second International Conference on the Fantastic in Literature and Film*. Westport, CT: Greenwood, 1986. Print.

Currie, Mark. *Postmodern Narrative Theory*. Basingstoke, Hampshire: Macmillan, 1998. Print.

_____, ed. *Metafiction*. London: Longman, 1995.

Delaney, Samuel R. "Skerries of the Dream." Gaiman, 1993. n. pag. Print.

Elam, Diane. *Romancing the Postmodern*. London: Routledge, 1992. Print.

von Franz, Marie-Louise. *Interpretation of Fairytales*. Zürich, Switzerland: Spring, 1973. Print.

_____. *Problems of the Feminine in Fairytales*. Dallas, TX: Spring, 1986. Print.

_____. "The Process of Individuation." *Man and His Symbols*. Ed. Carl Jung. New York: Dell, 1964. 157–254. Print.

Frye, Northrup. *Anatomy of Criticism*. London: Penguin, 1990. Print.

_____. *Fables of Identity*. New York: Harcourt, Brace and World, 1963. Print.

_____. *Myth and Metaphor: Selected Essays, 1974–1988,* Ed. Robert D. Dehham. Charlottesville: University Press of Virginia, 1990. Print.

Gaiman, Neil, Mike Dringenberg and Malcolm Jones III. 1990. *The Sandman: The Doll's House.* New York: DC Comics, 1990. Print.

Gaiman, Neil, et al. *The Sandman: A Game of You.* New York: DC Comics, 1993. Print.

_____. *The Sandman: The Kindly Ones.* New York: DC Comics, 1996. Print.

_____. *The Sandman: Preludes and Nocturnes.* New York: DC Comics, 1991. Print.

_____. *The Sandman: Worlds' End.* New York: DC Comics, 1994. Print.

Genette, Gerard. *Narrative Discourse,* Trans. Jane E. Lewin. Ithaca, NY: Cornell University Press, 1980. Print.

Graves, Robert. *The White Goddess.* London: Faber and Faber, 1961. Print.

Holland, Peter. Introduction. Shakespeare 1–117.

Hume, Kathryn. *Fantasy and Mimesis.* London: Methuen, 1984. Print.

Hunt, Peter. *An Introduction to Children's Literature.* Oxford: Oxford University Press, 1994. Print.

Jackson, Rosemary. *Fantasy: The Literature of Subversion.* London: Methuen, 1981. Print.

_____. "Narcissism and Beyond: A Psychoanalytic Reading of *Frankenstein* and Fantasies of the Double." Coyle 45–53.

Langley, N., et al. *The Wizard of Oz.* Dir. Victor Fleming. Metro-Goldwyn-Mayer, 1939. Film.

Latour, Bruno. *We Have Never Been Modern.* Trans. Catherine Porter. New York: Harvester Wheatsheaf, 1993. Print.

Leach, Edmund. *Genesis as Myth and Other Essays.* London: Jonathan Cape, 1969. Print.

_____. *Lévi-Strauss.* London: Fontana, 1970. Print.

Lévi-Strauss, Claude. *Myth and Meaning.* London: Routledge and Kegan Paul, 1978. Print.

_____. "Structure and Form: Reflections on a Work by Vladimir Propp." Propp 1984. 167–188.

Lyotard, Jean-Francois. *The Postmodern Condition: A Report on Knowledge.* Manchester: Manchester University Press, 1984. Print.

McCloud, Scott. *Understanding Comics: The Invisible Art.* New York: HarperCollins, 1994. Print.

Niederhausen, Michael. *Signifying in Comic Books.* Unpublished Master's thesis, Cincinnati, OH: Xavier University. N.p. N. Pag. Web. 18 April 2002.

Propp, Vladimir. *Morphology of the Folktale.* 2d ed. Austin: University of Texas Press, 1968. Print.

_____. *Theory and History of Folklore.* Manchester: Manchester University Press, 1984. Print.

Rauch, Stephan. *Neil Gaiman's The Sandman and Joseph Campbell: In Search of the Modern Myth.* Holicong, PA: Wildside, 2003. Print.

Rose, Jacqueline. *States of Fantasy.* Oxford: Clarendon, 1996. Print.

Scholes, Robert. "Metafiction." 1970. Currie (1995) 21–38.

_____. "Towards a Poetics of Fiction: An Approach Through Genre." *Novel* 2.2 (1969): 101–111. Print.

Shakespeare, William. *A Midsummer Night's Dream.* Oxford World's Classics. Oxford: Oxford University Press, 1998. Print.

Strelka, Joseph P., ed. *Literary Criticism and Myth.* University Park: Pennsylvania State University, 1980. Print.

Todorov, Tzvetan. *The Fantastic: A Structural Approach to a Literary Genre.* New York: Cornell University Press, 1975. Print.

Traill, Nancy H. *Possible Worlds of the Fantastic: The Rise of the Paranormal in Fiction.* London: University of Toronto Press, 1996. Print.

Warner, Marina. *Fantastic Metamorphoses, Other Worlds: Ways of Telling the Self.* Oxford: Oxford University Press, 2002. Print.

_____. *From the Beast to the Blonde.* London: Vintage, 1995. Print.

_____. *No Go the Bogeyman.* London: Vintage. 2000. Print.

Waugh, Patricia. "What is Metafiction and Why Are They Saying Such Awful Things About It?" Currie (1995) 39–54.

Zipes, Jack. *Breaking the Magic Spell,* Lexington: University Press of Kentucky, 2002. Print.

_____. *The Brothers Grimm,* London: Routledge, 1988. Print.

4

Thirty-Two Floors of Disruption: Time and Space in Alan Moore's "How Things Work Out"

RIKKE PLATZ CORTSEN

The critical interest in the opposition of visual and verbal, painting and poetry and how space and time relate to them goes back centuries. Comics scholar Douglas Wolk describes the shift from this traditional opposition of word and image to the modern hybrid medium of comics this way:

> Here's where Gotthold Ephraim Lessing's 1766 essay *Laokoön* comes in. Lessing rebutted the *ut pictora poesis* principle; space, he claimed, was the domain of painting, and time was the domain of poetry. Any particular panel of a comic book can encompass as much space as a person can see at once (projected onto a two-dimensional picture plane) … Time, on the other hand, has to be shaved very thinly to fit in a comic panel, which is generally understood to be an image of a single moment [128].

In the comics the reader's perception of time and space is not always that time is strictly related to text and that space is the domain of the visual, but rather that these are mixed together. Comics can conflate the dimensions of time and space on the page of the comic book in a way that Lessing probably never imagined. The idea that spatial and temporal relations can be explored productively is one that comics writer Alan Moore has toyed with in a number of his works throughout his career. Collaborating with different artists, he has investigated time, space and how these can be negotiated and challenged on the page of the comic book. In this essay I want to examine closely a small piece of his immense production in order to understand how the spatial and temporal relations can be represented in a way that plays with the reader's traditional understanding of both. The idea is to show how the medium of comics can be utilized to enact narratives crossing time and space that give the reader a unique experience of reading comics. In the eight-page narrative of "How Things Work Out" from *Tomorrow Stories* Alan Moore uses a building as a frame for his story, and in this complex example of what the image and text juxtaposition in comics can achieve, the building simultaneously represents both time *and* space.

By examining the various details and mechanisms at work in this comic, this essay will argue that in this case it is the media-specific mix of images and text in collaboration with the structural device of the building that are put into play to break conventional barriers of how time and space can be perceived. This brief example of Alan Moore's work foregrounds his complex understanding of the comics medium as one that allows for the transgression of temporal continuity and spatial consistency.

In "How Things Work Out" the pages show the same house with its individual floors representing different periods in time, which interferes with the reader's experience of a building's elements existing at one point in time as a whole. The disruptions of time and space Moore creates here also serve to reflect a complex understanding of human agency. The characters in "How Things Work Out" never realize that their fates have already been decided for them and they live their lives accordingly. For the reader, however, everything has always already occurred, and the frame of the house establishes a claustrophobic field of action where time is non-linear and simultaneous. The inevitability of human destinies is made bearable here by an expanded narrative field in which the reader can proceed simultaneously in a variety of directions, taking pleasure in alternative aesthetic continuities that cut across the conventional limitations of time and space.

Alan Moore and the nod towards Eisner

Tomorrow Stories is a serialized comic book anthology written by Alan Moore for Wildstorm's ABC (America's Best Comics) series. It is now published by DC Comics and contains stories featuring Cobweb, Jack B. Quick, Splash Brannigan, Greyshirt and First American, all characters invented by Moore for this series, each parodying some comic book genre or character type. "How Things Work Out" is part of the series within the series based on the adventures of the character Greyshirt. As with all the heroes of *Tomorrow Stories* Greyshirt is a new creation of Moore's that reveals Will Eisner's influence. The inspiration from *The Spirit* in the Greyshirt stories is clear in Moore's experiments with the way the titles are worked into the visual appearances of the page as well as in the character of Greyshirt. The appearance of Eisner's hero with a small black mask just covering his eye region and wearing gloves, resembles Moore's Greyshirt masked by a red scarf covering his mouth and a hat. Moore is also influenced by Eisner's habit of occasionally shifting the main focus of his narrative from the Spirit, showing the hero only on the final page, arresting the criminal. This made it possible for Eisner to tell the stories of the often overlooked people involved in the narratives, the otherwise unnoticed everyday men and women, instead of limiting his narratives to fast-paced action sequences. In that tradition, Greyshirt is not the most prominent character in the stories about him and in "How Things Work Out" he is even cast as the victim who needs rescuing by the unlikely hero, Sonny.

In the use of a building as the frame for the story, Alan Moore might also have looked in the direction of Eisner, only this time at his comic books about tenement life, such as *A Contract With God, A Life Force,* and *Dropsie Avenue,* the latter's original cover showing the people of a building sitting in the windows of their apartments. Eisner also did a story called *The Building* in 1987 that has a building as its main character; the people come and go, but the real interest is in the building's decay and the history of how it shapes the tenants' lives. In spite of Moore's claim that the choice of a building as the frame for the story in "How Things Work Out" is merely "some interesting little visual storytelling device we thought of trying out," it is significant in the way the story reads (Cooke 47). I argue that the use of the house provides Moore and Veitch with a device by which they can circumvent the reader's experience of temporal and spatial relations. The Building becomes the place *and* time where (and when) the characters can act across these divisions and dimensions as time and space implode and become one within the structure.

Buildings, stories and comics

In the realm of comics scholarship, an on-going discussion has been (and will most likely continue to be) the question of how to define the medium, and whether there are certain media specific qualities or elements that must be the core of any definition of comics. I have no intention of engaging in this debate, but I would like to start with one attempt at defining the comic that ties in with my analysis. In a recent article, Hillary Chute argues that Art Spiegelman perceives comics as architectural and that this is particularly evident in *In the Shadow of No Towers:*

> In his 1977 collection Breakdowns (which is rare and out-of-print but is soon to be republished by Pantheon), Spiegelman writes: "My dictionary defines COMIC STRIP as 'a narrative series of cartoons....' A NARRATIVE is defined as 'a story.' Most definitions of STORY leave me cold... Except for the one that says 'A complete horizontal division of a building [which is] ([From] Medieval Latin HISTORIA ... a row of windows with pictures on them)'" [235].

Moving from an abstract definition to something concrete and historical, Spiegelman's definition adequately accounts for the way the story is structured in "How Things Work Out." Alan Moore is acutely aware of the many connotations this association of comics and architecture might bring: On the index page, the narrative is presented as "Four Floors of Fear in Alan Moore's Tomorrow's Stories," and the following other components of the anthology are presented as "also in this building." Moore plays with the metaphor of the comic book being a building, but also very explicitly structures the narrative as "A complete horizontal division of a building."

As one of the *Tomorrow Stories,* "How Things Work Out" redefines both the temporality of narrative and the spatial context in which it is set. In this short piece, the building (space) and the history of decades portrayed on each floor (time) are both foregrounded in text and image, and this pattern is something that recurs in all the narrative in the series. "Tomorrow Stories" are at the same time narratives of the future and spaces of anticipation. The pun on stories as temporal narrative and stories as floor levels in a building echoes in the series' play with the conventions of space and time. However, this game is never as concrete as in "How Things Work Out" where each individual story exists simultaneously with its continuation in future decades, depicted on other floors of the same building.

Breaking down the house

In an essay on Chris Ware's comics Thomas Bredehoft discusses how architecture can be used in comics, and in turn he further examines how the medium of comics can utilize its two-dimensionality and its media specific elements such as panels, breakdowns and text to represent complicated notions of time and space: "In contrast to film or language-based narration, however, the medium of comics offers the possibility of a narrative mode that disrupts the time-sequencing itself, and it appears to be the case that it is the specifically two-dimensional architecture of the comics page that allows comics narration to break the linearity of a time-sequenced narrative line" (872). This breaking down of linearity is central to Bredehoft's argument. It is in the tension between the reader's experience of linear time and the comic's actual disruption of it that the particular act of reading comics becomes most compelling. In reading "How Things Work Out" the linear perception of time can be both emphasized and disrupted, producing traditional linear narrative as well as fragmenting it. Bredehoft later comments that "The two-dimensional architecture of the comics page allows the simultaneous presence on the page of panels depicting various points within a chronological or narrative sequence" (873). Alan Moore gives this aspect of the comics medium a literal realization in this short narrative, aligning the different points in time not only within the same space on the page, but within the same stage of representation: the building.

The page = the building[1]

A reader taking in the first page of this Greyshirt story immediately notices that the layout of the page is of great importance. The usual horizontally divided panels of the comic literally form a building with four floors. And what is more, each panel is marked on the left with a year; starting on third floor with 1999 and going backwards with twenty year intervals as the floors descend: from the '70s back to the '30s. When reading from top to bottom, the numbers take the reader in reverse through time, thus disrupting the normal habits of reading that usually take the reader forward in time, as her eyes move downwards on the page. When the back of the building is revealed at the end of the story, the years appear again, this time on the right hand side of the panels. Represented only from the front, the individual panels would have been too much like screens or stages; by insisting on the 3-D aspect of the building a sculptural register is introduced, which emphasizes the representation of something real. As with speech balloons, the white numbers on the page here is a convention in the medium of comics that does not disturb the reader's sense of reality. Even if the numbers take up space in the visual depiction of the panel or the page, the reader will experience that script as legible but "transparent" in that it is simultaneously present and not present in the story. As noted, Will Eisner excelled in ingenious integration of the title and other texts external to the narrative into the actual space of the comic book page, appearing as part of the story told. In "How Things Work Out" this Eisner-esque technique is carried on: At the right hand side the whole page is framed by the name of the hero GREYSHIRT. The sign spreads down through all the panels, but the writing changes in each panel, thus at the same time breaking the illusion that this is the same sign at the same time, as well as confirming it. Through the different time periods the sign has been changed, so what the reader looks at are four different incarnations of the sign, moving from black Art Deco style at the bottom panel via noble green writing in the 1950s to the fragmented digital style of the nineties. This sign is not actually on the building at the narrative level, but remains writing that only the reader of the comic can see. Nevertheless, it is incorporated in the drawing like a marquee on a theatre, framing the building. The bottom of the page is also framed by text announcing the title of this particular Greyshirt story: HOW THINGS WORK OUT is not part of the reality the characters move in, yet it is integrated into the architecture of the building as if it were a fence or entryway. Directly under the cat head at the top of the building, the reader encounters writing that is actually part of the represented house, which is inscribed with its name: KATZ BUILDING. Later on the reader will realize that Katz is also a character in the story — the owner of the building. This label on the top of the building thus points toward one theme of this narrative: that the fates of people and buildings are in some ways intertwined.

The appearance of the building, like that of its human inhabitants reflects the passage of time as the reader moves forward down the page, but backward in time. The building at the bottom panel is brand new, but taking in the whole page at once, the reader can observe that it is decaying in the reverse direction of the reading, with the bricks of the house in 1:1 looking worn and the railing in front of the window falling completely apart. The windows that appear spotless in 1:3 become more and more cracked as the reader glances upwards. The flower tray that carries blooming flowers below, loses its flowers and deteriorates, and then vanishes altogether. Although each floor is different, the similarities give the impression of continuity and change. The differences also signal technical advances through the decades: The ventilator is replaced by an air conditioner, and finally by a satellite dish on the roof. In spite of this evidence of modernization, The Katz building gradually decays as the stores and buildings around it move in the opposite direction towards renewal and renovation. The confusion of the building, out of sync with its surroundings is intensified by the confusion within its walls, which is represented through the simultaneity of multiple moments in time. Here is the disruption of time sequencing Bredehoft associates with the two-dimensionality of comics, as the passing of time is running in the opposite direction of what the reader expects.

A walk through the house

Moore's technique of situating time by displaying it in space continues on the following pages, where a detail in a given panel signifies that panel's specific era. A reader will recognize the lava lamp as a reference to the '70s, or women's different hairstyles as signifying the '30s with a slick and short style, the '70s with a "disco frizz," or the '90s with a rainbow "wavy bop." The two protagonists, Mr. Katz and Sonny, get visibly older, their hair showing not so much changes in fashion as the natural aging process: Mr. Katz from shiny black to his final tonsure and Sonny losing his curls. Time has also taken its toll and the end result of smoking shows up as we read through the pages and Mr. Katz who is always carrying a big cigar in the 1930s, '50s and '70s, has been put in a wheel chair with an oxygen tank in the 1990s, his speech constantly interrupted by insistent "koff koff"s." During the course of the narrative, Mr. Katz's fancy suits change according to the times,[2] but Sonny never alters his brown pants and green turtleneck. Thus he is singled out and seems to ground the narrative in defiance of time. He gets older, yes, but his clothing sends a signal to the reader that implies, that though a lot of things change, Sonny stays the same.

The flipping of the pages also reveals something else for the reader: while reading from top to bottom one moves through time, but reading from left to right across the pages takes one through the space of the building. The perspective changes from the full front of the Katz building on page 1, to the actual rooms of the building on page 2, then the story moves out on the stairs and landings on page 3 and 4, and moves from the rooms to the backside of the house, so that the last page 8 shows a full frontal view of the back of the building. The change of perspective emphasizes the 'realness' of the house by showing it in three dimensions, instead of limiting the point of view to the viewer looking in from the front. The reader is faced with several simultaneous narratives here. The horizontal time-sequencing from page to page is linear, and the linearity in the horizontal panels opens up for a reading of the top panels all the way through. The final decision of how to proceed through the story and combine space and time is left up to the reader, as she can take in the alternating time floors at the same time as following the linear time sequence through the pages. The various decades are represented side by side with the small time sequences within them.

Verbalization across time[3]

The different time periods are indicated in image as well as text: visually by the speech being written in different writing styles, corresponding to the current time frames, each one with its own font and speech balloon shape. When the reader turns to the speech balloons and the individual panels in this story, she notices that the grounding of the narrative in time is also present in the conversations. Mr. Katz comments on the decay in 1:1: "This rooms looking as shabby as this whole buildin'" whereas Sonny's father professes in 1959 that "Neighborhood's still nice, like when we moved in" and Mr. Katz introduces the small family's new home in 1939 by saying "See my beautiful apartment building? Brand new!" So even if we had not noticed the visual markers of the time passing, the characters conversations will make sure we understand the "time difference." Their conversations in some instances also serve to add on to the white numbers on the left hand side by indicating the time period like when Mr. Katz and his girl are going "discodancin'" in the '70s (1:2) and when Sonny's father take solace in the fact that Mr. Katz "aint no communist like your beatnik pals" of the '50s. In this way the logical chronological sequence of the narrative is reinforced by image and text. However, there are also disruptions of this sequencing, disruptions that can be attributed not only to Moore's experimentation here, but as a potential inherent in the comics medium.

Thomas Bredehoft has commented on how causality can act in comics. After discussing a small comic narrative that plays on the juxtaposition of different times, he notes:

> the logic of causality, in which causes always precede effects. Except in cases like the one at and (or, for example, in time-travel narratives), causality usually overlaps chronology: the order of events is hardly separable from the logic of cause and effect. But in the case of Feazell's page,[4] the page layout and fishing line serve to disrupt causality (thus allowing effects to precedecauses) precisely because the vertical juxtaposition of two panels clashes with the use of horizontal space to indicate time-sequencing [873].

This misuse of horizontal time-sequencing and its juxtaposition with vertical sequencing to disrupt causality is what Alan Moore does in "How things Work Out." Because we are so used to causality and chronology being interdependent, a natural response would be to attempt to read the narrative from the bottom up. It goes against our Western way of reading from the upper left corner to the bottom right, but chronologically it makes sense. Also, it corresponds with our bodily experience of walking up the stairs in a house. You start outside at the ground floor and move your way up, in this case also complying with the chronology of diegetic time. Following a reading that goes from the top floor to the bottom, the reader defies the linear concept of time and the laws of physical space (a jump from 1:4 to 2:1 is a jump from the first to the fourth floor). Alan Moore's structuring of this story promotes the reader's confusion and challenges causality. Nevertheless, Moore provides some guidance for the reader through the text that helps us bridge the gutters from panel to panel. Almost every time the reader crosses a gutter, whether horizontally or vertically, the passage is facilitated by language and often in the images as well. Sometimes the speech balloons in the panels following each other will be close to identical, like the repeating of "Nossir" in both 1:4 and 2:1, the "Jesus" and "Jesus Christ" that links 2:1 and 2:2, and the "Ahh, Who cares? Aint important" that is at both sides of the gutter between 4:3 and 4:4. Other times the link will be less literal, such as the transition from 5:4 to 6:1 with Mr. Katz's concern that "We don't want you or the kid bein' responsible for no sudden explosions." Turning the page we see Sonny (the kid) exploding suddenly and thus fulfilling Mr. Katz's concern 60 years later, albeit in a more metaphorical way. A speech balloon that actually ties one panel to the next four in 6:4 is when Mr. Katz denies being a bad guy: "I'm just complicated is all. Sometimes, I'm a regular **guy**, sometimes I'm sweet like **music**. Sometimes I'm comfortable as an old **fedora**, and, yeah, sometimes I'm an **animal**." By moving her eyes just a fraction to the right and taking in the whole page 7, the reader can see the words appearing in bold in the speech balloon being thrown out the various windows in the building: a guy (Mr. Katz himself), music on sheets, a fedora and an animal. This reading changes Mr. Katz's somewhat innocent exclamation "Whoah! My Life!" (7:4) to a more sinister and ironic comment that only the reader understands, since we have just seen his life in its many incarnations go out the window and land in the mud. As the whole page is included in the previous comment from Mr. Katz, the reader can decipher that Mr. Katz's life is being thrown out the window, down the drain. The experience here is closer to the conventions guiding the reading of verse than to the reading habits associated with prose narrative. Moore utilizes not only the intermingling of literal and figurative meanings, but allows the reader to take in the work at once horizontally (in the linearity of textual grammar) and vertically, linking end rhymes and rhythms that coexist on the page. We can read the narrative horizontally within the different time periods or vertically from the present to the past. What we cannot do is try to make chronology and causality meet.

What is the use?

All these cleverly thought out details might be considered to be just a knowing wink shared between creator and reader, but I want to argue that our perception of the story's themes are in many ways underlined and emphasized by its structure. "How Things Work Out" is on different levels a story about the choices people make and the causalities or lack hereof. It is about time passing and the inability of people to do anything to change this. Part of this is the tragedy of Sonny the protagonist. The way Alan Moore has chosen to defy time and causality has the implication that the reader knows things way before Sonny does. The tragic irony of Sonny's life is crystal clear to the reader, as he enthusiastically tells his father that "Dad, I'm not wasting **my** life here like you have, as soon as I'm over this **divorce**, I'm moving **out**, getting my **jazz band** back together" (2:3). The reader knows that Sonny will be stuck in the house, wasting his life like his dad, becoming his father as he takes on the role of care taker after the father's death. We also know that the saxophone will be put away and the only thing resembling a jazz career Sonny will have is his record collection and a poster from a festival.

Confining the action of the story within the same four walls of the building even though it bridges the decades gives the narrative a feeling of claustrophobia, but this sense of fatalism underlined in some of the incidents is contested in others. The attitude of the narrative is double or at least ambiguous. On the one hand we experience Sonny mirroring his father and repeating his steps, but we perceive the actions backwards so the causality of the narrative gets confused. After having realized that Sonny never got away as he intended, the reader is presented with Sonny's father's words: "It's not like we'll be in this mess for very **long**" (4:4) with the following page emphasizing how wrong this intention turns out to be: "Jeez, look at this **mess.**" (5:1). Decades later Sonny is still caught in Mr. Katz's mess, cleaning it up and hiding it just like his father before him. On the one hand, history seems to be repeating itself with all the initiative taken away from Sonny and his father, a strong causality and determinism guiding their lives. On the other hand, the narrative opens up for a free will and possibility of agency with the repetition of the words from the title. Both on the level of the form and content, this story is concerned with how things work out. In his autobiographical anecdote, Mr. Katz says that: "My **pop** was a **little** guy. He thought I'd amount to **nothin'**, like **he** did. Funny how things work **out**, ain't it?" (2:4) here linking Sonny and his father (the little guys) with his own social climbing. Mr. Katz airs the possibility of not becoming like your father, not repeating his mistakes, but the reader already knows that Sonny will to some degree do exactly this. The last aspect of the title phrase is the ending of this picture novella at the bottom panel where Mr. Katz expresses his prospect of the future: "Guess we'll see how you work **out**, eh, boy?"(8:4). Because of the disruptive presentation of the narrative, the reader is already in possession of the answer to this question: Sonny will both become his father and end up defying his weakness by working things out, killing Mr. Katz and ridding the building of its villain. The broken frame at (8:1) suggests that there is a way out of the confinement of the Katz building, one beginning with the murder of its namesake, and the reader is staring right at it.

However, when the reader reaches the bottom panel of page eight, it is clear that the act of freedom that Sonny performs by pushing Mr. Katz has been inevitable or at least intended all along the different decades. The promise Sonny speaks of in (8:1) is indicated at (8:4) and the story seems to end on a note that suggests a determinism at hand that Sonny father comments on just above the panel in (8: 3): "Who **knows?** Maybe there's some **plan** to things, and everything just happens how it **should**. Maybe we can't see the whole **picture**." There is indeed a plan, thought out by the writer Alan Moore and the one who has the privilege of seeing the whole picture is the reader.

In an article dealing with the historiographic vision of Alan Moore, Sean Carney sums up Moore's view of the forces of time and history:

> What emerges from an overview of Moore's oeuvre to date is a concern less with concrete historical events per se than with the representation of the dialectical contradiction of history itself: it is made by human beings in historical moments, but is also the seemingly trans historical force that makes and drives humanity forward, and so it takes on the appearance of an impersonal tide even while this tide remains the result of human agency [4].

"How Things Work Out" uses a disruption of linear time to convey this conception of history and humanity's possibility of agency within it. There are fragments of time in the individual panels and there is the overall combination of these as history in the course of the story, and Alan Moore uses the breakdown of the comic's pages to represent this. The characters in "How Things Work Out" are simultaneously parts of a small fragment and a bigger whole and the interpretation of their meaning as human beings, their potential for free will is in the hands of the reader as she chooses which way to read the narrative, and the open ended experience of the reader mirrors that of the characters. Whether or not they are to surf the tides of history or be swept underneath it is all in the eye of the beholder. Carney also places the concept of simultaneity as central to Moore's understanding of time, something he locates in a multitude of Moore's works. This perception of simultaneity and the conflation of time and space are presented to the reader by means of the medium of comics and the structure of a building as a function of time and space.

Conclusion

In this reading of an 8-page comic book narrative I have touched on a number of issues in relation to the medium of comics whose broader significance should be summed up.

First of all "How Things Work Out" shows how the medium of comics have its own history and masters that can be reinvented and used in intertextual references. Moore's nod towards Eisner is one both of recognition, praise and mental stepladder. In his paraphrasing of The Spirit Moore underlines the heritage of comics as well as takes it to a new level. The formal experiment that runs through this story emphasizes the visionary aspects of Will Eisner and insists on taking it a step further. In acknowledging Eisner's influence implicitly, Alan Moore pays tribute to a master of formal experiment in comics as well as using Eisner as base for an even wilder formal exercise.

Secondly, the use of the building as structural device not only links the medium of comics with architecture but ties in with the potential for representation of time and space in comics. In comics time and space can be one and the same, and the radical structure of "How Things Work Out" uses this to circumvent the reader's expectations towards narrative progress. Causality and time are disrupted a number of times as the reader progresses through the narrative, and as Thomas Bredehoft states, this is an inherent quality of comics: the potential for the construction of time and space that does not comply with the reader's empiric experience. The division of the page into different floors of a building to coincide with various decades allows for a freedom in the way the reader chooses to take in the story. She can progress vertically or horizontally and the story varies accordingly.

The third aspect of my reading is the way the formal use of comics can be activated in the themes of the narrative told. The many disruptions of time and space and the subversion of causality in "How Things Work Out" adds to the impression the reader gets of the characters and their lives. Sonny's life is not ruled by determinism but neither is he a free agent. The simultaneity in this story both emphasizes the inevitability of Sonny's duplication of his father as well as allows for Sonny to revolt against Mr. Katz. There is information and conclusions that are only available to the reader and this issue of free will opposed to a determined future is one of the themes that are complicated as a consequence of the way Moore uses the medium.

In the spatial and temporal structuring of a comics narrative, the writer/artist can deeply influence the lives of his fictional characters as well as manipulate the reader. In the example of "How Things Work Out" medium-specific characteristics are activated in order to free the reader's decoding of the narrative and allow for multiple pathways through the tale told. Here Moore takes advantage of the complexity of the medium of comics in that it can be decoded in one moment in the simultaneous taking-in of the page as well as progressing forward through the reading of panels after panel. In comics, time and space are not always distinct categories but rather function as a space-time amalgam.

Notes

1. In the following reading of "How Things Work Out" I am going to refer to the pages and the panels with numbers, numbering the panels from the top down with the direction of reading in Western countries (e.g. 3:4 meaning page 3, bottom panel).

2. Notice how in 1979, Mr. Katz not only is wearing a suit like John Travolta in *Saturday Night Fever*, he is also posing like him (3:2).

3. For this section I will cite the text of the comic in lower case letters although it appears in capitals in the actual book.

4. The Feazell page shows a man stealing money from himself in the future to use in the past, hereby defying causality.

Works Cited

Bredehoft, Thomas. "Comics Architecture, Multidimensionality, and Time: Chris Ware's *Jimmy Corrigan: The Smartest Kid on Earth.*" *Modern Fiction Studies* 52.4 (Winter 2006): 869–890. Print.

Carney, Sean: "The Tides of History: Alan Moore's Historiographic Vision." *ImageText* 2.2 (2002) N.p. Web. n. pag.

Cooke, Jon B. "America's Best Apocalypse? The Scribe on ABC and His Possible Retirement Comics." *Comic Book Artist* 1.25 (2003). N.p. Web. n. pag.

Doherty, Thomas. "Art Spiegelman's *Maus*: Graphic Art and the Holocaust." *American Literature* 68.1 (1996): 69–84. Print.

McCloud, Scott. *Understanding Comics.* New York: Harper Perennial, 1994. Print.

Moore, Alan, and Rick Veitch. "How Things Work Out." *Tomorrow Stories # 2.* ABC Comics, November 1999: N. pag. Print.

Wolk, Douglas. *Reading Comics and What They Mean.* Cambridge, MA: Da Capo, 2007. Print.

PART II

READING ETHNICITY

5

Picturing Books:
Southern Print Culture in
Howard Cruse's *Stuck Rubber Baby*

DAVID BORDELON

For an essay on a graphic novel set in the civil rights–era Deep South, I'd like to begin at what may seem like an odd time and place: sixteenth century Germany. It was at that time and place that Albrecht Dürer published the first in what became a series of prints depicting St. Jerome in his study. In the prints, St. Jerome is usually seated at a desk facing a book on a stand with other volumes and manuscripts scattered throughout the room. These images remind the reader of Dürer's place in the literate culture of the time — in particular his translation of the Bible into the Latin Vulgate. This emphasis on the importance of the word — *logos* — points towards the period's embrace of learning. Like other renaissance artists, Dürer uses books in these prints because they form a "lexicon of images" (Varnum and Gibbons xii), pictorial elements with stable culture meanings. As such, these elements are not merely "filler"; they function as signifiers, in this case of erudition, the knowledge that comes from reading and contemplation. And this "lexicon" can accrue multiple meanings. For St. Jerome and the Christian fathers, *logos* retained its specific religious connotations: reading and learning were valued mainly as a means of transmitting the word of God. For Dürer and other figures of the Enlightenment, *logos* lost its strictly ecclesiastical connotations: reading and learning were valued as a means of transmitting more secular knowledge. Yet in both cases books and reading signified growth.

In *Stuck Rubber Baby* (hereafter, *SRB*), Howard Cruse follows this long tradition in art history: He too uses images of print culture — books, periodicals, reading — to signify knowledge, but in the longer context of a graphic narrative, provides a more nuanced view of their qualitative value. The novel recounts the social and sexual awakening of the white, working class narrator, Toland Polk, as he overcomes his racist upbringing and acknowledges his homosexuality. The setting, 1960s Alabama, freights this awakening

107

with both violence and hope. The beating of Toland and others who challenge the prevailing conservative codes and beliefs and the brutal murders of activists and of his openly
gay friend, Sammy Noone, reflect the institutionalized violence of the South's response
to the civil rights movement. Hope arrives at the end of the novel in the shape of Toland
and Ginger Raines' daughter (conceived because, as the title notes, prophylactics sometimes malfunction) and Toland's eventual acceptance of his homosexuality. The narrative
itself, related in a series of flashbacks, mirrors this sense of hope and haunting as an older
Toland, having physically escaped the South, reflects on things past — the memories of
Southern tolerance and violence — revealed in the print culture surrounding him.

Given the complexity of the narrative, both in form and content, the cultural resonance of print and reading, unlike the Dürer prints, cannot be reduced to a simple chain
of signifiers: books = knowledge = good. In *SRB* images of print culture illustrate both
the problems of and solutions to prejudice. Specifically, these images reveal the duality
of reading and knowledge in the South: in the hands of the prejudiced majority, they
legitimize and reify discriminatory racial and sexual codes; in the hands of Toland and
others, they provide an escape from the segregation, violence, and social restrictions of
the Jim Crow South.

More broadly, exploring the interpretative possibilities of a specific image pattern
throughout the novel — in this case images of books and reading — illustrates how graphic
narratives work. Less intrusive than blocks of descriptive text, these images function like
the background set in a film or props in a play, adding layers of meaning beyond the
action or dialogue on the screen or stage. Moving them to the center of discussion illustrates how "things" in a graphic text — a neatly ordered bookcase, a newspaper headline,
a book cover — can provide contextual information to support broader thematic elements.
They also provide a window into the medium itself, and show how picturing books can
be more effective than describing them.

At this point, if this were an essay on a more canonical text, a survey of the criticism
on the particular work at hand would be in order. For graphic novels, this poses a problem
because unless the author's last name is Spiegelman, Pekar, or Ware, the academy is largely
silent on works by individual artists.[1] For Cruse, this is all the more surprising given one
critic's view that the novel represents the "Gold Standard" of historically based comic
fiction (Buhle 318). This emphasis on history informs my approach to *SRB* and provides
a theoretical basis for understanding its cultural resonance. Grounded in the work of
scholars such as Jane Tompkins, who argued in *Sentimental Designs* that "novels and stories
[…] offer powerful examples of the way a culture thinks about itself, articulating and
proposing solutions for the problems that shape a particular historical moment" (xi), this
essay examines a "particular historical moment" and culture — the early 1960s in the American South. But this essay redirects Tompkins' reader response point of view: where she
looked outward from a text to examine what that work meant to its audience, my focus
is inward, examining what an image within a text reveals about a particular character or
the culture depicted in the novel itself. Thus, instead of focusing on how "the book" —
the material object under scholarly study — was received by readers, I am interested in
how books and periodicals within "the book" shaped characters and reflected the cultural
attitudes of the period portrayed in the novel.

This focus draws its impetus from book history theory, which in Robert Darnton's classic formation, explores "how exposure to the printed word affect[s] the thought and behavior" of culture (9). In *SRB*, images of the "printed word"—and more generally print culture[2]—have a powerful effect, negative and positive, on the characters that inhabit the deep South of the novel. Taking a cue from more recent work by Sarah Wadsworth which stresses the necessity of "reattach[ing a text] to as many of its original contexts as possible" (11), this essay connects the print culture of the historical South with its depiction in the novel.

Graphic narrative scholars often focus on the spatial—the physical layout of panels—in their criticism. Scott McCloud and Will Eisner, seminal practitioners and theorists, deem this one of the essential elements of graphic narratives (66, 23–26). Hillary Chute and Marianne DeKoven suggest the interpretive potential of such a focus, noting that "[t]he diegetical horizon of each page, made up of what are essentially boxes of time, offers graphic narrative a representational mode capable of addressing complex political and historical issues with an explicit, formal degree of self-awareness" (769).[3] My reading of *SRB* suggests that within this "diegetical horizon" lie images that are indeed explicit and worthy of critical attention. More specifically, the novel illustrates how images of print culture inform and shape the "political and historical issues" of racism, religion, and homosexuality faced by the characters in *SRB*.

While reading traditionally symbolizes intellectual growth—consider Thoreau's famous exhortation from *Walden*: "How many a man has dated a new era in his life from the reading of a book!" (408)—it can also be used to incite hatred and violence: what if that book is *Mein Kampf*? It is this latter use of texts that I want to explore first. The post *Brown v. Board of Education* South was filled with segregationist texts decrying each step toward racial integration and warning of the resulting (or so they believed) social breakdown and violence. These texts attempted to establish a veneer of legitimacy to an undemocratic endeavor: segregation. As such they gave shape to the intellectual philosophy behind segregation, and thus the philosophy underpinning the beliefs and values of many characters in *SRB*. Tom P. Brady's 1955 *Black Monday*, which took its title from the day of the week the *Brown v. Board of Education* decision was issued, was one of the best known of these extremist works. Three aspects of this polemic bear especial resonance for *SRB*: denigration of the intelligence of blacks, a conflation between desegregation and communism, and violence. In a comment typical of the substance of the text—and typical of the beliefs espoused by the majority of Southerners in *SRB*—Brady argued that blacks possessed the mental capacity of a "chimpanzee" (12). And like many characters in the novel, he links communism with the civil rights movement, which explains his odd dedication for a book ostensibly about school desegregation: "This book is dedicated to those Americans who firmly believe socialism and communism are lethal 'messes of porridge' for which our sacred birthright shall not be sold" (n.p. Brady). Finally, while Brady is careful to distance himself from using violence to further his agenda, the white-hooded men with clubs and the exposed canines of police dogs in *SRB* find their historical correlative in comments from other segregationists. For instance, Brady approvingly quotes from an editorial by Major Frederick Sullens of the *Jackson Daily News*: "Human blood may stain Southern soil in many places because of this decision, but the dark red stains of that blood will be on the marble steps of the United States Supreme Court building" (quoted in Brady 41–2).

In a similar vein, Carleton Putnam's *Race and Reason* (1961) trots out warnings against communism and indulges in thinly veiled threats of violence. The difference between this text and Brady's was its wider distribution — 60,000 in its first six months according to its publisher (McMillen 166)— and its sheen of respectability.[4] For Putnam the flaws in the *Brown* decision are systemic: he argues that since the ruling was based on the work of the anthropologist Franz Boaz whose "doctrines," according to Putnam, are "unsubstantiated" and "so saturated with wishful thinking as to be pathetic" (23), the decision was flawed and its arguments untenable.[5] Like Brady, Putnam's aim was to make segregation acceptable to a middle class that sympathized with segregationist aims, but balked at the specter of burning crosses and lynchings. To this end his argument mimics the objective, scholarly approach of academic criticism. Written in a dry, pseudo-objective tone replete with footnotes and references, the book reflects the refined racism of the majority of Southerners, a refinement, as will be shown, exhibited by Toland's father, mother, and other characters in *SRB*.

Those who liked their racism raw turned to periodicals that appealed to baser instincts. On his website, Cruse cites one such tabloid, Roy V. Harris's *Augusta Courier* (1947–1974), as a model for the invented paper *The Dixie Patriot*, a work which figures prominently in the novel ("Barefootz"). Instead of the appearance of objectivity and an appeal to seemingly rational arguments, the *Courier* went straight for the jugular. One article rails against the sympathy for Martin Luther King's Southern Christian Leadership Conference engendered by the murder of Civil Rights workers: "They got themselves some dead bodies at Selma and, as result, they have been able to appeal to suckers all over the nation" ("Dead" 1). And like Brady and Putnam — and many characters in *SRB*— Harris remained convinced that "communists" were behind black discontent. One headline from 1964 reads "Race Riots in U. S. Communist Plots" ("Race" 1).

This sampling of the historical print culture of the South provides a contextual background for the fictional examples of segregationist literature in *SRB*, supplying the historical basis for the densely textured images in the novel. These images act as mirrors, reflecting both how books and periodicals undercut social progress in the historical South, and how such texts constrain his characters' lives. Early in *SRB*, a pair of panels echoes this sentiment of books as restraint by revealing a major cause of Southern racism: ignorance. In response to Toland's question about physical differences between blacks and whites, Toland's father offers a variant of Brady's "chimpanzee" analogy: he tells Toland "negro bones are probably tougher, since colored folks are closer to the animal state than we are and have gotten stronger from havin' to get by in the wild" (2).[6] Moving to cognitive differences, he adds that "white people's brains are more *developed*, it's been scientifically proven" (3).

This set up leads directly to two panels showing what the young Toland had believed was the source of his father's scientific knowledge: books. Symbolically, these twin panels represent the façade of white superiority, a façade that, as the texts by Brady and Putnam illustrate, was propped up by books.[7] In the first of the panels, Toland reaches for a book from a floor to ceiling bookcase covering two walls — with another bookcase peeking

These twin panels represent the façade of white supremacy as they move from Toland's youthful belief that books established the authority of his father's racist views to the empty logic of Southern prejudice (*SRB* 3).

through a doorway from a back room —filled with "truckloads" of books (3). The accompanying text reinforces the importance of the wall of books; in response to his father's ideas on blacks, Toland reasons "I assumed he knew what he was talking about because of all the *books* we had in the house" (3). The first bookcase panel literally illustrates the basis of Toland's acceptance; the neat orderly rows of books, filling the panel, lend textual weight to his father's pronouncements. Like the books in Dürer's print of St. Jerome, they occupy their traditional role as symbols of authority, an authority that some writers used to legitimize and rationalize their Jim Crow views.

In the second panel, an older Toland and his sister Melanie face the same, though now almost empty, bookcases as they pack the books after their parents' death. Here Southern prejudice — as signified by a print culture that espoused racial differences — meets a symbolic representation of its logic — empty bookcases. This panel undercuts Toland's earlier assumptions about books as vessels of knowledge, suggesting instead that while they occupy physical space, they can be "empty." As *Black Monday* and *Race and Reason* demonstrate, Southern books too often promoted a cultural view — racism — that Toland, unlike his father, did not endorse and which represent the prejudiced, limited, and stereotyped thinking — in short, the intellectual bankruptcy — of the segregationist South.[8]

While most of the images of books in this section of the novel serve an iconic purpose, denoted in generalized book shapes with squiggles or lines for titles[9], two books pictured in Toland's hands, *The Status Seekers*, Vance Packard's 1955 critique of American materialism and class lines and an invented title, *An Analysis of Social Darwinism*, provide examples of texts which supported segregationist views. Packard's book criticizes the workings of the ruling elite, especially the mechanisms of oppression that keep the middle and lower classes in line, and admits that "[a]mong Negroes, the color of their skin is almost universally recognized as a barrier to full dignity of treatment from their fellow citizens" (53). But this acknowledgment is tempered by his observation that "there is evidence that Negroes are no longer the lowest-prestige group among the nation's ethnics" (55). This suggestion that racism is abating in the United States is more explicit in his quotation from the linguist S. I. Hayakawa: "The Negro, to a degree hitherto impossible, can set the tone of social and business intercourse by the clues he gives in his speech and behavior as to how he expects to be treated[....] [I]f you are a biochemist or a parent and expect to be treated as a Negro, people are going to treat you as a Negro" (quoted in Packard 334–5). Packard's over-reliance on class blinds him to the reality of racism in the South, where blacks, regardless of income or profession, were treated as second-class citizens.

The title of the other book, *An Analysis of Social Darwinism*, suggests a reason for Southern acceptance of racism. In their quest for "scientific" rationales for segregation, many Southerners turned to Darwinian notions of the law of the jungle for "objective" support to their beliefs.[10] In 1956 Senator Sam J. Ervin of North Carolina resorted to Darwinist language in his defense of segregation, referring to it as "a basic law of nature — the law that like seeks like" (quoted in Zanden 389). The title of the book —*Social Darwinism*— acts almost as an inside joke; in effect, *SRB* suggests that outdated theories such as these were the basis of Toland's father's "fucked up" (in Toland's words) explanations of racial differences (3). Taken together, the books portray a collective mindset clouded with intellectual diversions: instead of confronting "the color line"— the salient issue underscoring all aspects of Southern life — *The Status Seekers* reduced racial problems to class issues, and *An Analysis* reduced them to the "survival of the fittest." These particular books, like Brady's and Putnam's, would not provide readers with the intellectual stimulus to move beyond the prevailing racial norms. Instead they symbolize an outdated and repressive social system.

Cruse supplies a more direct example of print culture reinforcing segregationist policies and culture in the fictional newspaper *Dixie Patriot*. Discussing the historical background of the paper, Cruse notes that "[o]n the virulence scale *The Dixie Patriot* [...] lies somewhere between the *Birmingham Independent* [...] and an even more hate-filled Georgia-based paper of that era called *The Augusta Courier*." He adds, "The *Birmingham Independent* made a habit during the turbulent '60s of publishing the names, addresses, and (when possible) photographs of any white Birminghamians who were spotted participating in protests against racial segregation" ("Barefootz"). This inclusion of names and addresses becomes a central plot device in *SRB*, leading to the death of Toland's friend Sammy.

Cruse connects the murder of Sammy to Southern print culture by illustrating the collusion between the media — specifically the *Dixie Patriot*— and this violent response to desegregation and homosexuality. After a bombing which kills several children in a choir and severely injures their choirmaster (an allusion to the 16th Street Baptist Church massacre), Sammy faced a television camera and unleashed a tirade implicating the Clayfield police commissioner, Chopper, in the attack. This outburst, and a still from the news coverage, lands Sammy on the cover of the *Dixie Patriot* as a "Pervert On Payroll Of Racemixing Church" (122).[11] The public outing, both of his sexual orientation and of his activism, turns deadly when a drunken Sammy goes to the *Patriot*'s office for a reproduction of his photograph and blurts out his address before a sober Toland, realizing the danger, can cover Sammy's mouth. Later that same night, Toland is beaten and Sammy is hanged (177–180). In *SRB* (as in the historical South) the press, instead of an instrument of justice in the war on southern intolerance, could function as an instrument of oppression — and violence. Playing the role of agitator, ironically a charge the *Patriot* leveled at those opposed to segregation, the newspaper becomes an accomplice to murder.

But the same paper that preaches intolerance could, in the hands of a sophisticated reader, reveal the flaws in racist logic. Cruse sets up this dichotomy through a confrontation between Toland's friend and roommate Riley Wheeler, a character who embodies openness and tolerance, and Toland's brother-in-law Orley, the resident bigot.[12] Cooling his heels in Orley's backyard during a barbeque, Riley thumbs through the pages of the *Patriot*. His comments demonstrate a clear understanding of the political dimensions of Southern racism: "I see you're reading *Nazi propaganda* now, Orley. Thinkin' 'bout signin' up with the *Brownshirts*?" (98). Orley responds, "There's not a *thing* about any *Germans* in that newspaper, Riley" (98), revealing either his refusal to rise to Riley's bait or an ignorance of the structural elements of the segregationist South. The likelihood of the latter is shown when Orley adds "The people that put out the Dixie Patriot are good *Americans*" (98). This conflation of patriotism with blind allegiance is fostered, as noted earlier, by segregationist attempts to marginalize any social activism by linking it to communism, which in the years after McCarthy and in the run-up to the Vietnam War acted as an effective bogeyman to a frightened public.

This Southern public includes people like Toland's date, Sybil Louise, who shares Orley's racist political and social views. As they are leaving the party, she objects to Riley's criticism of Southern values and echoes Orley's party line response, telling Toland "As for that newspaper [...] it may be *extreme* in some *aspects* but it *is* trying to *warn* us about what the communists are *up* to [... and] that's [not] something to *ridicule*" (100). Orley's and Sybil's defensive reaction to criticism of the newspaper mimics the way its name — *Dixie Patriot*— plays on the twin appeal of segregation: states' rights and fear of communism. According to its publishers, and obviously many other Southerners, you're a "patriot" only if you subscribe to older, "Dixie" values. Riley and Toland, unlike Orley and Sybil, refuse to accept such fear mongering, resorting, in Riley's case, to satire, a tool of the intellect. Toland's and Riley's default response to this kind of narrow thinking — logic — reflects Cruse's own experiences growing up in the early '60s South. In a private email he writes that such right-wing papers helped him discover "that the written word could be used to deceive, not just entertain or enlighten" and that criticizing the dangerous irrationality of such papers "gave me the [mental] tools I eventually needed to inoculate myself against the homophobic writings I encountered" ("Re: Questions").

While the rabid racism of a paper like the *Dixie Patriot* is easy to denounce, an image from mainstream media shows that even the more "respectable" Southern press contributed to the racist mindset. On the background of a page describing the Ku Klux Klan murder of Sledge Rankin, a black activist, lies an image illustrating where Toland learns of the crime: the "Negro News" section of the fictional *Clayfield Banner* (50). Both the separate section and the placement of the news item are relevant here. The castration and murder of a family man at the hands of the KKK is printed in a separate section; forced to the back of the bus, it's relegated to the inner pages, where the gaze of the dominant white culture can easily pass over it. Exploiting the nature of the medium, Cruse overlays images that advance the narrative while the "Negro News" section looms in the background, documenting the historical reality that even mainstream newspapers operated under a color line, segregating news into "Whites Only" and "Negro" sections.

The placement of the image itself is symbolic. As Thierry Groensteen observes, when an image, instead of the traditional white or black space, forms the background of a page, the symbolic power of that "background panel" is "magnifie[d]" (86). In this case the image reflects Southern racist attitudes; the background is a mirror "image" of the background prejudice that "colors" all aspects of life. While people like Sledge and Toland try to fight it, even the "good" whites, the ones, like the waitress later in the novel who calls the *Dixie Patriot* "awful," cannot see blacks as equals (78). This same waitress adds "Of course, I *do* think they have a *point* when they say it's probably the communists who're convincing the negroes that they're so dissatisfied" (78). Apparently, she doesn't read the "Negro News" section of the *Clayfield Banner* or she'd find a clearer rationale for their dissatisfaction. The novel makes clear that it is the presentation that counts: the waitress continues "it's the ugly way they [the *Patriot*] say it" (78). The cool, objective tone of the *Clayfield Banner* separates it, in the minds of the majority, from the hectoring, hate-mongering tone of the *Patriot*. Yet both provide textual "cover" and legitimize Southern racism. For all of its pretensions of objectivity, The *Banner*, and by extension those who subscribe to its values, are complicit in creating a climate of intolerance that will only perpetuate the Jim Crow South.

While the novel clearly illustrates the corrosive effects of reading in the South, it also reveals its potential emancipatory effects. On page two of the novel, a series of panels show how reading can expand a person's consciousness. While playing a game of Monopoly, a friend asks a young Toland "Wanna see somethin' *gross?*" (2). Naturally Toland says yes and the rather smarmy looking friend reaches into a drawer saying, "I found a nigger magazine in a trash can downtown. Look at this *picture*" (2). The next panel shows Toland, sweat beading his forehead, looking at a *Jet* magazine containing photographs of Emmett Till (2). This small image provides a wealth of historical symbolism. The September 15, 1955, issue of the magazine famously published images of Till's battered body, resulting in an outburst of indignation and sympathy for black southerners. Commenting on the primacy of these images, Christine Harold and Kevin Michael Deluca in "Behold the Corpse: Violent Images and the Case of Emmett Till," argue that the pictures "became a crucial visual vocabulary that articulated the ineffable qualities of American racism in ways words simply could not do" (265). Echoing the power of that image on the greater American consciousness, Toland identifies with Till: the panel following his reading of the magazine shows Toland lying in bed that night with pieces of his shattered skull flying loose as he remembers the images. It is this identification, this sense that the boy in the photo could well be him, that seems to trigger Toland's moral consciousness. His focus is not on the words accompanying the images in the magazine, but on the image itself, much like the readers of *SRB* who focus their attention on the image of Toland, wide-eyed and with shards of skin floating above his head, rather than the rather laconic text "I was worried about my *skull*" (2). The inclusion of a realistic print image—*Jet* magazine — acts as a counterweight to the fictional *Patriot* and *Clayfield Banner*, providing the black perspective that the segregationist press is so keen on suppressing. And while many white Southerners dismiss *Jet* as a "nigger magazine," for Toland it marks the beginning of a disenchantment with the prevailing racial codes of the pre–civil rights era South.

But it is not only the racial codes that spark Toland's discontent. He recalls his childhood fascination with a book titled *Seeing Through the Lord*, another of Cruse's invented texts that, as Toland recalls, "purported to *prove*, with logic as *elegant* as y'could *ask* for, that God didn't — and *couldn't possibly — exist*" (36).[13] For Toland, this becomes connected to larger questions of logic and reality: he reasons that "if somebody had *proved*, *once* and for all in a thoroughgoing way, that there *wasn't* any *God* ... and if that somebody had *published* the proof in a *book* for all to see ... then how come all the *churches* in Clayfield were proceeding on their merry way every Sunday without missing a *beat?*" (37). This gap between what to Toland seemed so obvious — no God should equal no religion — acts as a corollary to the Civil Rights movement: it too is obvious — no difference between humans should equal no discrimination. For Toland, a reader from a young age, logic and reason should prevail over the qualities he believed religion and segregation shared: superstition and ignorance. And while religion, particularly in black churches, provided a moral basis for civil rights in the South,[14] the view from white churches was mixed. For instance, while most established churches condemned segregation, the actions of their congregation revealed a schism. Consider the following from D. B. Red's 1959 pamphlet "Race Mixing A Religious Fraud": "all of the larger denominations are pushing us down the Devil's highway of racial integration and on toward national perdition" (n.p.). This denunciation leaves the door open for regional denominations, such as Southern Baptists, to denounce "race mixing." Indeed, a year later, a professor at a Mississippi Baptist college provided religious cover for racism by arguing that "Southern segregation [...] is the Christian way" (quoted in Dailey 125).

This connection between Southern white religious beliefs and segregation is made explicit in the novel through a tiny image of the *Patriot* imbedded in a larger panel. The headline reads "What Jesus said about Miscegenation" (99) — given its placement in the *Dixie Patriot*, I'm assuming it wasn't good.[15] But Toland was immune to such demagoguery. Though he realizes the power of religion, particularly in providing moral support for black unity, it only oppresses him. Over a background picturing him seated in the audience at a "Biracial Equality League [meeting] at Smith City Baptist," Toland, now looking back on the experience, writes "*Churches!!* There's no goddamn *escape* from them down south!" (55). A self professed "atheist" (55), instead of temples of sustenance, he views churches as symbols of oppression.

The importance of *Seeing Through the Lord* is evidenced by its multiple appearances in the text. It is first mentioned when Toland and Melanie are clearing the bookcases. Toland tells her "I tried *forever* to get Daddy to read this book." He adds, " I wanted to *talk* to him about it. But he never *would*" (12). Melanie's response, "Daddy always had *trouble reading* — but nothing could make him *admit* it" (12), is mirrored in a later scene where a youthful Toland hands his father the book, asking if he had ever read it and is told that "I can't recall ever findin' the time to sit *down* with it" (37). Together these two references underscore his father's prideful ignorance, an ignorance that kept him and

Through his invented *Dixie Patriot* headline, Cruse connects Southern white religious beliefs to the superstition and ignorance that sustain segregation (*SRB* 99).

many other Southerners from confronting the truth about racism. The book makes its final appearance, in name only, during a discussion of religious "philosophy" (136) between the Rev. Harland Pepper, a leader of the black community, and Toland. Enjoying the conversation, Toland wants to ask him "if he had ever read *Seeing Through the Lord*" (111), but is interrupted. Significantly, Toland wants to continue a discussion on religion, but instead of basing it on the Bible, he wants to discuss *Seeing Through the Lord*. For him, religion is not faith based, but a "philosophy" to be debated and argued, an intellectual rather than spiritual concept.

Philosophy in *SRB* takes on a decidedly secular shape in the form of a '60s radical print culture staple, *Playboy* magazine. Toland subscribed to the magazine (6) and Riley was a regular reader — as Toland notes "Riley could hold forth for *hours* about Hugh Hefner's Playboy Philosophy essays" (7). This remark is followed with an image of Toland leaning back on a couch, hand under chin in the classic "thoughtful" pose, reading an issue of the magazine. The text in the panel reinforces the idea of Hefner as an astute observer of American culture: "There was definitely something to Hef's sociological views" (7). "Hef's" essays, first appearing in 1962, were part of the magazine's efforts at both rebutting criticism about its content and advancing its editorial credo of "the privilege of all to think differently from one another [...] and the right to hoot irreverently at herders of sacred cows and keepers of stultifying tradition and taboo" (Hefner "Part I"). This series of essays seemed perfectly attuned to the skeptical, questioning mindset of Toland and his friends, providing them with the rhetoric and insight that helped them "hoot" on their own.

A review of the February 1963 "Playboy Philosophy" illustrates their connection to two themes relevant to *SRB*: American racism and the dubiousness of the connection between dissent and communism. Hefner, like Toland and unlike the majority of Southerners portrayed in the novel, believes that instead of discrimination, blacks should be included in society. He writes:

> Erasing the color line in education will, in the future, permit American Negroes to receive a far better and fuller education that they could have hoped for previously. This will benefit both the individual Negroes and the nation, for the total brainpower of any country is one of its most valuable natural resources ["Part III"].

Blacks are transformed here from a separate and unequal class to an integral part of America, a "natural resource" that should be nurtured instead of pigeon holed into stereotypical occupations — like the yard hand, preacher, and musician portrayed in *SRB*.

In the same article, Hefner warns against the red-baiting used by the Southern press to silence those who questioned segregation, noting that "[a] few neofascist and hate groups have persisted up to the present, using the fear of the omnipresent Communist menace and/or the hate of Negroes, Jews, Catholics, [...] or some other suitable group as their scapegoats" ("Part III"). "Neofascist" recalls Riley's connection between the *Dixie Patriot* and the brownshirts, grounding his politics — and by extension Toland's — in the rhetoric of an alternative print culture, a culture that actively protested against stereotypical Southern views. Exposure to the rational, skeptical outlook fostered by magazines such as *Playboy* and books like *Seeing Through the Lord* provided Toland with the intellectual ballast to reject the prevailing bigotry and prejudice and discover his own values; to be, as the financier J. Paul Getty wrote in an 1962 article which also appeared in *Playboy*, one of the vital but "vanishing Americans," who "question, doubt, probe, criticize and object [to the] existing social, economic and political forms" (152, 148).

One of the social forms that Toland questions is his own sexuality. And just as sites of reading figured in his political growth, they chart his sexual awakening.[16] At first, reading is used to block his homoerotic impulses. *Playboy* again makes an appearance, though this time in its more customary role as a projection of male — and in this case heterosexual male — sexual fantasy. Early in the novel, still struggling with his sexual identity, Toland makes an "absolute *rule*" to only masturbate while "looking at one of the *centerfold playmates*" (6). The image accompanying this shows Toland with one hand in his pants and the other clutching a *Playboy* magazine while a parade of bare breasts fills the rest of the panel. For Toland, the magazine acts as a prophylactic, protecting him from what he believes are unnatural desires.

But just as the novel portrays reading as an instrument of both support and dissent regarding racism, it lends the same duality to sexuality. While one magazine, *Playboy*, helped him suppress his desire, another magazine, *Life*, liberated it. After his first night with a male lover leaves him smitten, he sees a picture of Sal Mineo in *Life* magazine and realizes that the "yearning *ache*" he felt "had to do with *more* than some *one guy* I'd had my arms around in a *motel*" (151). Here he begins to realize that despite all his protestations to the contrary, his "ache" was not going away and could not be satisfied with a one-night stand; he begins to see that he was, indeed, a homosexual.[17] As with *Playboy*, instead of an iconic image represented by squiggly lines, *Life* magazine's masthead is clearly depicted. The specificity of the title — "Life" — and the magazine's distinctive cultural weight in post-war culture requires the reader to decode a wealth of meaning. From its founding, the magazine had a history of directly addressing social taboos, especially America's puritanical sexual mores — consider, for example, the famous February 15, 1937, photo essay "How to Undress in Front of Your Husband." In 1964, roughly the time period of the novel, *Life* published a two part essay on "Homosexuality in America," a remarkably frank and, for the time period, progressive discussion of the topic. While it referred to homosexuality as a "social disorder" (Welch 67), it reported that personality tests revealed "no significant differences" (Havemann 79) between homosexual and heterosexual men. The

The placement of books in Toland and his partner's apartment establishes the men as readers and books as the intellectual capital that provided Toland a mental ticket out of Clayfield (*SRB* 207).

novel appropriates the cultural resonance of *Life* magazine — one of the most popular mainstream periodicals during the early '60s — lending a kind of "Good Housekeeping" seal of approval to Toland's sexual awakening, a sense that his orientation is tacitly approved by a widely accepted cultural touchstone.[18] Tying this epiphany to the magazine suggests that instead of an aberrant behavior, his homosexuality is normal, a part of "life" itself (the pun may be intended on Cruse's part) and as such, should not be subject to the prejudice, bigotry and, as we see with Sammy Noone, violence of the dominant Southern culture.[19]

By the end of the novel, books and reading have come full circle. Instead of the unread or empty bookcases pictured in the beginning, *SRB* ends with Toland and his partner in their book strewn urban apartment, shaking the snow off their clothes. The high-rise balcony and snow provide a clear indication that Toland has indeed emigrated from what Riley had derisively labeled the "cracker box" (99) — Clayfield and, more generally, the South. Instead of the neat orderly rows of books from his youth which symbolized books as ornamentation, the haphazard arrangement of texts on the shelves and their scattered placement throughout the apartment make it clear that the people who live there are readers, that print is a central part of their lives.[20] For Toland these books provided a mental ticket out of Clayfield, offering the intellectual capital to move beyond the racial and sexual boundaries of the dominant Southern culture and find a world where he could be comfortable with his own views. For the reader, they are a reminder that the books and magazines which helped Toland overcome the limits of his birthplace remain a central part of his life.

In Kate Chopin's *The Awakening*, a textual connection between her emotional and sexual declaration of independence is signified, rather obviously, when the narrator notes that she "sat in the library and read Emerson" (70)—he of "Self-Reliance" fame. But in a graphic medium, this kind of background information can be supplied more subtly. For instance, as the reproduction of the "What Jesus Says About Miscegenation" headline shows, an image can be minuscule—I had to remove my bifocals and squint to make it out—and still retain symbolic power. Yet a similar subtlety would be difficult to achieve in a written text: writing out the headline would draw undue attention and its wry, snarky character would be lost.

Consider the books pictured in the final pages of the novel. The main narrative is building towards the final double page which resolves the theme of music and forgiveness, another important motif in the novel. In a text based novel, describing the books and magazines would have been too weak or too disruptive. A generic description to match the iconic images—"bookcases filled the room and magazines lay scattered about"—doesn't convey the physicality and thus the presence of print culture in their lives. Conversely, a detailed description or even listing of several titles would slow the narrative as it builds to its conclusion, detracting from its emphasis on music which culminates in Toland's marvelous dream vision of springtime and racial harmony in Clayfield. Instead, the images of books and magazines subtly echo the opening, when a younger Toland was first challenged and then, to borrow Chopin's word, "awakened" by magazines, newspapers and books.

While my reading of the novel is rooted in book history, this emphasis on tracing the ramifications of image patterns opens other interpretative possibilities in *SRB* and in other texts. For instance, an analysis of the music motif noted above could examine how narrative rhythms in the panels echo the jazz and blues being played; it could also trace the historical background of the music, which, like the images of texts, contains both created and actual titles.

The interpretative possibilities of a book history approach to graphic narratives are not exhausted by *SRB*. Consider, for example, the opening pages of Daniel Clowes' *Ghost World*, where the spines of *Scooby Doo*, and *2000 Insults*, share shelf space with the *Encyclopedia of Unusual Sexual Practices*, cataloging Enid Coleslaw's psychological dilemma — the tension between childhood and adult worlds. Later references to 'zines and the prominent placement of a symbol of '80s commercialized subversiveness—*Sassy* magazine (9)—root the novel in a particular time and help shape Enid's character as an acerbically intelligent and hyper ironic young woman. In Peter Kruper's wordless novel *The System* (as in many other wordless novels) images of newspapers and print flyers play a more dominant role, revealing the names of characters and providing information that propels the narrative. And Alison Bechdel's *Fun Home*, filled with images of documents and references to writers from Edgar Albee to Oscar Wilde, begs to be examined from this perspective.

An instructive analogy to this interpretative method is found in what Clifford Geertz labels "thick description," an anthropological approach to understanding a culture which draws "large conclusions from small, but very densely textured facts" (28). These "facts" become part of the "symbols" through which people "communicate, perpetuate, and develop their knowledge about and attitudes toward life" (Geertz 89). In graphic texts authors create cultures — through images and text — where characters "communicate" and "develop their knowledge." A thick description of *Stuck Rubber Baby* reveals the trail of print — images of the books and magazines Toland read — which formed the basis of his egalitarian attitudes. These images demonstrate that pictures of books, like the words actual books contain, can carry a semiotic weight. *Stuck Rubber Baby* reverses the old saw: It turns out that a picture of a book may take a thousand words, or more, to explain.

Notes

1. See Hillary Chute's "Decoding Comics" (2006) for a recent survey of graphic narrative criticism.

2. Print culture includes the range of material (books, periodicals, bookcases, libraries, etc.) and mental apparatus (reading, writing) involved in the production, transmission, and assimilation of printed matter.

3. Consider also Joseph Witek's belief that "The move to history in comic-book form is an implicit rejection of the death grip that fantasy has long held on the medium[....] Comics are much less linear than prose and more simultaneous in the narrative effects that are possible, while they remain connected to traditional prose narratives by their extensive generic and thematic heritage" (153).

4. Southern state officials were particularly enamored with this text. In Mississippi, "governor Ross Barnett [...] declared October 26, 1961, as 'Race and Reason Day'" (Jackson 119). The Louisiana State Board of Education purchased 5,000 volumes and, along with Virginia, made the book "required reading" in their schools (McMillen 167, Jackson 120). And in a more "liberal" environment, full page advertisements for the book appeared at least twice in the *New York Times Book Review* (Black 66).

5. Later, he offers Cornelius J. Connolly's *The External Morphology of the Primate Brain* (1950) and Ward C. Halstead's *Brain and Intelligence* (1947) to support his views (40–41). The book is peppered throughout with references to anthropological articles and texts in an attempt to provide scientific weight to his arguments.

6. As in many graphic novels, Cruse uses all caps for dialogue. For the sake of legibility, I have silently normalized the case and substituted italics for bold print.

7. The duplicate panels reinforce the importance of books — as Thierry Groensteen notes, such "rhym[ing]" images reinforce the impact on the reader (7).

8. Melanie's comment, "Don't tell me you thought Daddy had read all those things" (3), further reinforces this bankruptcy. Just as reading the wrong books can spread ignorance, *not* reading at all can hinder intellectual and moral development. Much like the row of Charles Bovary's medical tomes in Flaubert's *Madame Bovary*, the books in Toland's house were meant to convey respectability, authority, and knowledge. And just as the uncut pages of Charles's medical library demonstrate his ignorance, the unread books in *SRB* symbolize his father's ignorance. Together, these twin panels, positioned early in the novel, reveal the importance of print culture in the novel. They suggest the problems of reading at this time in the South: Many of the books written by Southerners for Southern consumption served to perpetuate the racial divides. And illiteracy, as Toland's father shows, was another factor holding back the intellectual and moral development of the civil rights era South.

9. What Anne Marie Barry refers to as a "Gestalt" form (113) and what Scott McCloud labels "closure" (63).

10. See James Zander (396) and Rutlege Dennis (244–247) for brief discussions of Social Darwinism's role in Southern racism.

11. For Cruse, the civil rights movement carries both racial and sexual meaning. He sees the movement toward racial parity as a "parallel narrative" to gay rights (Keller).

12. Orley's proto-Archie Bunker status is also illustrated (literally) by print culture. He's pictured

reading a *True Stories* type magazine with "I Rode in a U.F.O." as a headline (20) and writes a letter to the editor of the *Clayfield Banner* (fictional mainstream newspaper) protesting the black boycott of local businesses (21–22).

13. The autobiographical nature of this is seen from Cruse's report that, as a child, he drew inspiration from Twain's *Mysterious Stranger* which "propelled me headlong into a life-changing 'crisis of faith' when I read it" ("RE: Questions").

14. See John M. Giggie's "The Third Great Awakening: Religion and the Civil Rights Movement" (257) for a succinct overview of, as his title notes, religion and civil rights.

15. Consider as well the "white preacher" Toland hears on the radio: "O Lord, help us know that thou art a Prince of Peace, not Strife ... and that Thou dost not protest noisily in the street, but rather whispereth sweet psalms of salvation in the heart" (55), a not-so-subtle reference to economic boycotts, a staple of the civil rights movement. And for a historical view on religion and miscegenation, consider the following passage from Brady's *Black Monday*: "the loveliest and purest of God's creatures, the nearest thing to an angelic being that treads this terrestrial ball is a well-bred, cultured white woman or her blue-eyed, golden-haired little girl" (45).

16. Cruse's exploration of homosexuality fits broader trends in mainstream comics; the later 1980s and early 1990s featured a rise in openly homosexual characters (Franklin 222).

17. The "begins" is crucial here. As a realistic novel set in the 1960s, Cruse does not chart a clear path to Toland's embrace of his homosexuality: His "Baby" of the title and his love for Ginger suggests his struggle with sexuality did not lend itself to clear boundaries.

18. A text by another cultural touchstone, Nathaniel Hawthorne, echoes an earlier time of repression in America. After attending the funeral of the girls killed in the church bombing, Ginger expresses her disgust at the inane comments of students in the college cafeteria who are oblivious to the suffering of their neighbors by throwing a collection of *Hawthorne's Tales* across the room. Just as Hawthorne's Puritan tales were meant to provoke readers with dark visions of secrets nestled in the bosoms of supposedly pious people, the reaction shots of students following the book's tumbling passage through a series of eight panels, illustrates the literal power of a book — in this case when used a projectile — to disturb and provoke. This seemingly minor incident gains power from its placement in the narrative, occurring right before she is impregnated by Toland (117). Both Ginger and Hester Prynne, Hawthorne's most famous heroine, find themselves pregnant without a husband and facing cultural ostracization; however Ginger, unlike Hester, decides to give up her baby for adoption. While Ginger is "free" to live her life, hundreds of years after Hester and Pearl, the novel makes clear that pregnancy can still carry a stigma.

19. The same issue contains a report titled "The Klan Scourges Old St. Augustine," detailing the infiltration of local law enforcement by the Klan. It describes a demonstration similar to the Russell Park protest in *SRB*: "Between the mob and its targets — the marchers — stood only the crew commanded by Sheriff Davis[....] The demonstrators — dedicated to the principles of nonviolence — were set upon by the waiting whites. They were slugged and stomped, arose to be attacked and fall again, while the sheriff's men stood by and watched" (McMillan 21).

20. This is another autobiographical connection between Toland and Cruse. Recalling his childhood, Cruse writes that "Since we didn't own a television until I was eight, I established a reading habit early and life in a rural southern town provided plenty of time to fill" ("Re: Questions").

Works Cited

Barry, Ann Marie Seward. *Visual Intelligence: Perception, Image, and Manipulation in Visual Communication.* Albany: State University of New York Press, 1997. Print.

Bechdel, Alison. *Fun House.* Boston: Mariner, 2007. Print.

Black, Isabella. "Race and Unreason: Anti-Negro Opinion in Professional and Scientific Literature Since 1954." *Phylon* 26 (1965): 65–79. Print.

Brady, Tom P. *Black Monday.* Winona: Association of Citizens' Councils of Mississippi, 1955. Print.

Buhle, Paul. "History and Comics." *Reviews in American History* 35 (2007): 315–323. Print.

Chopin, Kate. *The Awakening.* New York: Norton, 1994. Print.

Chute, Hillary. "Decoding Comics." *MFS Modern Fiction Studies* 52 (Winter 2006): 1015–1027.

_____, and Marianne DeKoven. "Introduction: Graphic Narrative." *MFS Modern Fiction Studies* 52 (Winter 2006): 767–782. Print.

Clowes, Daniel. *Ghost World.* Seattle: Fantagraphics, 1998. Print.

Cruse, Howard. "Barefootz and Blood." *The Long and Winding Stuck Rubber Road.* N.p. n. pag. Web. 12 June 2007.

_____. "Re: Questions on Stuck Rubber Baby for Literary Conference and Chapter." Email from author. 5 April 2008.

_____. *Stuck Rubber Baby*. New York: Paradox, 1995. Print.

Dailey, Jane. "Sex, Segregation, and the Sacred after *Brown.*" *Journal of American History* 91 (June 2004): 119–44. Print.

Darnton, Robert. "What Is the History of Books?" *The Kiss of Lamourette: Reflections in Cultural History*. London: Faber and Faber, 1990: 107–36. Rprt. in *The Book History Reader*. Eds. David Finkelstein and Alistair McCleery. London: Routledge, 2006. 9–26. Print.

"Dead Bodies at Selma Hit the Jackpot for Rabble Rousing Preacher." *The Augusta Courier* 21 June 1965: 1+. Print.

Dennis, Rutlege M. "Social Darwinism, Scientific Racism, and the Metaphysics of Race." *The Journal of Negro Education* 64 (Summer 1995): 243–252. Print.

Eisner, Will. *Comics and Sequential Art*. New York: W.W. Norton, 2008. Print.

Franklin, Morris E. "Coming Out in Comic Books: Letter Columns, Readers, and Gay and Lesbian Characters." *Comics and Ideology*. Ed. Matthew P. McAllister, Edward H. Sewell, Jr., and Ian Gordon. New York: Peter Lang, 2006. 221–250. Print.

Geertz, Glifford. *The Interpretation of Culture*. New York: Basic, 1973. Print.

Getty, John Paul. "The Vanishing Americans." *How to Be Rich*. Chicago: Playboy, 1965. 147–157. Print.

Giggie, John M. "The Third Great Awakening: Religion and the Civil Rights Movement." *Reviews in American History* 33 (2005): 254–262. Print.

Groensteen, Thierry. *The System of Comics*. 1999. Trans. Bart Beaty and Nick Nguyen. Jackson: University Press of Mississippi, 2007. Print.

Harold, Christine, and Kevin Michael Deluca. "Behold the Corpse: Violent Images and the Case of Emmett Till." *Rhetoric and Public Affairs* 8 (2005): 263–286. Print.

Havemann, Ernest. "Scientists Search for the Answers to a Touchy and Puzzling Question: Why?" *Life*, 26 June 1964: 78–80. Print.

Hefner, Hugh. "Part I: The Playboy Philosophy." *Playboy Magazine*. December 1962. n. pag. Web. 12 June 2007.

_____. "Part III: The Playboy Philosophy." *Playboy Magazine*. February 1963. n. pag. Web. 12 June 2007.

Jackson, John P. *Science for Segregation: Race, Law, and the Case against Brown v. Board of Education*. New York: New York University Press, 2005. Print.

Keller, Katherine. "Stuck on Howard Cruse." *Sequential Tart*. N.p. n. pag. Web. 21 March 2008.

Kruper, Peter. *The System*. New York: DC Comics, 1997. Print.

McCloud, Scott. *Understanding Comics: The Invisible Art*. New York: HarperCollins, 1993. Print.

McMillan, George. "The Klan Scourges Old St. Augustine." *Life*, 26 June 1964: 21.

McMillen, Neil R. *The Citizens' Council: Organized Resistance to the Second Reconstruction 1954–64*. Urbana: University of Illinois Press, 1971. Print.

Packard, Vance. *The Status Seekers*. New York: David McKay, 1959. Print.

Putnam, Carleton. *Race and Reason: A Yankee View*. Washington, D.C.: Public Affairs, 1961. Print.

"Race Riots in U.S. Communist Plots, New Hampshire Newspaper Editor Says." *The Augusta Courier*, 10 August 1964. 1+. Print.

Red, D. B. "Race Mixing a Religious Fraud." Pamphlet. 1959. University of Southern Mississippi Digital Library. Web. 20 March 2008.

Thoreau, Henry David. *Walden*. Library of America. New York: Literary Classics of the United States, 1985. Print.

Tompkins, Jane. *Sensational Designs: The Cultural Work of American Fiction, 1790–1860*. New York: Oxford, 1985. Print.

Varnum, Robin, and Christina T. Gibbons. "Introduction." *The Language of Comics: Word and Image*. Jackson: University of Mississippi Press, 2001. ix–xix. Print.

Wadsworth, Sarah. *In the Company of Books: Literature and its "Classes" in Nineteenth-Century America*. Boston: University of Massachusetts Press, 2006. Print.

Welch, Paul. "Homosexuality in America." *Life*, 26 June 1964: 66–74. Print.

Witek, Joseph. *Comic Books as History: The Narrative Art of Jack Jackson, Art Spiegelman, and Harvey Pekar*. Jackson: University Press of Mississippi, 1989. Print.

Zanden, James W. Vander. "The Ideology of White Supremacy" *Journal of the History of Ideas* 20 (June–September 1959): 385–402. Print.

6

Iconoclastic Readings and Self-Reflexive Rebellions in Marjane Satrapi's *Persepolis* and *Persepolis 2*

PAMELA J. RADER

As Gillian Whitlock observes in "Autographics: The Seeing 'I' of the Comics," comics and sequential art in contemporary American culture are often associated "with juvenilia, and our earliest reading experiences" (967). Moreover, sequential art conjures up the section of the Sunday paper that is quickly forgotten by Monday, and serial comics have long been thought of as disposable; collectors aside, unbound narratives were consumed by minors in the backseat and were not to be taken seriously. However, as the longtime stepchildren of the subterranean literary and art worlds, comics and graphic literature, with the help of Hollywood, have emerged into mainstream culture, particularly in public libraries and in academia. From first year writing classes to women's literature courses, graphic narratives are widely adopted in university curriculum. For example, Art Spiegelman's *Maus I* and *Maus II* can be found on the shelves for a variety of history, literature, and writing classes. Continuing to reap accolades, and now a feature film, Marjane Satrapi's *Persepolis* dyad has cross-cultural and cross-gender appeal.[1] The author-artist Satrapi handles with illustrative and verbal aplomb a rendition of the real; she meshes her personal story and the history of the Iranian Cultural Revolution in Iran. In a graphic medium, Satrapi's two part graphic memoir has not only reformed the mainstream American views of comics as trite, juvenile pulp, but has also debunked our expectations for the prose autobiography.

Differently from straight prose, graphic narratives bring a fresh gust of interpretation to the story as the author-artists see it and foreground the storytelling process by rendering it visual. Fusing visual and verbal texts, the author-artist of the graphic memoir debunks expectations for the straight prose autobiography and for the picture-book as naïve or *simple*. I posit that Satrapi rebels against the conventions of serialized and sequential comics, the autobiography, and Islamic art. Like American Art Spiegelman, Canadian

Seth and Frenchman David B., Iranian-born Marjane Satrapi borrows the comic medium of fantasy for a historical and personal reality, and she breaks from the collaborative efforts of a writer, illustrator, inker, letterer in fantasy or superhero comics to author and illustrate her story. As a memoirist Satrapi does not follow the autobiographical traditions of the verbal narrative, such as the "as told to" and prose tales; rather, she adopts one crafted in words *and* drawings — a graphic narrative, or what life studies scholar Gillian Whitlock calls "autographics." Opting to create multiple personal perspectives, Marjane Satrapi self-reflexively defies a one-dimensional representation of the first person point of view, which cannot be imitated in the prose memoir or autobiography. Touching a humanist nerve, her innovative graphic trinity of selves challenges and forever alters the way we read within literary genres, cultures, and our construction of selves.

Words and Images: Simultaneous Reading

Before the alphabet and written language, early humans left behind walls and caves of pictographs and petroglyphs, narrating their experiences. As human communication and language evolved, so did a variety of readable didactic iconography to grace cathedral façades, imparting biblical stories in medieval Europe. Although we associate literacy with the printed word, we must still read images. In a *Bookslut* interview with John Zuarino, who asks why comics and not prose, Satrapi explains, "I didn't have any other way. My brain functions with images. Just the words is [sic] not enough" (Satrapi quoted in Zuarino). She further illuminates the creative process as one where the drawing and writing are "more of a simultaneous experience. [...] All of it grows at the same time" (Zuarino). The simultaneity of words and images — that Satrapi speaks of— is paramount to humans' contemporary reading experience as well. Peggy Phelan, in her article, "Lessons in Blindness from Samuel Beckett," calls attention to Beckett's bilingualism, which "allowed him to apprehend the duality of the expressive registers of the visual and the verbal with astonishing fluidity. He was both bilingual and biocular, as it were: he saw the visual as worded and he understood that the act of speaking inevitably created a pictorial image" (1285). An English-speaker who wrote in French, Beckett was clearly bilingual in the traditional sense, as is Marjane Satrapi, a Persian speaker who writes in French, yet both redefine writing by creating a signature pictorial language. Phelan aptly articulates Beckett's self-reflexive language of biocularity: "Seeing was always already a way of saying for Beckett, and so too was saying a way of seeing" (1285). Through her concept of biocularity, Phelan reminds Beckett's readers that his plays are not just about reading, but about seeing — stage design, human movement as language, and the overall performance.

Phelan's biocularity can be appropriated to make sense of an evolving imagistic world. In a global world of advertising we revise and adhere to our collective penchant for icons through our creation and recognition of logos, brands, and even celebrities. And while the world is image-laden, it requires new attention to read these images, as *PMLA* editor Marianne Hirsch argues in her column. Another reality of the twenty-first century is the virtual realities; cyberspace testifies to the global market for virtual games — such as role playing and creating personas — where players may select or design avatars that stand in for them in the gaming realm and where one can appropriate a role or avatar that is like or unlike oneself— something altogether different. Satrapi's texts ask that we re-examine icons, iconography, and avatars for the printed page, which challenges, yet abets our reading experience.

In her essay, Gillian Whitlock also reinforces the "biocularity" of the graphic narrative, which invites a more complex reading experience, fusing the otherwise bifurcation of visual image with visible captioning practices. As Phelan and Whitlock note, the notion of "text" becomes further complicated with the conjoined visual (on stage or in print) and verbal texts that collude to invite a contrapuntal reading practice. Perhaps, Phelan's notion of biocularity contributes to Satrapi's Western readers' reverent reception of this graphic narrative for adults and young readers alike: images show and assault the viewer where verbal lexicon fails. Instead of focusing on the graphic memoir as a narrative of trauma or a genre that requires a new kind of visual literacy, this author will examine further the literary and cultural complexity of self-representation in the graphic memoirs, or what Whitlock has aptly coined as "autographics," in Marjane Satrapi's *Persepolis* and *Persepolis II* by going behind the eye to the narrating "I"s.

Eyes Reading the Three "I"s

Satrapi opens *Persepolis. A Story of a Childhood* with a small frame of a solitary veiled girl with the caption, "This is me when I was 10 years old. This was in 1980" (3). However, this "me" inked by Satrapi is in effect her self-designed avatar: a self-representation. In these first two sentences, she establishes the narrative as an autobiography with an avatar and roots her story in a specific moment in time, giving it a historical context. The seminal university student discussions on *Persepolis* invariably comment upon the self-reflexive quality of the story wherein a handful of readers raise the question of the two Satrapis: the author-artist and her narrated self, a character. There is, however, a third Satrapi: the narrator. At times, for the readers, the narrating voice collapses into the point of view of the figurative character on the page, or this voice becomes synonymous with the author-artist's voice. A slippery yet independent voice, the narrator becomes a kind of liminal avatar: it does not share an illustrated body with the character-avatar, nor can it be subsumed as the author's definitive point of view.

Here, to better understand the complexity of reading images and words, we must distinguish Satrapi the author-artist from Satrapi the narrator, and Satrapi the avatar created by the author-artist and narrating avatar. A memoir author who works with prose alone can play with point of view and style, while subverting or commenting upon the natures of fiction and truth. Drawing from and embellishing on personal experiences, however, the author-artist not only self-represents in prose, but in images. She must design how she will humanize her self, or selves, on the published page. In the unique case of *Persepolis* and *Persepolis 2*, Satrapi creates a pictorial avatar that is a character in human form, a likeness of an earlier, younger self. Furthermore, she creates a narrating avatar whose mature voice and perspective require interpretation of memory and offer commentary through tone. This narrating avatar's voice so subtly steers our reading and interpretations of the pictorial avatar that we may forgetfully collapse the narrator into the younger version of the author-artist.

Biocularity: Cooperating Texts, Collaborating Avatars

The author-artist who is charged with the verbal and pictorial narratives complements and revolutionizes the traditional memoir with the illustrative vocabulary. With visual text the author need not verbally describe her young avatar's perceptions nor is the reader left to speculate or imagine the child's perceptions. For instance, we find a child caught between two worlds, the secular and religious (6). There is room, however, for speculation in the narrator's tone as she toys with her six-year old avatar's precocious self-awareness and her proclaimed seriousness. Here, the accompanying image is divided in half, as is its avatar. On the left-side, the avatar's unveiled head shares space with representations of tools evocative of engineering and technology, perhaps a pseudo-commentary on the educated, more secular Iranian population. The right half of the same cell offers a veiled head with the decorative arabesques adorning the figure, suggestive of Iran's Persian past and then current reform. Drawing a parallel to the imagination of the child and the imagination of an artist, the adult artist-author Satrapi provides a richer commentary on the revolution.

As an author-artist narrating her life story, this Satrapi can literally *and* visually represent the two worlds of an Iranian girl torn between the secular and Muslim through the eyes of the adult narrator. But this narrative complexity is heightened further by the juxtaposition of the adult's metaphorical representation of a childhood — her own — in hindsight with the adult author's representation of childhood through the eyes of a child, the avatar Marjane, and a narrator betwixt character and author. Through the narrating avatar's voice, Satrapi's text explains to the readers a source of personal conflict: the revolution forced Iranians to choose between traditional and modern beliefs. To reflect the child-Satrapi's confusion between two different ideologies, the adult author-artist Satrapi recreates — from memory — an interpretive image of the child-character, or avatar, and her conflict. Finally, within this same image, we read stark contrasts in the symbolic division between the

The divided image of the unveiled and veiled avatar presents a child caught between the secular and the religious worlds (*Persepolis* 6).

iconography of "modern and avant-garde" in the left half and veil and the religion-inspired veil associated with the Cultural Revolution in the right half. As a graphic narrator, Satrapi has the tools to illustrate her memory of the harsh reality where she felt divided by two very different worlds; when such a photograph does not exist, memory shapes how one opts to draw a representation of a conflicted child. The author-artist's memory of a childhood in Iran, the creation of the child character-avatar, and the narrator-avatar's commentary collaborate to tell a complex verbal-pictorial story infused with memories and its emotions without detracting from the memoir's realism.

Reinforcing the autographic text as a highly self-reflexive narrative, Satrapi continues to rebel against the conventions of the autobiography as a linear, singular first-person, prose genre by employing her imagination to convey realism and memory with images. Pairing a likeable, human character in her child-avatar with the dead-pan adult narrator-avatar reinforces the author-artist's awareness of an audience and calls attention to the text as such: a self-reflexive autographic story. For instance, in a good humored caption, the avatar confesses that she "was born with religion," made visible by the emanating, halo-like light around the baby's head (6). In the next frame, the caption's first sentence reads, "At the age of six I was already sure I was the last prophet," and it is accompanied by the recognizable face of the avatar Marji, but whose face is set in a hyperbolic sun-like halo, with four genuflecting, reverential disciples who call her "O'Celestial Light!"(6). Curiously, sequential art may render a character's inner thoughts quite pictorially without the verbal explanation, which requires straight prose and its manipulation of tone. Here, the disciple's cry and the avatar's matter-of-fact "I was already sure I was the last prophet" work with the image to convey both cross cultural humor and an Iranian girl's humanity. Then, the character-avatar — through the narrator — is aware of being seen as a character or actor in her life story and her country's story, who calls attention to herself as following the script created for her by the artist-author. Like a nesting doll or one of Borges's narrative labyrinths, the character-avatar as "Celestial Light" becomes something else: the author-artist's narrator creates a child-avatar character that then imagines she is a prophet — another avatar.

Conscious of herself as a character in her own narrative, Marjane the character-avatar often speaks to the reader, signaling a kind of meta-autobiographic moment. Self-reflexively, the author-artist calls attention to distinctions of written text: captions are used for the narrator-avatar's voice, and bubbles for the speaking character-avatar. For instance, explaining the war and revolution to her readers, twelve-year old Marjane raises her arm and points an authorial finger proclaiming her adulthood, she says, in a bubble for reported speech, "With this first cigarette, I kissed childhood goodbye," which is accompanied by the matter-of-fact, deadpan caption, "Now I was a grown-up" at the bottom of the frame (117). The avatar looks at and speaks directly to her readers, through our eyes, using the endearing humanizing form of a girl eager to be older and wiser; almost synchronized, the character and narrator make use of direct, public speech in the balloon and the inner thoughts of the caption, respectively. As the character-avatar contemplates her first cigarette, she, as an instrument of the author-artist, abets the readers' understanding of the revolution with images and captions of dissidents' arrests and their pending executions (117). It is the stark human images that assault the eyes and their verbal accompaniment that collude to chronicle the personal and collective history of a young Iranian person during the Cultural Revolution; the images render the reality human and the words anchor the carnage in time.

With an outward-gazing character-avatar, Satrapi's story implicates her readers; simultaneously, we read the caption, bubble, and image, and we read the avatar's attention to our presence in the act of reading. Moreover, the author-artist seems to deliberately opt for a pictorial narrative paired with captions and bubbles for the character-avatar's direct speech. Without the character's ability to speak, the story would have been told through images and captions, or solely by the narrator; to permit the created character to verbalize her thoughts or beliefs further humanizes the story. Perhaps the author-artist's images and her avatars' commentaries encourage remembering and educate people to about "the other point of view of Iran" in a "linear reading" of that time (Zuarino); Satrapi successfully, in Barthesian terms, "wounds" the viewer/reader's eyes with the harsh historical and human realities (Barthes 21). The readers are forced not to just to see Satrapi the memoirist's point of view, but another point of view of Iran. The interplay of author-avatars and words-images collaborates to tell the story of a period in Iran and attempts to portray a person named Marjane Satrapi, the author-artist. The wounding realities witnessed by an individual alter how the readers "see" a nation. In a broader scope, sequential art can be instrumental in refuting humans' ethical blindness of war and its senseless atrocities.

The Humanist: Complex Self-Portraits

THIS WAS OKAY WITH ME. I REALLY LIKED HEIDI.

In addition to the complex nexus of avatars and self-representation through imagination and memory, the autographic rendition reminds its readers that this is a "real" story of a "real" girl by making her human. Perhaps to further complicate the artist-author's duty to represent herself or selves, Satrapi elects not to show herself in an extraordinary or favorable light. In *Persepolis 2*, she reveals her humanity with her expectations for her new Tyrolean roommate to resemble the storybook Alpine heroine, Heidi: "I really liked Heidi" (1). In illustrating Heidi, Satrapi depicts a tall, solid blond girl with braids in a patterned dress and possible clogs next to the all black-clad, black haired adolescent Satrapi; here, the author-artist reveals both the narrator- and character-

The stereotyping of her Tyrolean roommate reveals the narrator-avatar's humanity and honesty (*Persepolis 2* 1).

avatars' humanity through stereotyping. While the Tyrolean Lucia is
indeed blond, she does not resemble
Heidi. Often viewed as a negative
practice, stereotyping does, however,
reveal the narrator-avatar's honesty
and humanity; the readers may also
participate in stereotyping and may
have imagined a Tyrolean girl to
resemble Heidi. And, although Iranian, Satrapi taps into and shares her
Western readers' familiarity with the
story of the mountain heroine, enabling her to build bridges across any
cultural gaps she may have had with
her audience.

The narrating avatar's perception of her adolescent transformation as a hulk-like figure emphasizes her humanity, bridging cultural gaps between the heroine and her audience (*Persepolis 2* 35).

Through stereotyping, Satrapi
creates honest, human, and credible
avatars. To convey the personality of
the precocious albeit naïve Marji, the
artist-author uses hyperbolic rendi-
tions to simultaneously convey a self-reflexive humor and imagination as when Marji
believes she is the last prophet. Joining frequent commentaries on her perceived personality
Satrapi also exhibits her self-deprecating humor with her physical self. For instance,
Perseopolis 2 discloses the author's and avatars' perceived awkward adolescent transformation which, in its first frame, compares her normal growth process to that of a hulk-like
figure bursting out of its clothes (35). The hulk-like figure, surrounded by highly-charged
squiggly lines, communicates and serves as a kind of Kafkaesque metaphor: the narrating
character — still a creation of the artist-author — perceives this "physical metamorphosis"
as her adolescent reality (35). Like Kafka's Gregor Samsa, she becomes the metaphor: a
monstrous figure. In the subsequent frames, she draws her metamorphosis step by step.
In a head shot, with a longer face, and one enlarged eye, the caption reads, "Then my
right eye grew," leaving the left eye disproportionately smaller, and in a new frame, "followed swiftly by my chin which doubled in length" (35). When the chin has grown, we
note that at least both eyes have reached the same size. And the catalog of transformations
continues to incite humor through the artist-author's cartooning as caricature; this schism
between the real, gradual physical changes into an adult and the self's alleged grotesque
hulk-like persona reveal the narrating avatar's self-perception as a hyperbolically awkward
self as seen through its body. Moreover, the author-artist uses the graphic medium to
illustrate her self-consciousness about her appearance at this stage; drawing on universal
experiences, Satrapi connects again to her audience, emphasizing her human-ness or
humanity. While the author-artist has already won over her readers with her endearing,
imaginative and outspoken child-avatar in *Persepolis*, her maturing adolescent-avatar in
Persepolis 2 becomes more human, growing up and making difficult choices.

An example of the maturing avatar's narrating candor shifts its focus to ethics. In one such incident the character-avatar fears arrest when she and her boyfriend Reza have arranged to meet outside a bazaar. Spotting a car full of guardians of the revolution, she fears that they will arrest her for wearing lipstick, but, to thwart a possible arrest, she devises a scheme. A guard is called over and says, "Yes my sister!" to which Marjane responds, "There is a guy who said something indecent to me" (131). The man, an innocent bystander, is arrested because she compromises his safety to procure her own wellbeing; her feigned honor distracts the guards from her personal choice to wear the verboten lipstick. Such a scene could easily be omitted when one is one's own biographer, but perhaps Satrapi includes the scene to highlight her narrator and character avatars' human flaws — as well as her own — and to underscore the social political climate influencing her choices and actions. As a result of these numerous self-reflexive instances, the narrator- and character-avatars gain the readers' trust when they refuse to self-censor such memories in order to tell the larger national story.

Satrapi consistently constructs this biocular composition of "wounding" the viewer-reader with pictorially rendered historical realities, conveying a complex portrait of selves. Entwining seemingly conflicted practices of stereotyping and opportunism, Satrapi's text enunciates a humanizing tendency to tell the truth, which she reinforces in an interview: "I am a humanist. I believe in human beings" (Satrapi quoted in Tully). As a humanist telling a human story, the author-artist commits the rebellious act of drawing the human form to tell a personal and national story of the Cultural Revolution. The author-artist defies the religious regime, when she exercises her secular rights to render the otherwise verboten human form in graphic form, as visual art. While the graphic realism of suffering or morally conflicted human forms may be what wounds readers, these drawn forms allow the readers to read or see the humanity in Iranians needed for empathy and for healing.

Innocence Lost, Innocence Retained

While human likeness is found in the sculpture of ancient Greek deities and the iconography of medieval Europe's cathedrals, these stone texts served as a didactic narrative tool, passing on to the illiterate polytheist mythologies and teachings of the Church, respectively. Furthermore, the age-old, cross-cultural practice of propaganda manipulates the combination of text and images to impart value systems. Allusions to Christian iconography and to markers of Islam, Satrapi's text uses icons to humanize, not deify or lampoon, her representations of martyrs, a mullah, and veiled Iranian women. Aside from her appropriation of Catholicism's Pièta, her figures do achieve a kind of iconographic status that resists stereotyping; as Whitlock points out the familiar Pièta image becomes a rebellious icon of compassion in the context of the Iranian Cultural Revolution.[2] Satrapi's use of images and icons act as poignant testaments to the impact of war, revolution, and their figureheads on a child.

In a section of *Persepolis* called "The Heroes," two political prisoners, friends of the family, are released from prison and share their experiences with Marji's parents who forget to send her out of the room. Mr. Satrapi's avatar asks if the men have any news of

The mise-en-page reconfigures the clothes iron, an icon of domesticity, as a dehumanizing emblem of the Revolution (*Persepolis* 51).

Ahmadi. In the middle of the page, un-framed, the narrating self reveals the avatar's inner impressions of Ahmadi's torture and death; in three drawings he is shown genuflect with a bleeding back onto which his torturer urinates, strapped to a cot and whipped, and finally branded with a domestic iron. In a long, narrow horizontal frame at the bottom of the page, a caption reveals the avatar's harsh realization, "I never imagined that you could use that appliance for torture" (51). While this elongated horizontal panel appears to be divided into three sequential panels because the stark black and white contrasts move the eye from left to right, it also bears the psychic weight of the borderless renditions of Ahmadi's torture. Through the page layout, or what Jesse Cohn calls the mise-en-page, the familiar household appliance becomes tainted for young Marjane. No longer an item that simply presses clothes, the iron and its function have been perverted by the torturers as an instrument of violence. An icon of domesticity becomes reconfigured as a dehumanizing emblem of the Revolution.

Moreover, the author-artist discloses illustratively that even a child sees — albeit literally — war and execution as butchery — with Ahmadi's body chopped into parts (52). This child-like depiction of a neatly dismembered body imparts both the narrator- and character avatars' sensibility of dogma's inhumanity and indifference to human life; in the eyes or rather the imagination of a child, dismemberment becomes akin to a disassembled doll; the imaginatively dismembered Ahmadi somehow resembles a puppet. Ironically, this attendant innocence offers a visual testament of the child's lost and lingering innocence: she has been made aware of torture, while her imaginings of torture remain rather neat and clean. Here, the child's imagination, without seeing firsthand, omits the reality of wounds and dismemberment because it retains its youthful naiveté, distinguishing it from what the adult imagination knows; Satrapi the artist-author chooses to illustrate that paradox of innocence-lost and innocence-retained. Finally, for the readers, torture and violence have been humanized by the visual text through the child's eyes and through the remembrance of Ahmadi's experience.

Iconographic Rebellions

Religious figures have long been vulnerable to stereotyping, pastiche, and often been reduced to stock characters. Instead of coasting on a bandwagon of secular distaste for Iran's religious leaders, Satrapi offers a glimpse at religion through spirituality. The author-artist thwarts her western readers' attendant anticipation for a fundamentalist mullah; instead she reports a conversation about the veil and prayer between two people in the designated bubbles for speech, without the commentary provided by the narrator's captions. In *Persepolis 2*, Satrapi the student, now back in Iran and seeking admittance to an art program, must pass an ideological test administered by a mullah who, in the cells, remains a faceless, bespectacled silhouette: a black form outlined in white (130). He does not test her on the Koran, but asks her about her veil and prayer practice; when he asks the veiled Marjane if she knows how to pray, she responds negatively, and explains, "Like all Iranians, I don't understand Arabic. If praying is talking to God, I prefer to do it in a language that I know. I believe in God, but I speak to him in Persian" (130). The mullah dismisses her shortly after she cites the prophet Mohammed, and concludes by seeking affirmation, "God is always with us. He is in us! Right?" (130). Conducted in bubbles without any commentary in captions, this exchange could have cost Marjane her admission into the art program. Contrary to stereotyping all religious leaders as fundamentalists who seek regurgitation of holy texts or their interpretations of those texts, Marjane's depiction of a religious leader gives him a physical presence in her figurative drawing. Where his dark, anonymous iconographic form could have reinforced a stereotype (i.e. he wears a turban and spectacles), it gives weight and credence to his humanity and individuality. Satrapi the artist-author reveals how the mullah debunks her own, or her avatars' (character's and narrator's) expectations and her readers' for not reinforcing the stereotype of a religious man.

Again, known for its abstract ornamentation, Islamic art does not subscribe to representation of the human form. However, Satrapi, once an art student now an autographer, rebels against the then current regime with her figurative art in which she shows the veil as a cultural reality that detracts from individuality and effects an abstraction: women can be perceived as abstract black shapes. So the veil and its covering function are the topic of many frames in Satrapi's two-part memoir. On the first page of *Persepolis*, we are playfully told that the second frame is "a class photo" in which four veiled classmates are shown. Reminiscent of French surrealist painter René Magritte's "Ceci n'est pas une pipe,"[3] the narrator tells us with verbal authority that this is a class photograph, but it is not; she uses a drawing to embed the said-photograph into a hand drawn image-text. While the very first image or frame in the book is the avatar of

The mullah's stereotypical image is countered by his acceptance of the narrator-avatar's responses, lending credence to his humanity and individuality (*Persepolis 2* 130).

AND THIS IS A CLASS PHOTO. I'M SITTING ON THE FAR LEFT SO YOU DON'T SEE ME. FROM LEFT TO RIGHT: GOLNAZ, MAHSHID, NARINE, MINNA.

While the veil has the ability to conceal, in Satrapi's drawing of the class photograph she does not render the girls anonymous but individualizes them, rendering her interpretation of each girl's distinctive features (*Persepolis* 3).

young Marjane, the author-artist deliberately cuts her avatar from the class photograph, leaving only a glimpse of her fingers and elbow. Arch, yet sincere, the author-artist inks a representation of that familiar grade school class photograph (3). From left to right the girls are illustrated with distinguishing features in mind: Golnaz with a forehead covered in thick fringes; Mahshid with curlier bangs and closed lash-ladden lids; Narine's bangs create an upside-down V while looking a little cross-eyed; and Minna's bangs reveal arched brows and a mouth that is not down-turned like the others. Illustration, unlike photographs, could arguably serve as an individualized tool for interpretation: the artist as individual must recall and render her interpretation of each girl's distinctive features. While the veil has the ability to conceal, in Satrapi's drawings, she does not render the girls anonymous, but individualizes them. Finally, the veiling of the pictorial — the photograph for the drawing — occurs through verbal narration, reminding the readers of their required participation to read words and pictures simultaneously of their biocularity.

Furthermore, in *Persepolis 2*, Marjane the narrating-avatar describes her university peers' individuality as a text that can be read — if one knows how to read. For example, in a large frame, three young women are depicted twice; from left to right, their veiled heads and covered bodies are accompanied by an interpretive drawing, as if with X-rays, of what the chador and veil conceal (140). While common in super-hero comics, neither the artist-author nor the narrator have X-ray vision, the narrative does seek to show the simultaneity of the young women's stipulated sameness (by the regime) and their hidden

WITH PRACTICE, EVEN THOUGH THEY WERE COVERED FROM HEAD TO FOOT, YOU GOT TO THE POINT WHERE YOU COULD GUESS THEIR SHAPE, THE WAY THEY WORE THEIR HAIR AND EVEN THEIR POLITICAL OPINIONS. OBVIOUSLY, THE MORE A WOMAN SHOWED, THE MORE PROGRESSIVE AND MODERN SHE WAS.

Marjane the narrating avatar describes the individuality concealed by the chador and veil as a text that can be read — if one knows how to read (*Persepolis 2* 140).

sense of self or individualism. Under the exterior covering, one distinguishes the individualized hairstyles and body shapes. The use of the supernatural X-ray is at once self-reflexive as graphic narrative/memoir and as the genre's tool to show how the author-illustrator liberates both the memoir and Iranian women from their assumed conventions. Like Satrapi's autographic text, Iranian women find ways to subvert and rebel against conventions. Comics and now autographics can suspend another kind of disbelief that straight prose cannot; the subversive graphic narrative can simultaneously reveal and conceal what rebellious individualism lies under the headscarf and the black drapery of the chador. Although the self-reflective nature of graphic memoirs has been established, it is arguably further complicated by the cultural milieus it crosses. Drawing human, particularly female, forms Satrapi the secular artist defies the traditionalist regime of Iran, while the narrator-avatar's caption emphasizes hidden subjectivity and rejects objectification of the female form.

Seeds of Secularism: Illustration and Education as Acts of Rebellion

Schooled in the history of Palestine and western thought, the young avatar reads avidly before becoming an artist who draws human forms. She comes from a modern and avant-garde family, which points to their secular interests. The seeds for these pictorial and autobiographic rebellions are sown in Satrapi's youth, as her avatar explains. In *Persepolis*, Satrapi's young avatar, seated on a stool and surrounded by towers of stacked books, illuminates her parents' occidental tendencies in their choice of literature when she speaks in the balloons reserved for direct speech and for the readers, "To enlighten me they bought books" (12). In the subsequent frame, the young Marjane states that she "knew *everything* about the children of Palestine" in caption format (emphasis added, 12). Although wise for her years, her avatar's boast even seems a bit innocent. She then catalogues her reading list and testifies to the early impressions of Karl Marx when she states: "But my favorite was a *comic book* entitled 'Dialectic Materialism'" (emphasis added, 12). Reading historical accounts about people and events outside of Iran not only demonstrates her parents' bibliographic consent, but further underscores their secular tendency and their loss of that autodidactic freedom under the government of Islamic fundamentalists. The avatar Marjane even suggests that, in her rapidly changing country, her favorite reading was both a secular philosophical text and a comic book wherein Marx's material reality debunks Descartes' logic; under the more secular Shah, Marjane would have had access to the ideologies of the "West" embodied in their philosophers and the figurative lay comic medium. Furthermore, to dispel the boast in the earlier cell, the narrator-avatar admits that the character reads an abridged graphic summary of Marx's seminal text. Here, the author-artist and narrating-avatar collude to subvert the simplicity or triteness of comics: graphic texts have the power to educate their readers.

Satrapi the author-artist creates a deliberate, non-speculative visual vocabulary when she renders her comparative drawings of God — whom she names so and not Allah — and Karl Marx. Her basis for Marx's physiognomy stems from the "Dialectic Materialism" comic, showing him bearded with curlier hair: "It was funny to see how much Marx and God looked like each other. Though Marx's hair was a bit curlier" (13). The seemingly naïve yet subversive comparison illustrates the elevated status of both God and Marx, through a child's eyes, specifically through the narrator-avatar's eyes.

Through the subversive comparison of God and Marx, the author-artist and narrating-avatar collude to subvert the simplicity of comics, evidencing that graphic texts have the power to educate their readers (*Persepolis* 13).

Early on in *Persepolis* then the avatar underscores her cultural otherness on several levels: she reveals that her art trumps traditional Islamic notions of art as strictly ornamental and non-figurative. Moreover, the autobiographical avatar represents a likeness of herself—a sometimes veiled female form in a visual context. Perhaps a revolutionary aspect of this story in particular is the pictorial rendering of a young Iranian girl in Iran at the time of the Cultural Revolution and that young avatar's development into a young Iranian woman living abroad in exile in *Persepolis 2*. However, the author-artist's role is not simply twofold — fusing drawings and words — but further complicated by languages. Co-reading the image-text with the verbal-texts (captions and bubbles) not only demands reader participation, but a synthesis of story; verbal text also brings to mind the language in which *Persepolis* and *Persepolis 2* were written: French. A polyglot, Satrapi's mother tongue is Persian, and her adopted literary tongue French. Not only does the artist-author demonstrate narrative agility in verbal and iconographic texts, but in the translation of her texts. Like playwright Samuel Beckett, Satrapi writes in French, and she works within two types of languages — Persian and French — and images and words. Perhaps the pictorial and the worded texts harken back to what Satrapi called their simultaneity for an achieved verisimilitude.

Iconoclastic Readings

While drawings may not require translation, Satrapi wrote the dyad in French published by L'Association, and remarked that "in any translation you lose a little bit" (Satrapi quoted in Tully). Nevertheless, she carries her narration with a verve for cross cultural, translatable humor, making the reader forget the transgressive acts of employing figurative art to narrate an increasingly Islamic Iran and of embedding avatars to show and tell her story. Perhaps the success of the *Persepolis* narratives in the classroom and in bookstores lies in their humanity: Satrapi the artist-author creates a complex, ever-evolving character avatar and multifaceted narrator avatars with which readers can identify or for which they feel compassion despite cultural differences, while enacting an artistic rebellion of her own in figurative drawings frowned upon in Islamic art. Even if allusions reveal a gratitude for diverse secular aspects of U.S. and European cultures, the visual-verbal narrative touches upon another unspoken paradox. The unifying experience of feeling Marji's humanity is predicated on the notion that Marji the character-avatar appears the same to each reader — she cannot be visually imagined otherwise, and her reported thoughts are even interpreted for us, such as the literalness of the torture and martyrdom scenes in *Persepolis* (45; 115). Satrapi the autographer, to reinforce and embrace Whitlock's neologism, controls not only how her avatars will represent her, but that her character — and narrator-avatars serve as emissaries of how her readers may conflate the character and narrator with the author, thus readily embracing her complex selves for an endearing, singular Marjane.

Notes

1. In 2007, the motion picture was released, and Pantheon issued *The Complete Persepolis*.
2. Gillian Whitlock reads Satrapi's two renditions of La Pièta —first in *Persepolis* and then in *Persepolis*

2; Whitlock notes importantly "that the tendency to glorify martyrdom and suffering in propaganda is not peculiarly Iranian or Muslim" (976).

3. Magritte's text and icon translate as if to say, this is not a pipe, but a painting or a representation of a pipe.

Works Cited

Barthes, Roland. *Camera Lucida: Reflections on Photography*. Trans. Richard Howard. New York: Hill, 1981. Print.

Cohn, Jesse. "Mise-en-Page: A Vocabulary for Page Layouts." *Teaching the Graphic Novel*. Ed. Stephen E. Tabachnick. New York: Modern Language Association, 2009. 44–57. Print.

Hirsch, Marianne. "Editor's Column: Collateral Damage." *PMLA* 119 (2004): 1209–15. Print.

Phelan, Peggy. "Lessons in Blindness from Samuel Beckett." *PMLA* 119 (2004): 1279–87. Print.

Satrapi, Marjane. *Persepolis: The Story of a Childhood*. Trans. Mattias Ripa and Blake Ferris. New York: Pantheon, 2003. Print.

_____. *Persepolis 2. The Story of a Return*. Trans. Anjali Signh. New York: Pantheon, 2004. Print.

Tully, Annie. "An Interview with Marjane Satrapi." *Bookslut*, October 2004. Web. 24 July 2007.

Whitlock, Gillian. "Autographics: The Seeing "I" of the Comics." *Modern Fiction Studies* 52.4 (2006): 965–979. Print.

Zuarino, John. "An Interview with Marjane Satrapi." *Bookslut*, November 2006. Web. 24 July 2007.

7

Drawing the Trauma of Race: Choices and Crises of Representation in Art Spiegelman's *Maus*

Luminita Dragulescu

For approximately three decades critics have crossed their intellectual swords over the relevance and ethics of bestial representation in *Maus*; a cat and mouse comic book rendition of the Holocaust was bound to create controversy. Art Spiegelman's choices of representation regarding the genre, medium, and artistic view to convey one of the most scrutinized human catastrophes continue to galvanize readers' and critics' response. Western culture has become cautious of animal signifiers for various ethnic and racial groups after learning about the subhuman treatment generated by racism and xenophobia to which these groups were subjected during World War II. So why did Spiegelman choose to depict his characters as anthropomorphic animals or as humans with animal-faced masks in his drawings and in particular, to represent the most victimized group as vermin, as mice? The inquiry extends beyond the mere thematic requirement of *Funny Animals* (1972), the "comix" anthology to which Spiegelman was invited to contribute.[1] *Funny Animals* merely provided the occasion to transmit the inter-generational burden of the Holocaust trauma through a genre that, though at odds with tragedy, has the invaluable potential of the non-verbal account. In effect, Spiegelman does not only break taboos of the ethics of representation in regards to Holocaust and is altogether inconsistent in his choices, but he also rethinks the possibilities offered by the graphic art to accommodate non-fictional narratives and address a whole new audience. Moreover, graphic art makes available exceptional choices of representations which I deem relevant for the politics of (racial) identity difference that were generative of the Holocaust trauma in the first place.

For trauma studies, for which "unspeakable" and "unrepresentable" are key words, as well as for race theories, where the unreliability of visual markers are notorious, Spiegelman's graphic art points towards both the possibilities and also the limits of illustrating race and trauma. In his attempt to represent "the unrepresentable" of trauma through a medium commonly meant to entertain if not to amuse, Spiegelman resorts to a genre that both simplifies and also complicates the narrative(s).[2] The graphic art of *Maus* offers prolific grounds for both discursive and iconic modes of representation. Where the verbal account is reduced to un-dramatized conversation, the carefully detailed panels construct complex signifiers. While representing the Holocaust through comics may appear idiosyncratic, Spiegelman combines the metaphorical pictorials with the verbal, conversational record to draw human emotion, memory, and history related to one of the biggest catastrophes of the twentieth century.

The choice of depicting a Holocaust survivor's story with animal or zoomorphic characters serves Spiegelman's strategy to represent difference, be it ethnic, racial, or national. This choice of representing the people involved in the Holocaust as well as those populating the postwar world of Art Spiegelman as anthropomorphic animals or animal-masked humans caricaturizes, as I will demonstrate, the very foundation of the Nazi ideology which triggered the Jewish people's trauma, the extreme intolerance towards the racial and ethnic Other, veiled as scientifically (biologically) founded theories. Ideologically consistent with the period that the Holocaust survivors recall and that arguably constitutes the main timeframe of the book, characters are portrayed to fit the biologically justified theories of racial difference which scientists endorsed until after the end of World War II. Spiegelman ridicules these theories' absurdity through his choices of representation in *Maus*. The irrational Nazi ideology, which generated the Jewish trauma and triggered Spiegelman's own trauma, constitutes the bitter fountain from which Spiegelman draws (in both senses) his indictment of racism and xenophobia.

With stories that spread out as comic strips, *Maus* unfolds an allegory of familial and cultural catastrophes that are representative of the ghosts of traumatic memory which haunt the survivors of the Holocaust and their descendents.[3] Spiegelman brings together the time frame of his father's Holocaust testimony and the very time of the artistic creation of *Maus*. The two time frames are superimposed at times in an effort to reveal the identification of the descendant with his ancestors through what Marianne Hirsch describes as "postmemory." The artist is also a character, a protagonist no less, Artie, who wants to find answers for his mother's suicide, which threw him into depression, and to learn about his parents' harrowing history. Markedly, the trauma of the Spiegelmans, accounted for through Vladek's recollection of the Holocaust, is inseparable from the communal trauma of the Jewish people during the Nazi era in Europe and inevitably appears to be the source of Artie's personal trauma.

With such strong emphasis on illustrating trauma in its individual and cultural varieties, it is not surprising that virtually every critical reading of *Maus* takes a position in regards to the work's representation of the Holocaust. The field of trauma studies has faced since its inception the challenge of representing the experience and apprehension of human tragedy in narratives of both individual and communal trauma. Representation, as a crucial locus of intersection between past and present, memory and testimony, witness and hearer, patient and clinician, has become the key term that resonates through the field's difficulties and possibilities. Some theorists consider trauma, more often than not, "unrepresentable," yet others argue that trauma in fact can be conveyed to certain extent through a process that relies equally on the narrator as much as on the hearer of the traumatic event (who can act also as an observer of the manifestations of trauma).[4] Emphasizing the role of the hearer in "the testimony to the trauma," particularly the Holocaust trauma, psychiatrist Dori Laub characterizes that individual as "the blank screen on which the event comes to be inscribed for the first time" (57). As both the hearer of his father's testimony and the narrator of his father's trauma (and his own), in the two volumes of *Maus: A Survivor's Tale, My Father Bleeds History* and *And Here My Troubles Began* (1973, 1983), Art Spiegelman chooses to draw as well as discursively write (on) this blank slate. As a result, *Maus* conveys different — yet contingent — narratives of traumatic remembrance. By employing a narrative which is as much pictorial as verbal, as historian Hayden White emphasizes, *Maus* raises "all of the crucial issues regarding the 'crisis of representation' in general" (42). As readers, we must grasp the (historical) narrative not only as discovery, finding of the past, but as an invention/creation as well.

The question of the ethics of representation in what regards history, trauma and race, is unavoidable in any analysis of *Maus*, as Marianne Hirsch observes, because "[c]omics in relation to such events as the Holocaust and 9/11 is bound to be extremely provocative," explaining that "the important thing about the medium [...] is precisely that it forces you to foreground the question of representation" ("Intimacy" 15). In fact, Spiegelman himself expresses concerns pertaining to the reception of his art: "One of the problems is that the word comics itself brings to mind the notion that they have to be funny.... I prefer the word co-mix, to mix together, because to talk about comics is to talk about mixing together words and picture that tell as story" (*Comix* 74). Many critics enthusiastically welcomed the graphic art's potential for historical representation. Hayden White characterizes *Maus* as a "masterpiece of stylization, figuration, and allegorization" and a "critically self-conscious" contribution to the debates around Holocaust representation (41–2). Michael Rothberg asserts that "[b]y situating a nonfictional story in a highly mediated, unreal, 'comic' space, Spiegelman captures the hyperintensity of Auschwitz" (206). For James E. Young, Spiegelman's "comix" displays superior possibilities of representation, because "unlike a more linear historical narrative, the 'comix-ture' of words and images generates a triangulation of meaning — a kind of three-dimensional narrative — in the movement among words, images, and the reader's eye" (18). Nevertheless, as a genre, as Marc Singer warns, "[c]omics rely upon visually codified representations in which characters are continually reduced to their appearances" (107). By signifying the volatile concepts as race and racial difference through visual representation alone, the artist exposes the instability, hence the relevance, of such constructions in the first place.

To the already overwhelming challenge of representing not only the Holocaust's traumatic events but their consequences on individuals and communities, Spiegelman adds the challenge of self-representation. The author admits that ultimately, "*Maus* is not what happened in the past, but rather what the son understands of the father's story.... It is an autobiographical history of my relationship with my father, a survivor of the Nazi death camps, cast with cartoon animals" (*Comix* 61). Furthermore, *Maus* is not only how the son understands and depicts his father's story, but how the father himself remembers and chooses to share it. Thus, the story functions more as a signifier of personal trauma rather than restorative history. *Maus* depicts a masked history that reveals through symbols. We do not see faces, but we understand and "see" the story.

If indeed, as a form of self-promotion and under the impulse of the desire for recognition, autobiography tends to defend and beautify one's character and to dramatize one's life experiences, Art Spiegelman's self-representation and his meta-commentary on his conflicted rapport with his father's recollections display remarkable effort to be neither apologetic nor defensive. In fact, both Vladek and Art exclude self-representation as an *apologia pro vita sua*. Spiegelman vies for historical accuracy when interviewing his father, although, as critic Timothy Dow Adams notes, autobiography is "the story of an attempt to reconcile one's life with one's biography … not … meant to be taken as historically accurate but as metaphorically authentic" (ix). Testifying to his efforts to reconcile life and biography, Spiegelman obsessively reports on his self-conscious efforts to make the best choices of representation and his concerns with the inevitable representational crises. Much like the curtailed story that the father *allows* himself to share with Art (and far less with the world via his son's art), Artie's (Spiegelman's narrative persona) drawings show bits and pieces of mixed temporal frames, meta-commentary, and the few physical remnants (photographs) of a catastrophic past. It is this curtailing however, together with the omissions, the silence, and the lost (or discarded) documents, that is characteristic of the problematic representation and interpretation of trauma.

As a listener to Vladek's story, Artie's project is not merely to record the story, but to represent it to the best of *his* artistic abilities. Since representation is always already interpretation, we must acknowledge that ultimately it is Artie's pen that draws the "truth," a "truth" which has been already shaped by his father. This is a caveat that the book suggests time and again, with every meta-commentary of Artie's toil and doubt of how to best illustrate his story. For one thing, Artie is continually mediating between his role as a listener and as a(n) (auto)biographer. James E. Young envisions this mediation as osmosis: "Artie is not just a shaper of testimony during its telling, or after in his drawings, but an integral part of its very genesis, part of his raison d'être. By making this telling and receiving the subject of *Maus* Spiegelman acknowledges multiple levels of creativity and knowledge-making in the telling and his subsequent drawing" (24). The complicated relation that the author has with his subject, his father, echoes in how he records the story and its making. A listener to a trauma victim's account, as Dori Laub notes, "must *listen to and hear the silence*, speaking mutely both in silence and in speech, both from behind and from the speech" (58, author's emphasis). From this perspective, Artie appears to struggle to connect with his father's story, to make sense of it, and all the while he needs to protect himself from "borrowing" it, from identifying with it, thus making it his own. Laub's ruminations on the role of the listener gesture towards Artie's dual position when she cautions: "the listener … has to be at the same time a witness to the trauma witness and a witness to himself" (58). Spiegelman repeatedly communicates the thorny position he assumes as a listener and his torment in the process, the struggle to order and clarify his father's account, the frustration with the prominent absence of his mother's testimony, and the anger at discovering that his mother's testimony (addressed to him in her journals) was intentionally destroyed by Vladek.

A second generation descendant of Holocaust survivors, Spiegelman has inevitably appropriated what Marianne Hirsch calls "postmemory," a concept that, not surprisingly, the theorist coined in relation to *Maus*, and which "characterizes the experience of those who grow up dominated by narratives that precede their birth, whose own belated stories are evacuated by the stories of the previous generation shaped by traumatic events that can be neither understood nor recreated" (*Family Frames* 22).[5] Spiegelman depicts his persona as experiencing this specific memory that transcends mere verbal communication or even direct contact between Holocaust survivors (and victims) and their inheritors, but which impacts the second (and likely the following) generation(s). Hirsch clarifies in a later text that postmemory "is a question of adopting the traumatic experiences — and thus also the memories — of others as one's own, or, more precisely, as experiences one might oneself have had, and of inscribing them into one's own life story" ("Projected Memory" 9). Artie's involvement with Vladek's testimony makes postmemory almost palpable, a fact illustrated by the piles of cartoon corpses that surround Artie in his moments of emotional connection with the memory of the Holocaust that he resurfaces. Artie's project inseparably ties, as I mentioned earlier, the traumatic history of the Spiegelmans with the communal trauma of the peoples whom the Nazis undertook to exterminate. The artist's effort to present the survivor(s) stories and his emotional investment with the narrative osmotically links the past with the present, memory with postmemory. The memories that Vladek and Mala share with Artie permeate his postmemory and results in Artie's uncanny appropriation of his parents' harrowing past. The flies that infest the corpses of the Auschwitz camp buzz around Artie and the smoke of his omnipresent cigarette blends with that from the crematoriums' chimneys. The bodies of four Jewish girls, whom Vladek recalls were "good friends of Anja's" hanged in the Nazi-occupied Poland, materialize dangling from trees in the Catskills as Artie drives his wife and his father to the supermarket in the late 70s (*Maus II* 79). On the inside cover of the book, powerful markers of postmemory, the armed and uniformed anthropomorphic cats that guarded Auschwitz, are depicted outside the artist's New York studio, as Artie, mouse-masked, is working at his easel. The scene has multi dimensional depth and echoes Marianne Hirsch's conception of "not individual, but cultural memory," since it "reveals memory to be an act of the *present* on the part of the subject who constitutes [himself] by means of a series of identifications across temporal, spatial, and cultural divides" (6). In the same vein, the frames that superimpose past and present in images and make them coexist for Artie embody postmemory. Spiegelman crams certain markers of the past, such as "the camp tattoo, prewar photographs" and "Artie Spiegelman himself, framed by his father's body, his parents' postwar child, born in Sweden after the couple lost their first son to the Nazis," as Hillary Chute notes in her analysis of history representation in *Maus* (205).

Postmemory, which is fundamentally traumatic transference, does not necessarily claim accuracy. The reverberations of the past are more emotional than rational and post-memory is more empathetic than precise. In contrast, survivors of catastrophes such as the Holocaust, struggled to restore and "work through" the events they lived although trauma notoriously eludes exactness. Representing trauma confronts both the witness and the listener with the limitations and crises of apprehension and expression. With regard to the possibility of narrating trauma, Dori Laub asserts that trauma is defined by the gaps of knowledge of the traumatic event or instance, since "hardly anything of all gets explicitly said in words." Cathy Caruth shares the same position, yet a problematic one in the face of so many representations and memoirs of the Holocaust survivors. Trauma theorist Ruth Leys defines Caruth's and Laub's approach as a mimetic model, in which the subject cannot integrate the trauma into her/his perceptual and cognitive system. In her Foucauldian analysis of the genealogy of trauma studies, Leys expresses doubts about defining trauma only through its "gaps," one approach that, she argues, ignores the value of direct narrative in apprehending trauma (63).[6] Leys gives more credit to the antimimetic model which upholds that trauma is a completely external event that the subject can recall and comprehend with (professional) help. In reading *Maus* we should acknowledge that the challenge is to decipher trauma as both a mimetic and antimimetic phenomenon, as both understood and obscured. We need to comprehend what has not been represented in either words or pictograms and read the larger meaning of an (auto)biographical project that was not necessarily intended as a signifier for the Holocaust trauma but can stand as one. Dori Laub deems crucial that we acknowledge not only to the limits of representation in as far as the story *can* be told, but also how accurately it can be remembered, how well the victim *knows* the facts. For that reason, the representation of the "truth" may encounter the obstacles, on the one hand, of the victims' not wanting or not being able to share their traumatic story, and, on the other hand, the victims' sharing their distorted version of the "truth," honest as it may be, since the traumatized person *believes* it is true.

Spiegelman's project is an experimental representation of the trauma associated with the Holocaust and its survivors (and by survivors, I mean their descendants, as well). Choosing pictorial as well as verbal media to represent the narrative, the artist appeals both to the Lacanian Symbolic and the Imaginary Order, thus bringing into play equally linguistic and also non-linguistic communication. In Spiegelman's words, "[t]he strength of commix lies in [its] synthetic ability to approximate a 'mental language' that is closer to actual human thought than either words or pictured alone" (cited in Young 18). While the linguistic or verbal message is imperative for trauma representation, Spiegelman's non-linguistic politics of representation, of drawing the slate of trauma, demonstrates the extent to which such representation is possible and relevant. The episode of the Auschwitz orchestra allowed critics to demonstrate the vicissitudes of memory in general and the unreliability of traumatic memory in particular. One panel depicts Vladek recalling his entering Auschwitz, while the next illustrates the official version of the historical accounts which Artie consulted (*Maus II* 54). Vladek does not have any recollection of an orchestra playing while the new groups of prisoners marched to work although, as Artie tells him, "it's very well documented." All Vladek remembers were the "guards shouting." To reconcile individual and historical accounts, Artie covers the orchestra, which he depicted in a previous panel, with the prisoners marching; only the suggestion of the tip of the instruments and the head of the conductor remains behind the rows of prisoners.

Spiegelman, admittedly, did not draw *Maus* on a blank slate. His inspiration, as revealed in the interactive *The Complete Maus* CD-ROM, comes from propagandistic portrayals of Jews as rats by the Nazi ideological apparatuses. The artists brought these depictions to an unlikely merger with the anthropomorphic heroic mice of the American pop culture that has constituted the average American child's, and visibly Art's, source of entertainment. Yet the American cartoons that inspired Spiegelman were racist in their own right, as the artist recalls in *The Complete Maus*. Andrew Loman, arguing for links between American racism and the Holocaust in his analysis of *Maus*, notes that "[r]acist discourse on both sides of the Atlantic used bestialization as a trope and [that] there clearly exist continuities between Nazi and anti–Semitism and American anti-black racism of the 1930s" (554). Loman contends that "the nature of Nazi racial caricatures justifies Spiegelman in claiming that he was writing 'alongside Hitler,' appropriating Nazi racial discourses and subverting them" (554). Spiegelman specifically credits "Kafka's tale, 'Josephine the Singer, or the Mouse Folk,' [which] offered a precedent, as did the Saturday morning cartoons and comics of my childhood" ("Artist's Statement" 44).

Characterized as a non-human race by the Nazis (*Maus* opens with Hitler's statement in that sense), the depiction of choice at the time was that of a rat, mouse, or blood-sucking bat, in short, reviled vermin. Spiegelman deconstructs the ubiquitous rodent representation of Jews of the Nazi era from the position of oppressors of the masses, to that of victims of mass oppression. In the process, he replaces the figure of the grotesque, filthy, and terrifying rat with that of the vulnerable, powerless, and ultimately sympathetic mouse. Spiegelman's mouse, however, does not share the attitude and fate of the always-victorious American cartoon mouse. To complete the scene, the artist makes the victimization clear with the depiction of the Germans as (anthropomorphic) cats, mice's eternal doom. In relation to this choice of representation Marianne Hirsch comments that "[i]f Jews and Germans are cats, then, they seem to be so not immutably, but only *in relation to each other* and in relation to the Holocaust and its memory. They are human except for the predator/victim relationship between them" (*Family Frames* 27, author's emphasis). Nevertheless, the animal depiction of the characters that populate *Maus* is not reducible to either the predator/victim relationship or to the Jews relationship with each other or with the Holocaust and its memory. That interpretation, Hirsch admits, would not explicate the zoomorphic representations of other ethnic or national groups whom Artie depicted in the timeframe of the 1980s (127). Hirsch lists them as "a number of contradictions and incongruities," but I argue that this choice of representation is deliberate (27). The very choice of deconstructing the propaganda imagery of the Nazi era and of turning its significance on its head testifies for this premeditation.

By not depicting Germans as humans (which would have been consistent with their depiction by the anti–Semitic propaganda), Spiegelman establishes his position in regards to hierarchies of racial/ethnic difference and with the ethics of representation in general. He bases his politics of representation on an equalitarian stance, to represent every race, ethnicity or nationality on the same level, either as anthropomorphic animals *or* as masked humans, but never some as humans *and* others as anthropomorphic animals in the same frame. Even when the author adds the few photographs to the comic strips, they are not in the same frame with the drawings of anthropomorphic animals. They stand on their own, such as, for instance, the positioning of the photograph that Vladek took in a borrowed prisoner uniform, after the war in the proximity of the drawn characters (134). The only exception is the instance in which the artist endeavors to represent postmemory, when the masked Artie is juxtaposed on the background of the Auschwitz scene. The "Time Flies" chapter title accompanies the visual pun of the flies, which infested the corpses at Auschwitz, swarming in Artie's studio.

While the Nazi propaganda represented Jews as non-human, detested creatures, in contrast to the "superior," human Aryan race, Spiegelman depicts everyone as either (anthropomorphic) animals or as humans with animal-faced masks. Unlike the Nazis who insisted on the subhuman nature of the non Aryan races, Spiegelman emphasizes the human fabric, be it at its best or its worst, in all his characters, regardless of their racial or ethnic differences. At all times the artist reminds us that the animal characters signify humans. The paraphernalia of glasses, pipes, cigarettes, pens, or weaponry completes the illustration of the anthropomorphic animals in human attires and dwelling in human lodgings. Regardless of the zoomorphic choice of representation, some human shapes and markers are consistent throughout the project. I will not go so far as to regard the choice of associating certain peoples with certain animals as based on those animals' culturally accepted characteristics matched with some national stereotypes, although reading *Maus* as an animal fable is not new territory.[7] That discussion is open and it likely goes farther than merely thinking of cats as predators, of mice as victims, or of dogs as protectors or rescuers.

Nevertheless, it would be superficial, if not dangerous, to reduce the artist's choice of representing Germans as cats and Jews as mice to a one-dimensional relationship of ancestral, innate antagonism, which is bound to be perpetual. Referring to representations of Holocaust in graphic novels, Robert Eaglestone cautions against arguing that *Maus*, "with its biological, animal metaphor, leads us to presume simply that Germans (cats) always prey on Jews (Mice) and that this is inevitable and unavoidable. If one is not a cat, one cannot be guilty." Moreover, the critic argues that Spiegelman's project "implicitly (if unintentionally) supports the 'Goldhagen Thesis,' that all Germans (cats) were willing to see Jews (mice) murdered" (328–9). It seems that Spiegelman specifically transitioned the Jews from anthropomorphic mice to mouse-masked humans in what constitutes the present time frame in the narrative. That Jews are not mice, or mice-like, becomes evident as such. But in the World War II era of xenophobic nationalism, the animal characteristics are more specific, perhaps suggesting a return to animalistic impulses that such times spawned, in which peoples, urged by propaganda, could act as either predators or prey.

Dismantling the politics of racial/ethical/national difference that "justified" and endorsed the Holocaust, Spiegelman's project lays bare that one race's "superiority" over another cannot be rationalized scientifically or morally; ultimately, the access to (totalitarian) power "validates" the extremist ideology that endorses the primacy of the white race over any racial Other. Since the racial/ethnic and even national norms are so volatile, their representation through markers of physical and moral difference is problematic. An attempt to differentiate faithfully and relevantly between groups, based on the three criteria mentioned above, complicates itself in geometrical progression. The author challenges any simplistic reading of his art when, for instance, he draws together anthropomorphic dogs next to the (cat-like) Nazi guards' German Shepherds or when he depicts the anthropomorphically drawn mice—Anja's parents and grandparents—in their mice and rat infested hiding. Spiegelman also imparts a subtle irony when depicting Artie's psychiatrist, a "Czech Jew, a survivor of Terezin and Auschwitz," as a mouse-masked human, whose place is "overrun with stray dogs and cats" and who keeps a framed picture of his cat on his desk (*Maus II* 43). All the same, Artie depicts with minute detail the lice which Vladek describes as swarming all over in the Dachau concentration camp, just as he depicts the gypsy fortuneteller, whom Vladek consulted after his liberation, as an anthropomorphic bee — the only insect in the representation of an ethnicity (*Maus II* 91, 133). These instances constitute a postmodern gesture towards the ambiguous lines on which basis the Nazi and by extension, any racist and xenophobic ideology, discriminated against the Other based on the supposedly innate superiority of one's race, ethnicity, nationality, or ... species.

Spiegelman's project displays an understanding of the categories of race, ethnicity, and nationality as exclusively social-cultural constructs, hence interchangeable. In order to undermine racial norms based on visibility, Artie chooses that nationality and not race takes the primacy for his own representational norm. He portrays Poles as pigs, French as frogs, Germans as cats, American as dogs, and Swedes as deer. He represents the black hitch-hiker as an anthropomorphic black dog (the animal of preference for representing American nationality), and not as a different species (*Maus II* 98–9). However, he consistently represents Jews either as anthropomorphic mice or as mouse-masked humans, regardless of their nationality, even when he draws a converted Jew, like his wife. The argument between Françoise and Vladek is particularly interesting for its display of racialist hierarchies. Vladek, abiding by the racist stereotype of Blacks as thieves, talks about the Blacks using a racist slur, "the way the Nazis talked about the Jews," as his daughter-in-law scolds him. In disbelief, Françoise expresses her indignation, "That's outrageous! How can you, of all people, be such a racist!" When he replies to Françoise that "It's not even to compare. The Shvartsers and the Jews!" Vladek conveys the hierarchy of difference by which he stands (99). As a victim of anti–Semitism, Vladek seems an unlikely proponent of any discriminatory ideology. However, considering the way trauma perpetuates itself through both traumatic remembrance and through compulsive psychic and bodily performance, part of Vladek's attitude can be identified as a traumatic behavior of irrational distrust in the Other, an unconscious habit which is perpetually reinforced by the ideology of white supremacy. His idiosyncrasies are deeply rooted in the reality of his Holocaust experience and reenacted compulsively. Yet Vladek does not discriminate in his mistrust either of Jews (like Mala, whom he considers suing for "robbing" him) or of non–Jews. Since there are no simple answers to a complicated problem, Artie's depiction of his father's history reveals a man with flaws and thus makes him even more human. Brought up in an ideology that acknowledged and promoted racial, ethnic and national differences and hierarchies, Vladek carries on the postmemory of his people's millennia-long history of oppression, together with the experiential memory of a reality that is long gone, yet which for him exists as a perpetual warning. For this reason, through mimetic impulse, he will always save money, count pills, worry about food, and warn his son to be suspicious of everything and everybody. Highlighting the congruence between American racism and the Holocaust illustrated in the hitchhiker panels, Andrew Loman, suggests that "Vladek's salvation from the murderously racist milieu will not be perfect, and that in America he himself will perpetuate, *mutatis mutandis*, the racism to which he was been subject in Germany and Poland" (158). The survivors of the Holocaust made it through the oppression, but not through the ideology of oppression.

One of the first frames of *My Father Bleeds History* depicts the old Vladek riding his stationary bike superimposed over a cartoonish rendition of *The Sheik* (1921) poster. He proudly recalls that "[p]eople always told me I looked just like Rudolph Valentino" (13).

Throughout the narrative, we learn more about Vladek's good looks and charm, "really a nice, handsome boy," and how his *physical* appearance worked to his advantage in both the best and the worst of times (13). But beyond the statement's reference to Vladek's once appealing looks, Art Spiegelman uses his father's resemblance to the movie star to put across a different kind of statement. Since Valentino was not Jewish, his portrayal as a mouse-faced human with a mouse-faced swooning woman in the iconic poster for *The Sheik* merely reflects the Latin lover's resemblance to the young Vladek. As follows, the mouse-face, though representing Jews, is unreliable as a physical marker of the body, much like the Jewish bodily indetermination, despite the obsessive taxonomies with which the Nazi "scientists" would "norm" the Jews according to their biological features, to their phenotype. Noting the absurdity and futility of designating Jews with specific, unifying physical characteristics that would position them as non-white, or as whites' Other, as the Nazi ideology professed, Matthew F. Jacobson explains that "[a]nti-Semitism is incomprehensible *primarily* because Jewish 'difference' is called into question by an unreliable Jewish physicality" (128, author's emphasis). In that sense, Artie's bringing together Vladek and Valentino, drawn as anthropomorphic mice, suggests the unreliability of the visual/phenotype descriptors in differentiating the Jews from whites, or from other whites "of a different color," in Jacobson's words. Vladek can easily pass for a non–Jew, for a (more) "acceptable" Pole during the war, much like the Italian Valentino who had, as Jacobson remarks, "the physiognomical ability to be both the exotic, racial Other and the acceptable, chivalric European" (5). Appropriately, Spiegelman's depiction of the famous actor as the Sheikh in the same frame with Vladek reinforces by proxy Vladek's otherness as well as his bodily racial indetermination. Yet in the same breath, the artist challenges any fixed depiction of this Otherness when he depicts the white, Gentile actress Agnes Ayres, Valentino's love interest in *The Sheik*, as a mouse-faced woman. This could appear as an inconsistency, if not a crisis of representation, but then again, can one represent difference with consistency? This is the impossibility towards which Spiegelman's art gestures.

The complications that arise from the visual representation of bodily differences are evocative for the politics of racial representation based largely on visibility. As such, *Maus* contributes to a long history of racial Jewishness, which, in Jacobson's view, "is not merely the history of anti–Semitism; it encompasses the ways in which both Jews and non–Jews have construed Jewishness — and the ways in which they have *seen* it — over time" (175, author's emphasis). Art Spiegelman's text marks the role of visibility, of the biological difference in classifying Jewishness; it can be construed as a means of understanding the Jewishness through the lens of racial, maybe even more than ethnic, difference. Notably, the author chooses to draw his characters (and himself) as anthropomorphic animals when illustrating Vladek's narrative and also his meta-narrative, the episodes that address directly his conversations with his father, Mala, or Françoise about the making of *Maus*. However, while Spiegelman represents episodes outside his involvement with the project, his bearing witness to his father's and Mala's narratives, the portrayal of choice is that of a mouse-masked human, a mask which resembles the ones his parents wore while performing (racial) passing (*Maus I* 136–55). Jewishness, even when acquired through conversion, we understand, takes precedence over the Polish (in Vladek's case), American (in

Artie's case), or French (in Françoise's case) nationality. This precedence is possibly a form of postmemory, an interconnectedness of those who have suffered during the Holocaust specifically for being Jews (or Gypsies, etc.). Nevertheless, these masks do not carry out the same representational function throughout *Maus*. That Artie wears the mouse-faced mask — the signifier for the Jewish identity — while visiting his psychiatrist (who also wears one) means that this aspect of the wearer's identity could be discretionary to certain extent, a matter of choice, hence disposable at will. Since it is only a mask and not a physical attribute, the signifier suggests a decrease in the importance of the Jewish identity as the dominant feature of the bearer. Beyond the strict oppositional structure white (Aryan) and Jew that founded the anti–Semitic ideology, the characters of Jewish descent may live "outside" their Jewishness to certain extent, giving far less importance to this aspect of their identity. Dominick LaCapra argues that while interviewing Vladek, Artie is or becomes a Jew: "Indeed, in certain ways, [Artie] becomes a Jew or assumes a Jewish identity ... through his concern with the Holocaust — a concern that nonetheless escapes sufficient critical examination" (177).[8] Evidently, in this case the mask is ideological, or, in other words, the appropriation of a Jewish cultural, not "biological," identity. Françoise's depiction as a mouse, despite her Gentile French identity, reinforces Artie's portrayal of Jewishness as an ideology that one can appropriate (or discard); "if you're a mouse, I ought to be a mouse too. I converted, didn't I?" argues Françoise (*Maus I* 11). Interestingly, Françoise *becomes* a mouse once converting to Judaism and not a masked human with a mouse face. Judaism as a social construct takes precedent over the Jewish phenotype, over kinship, by which racialist theories are founded.

On the contrary, the masks depicted in "Mouse Trap," the final chapter of *My Father Bleeds History*, perform quite a different function. The mask here stands for a prescribed identity that for the most part depends on visible biological descriptors. Since one cannot dispose at will of the biological markers, albeit flawed and unreliable in their inherent inconstancy, that the Nazi era equated with racial, and even ethnic and national identity, the choice of masks points towards the need to pass as a socially acceptable identity. Unlike the "ideological" mask, which can be adjusted to fit the individual, the "biological" mask is imperfect because it cannot in fact alter the visible characteristics by which, for instance, the Jews were described. Spiegelman points towards the difficulty of passing for a non–Jew when he draws Anja with a telltale tail (*telltail?*) while her mouse-face is covered with a pig-face mask. She thus assumes the more tolerated Polish identity. The revealing tail becomes a signifier of her Jewish physicality (stereotyped by the Nazi description), because, recalls Vladek in his imperfect English, "you could see more easy she was Jewish" (*Maus I* 136).

The animal mask, which covers either a zoomorphic face or a human face, is drawn to signify Jewish, American, Polish, or other identity, but *mutatis mutandis*, it also reflects the change in race theories since the time of the Holocaust. As race theorist Kenan Malik specifies, in the postwar world "discussions of human differences were dominated by the categories of 'culture' and 'history' rather than those of 'race' and 'biology'" (127). That is not to say, however, that racial/racist hierarchies became outdated. Significantly, we can never actually get a glimpse of Artie's face or anyone else's in *Maus* other than the few photographs and "The Prisoner of the Hell Planet," which is based on a different premise of artistic representation altogether. The concealing of the human face behind the animal mask is an indication that, may it be ideologically or biologically constructed, racial, ethnic, and national identity is ultimately inescapable, although to certain degree, it can be mimicked or exchanged, substituted. If Spiegelman represents racial difference through anthropomorphic animal species, the masked Artie at his psychiatrist suggests the author's compliance with race only as a social construct and his rejection of race as biologically justified. In order to create that equalitarian base on which he founded this animal fable and to be consistent in his politics of representation, Spiegelman represents his psychiatrist, as well as the media and business people, as equal, yet racially, ethnically, or nationally different — with a mask. The artist's choice of illustrating difference is consistent with race conceptualizations during and after War World II. It resonates with Malik's assertion that the consequence of the Nazism "was to throw into disrepute the biological arguments for racial superiority and to discredit the overt expressions of racism" but, he warns, "while maintaining intact all the assumptions of racial thinking — in particular that humanity can be divided into discrete groups, that these divisions are to some degree immutable and that they have social consequences" (127). Although echoing these beliefs, Spiegelman does not endorse them, but exposes their irrationality. Spiegelman's representation reaffirms racial, ethnic and national difference but it does so by warning about the risk of equating difference with hierarchy. Troubled by contradictory conceptualizations of race and ethnicity and conflicting interpretations of history, decades after World War II, the artist reflects these inconsistencies through his choices and crises of representation.

Notes

1. In *The Complete Maus* CD-ROM, Spiegelman recalls how *Maus* came into being, as a "comix" that involved anthropomorphized animals. After having watched old cats and mice "racist cartoons," and noticing that "Al Jolson was Mickey Mouse without ears," his first impulse was to approach racism in America. As he recalls, "at this point I said, 'I have it: I'll do a comic-book story about the Ku Klux Kats, and a lynching of some mice, and deal with racism in America using cats and mice as the vehicle.' And that lasted about ten minutes before I realized that I just didn't have enough background and knowledge to make this thing happen well ... and I realized that I had a metaphor of oppression much closer to my own past in the Nazi Project."

2. In an apt consideration of Spiegelman's relation with the tradition of fables, cartoons and comic books, Andreas Huysen notes: "Spiegelman draws on the comic as a mass cultural genre, but transforms it in a narrative saturated with modernist techniques of self-reflectivity, self-irony, ruptures in narrative time and highly complex image sequencing and montaging. As a comic, *Maus* resonates less with Disney productions than with the whole tradition of popular animal fables from Aesop to LaFontaine and even Kafka. At the same time, it evolved of course from an American comic book counter-tradition born in the 1960s that includes works such as Krazy Kat, Fritz the Cat, and others. At the same time, *Maus* remains different from the older tradition of the enlightening animal fable. If the animal fable (taking George Orwell's *Animal Farm* as a twentieth-century example) had enlightenment as its purpose either through satire or moral instruction, *Maus* remains thoroughly ambitious, if not opaque, as to the possible success of such enlightenment" (67).

3. From here on, in parenthetical citations, I will refer to *My Father Bleeds History* as *Maus I* and to *And Here My Troubles Began* as *Maus II*.

4. Theorists Cathy Caruth, Dori Laub, and Shoshana Felman, among others, as well as writers such Toni Morrison argue for the "unrepresentable," "unspeakable" nature of trauma, a position however disputed by theorist Ruth Leys and literary critics like Suzette Henke, Leigh Gilmore and others, who argue for the possibility of representation of trauma, albeit with limitations.

5. Hirsch clarifies her concept: "I propose the term 'postmemory' with some hesitation, conscious

that the prefix 'post' could imply that we are beyond memory and therefore perhaps ... purely in history.... Postmemory is a powerful and very particular form of memory precisely because its connection to its object or source is mediated not through recollection but through an imaginative investment and creation. This is not to say that memory itself is unmediated, but that it is more directly connected to the past" (*Family Frames*, 22).

6. In "The Pathos of the Literal: Trauma and the Crisis of Representation," Leys casts a shadow of doubt on the urgency with which trauma theorists, such as Laub, Felman, and Caruth use (or abuse) Freudian psychoanalysis to validate their conceptualization of trauma as "infectious" from the witness to the listener, as unrepresentable, yet performative, and the stress on trauma's "latency," its belated manifestation (*Trauma: A Genealogy*. Chicago: University of Chicago Press, 2000: 266–98).

7. James E. Young argues that Spiegelman must have created the other animal figures insofar as they are related to mice: "the wily and somehow indifferent cat is the obvious natural enemy and, as Germans, the principal killer of mice here. The hapless Poles are saddled with a more ambiguous figure: though not a natural enemy of the Jews during the Holocaust, as pigs they come to symbolize what is *treif*, or non–Kosher. They may not be as anti–Jewish as the cats, but they are decidedly un–Jewish. The only animal to resonate a Nazi cast would be a friendly, if none-too-bright dogs as stand-in for Americans, regarded as a mongrel people by Hitler but pictured here as the natural and more powerful enemy of the cats. The rest of the animals are literally benign: reindeer for the Swedes, moths for Gypsies. But none of these, aside for the mouse, is intrinsic, witness Spiegelman's deliberation over to make his French-born wife, Françoise, a frog or a mouse (technically speaking, she has to be a mouse)" (34). Of course, my argument aims to show that these choices of representation display more complex intentions.

8. Dominick LaCapra is concerned with what he believes is Artie's lack of self-reflectivity in motivating his project, that is, his interrogating his father. Writes LaCapra, "Artie has an insistent and pervasive preoccupation with recording his father's story, which is dangerously close to becoming the master narrative of his own life. But he nowhere sits himself down and asks about his own motivations and reasons or directs at himself the dogged scrutiny to which he subjects his father" (177). Unlike the theorist, I believe that Artie does in fact reveal, or at least suggests the "motivations or reasons" for recording and representing his father's story just as he interrupts it with episodes of self-scrutiny. Artie is as much in pursuit of his own trauma — his mother's suicide, the "sibling rivalry with a snapshot" (*Maus II*, 15), and the estrangement from his father — as he is of his father's and his people's. For instance, "Prisoner on the Hell Planet" (*Maus II*, 100–3), clearly hints to (one of) Artie's motivation(s) for interviewing his father, his mother's suicide, which was inexplicable at the time he drew the story. As his father's story unravels for Artie, he rationalizes not only the roots of his own trauma, but also the connection with the collective trauma of the Holocaust.

Works Cited

Adams, Timothy Dow. *Telling Lies in Modern American Autobiography*. Chapel Hill: University of North Carolina Press, 1990. Print.

Chute, Hillary. "The Shadow of a Past Time: History and Graphic Representation in *Maus*." *Twentieth-Century Literature* 52.2 (Summer 2006): 199–230. Print.

Eaglestone, Robert. "Madness or Modernity? The Holocaust in Two Anglo-Saxon Comics." *Rethinking History* 6:3 (2002): 319–30. Print.

Hirsch, Marianne. *Family Frames: Photography, Narrative, and Postmemory*. Cambridge: Harvard University Press, 1997. Print.

_____. "Intimacy Across the Generations: Memory, Postmemory, and Representation." *disClosure* 15 (2006): 32–8. Print.

_____. "Projected Memory: Holocaust Photographs in Personal and Public Fantasy." *Acts of Memory: Cultural Recall in the Present*. Mieke Bal, et al., eds. Hanover: University Press of New England, 1999. Print.

Huyssen, Andreas. "Of Mice and Mimesis: Reading Spiegelman with Adorno." *New German Critique* 81 (Fall 2000): 65–83. Print.

Jacobson, Matthew Frye. *Whiteness of a Different Color: European Immigrants and the Alchemy of Race*. Cambridge: Harvard University Press, 1999. Print.

LaCapra, Dominick. *History and Memory After Auschwitz*. Ithaca, NY: Cornell University Press, 1994. Print.

Laub, Dori, M.D. "Bearing Witness or the Vicissitudes of Listening." *Testimony: Crises of Witnessing in*

Literature, Psychoanalysis, and History. Shoshana Felman and Dori Laub, M.D. New York: Routledge, 1992. Print.

Loman, Andrew. "'Well Intended Liberal Slop': Allegories of Race in Spiegelman's *Maus.*" *Journal of American Studies* 40.3 (2006): 551–71. Print.

Malik, Kenan. *The Meaning of Race: Race, History and Culture in Western Society.* New York: New York University Press, 1996. Print.

Marsella, Anthony J., et al. *Ethnocultural Aspects of Posttraumatic Stress Disorder: Issues, Research, and Clinical Applications.* Washington, D.C.: American Psychiatric Association, 2001. Print.

Rothberg, Michael. *Traumatic Realism: the Demands of Holocaust Representation.* Minneapolis: University of Minnesota Press, 2000. Print.

Singer, Marc. "'Black Skins' and White Masks: Comic Books and the Secret of Race." *African American Review* 36:1 (2002): 107–19. Print.

Spiegelman, Art. "Artist's Statement." *Jewish Themes/Contemporary American Artists.* Susan Tumarkin Goodman, ed., vol. 2. New York: Jewish Museum, 1986. Print.

_____. *Comix, Essays, Graphics and Scraps.* New York: Raw, 1998. Print.

_____. *The Complete Maus* CD-ROM. New York: Voyager, 1994. Print.

_____. *Maus: A Survivor's Tale: My Father Bleeds History/Here My Troubles Began.* New York: Pantheon, 1993 (1973, 1983). Print.

White, Hayden. "Historical Employment and the Story of Truth," in S. Friendländer, *Probing the Limits of Representation: Nazism and the "Final Solution."* Cambridge: Harvard University Press, 1992: 37–53. Print.

Young, E. James. *At Memory's Edge: After-Images of the Holocaust in Contemporary Art and Architecture.* New Haven: Yale University Press, 2000. Print.

8

Mezclando (Mixing) the "Facts" and the Power of the Image in *Latino USA*

ELLEN M. GIL-GÓMEZ

The consideration of the comic medium is largely absent from Chicano/a studies. This is particularly surprising given that Latino/a cultures regularly embrace "popular" media and insist on mixing genres, styles and forms within the arts generally. These mixtures routinely serve as popular narratives and counter histories to those of the dominant culture and/or reflect the hybrid language, ethnic and racial categories so common in Latino/a experiences. For these reasons exploring Chicano/a comics is essential to show how Chicano/a artists and authors have utilized the medium as they imagine their own narratives of resistance that don't fit neatly between the poles of superhero or alternative commix.[1] In order to do justice to these projects, I place the emphasis of this study of the nature of creative processes rather than on an evaluation of the "authentic" nature of the product created. My goal then is to analyze the ways that author Ilan Stavans and cartoonist Lalo Alcaraz created their unique Chicano comic: *Latino USA: A Cartoon History.*

It has been posited by the likes of Scott McCloud and Charles Hatfield, and others, that comics form a specific and unique medium that is not any one thing — images, writing or their contexts — but all three, and simultaneously none of them (McCloud 17; Hatfield xiii). This complicated nature is very much evocative of Chicana feminist scholar Gloria Anzaldúa's arguments of the philosophical condition of the "new mestiza" who is "In a constant state of mental nepantilism, an Aztec word meaning torn between ways, *la mestiza* is a product of the transfer of the cultural and spiritual values of one group to another … in a state of perpetual transition, the *mestiza* faces the dilemma of the mixed breed" (78) from her influential *Borderlands/La Frontera.* However, the danger of simply applying Anzaldúa's theory of mestiza consciousness to the medium of comics — as Nericcio does when he describes the term as helpful as a "way of describing the lineage of a comic-book medium" (n. pag.) through locating comics as the "illicit progeny" of the "ménage a trios" of film, fine art and prose (n. pag.)—is that it assumes a false focus on the comic as representational of identity rather than on a dynamic creative process which can be changed and adapted by the artist and have a broader impact on the medium.

While I value the insistence on studying comics as a mixture, a wonderfully messy series of texts and contexts, it is inappropriate to usurp this racialized Spanish term—particularly after Anzaldúa's groundbreaking repositioning of the term within women of color feminisms and Border Theory—for anything that reflects mixture. It's an error to conclude that comics generally can or should be read through a "mestizo" approach or as an inherently "mestizo" medium due simply to its complexity because the term itself is tied to its linguistic, racial and ethnic origins and history even within Anzaldúa's theory of mestiza consciousness.[2] That said, I am interested in exploring here what Nericcio hints at: How can comics be "mestizo" texts in their creation? I would like to explore this question as it relates to methodology or creative vision rather than as tied to a product because authentic products tend to find their own location within the ghetto of "diversity" rather than as fundamental to the medium as a whole. Accordingly, I have not used mestiza or mestizo in my title as a description of a methodology or a text but rather the Spanish verb "*mezclar*"—"to mix" in order to analyze a specific kind of mixing here. It is fair to say then that like McCloud and Hatfield I am not interested in drawing boundaries or finding origins but analyzing a specific instance of how text can indeed reflect *mestizaje*—with the language, cultural and historical legacy of that word—via its author/illustrator engaging in the process of *mezclando*, mixing, in order to do so.

Chicano/a Arts, *Mestizaje* and Mestizo

Before considering the specific culturally resonant mixtures within *Latino USA* I will very briefly outline the foundations of and ingredients found within Chicano/a culture and arts. The ancestry of Chicanos is a mixture of American and Mexican, which are each inherently mixed identities. To oversimplify, Mexicans are most typically a combination of Indigenous and Spanish ancestry; the Chicano adds also the American, and consequently it is not a surprise that with these levels of racial/ethnic/linguistic mixture that Chicano culture and arts would reflect these myriad influences. In the United States, and likewise from a Latin American perspective, Chicano/a culture has been viewed as a minor, unfortunate or unsuccessful imitation of "American" or "Mexican." The Chicano/a supposedly does neither one well and ultimately combines both inappropriately. For example Spanglish, the language of many Chicanos/as is still seen as a "bastard" tongue from both sides. As Anzaldúa speaks of being punished for using the tongues intrinsic to her mixed identity she states: "So, if you want to really hurt me, talk badly about my language. Ethnic identity is twin skin to linguistic identity. I am my language" (75). While many may not agree with how Anzaldúa ties identity and language together essentially, clearly the usage of language is tied to both the experience and reflection of the world we inhabit. (In relation to comics it is helpful here to consider Anzaldúa's remarks about language to relate to not just written text but all comic "language" as in imagery and panel design.) Chicano/a arts, broadly speaking, rely and insist upon mixture, though the individual elements of the mixture may change. As George Vargas notes "Chicano artists draw from their *mestizaje* experiences in synthesizing ideas and making artistic forms" (195–6).

Good examples are shown in the emergence the public art styles of Chicano graffiti, poster and mural art. Like comics, graffiti art has its influences straddled between the relatively highbrow location of mural art and the solidly lowbrow style and materials of graffiti. Poster art emerged for more directly political purposes but also served as a way to "recreate," if you will, urban spaces with new aesthetics (Noriega 21, Pérez-Torres 124). The necessity for these versions of this public art is both within Mexican tradition — i.e., the Mexican masters, Rivera, Orozco and Siquieros who were trained artists wishing to break away from European influences — as well as simply the lack of access to traditional artistic venues, materials and monies. Indeed, Siquieros famously stated that "We repudiate so-called easel art and all such art which springs from ultra-intellectual circles, for it is essentially aristocratic. We hail the monumental expression of art because such art is public property" (Campbell). Thus in the 1970s artists such as Willie Heron, Gronk and Judy Baca expressed themselves on their neighborhood's walls which in turn led to public art as community statement and political activism as in the murals in Chicano Park. There is still a struggle between legitimizing Chicano art — as the Chicano performance ASCO collective did by signing the Los Angeles County Museum of Art and then calling it "art" as a protest against its exclusionary practices — and embracing this "outsiderness" as inherently part of an artistic vision. In public arts to a very large degree the medium is the message; this holds true with the comic medium.

The corrido, or folk ballad tradition, which has a longer history within Mexican and thus Chicano/a communities is another form of community art at the center of the Chicano imaginary, and it has been there long before the rise of public muralism. The corrido is essentially a form of musical story telling that communities would create as ways to remember and pass along important events and people. As a result there were corridos created for figures deemed outlaws or "bandits" in the nineteenth century southwest such as: Joaquin Murrieta, Gregorio Cortez, and Tibúrcio Vasquez; and later figures such as César Chávez. They served as subversive forms of communication and celebration of local history when Mexican American liberty was tenuous. This community-created form has been widely studied in Chicano literature as relevant to the development of the written texts of the Chicano Renaissance of the 1970s and beyond. For example, see the ground-breaking work by Americo Paredes *With a Pistol in His Hand*, which brought the corrido into academic terrain in the 1950s or Ramón Saldívar's important *Chicano Narrative* which brought its study from anthropology and folklore to literary genre studies and its impact on contemporary literature.

There are a multitude of other examples from the creation of collaborative theater companies such as El Teatro Campesino, to low rider culture, spoken word poetry, rock music, to the genre mixtures of Chicana feminist writers, poets, artists and comedians. Chicano/a arts then continually walks the tightrope of influences, between and amongst Latin America and the United States; language, between English, Spanish, Indigenous languages and mixtures thereof; race, white, black, indigenous and mixtures thereof; culture, between high culture and low culture, urban or rural; and ultimately authenticity. The terrain of representation is always one fraught with danger. Which mixture is the "correct" one? All of this slipperiness, all of these mixtures, obviously share much space with the medium of comics, by its very nature, and thus to synthesize this territory results in innumerable possibilities.

As demonstrated above, Chicano/a arts does have many similarities in that artists might draw, as Vargas claims, from "their *mestizaje* experiences" in order to create new mixtures. However, the danger in locating the centrality of mestizo/a *experience* in my view is that it presupposes the creation of the authentic person, or the legitimate subject, who then draws on authentic experience in order to create. Chicano/a creativity is fore-grounded within essential identity rather than on the purposeful methods of construct-edness. This brings me to the *mezclando* of my title. Because of the slippery nature of *mestizaje* itself, finding the meanings of "mestizo" identity are always relative because they are drawn from within historicized racial contexts and consequentially trying to "find" that which is truly mestizo is not viable. It is always already impossible because the mestizo as a concept is always in the process of undoing itself. The Latin American history of *mestizaje* is actually an argument for white supremacy; its argument assumes that the Indian will benefit from the whiteness of the European and thus the mestizo is actually a step closer to white. The Latin American history of race then is built upon that usage from within the imperialist caste system. An American perspective uses the same concept of mestizo as a mixture but for the opposite reason. Because Americans are assumed to be white, and always already privileged in so being, when a Chicano or U.S. Latino claims a mestizo identity it is a call for an accounting of brownness. Chicano usage highlights the erasure of the brown within white privilege; to highlight difference, in other words. So for a Chicano the mestizo is a step towards the indigenous, the "real," the origin of identity. I suggest though that these contradictory positions do not eliminate the usefulness of the term, in fact the absurdity exemplifies its merit not in forming essen-tial identity, but rather foregrounding the intentional constructedness of identity. I ulti-mately find it more productive, while keeping these contexts in mind, to abandon the need for nouns and focus instead on explicating verbs. Assuming that both Latin Amer-icans and U.S. Latinos/as are drawn to complicate their racial histories in these paradoxical ways, how do they navigate these terrains in order to create narratives? I want to explore what Chicanos *do* rather than what they *are* so that we get closer to understanding their texts.

To put it simply *mezclando* is creation; it is a process of making that is irrevocably tied to mixture. The specifics of what's being mixed differ depending on the particular experiences and contexts of the artist and are in the end not as important as the intent to find ways of communicating within paradox. The strategy of *mezclando* is at once a com-position but routinely through its contradictory "ingredients" if you will, it simultaneously de-composes. Indeed, perhaps what it tries to both demonstrate and to some degree capture is the movement between composition and de-composition, or perhaps the gap between them. *Mezclando* highlights ruptures, gaps, contradictions, conflicts, and to some degree composes them within language (be it text, structure or images). Rather than using the received rules that the ingredients and their contexts and histories demand (such as genre, vocabulary, iconography) to create composed products that enact their own de-composition, to *mezclar* is to utilize those rules and structures of composition, and their contexts, to emphasize what they *do* rather than what they *are*. This strategy then, through varying but deliberate de-contextualization, demonstrates that as one composes, creates image, or narrative, one simplifies mixtures rather than complicates them. *Mezclando* thrives with contradiction, with incongruence, as the mixtures reverberate with one another and accentuate the gaps rather than the welds; the subject, narrative, or story actually better reflects the identity and experience of *mestizaje*, albeit temporarily. Consequently, *mezclando* is mixture that calls attention to moments of possible, though shifting, meaning rather than fixed products with separate ingredients; it's mixture whose aim is not to combine together but to rather alter context itself. It is only from within these gaps of meaning that we can synthesize the views that the opposing sides have towards the middle.

¿Et Tú *Latino USA*?

In 2000 Basic Books published *Latino USA: A Cartoon History* that was a collaboration between Ilan Stavans, the preeminent scholar of contemporary Latino letters, and Lalo Alcaraz, nationally syndicated cartoonist of *La Cucaracha*. Stavans is professor of Spanish at Amherst College and has written numerous books and articles including: *The Hispanic Condition, The Riddle of Cantinflas, Growing Up Latino*, and was tapped to be the editor of W.W. Norton's anthology of Latino Literature, which he has worked on for more than a decade. It is fair to acknowledge that Stavans has benefited from the "star system" within academic publishing and has been allowed to focus his work as he chooses. He is without a doubt the single most sought after voice on all things Latino by major publishing companies and critiques of this bestowed representational power have included his identity as a light skinned, middle class, Jewish Mexican immigrant. This is evident in numerous newspaper articles surrounding the Norton project where he is described as a "czar," a "canon former," a "spokesman" for Latino literature (and ultimately identity) and also as an "outsider," and an "ambitious interloper" in the field (Richardson). Interestingly, all of the suspicions about Stavans' status as Latino power broker are displayed in Allatson's "Ilan Stavans's *Latino USA: A Cartoon History (of a Cosmopolitan Intellectual)*." Though certainly a substantial piece of scholarship it is dependent on acknowledging Stavans's "star power" analyzing the book as only a simulacrum of Stavans's power to represent rather than as an image text on its own terms. Indeed Allatson leaves out any discussion of the cartoonist beyond listing him.

Lalo Alcaraz is Chicano cartoonist nationally syndicated with Universal Press Syndicate who started his strip *La Cucaracha* in the local Los Angeles paper the *L.A. Weekly*. After giving up on editorial cartoons as a way to make a living, he began the daily strip which focused on the character La Cuco Rocha, who may or may not be human, and his family, friends, and neighborhood. He functions sometimes as Alcaraz's alter ego and as a general social commentator. Alcaraz describes the strip as being "political, in-your-face, edgy ... really bicultural, not watered down." ("Lalo") Alcaraz came to the *Latino USA* project by invitation from Stavans who enjoyed his cartoons and called him his "artistic soulmate" (Stavans xv). In an email interview I conducted with Alcaraz he said of the project that he wanted to learn how to create book length texts and work with Stavans whom he called "a prestigious author." When discussing the collaborative process he stated that Stavans supplied him with "a script" to work from which included some design elements such as specific paintings, historical figures or photographs to recreate in certain sections. Otherwise Alcaraz indicates that "I did pretty much assemble that whole damn book by myself. An indexer and an editor (and maybe a proofer) were the only ones other than Ilan or I that worked on it, and it was definitely different than drawing one cartoon on one topic" ("Alcaraz"). He also indicated that Stavans embraced the illustration of the conflict between the two—Alcaraz's cartoon characters routinely mock or "talk back" to Stavans' script. As Alcaraz states "When I didnt [sic] agree with something, I mocked it, as I had inserted myself as a character. It happened, and Ilan was very flexible about it, and he let me rewrite or balance out certain points." It is clear that though not the governing force of the *text* of the book Alcaraz certainly governed the majority of images, in their creation and in how they "talk back" to the text itself, and the page design, which are central to the entire text.

Latino USA is as its subtitle indicates a "cartoon history" of U.S. Latinos/as which has been largely ignored by scholars perhaps because it does not easily fit into any disciplinary category. Both of the creators of the book describe it as an academic publication, though the way it was marketed and received was as a juvenile overview of history. This is somewhat logical given the broad sweep of the "history" included but even more so because of the general reception of comic format. The packaging of the book itself seems to be geared towards a relatively general audience rather than for scholars of Latino/a history, literature or graphic texts. The "praise for Latino USA" on the back cover focuses on the text as a welcome vehicle to illuminate Latino history and "Hispanic Culture in the United States" focusing primarily on academic Stavans rather than Alcaraz, the cartoonist. It is consistent then that the reviews tend to evaluate the book from that approach and not as a literary text, a comic or graphic novel. For all of Stavans' words of his own culturally based intentions to collaborate on an imagetext from the book's introduction the book itself was received as at best a basic historical supplement meant for children or at worst a self congratulatory ego trip.

Border Comics: Imagetext as Narrative Device

Because of this discrepancy around what kind of text exactly *Latino USA* claims to be it serves to spend some time considering how Stavans positions it as genre, but more importantly as narrative device. Stavans does not begin his text without a lack of agenda. It's clear that Stavans is not advocating that *Latino USA* be seen as a traditional history text that uses an objective voice to delineate "the facts." Rather since he labels *Latino USA* quite clearly as "my own account" (xv) he focuses his foreword on explaining the "cartoon" part of the book's title. He locates its genesis primarily in his desire to both demonstrate, and speak, a variety of voices through combining "lowbrow" comics traditions with the "highbrow" of academic historical narrative. Importantly he locates his own personal passage into academia through the comic book of his childhood when he believed that the comic "could offer a better lesson in civics" (xi) rather than the singular voice of a history textbook. Here we see Stavans set the table for his part of the *mezclando* solely through his traditional textual narrative: the book is a history and also his own story, it is both traditional and non-traditional, academic and popular, visual and written, fact and fiction.

It's apparent that one of the main factors of importance to Stavans is to find an adequate narrative form for this story. In order to tell the story of Latinos/as in the U.S. he chooses to resurrect and reclaim an "indigenous" and popular Mexican storytelling tradition which he defines via its audience reception as he recounts los comics' "egalitarian" and "democratic" "mission" reflected in the clientele of the comic shop which catered to "Mexico's population in its entirety, men and women, children and adults, rich and poor, rulers and the populace." He rejects the argument that all Mexican comics were foreign imports bent on colonization and rather celebrates that his "strip heroes … were definitely locals" who broke stereotypes and routinely saved the universe with more style than Superman or Batman (xi). His argument goes beyond just lauding Mexican national identity as the content of these comics and posits that the medium of the graphic text is actually more indigenous and "inherent to Mexican culture" (xiii) than the written text, perhaps due to some combination of various pre–Columbian codices and language systems, the religious art tradition of the retalbo and the nineteenth century political satirist José Guadalupe Posada.[3] He sees the continued importance of image texts in the descendents of these origins in the many sources of public art in Chicano/a communities, as mentioned above, such as murals and graffiti art, or "street art" as he names it. He rightly concludes that these forms are continuing evidence of these cultures desire to solidly locate images and iconography at the level of the people (xiv). The masses are what give these image texts their value and currency. This of course inherently runs counter to the ruling ideology of value lying in the hands of the elite, within which Stavans would include himself, and in which he remains ambivalent. Thus *Latino USA* is his very real attempt to become "a manufacturer of kitsch" rather than remain bound to the formal rules of his elite professional career. He creates his kitsch with gusto though, as is clear throughout his text, through continuing and sometimes contradictory balancing acts with which he is not fully comfortable. This juggling does not lessen his goals for the book in fact it demonstrates them.

In order to understand the impact of Stavans's and Alcaraz's book we must consider it as its own "unfixable" text. It cannot be read as "history" with illustrations, or as a comic with a lot of writing in it but rather it must be read as an altogether separate medium. This is what Stavans is trying to argue for in his Foreword, not for a historical narrative innocent by way of its cartoon delivery but as an attempt to create a whole different category of "story." It certainly may be a slight overstatement that because of the book's form the "'unofficialness' translated itself into what I think is a less Europeanized, more democratic viewpoint" (xv). It's difficult to argue that if each making of history is one person's making of history that this document also must be so. It is in the book's imagery that Stavans' argument for a democratic style is perhaps almost accurate.

Most interesting in this effort is Stavans's usage of a chorus of sorts (though one never all singing the same song!). He includes multiple icons, cultural stereotypes and archetypes that become narrators and counter-narrators throughout the text. In addition to the appearance of the narrators themselves, and their textual dialogue, is Alcaraz's visual design indicating either supporting or opposing illustrative arguments throughout. The graphic nature of the text is not just an addition to, or backdrop for, Stavans' written arguments but is integral to the creation of its meaning. We must acknowledge Alcaraz's voice as present, as speaker, as including various rhetorical arguments in his visual representations. Thus *Latino USA*'s text becomes the voices of at least two authors and importantly so for Stavans' because they represent the tension of borders and their expanses "both south and north of Rio Grande" because of their personal heritage, history and experiences. Image and text then do "echo" (xv) and interact with one another to represent opposing contradictory forces in the text that are nonetheless both speaking under the same umbrella of "Latino."

Mezclando It Up in the *Latino USA*: A Cartoon History

I must begin with the choice of "cartoon" in the book's title to describe the collaborative image text and its contents. Rather than agreeing to the necessity of applying McCloud's now standard definition of "cartoon" as a single panel or image without sequential context as being distinct from "comic" which is a text that puts single panels together in sequence to form narrative structure (7–17), I would argue that to read *Latino USA* it is more illuminating to use instead the Spanish translations of "cartoon." Of most importance is the synonym *caricatura* or caricature. From Dictionary.com for example "any imitation or copy so distorted or inferior as to be ludicrous." This association is much more descriptive of this project in form, style and context. Consequently, the chosen term does not reflect that Stavans intends his "history" should only be meaningful in Stavans' invented vacuum but indeed as conceptually contextual or sequential.[4] Rather, if we allow the Spanish translation as distinct from the McCloud terminology (indeed there is no equivalent for McCloud's "comics"), we can then read the individual characters, sequences, and the entire project of something called "Latino history" as caricature itself. Simply, the whole project is a caricature of itself and to continually remind us of this fact we have "the author" and "the cartoonist" as "players" in the theater production to follow. It is one of the main ways that the author and illustrator force us to de-contextualize their narrative from expectations of the genre of history. As Stavans states, the relationship between image and text is "purposeful imitation" (xv) which both creators utilize in order to create gaps and echoes. When freed from the insistence of reading the text as Stavans's grab to control all Latino meanings, we can see the tongue firmly in the cheek throughout its pages. Caricature is the central conceit and is also a perfect way to "translate" the continually contradictory project of something labeled as "Latino." It is one of the important ingredients in the *mezclando* that follows.

Rather than provide an exhaustive review of the historical narrative here my analysis will focus on how a small sampling of the images and text work together within the framework of caricature to reveal the inherent process of the mixing, or *mezclando*, within this project. At its heart then I am interested in how the authors continually juggle contradiction to intentionally provide a more complex reflection of mestizo identity and ultimately history through *mezclando*. I will focus on how the authors of both written text and visual text present history as both "facts" and "myths" and in many ways practical only in the imaginary; how the iconographic characters function to represent and demonstrate mixture; and ultimately to consider how *mezclando* is a method of subversion unique to Latino image texts.

The first page of the book nicely states and demonstrates its major conceit and ideological stance towards the topic of Latino history as caricature. On the left page is the "Programa del Teatro Histórico: Introducing the Players" which includes textual descriptions of each of the iconographical, stereotypical or archetypical characters and clichés that Stavans listed as his multiple narrators and counternarrators in the Foreword. As the caricature of a theatrical playbill indicates, Stavans intends the focus to be on these characters as actors or performers in the text to come in order to indicate their power in making meaning as transient rather than permanent.[5]

The paired image on the opposite page only includes the title "Introduction" and demonstrates these relationships even better. The insistence here is on foregrounding the constructedness of the "play" to follow which shares its name with the book's title. We have an image of a stage with many of the already introduced characters present, they include both those that will function as narrators and others that function as thematic representatives of later "content." These characters are not merely listed, as on the prior page, but are placed in relationship to one another reflecting meaningful emotions, body language, and opinion via their visual location in the scene. The central figures on stage are three sets of characters that represent roughly conservatism/assimilation vs. revolution/ separatism. Beginning in no particular order of importance, to the left is the icon "Maestra" who has earlier been pictured and defined as: "In English it means *teacher*. Inspired by the author's 5th grade teacher, the real Maestra would be truly shocked by his progress." In addition to this definition, in the acknowledgements Alcaraz thanks his "lovely Chicana schoolteacher-wife, ... for being the visual inspiration for Maestra" (168) thereby revealing that Maestra is at once visually representative of an individual human — Alcaraz's wife, Victoria, representative of a different individual human — Stavans's fifth grade teacher, and in her function in the text, iconographic of a value system or ideological approach to Latino history. It's a marvelous *mezclando* that exemplifies how Stavans/Alcaraz both work together and at different purposes in order to create their meaningful iconography.

I suggest that Maestra's function in the text is as a voice of reason and balance; she continually attempts to de-politicize the history to create recognizable "facts" and boundaries, rather than engaging in open ended philosophical debates. This is not to say that Maestra does not engage in "personal" opinions nor does she shy away from challenging the view of history as simple or one sided. In this introductory section she demonstrates that she does not understand Spanish (4), posits that history is a "kaleidoscope" (4) of histories rather than one coherent one, argues that because the book/play is in English the river separating Mexico and the United States should be called the Rio Grande (5), angrily denounces the term "alien" (8), and locates the "start" of this history in Christopher Columbus's first voyage in 1492 (13). This information is by no means all agreed upon as representative of a "conservative" view of Latino history. I locate her role as conservative not in the content of her "views" but generally in her function. Her main functions are

The caricature of a theatrical playbill establishes caricature as the central conceit of *Latino U.S.A.*

to summarize the actions of people and events generally without commentary, to correct the author's tendency to get off track—"let's not get lost in needless 'ifs.' Our job is to chronicle **Latino History**"[6] she shouts at him in exasperation" (20)—and also to provide closure to questions rather than allowing them to remain open ended. On the last page of the text she is silent but wearing an apple on her lapel, which one imagines is a sign of her successful teaching (166).

On this first page Maestra and what appears to be a stereotypical bandit figure (from an U.S. perspective or a peon/campesino or soldier from a Mexican one another *mezclando*) are about to shake hands thus forming a pair. They both have stiff and almost formal posture, their eyes look a bit hesitant and unsure, but both wear a smile as they approach each other. The soldado has the typical sombrero, rifle, bullets across his chest, and huaraches representative of a rural soldier from the Mexican Revolution of the early twentieth century. This same figure, with or without the bullets and gun, is representative of the stereotype of Mexicans as bandits, or just generally sneaky, and untrustworthy, from early American "greaser" movies, and as cartoon figures such as Speedy Gonzalez or the Frito Bandito. As he is not a narrator in the text we do not learn of his particular context as defined by his function in *Latino USA* and thus can see the nexus of both of these figures at work in the image: the traditional stereotype as a bandit from U.S. perspective, and as a rebel with a cause from a Mexican one. The only other references to the image in the text are split between representations of rural peasants or campesinos of any nationality primarily located as laborers, or as imitations of very specific images of soldiers from the Mexican revolution including: Emiliano Zapata and Pancho Villa from an historical photograph and generally (66, 69), Valentina Ramirez who was a soldadera in a much reproduced and iconographic photograph (67) and an engraving by Posada entitled "The Farewell," which shows a male soldier kissing a woman (68).[7] This blending of images of general citizenry with specific historical images/figures of revolution within this figure I suggest locates it as a positive archetype. Thus in this image alone he also operates as *mezclando*: bad guy and good guy, negative stereotype and liberating archetype, victim and architect of history. In this first pair then what seems like an image of two opposing forces actually represents the false dichotomy of this kind of ordering to complicate both their meanings and their functions in the text. They serve as a visual representation of *mezclando* both together in their initial gestures towards one another, and as noted in their separate functions in the text as a whole.

The next pair stands to the right on the stage and is arguably the most visually set off from the other characters and thus most immediately noticeable. They are a female activist identified with a beret decorated with a closed fist thus is associated with the Brown Power movement or specifically as a member of the Brown Berets. Across from her is a man in a suit and glasses with a briefcase by his feet. He is much more generic with no other identifiable elements and thus we assume he is some sort of professional. Given the pattern of opposing forces at work in the imagery here, I would identify him as the everyman "Mr. Businessman." These two characters stand at a noticeable distance from each other, with very big frowns on their faces, their bodies in erect and open stances, as if to take up as much space as possible, and respectively, with hands on hips and arms crossed. They eye each other suspiciously and angrily, making only gestures of rejection and hatred towards the other. They are clearly the largest source of antagonism on the page. As with the soldado, neither of them have narratorial power and thus they function as stereotypes in this panel dependent upon the reader's own associations with them. Unlike the soldado/bandit example, these stereotypes have currency primarily within the Latino community rather than externally therefore they would draw upon some element of prior knowledge by readers through experience or education.

Starting with "Mr. Businessman" it is somewhat difficult to identify this figure specifically in any other of the pages in the book. However, I would argue there are a few versions of this type identified with a suit, symbols of money and/or a briefcase in order to trace his arc in this book. After his appearance on the stage on page one, the type, though not the exact copy of the original, appears on the very next page next to the narrator Cantinflas—famous Mexican comedian described on the players list—mouth agape taking in the argument that America is a continent rather than a nation. He looks most prominently at Calavera—associated with the satirical art of Posada and also introduced in the players list—who states that naming the river between the United States and Mexico not only demonstrates difference within language but "two opposing world views" (2). He appears to be stunned by these notions and is positioned as though falling to his knees. He next appears, again in a different specific version, in the discussion about identity and labels as related to population totals. After a statistic estimating the total Latino population in the United States in 2025, a number of characters comment about the number and its significance. Regarding another character's question if the estimate includes those undocumented "Mr. Businessman" answers "Of course not. How are you going to count the ones who refuse to be counted?" (9). His attitude seems to be one of disapproval as he wears quite an angry expression, and of course his dialog puts the responsibility squarely on the undocumented for choosing not to be counted rather than blaming the forces that make it necessary or a combination of both. The next image we encounter is more than half way through the text in the context of the Cuban Revolution where he represents the wealthy professional Cubans who left into exile to the United States because of Castro's forced redistribution of money and property. He is shown holding his briefcase with a dollar sign, a silhouetted shoe print on his backside, while ostensibly shouting expletives, represented by wavy lines, as he boards the "SS Exile" and being seen off by "los pobres," visually pictured as black Cubans, and our Calavera. The next two images are fairly similar in their associations: they show our suited man clearly selling out and grasping for wealth and mainstream icons of "success." He is shown at the end of the spectrum of characters identifiable within 1960s and 70s radicalism, as if all the work of the 1960s led to his choice to don suit, tie, briefcase and specifically the symbol of Ralph Lauren's polo line on his clothes. The next page shows this type on a treadmill with huge dollar signs in his eyes and his face dripping with sweat as Calavera concludes that "The only thing the Latino 'haves' wanted was to separate themselves from the 'have nots'" (138) as he gestures towards the running man. The very final appearance of this man is uncertain as his full body is not included and thus he is not shown carrying a briefcase. I include him here though because his face looks remarkably like his first appearance on the page one introduction except without glasses and his dialog is consistent with the values of his prior incarnations. This character has the last word of the entire book, at least in dialog because we do get "Fin" as the curtain closes, when he shouts up to the characters left on stage that "I'd like a refund for this show! Now!" (166). Again his comment is directly associated with the importance of money and also to a conservatism that would find the whole project (the play and book) of *Latino USA* to be a useless venture.

His central purpose, as with his visage, is difficult to nail down, but I would argue that he exists as a representative of a conservatism that sees value only in financial gain and would oppose anything, or anyone, that would jeopardize that. Thus he is directly connected to upper class mobility, to currency, to high brow fashion and to the disapproval of all kinds of revolution whether it occurs in the street or in the mind. I believe he, like the campesino, is cast in a variety of unique versions in order to show his presence in a number of locations, time periods and with a reaction to differing issues. But rather than being illustrative of the lives of the masses of Latinos he stands for the greedy few with minds closed tightly around a number of issues.

His partner in that first introductory stage meeting is clearly identified as a radical activist of the Brown Power movement, given the image of the raised and clenched fist on her beret, and her opposition to the value systems of "Mr. Businessman" is quite evident and logical. It is interesting that one of the characters in this pairing is of specific historical relevance though certainly not current obsolescence — the radical activist — whereas the other is a more slippery and amorphous one reference. Consequently perhaps the reason that these two cannot shake hands, as Maestra and bandit/soldado could at the beginning of the text, is that the battle between social and political revolution is still very much alive within the community. Her appearances are most discreetly within the discussion of the 1960s radicalism and this figure is pictured protesting with Tijerina's Alianza Federal de Mercedes, for "Chicana Power" in what appears as a general protest for the rights of Chicanos, arguably she is also present in a protest on behalf of La Raza Unida Party, and as a student protestor screaming "¡Venceremos!" or out of Vietnam (111, 113–4, 120). She appears again in a recreation of a photograph in reference to the creation of the Brown Berets in 1967 (125) and here she has the insignia of that group on her beret. She appears as a protester in the National Chicano Moratorium (131) and as a member of a representative crowd reflecting the cooperation among "all the have nots: Puerto Ricans, Chicanos, Blacks and Native Americans" (132). Finally she appears as a representative of MeCHa, a student group, and holds a textbook indicative of the community's activism in creating Ethnic Studies at the university. In a kind of timeline that is meant to represent 1970s recession, and one imagines not just financial, she exists on a timeline in the middle between a hippie and our "Mr. Businessman" with the polo emblem (137).

These two figures are indeed diametrically opposed; they begin in opposition on stage and by the end of the "play" our radical activist is completely lost. There is no middle ground when it comes to politics within *Latino USA* both sides are locked into a reactionary stance against the other. Important though is the fact that they are both included within the history presented here, they are not resolved and they are not directly put into clear ideological boxes. It seems that the 1970s "recession" led to the rise of "Mr. Businessman" who speaks back to the entire project by the end of the play, apparently demonstrating his power over it as a consumer. But of course he has had to read or watch the text in its entirety so it has in fact accomplished the goals of— in his eyes anyway — the revolutionary. These figures represent that there are completely opposing political views and modes of operating within Latino communities and yet they are entirely coherent within its diverse fabric. "Mr. Businessman" passively reacts to circumstances and ideas, and instead the activist is typified by her very specific political opinions and physical interventions. Our authors create the *mezclando* not by creating one figure that represents contradictory forces in itself, but by showing the divergent forces that do not mix and yet are both part of the whole. It is these political values, of revolution or assimilation, that most "call out" our authors onto their own pages and thus force them to become part of their own mixtura/mixture (more about that in the final section).

The final pairing on the introduction on page one is perhaps the most contentious in the book. On the left of the page and standing behind Maestra and the soldado are, standing quite closely together, a Spanish conquistador and an Indian. The conquistador looks quite sheepish, even in his armor, as he smiles very broadly and holds up a hand to request that the Indian, opposite him, "stop" his motioning for the Spaniard to "get lost." The Indian man is very stoic as he wears a frown and ceremonial robes. The two stand toe to toe and I would say fit somewhere between the emotional register of the previous pairs: they do represent opposing poles and yet they are not reflecting hatred or violence, or a willingness to compromise, but rather one forceful determination and the other sheepishness. Of note here is that they are not portrayed as victimizer and victim nor conqueror and conquered; indeed I would argue that they represent a kind of assignation. As we know the Spaniards did not follow the indigenous peoples' request to "get lost," which led to what some posit was genocide. In any case Stavans and Alcaraz do not create an immediate hierarchy of power here; though perhaps through the emotions and gestures imply a chronology: cause and effect. It is through the text's subsequent images that the relationship of the pair is better revealed.

Evocatively, the next time we see the costume of the conquistador it is worn by Stavans himself as he interjects, at the bottom of a page which defines and contextualizes the term "Latino," that he "like[s the label] Hispanic best." The image collapses Spanish identity into the costume of the conquistador which is appropriate within the visual language of caricature. Finally on this page Alcaraz replies to Stavans' claim that "'Hispanic' makes me panic!" which functions as a reminder of the gap in identity politics between the two creators (7). The artist though speaks as himself and not in another caricatured costume. The rest of the uses of this character are similar to the activist in that the costume is directly associated with the historical time period that it appeared and indicative of certain beliefs and activities. We see it a number of times on historic men: Cortés (14), Nuñez Cabeza de Vaca (15), de Soto and De Oñate (22). Finally we see it applied generally to colonizers to comment on various effects of the conquest: the building of churches (22) and the enslavement of Africans and Indians (19 and 47). These images focus on the above activities and do not show any active attacks on Indians or African slaves; however, they are always armed and prepared for violence in costume if not in physical actions. Thus they represent actions already known, and developed and explained through the text rather than visually.

As is logical in the diversity of natives colonized, the images of indigenous nations and individuals vary quite a bit more from those of the conquistadors. We have only one specific indigenous individual portrayed in Popé the leader of a revolt in the early seventeenth century (23). Otherwise the Indian figure, like the peon/campesino, generally stands for the masses of population but during the periods of colonization rather than throughout the entire history. Thus we have numerous representations of Indians as inhabitants of the "new world" (14–15, 17, 19–21) who are portrayed as uninterested or confused by the Spaniards or determined to block their trespass; slave laborers in service to the church, (22–23, 47) as representatives of Spanish myth (17) or Aztec myth (73) and finally as ancient originators of food and words then inherited by both Mexicans and Americans (97). Interestingly the Indians are placed solely in the narrative context of part one: "Conquest and Exploration" (12) and when they appear in other chapters they are included as ways to look back an either pre Columbian or conquest times. The contemporary version of the Indian is very different in appearance and costume and first appears in a crowd scene of activists for the grape boycott listening to Chávez, as a masked member of "EZLF" (122) which I assume is meant to be a Spanglish caricatured acronym. The final image is of Sub-Commander Marcos in the same costume and a hat with "EZLN" (the Zapatista Army for National Liberation) advocating for the rights of the "Indian population" (161).

Generally these two images are shown in relationship as conqueror and conquered with the actual military conquests made clear through written text rather than through violent actions. Although the Spaniards do routinely appear as armed overseers of Indian laborers, the violence happens "off stage" and is not portrayed visually. Actually the only time a weapon is brandished between them is in the hypothetical "what if" story of what might have happened if the Indians conquered the Europeans instead of the other way around. In one image an Indian man, in religious costume, holds a knife to the belly of a Catholic priest or monk in order to convert him. Therefore, the actual violence of the conquest is minimized though shown in the form of analogy in this section. I suggest that Stavans wants to delay any reaction that his reader might have when confronted by this period of history in order for us to consider that even though the conquest was violent it also was responsible for creating the peoples we know today as Latinos/as. Certainly not condoning this violence, nor minimizing its impact in writing, the absence of violent images serves to lessen the visceral impact. In fairness though the authors also do not show Indigenous wars or negative images of paganism or sacrifice, which have been seen as arguments for their need for "civilization." In any case the play and the book continues the matter of fact relationship introduced on page one: it's a relationship that's forced for an unspoken reason. One that both Spaniard and Indian are forced to inhabit.

In many ways then, this pair combines the *mezclando* of the two previous pairs. The two are locked in a sort of combat, as the activist and the businessman, but rather than focusing on the political, or even militaristic reasons for the combat, the authors translate it into cultural territory thus making the war a draw (no pun intended) and thus the source of the *mezclando* itself. Like Maestra and the soldado/bandit also the two figures are always evocative of multiple associations from differing perspectives: as conqueror/conquered, as white/brown, and as representative of cultural and/or language traditions. Ultimately this pair function both as combatants and as signifiers of signification itself: they are the origin, and consequence, of *mezclando* and as we will see later the utilization of *mestizaje* itself.

Revealing the Mezcladoras Behind the Curtain

I read the positioning of author and illustrator as characters as well as narrators in the play/book *Latino USA*, as well as the inclusion of various other elements representative of their "creators," as the final crucial element of *mezclando* that effectively demonstrates the subversive effects of this caricature. The repeated visual presence, of Stavans at least, has been read as representative of the author's narcissistic obsession with his own perspective resulting in a narrative that would be better labeled, as Allatson argues a "Stavans-centered Latino history" (25). I argue though that not also considering Alcaraz's inclusion as character and narrator, as well as various objects representative of him in the text, is to misread this trope as solely narcissistic rather than potentially subversive.

Stavans indeed lists himself in the players list as "The author: Scientific name Dues Obnoxious Spanglishicus. Responsible for the following mess. Most of us here ~~don't~~ really like him." (n. pag.) His primary role as this character is to pop in from behind the curtain and make side notes and express his personal opinions on the contents of the play which unfolds concurrently. As mentioned above in the discussion of Maestra, he routinely also introduces opposing and much more open ended philosophical questions that the other narrators dismiss quickly, in order to insert questions about the role of authorship in history, the nature of history and historical narratives, and in the "Epilogue" to sum up the point of this history and thus the book/play. For example, he pops in from a sewer access on the page about the "Seven Cities of Cibola," to declare "Yet another myth in Latino history!" (17); on a page focused on what might have been the outcome if the conquest had worked the other way around he states "What if our view of beauty had Indian women — bronze, svelte, stunning — as its ideal and not its Iberian counterparts?" (20); and regarding the rise of anti-immigrant sentiment in the 1980s he asks in exasperation:

> When will the United States realize that immigration is a two-way street? Unless Latin American countries increase their per-capita earning, the desire to look elsewhere for a better life will continue. Likewise, without immigrants where would the economies of Texas, California, Arizona and New Mexico be? [153].

In addition to this speaking role as commentator the character also routinely stands behind the main action silently but providing a clear physical response, and thus commentary, to a page's action and actors — reacting with for example, smiling, giggling, clapping, directed anger or puzzlement (4, 152, 53, 134, 36).

Other, mostly verbally silent, participation is also pictured as the author routinely participates directly in the diegetic action of the page by joining other characters, dressing in similar costume or in other ways joining the "plot" of the story. I suggest that this element operates in two main ways. First, it provides a connection between "past" and "present" by portraying the intrusion of the narrative construction on the plot of history (again in this case the book or play). We can read his shaping influence on the narrative in his body language and behavior in each scene. The author is quite recognizable in all of these panels standing out as an intruder and therefore we do not interpret his presence as a forced snapshot of "actual" history as if he really was an eighteenth-century Mexican founder of Los Angeles (25), an arrested zoot suiter (88), or present at a speech by Martin Luther King, Jr. (109). On the contrary, his presence reminds us of the caricature of the entire project rather than its truthfulness. The author's diegetic presence functions as representative of the impact of past events on the current views of Latino history, identity and culture. As a whole, it is another kind of "what if" we could ask if we were to go back in time to witness "history." We only know it is history in that present because we come from the future where that narrative has already been shaped. Indeed the author states at one point: "What is history if not a set of convenient collectible lies — a fiction?" (34) Secondly, the author's role in the action also heightens the impact of a collective history, built upon a collective memory, similar to Corky Gonzales's poem "I Am Joaquin" — mentioned in the text and quoted there — which uses a first person speaker who impossibly travels through time and speaks directly from different individuals' perspectives in order to paint a story of Chicano history and begin forging a Chicano identity. As Calavera states the speaker "Becomes the quintessential Chicano Spirit. The poetic voice of the struggle" (112). Similarly, the author's presence in historical scenes visually represents collective identity at specific historical events and, because they are multiple, through time, in order to create a communal, though imaginary, experience of history. The author as character, nor Stavans himself, never claim to be telling truth but rather continue to show the constructedness of truth (the author behind the curtain) and undermine the possibility of really knowing the truth. To put a very clear bias in the text the author routinely comments on his own book projects — or at least subjects — and even includes a "shameless plug" for his own book on Oscar "Zeta" Acosta (127). Alcaraz also includes Stavans's own book titles on the shelves of the library.

Another purpose of the author's participation as character is to interrupt the seamless chronicling of history to reemphasize the narrative quality of history itself even in the present reading/viewing of *Latino USA*. With the metaphoric positioning of the Rio Grande/Rio Bravo as the borderline between the United States and Latin America we begin the book's dialogue about the tools historians use to create truth. Calavera and Toucan interrupt the philosophical musings about the name of the river, which depends on where you stand geographically and what language you speak, to inquire when the "history" will begin. Calavera states "I was under the impression this was a cartoon history of Latinos. Does our author get paid to do that?" (4). In the context of the panels, Calavera is criticizing the previous time spent ruminating on questions of identity and the nature of language. The Calavera then suggests they have a talk with him, apparently to "correct" his approach, while the Toucan doesn't even realize the author exists. As the representative of magical realism it's logical that Toucan does not separate between "realities" of action whereas Calavera, the voice of satire, does. This section establishes different experiences of, and views toward, the narrative but also that these characters are at the author's mercy as they are his creation (4). They are embedded within their own genres and can see the text only from those contexts. The questioning continues with the first snap of the film clapboard titled "Part 1: Conquest and Exploration 1492–1890," which leads Calavera to immediately interrupt questioning the narrative's beginning with Columbus. The author immediately shoots back "How would *you* divide history? By definition, history has neither beginning nor end, but it is a neverending flux, it's the historians who are setting the limits" (12). He effectively skirts Calavera's question but also posits history itself as a function of the imaginary as he continues to insist by other means throughout *Latino USA*. Another example of this is in an aside that illustrates the carving of the historical narrative into numbered pieces; the characters consider the "milestones" of Latino history as huge rocks with the dates "1848" and "1898" on them. Another smaller stone labeled "1948" drops off a rope and falls and is abandoned as breaking the asserted number pattern. The author wishes to include another milestone "1998" to the list thus filling out the convenient 100 year span set up before. His argument for the date coincides with the writing of *Latino USA*'s text which he proudly asserts is a milestone at least for him. The ridiculousness of this scene points to the fact that personal views always affect the dating and categorizing of historically important events, and it is also his way to disrupt the innocence of creating periods and epochs in narrative sequence. As the author states, in disagreement with Maestra, "The past isn't unchangeable, only the future is" (58) thereby opposing this structuring of "facts." On the facing page he also suggests that all historical "facts" are intertextual and never "original" as he is pictured sitting in a library with his own authored books as well a many other volumes of Latino history, literature and culture (59). The volumes sit next to each other all as imagined approaches to their topics; all borrowing from each other and from other antecedents. Ultimately, the author concludes in the Epilogue that the lesson of this history "is that history is a theater of possibilities" after which he happily jumps of stage and leaves (166).

Including an analysis of Alcaraz's presence as the character of "the cartoonist: Este vato loco has been drawing crowds since childhood" (n. pag.) within the text helps us see how both author and cartoonist function in similar ways to those mentioned above though in unique ways as yet another counter balance to the power of the author. We first see the cartoonist appear as a small image placed behind the author when he states "I like 'Hispanic' best" (7) as discussed above. The cartoonist responds in his mind only "'Hispanic' makes me panic!" which a look of angry confusion on his face. Unlike the author, and other narrators, the cartoonist does not interject anything in spoken text. His power functions solely through the image and its relationship to other visual and written texts on the page and is yet quite clear. A stronger example of this verbally silent reaction is in the discussion of Richard Rodriguez's *Hunger of Memory* in which he argued against Affirmative Action and bilingual education. The author is shown with a heart over his head saying, "The prose is superb — rhythmic, persuasive..." while the cartoonist is shown directly opposite him in the next panel gagging himself with his finger and wearing a "Absence of Memory" t-shirt (144) to indicate his disagreement and disgust.

The function of the cartoonist becomes more complex in a discussion of corridos where he is shown as a small figure at the bottom corner of the page sitting at a table holding up "Gregorio Cortez T-shirts XL only" (41). Mixing the celebration of a folk hero with its marketing as merchandise is one of the familiar themes of Alcaraz as a cartoonist and satirist. He is well known for poking fun at the Spanglish mixture of Mexican or other Latino images crossed with American consumerism or politics. On the following panel when the author expresses sadness in America's ignorance about Gregorio Cortez as a folk hero as contrasted to the familiarity of the drinking song "La Cucaracha" the cartoonist appears as a small figure quite far behind the author. Wearing a smile on his face and a t-shirt with his own cartoon character "Cuco Rocha," who just happens to be a character in his syndicated comic strip "La Cucaracha," we have the allusion to multiple signifiers here. Alcaraz has said Cuco Rocha is a kind of cockroach version of himself or as he stated in an interview "he's a Chicano that got so pissed off, he turned into La Cucaracha" ("Lalo") providing commentary on all things Latino. La cucaracha is also a cultural marker of Mexicans as a people which Alcaraz uses as a signifier in his own comic.

Thus this panel uses the author's text to make an ironic statement, but also layers that with the image of the cockroach, its national symbolism, Alcaraz's work in general and specifically his use of that symbol for his own satiric Chicano purposes. On one hand we could read this as self aggrandizement, however I suggest that the interaction between author and cartoonist here better shows the intertextuality at work within history as it's imagined and translated by others. Another example of the author's and cartoonist's functions reacting and replicating is on the aforementioned library shelves holding Stavans's own titles also sit Alcaraz's. Thus we have titles *La Cucaracha* and *Pocho.com* (59). Clearly not standard library fare especially as neither is a printed volume. I believe this library is rather a kind of vault of inspiration with the important texts that they used to shape their own authorizing of history. Even though the cartoonist is not visually portrayed as a character in the room he is nonetheless present. Alcaraz himself declares that he included these references "because I am a shameless self promoter, and any artist worth his salt is too" ("Alcaraz").

Other instances show the cartoonist as silently watching part of the plot of the history take place. Thus he sits at a table drinking at a Cuban nightclub/casino before the Cuban Revolution (102), sleeps during a lecture by the president of the University of Wisconsin in 1897 which consists of stereotyping Spain as a useless culture (51), again sits drinking with the author and a calavera as the importance of the artist Posada is discussed — and Alcaraz's drawing skills are critiqued (70).

In another silent approach to infusing a level of critique into the text Alcaraz uses a variety of visual inspirations for his images including political cartoons from the nineteenth and early twentieth centuries put in very different contexts (27, 50, 60) historical photographs of actual events and incidents (24, 46, 66, 67, 88, 94–5, 100, 108, 118, 125) recontextualized recreations of magazine and newspapers (32, 90, 120, 151–152), images from popular culture (8, 14, 44), and copies of partial or entire Latino art works (68, 71, 117, 124). This effectively locates history in a range of different places including historical documents as well as murals, street signs, the work of artists, and of kitsch culture. It blurs the line between makers of history and recorders or translators of history and thus effectively loosens "history" from specific kinds of documents, images and narratives.

In the epilogue we have three interesting images of the cartoonist and the cartoon. First is the cartoonist himself playing TV reporter for the network "Pocho TV," a play on his Pocho.com and his work on "Pocho Hour of Power" on Los Angeles radio station KPFK, asking the author what the lesson of history is (164). Following that are images of Cuco Rocha and a cockroach on the very last pages of the book. At the end of the play when the author is answering the question about the lesson of the book there are a number of figures on stage including Cuco Rocha peeking in from behind the curtain. It is not clear if he "stands" for Alcaraz here, as his alter ego ("Lalo"), or as a representative of the Latino masses, or just one really pissed off Chicano. He is looking rather sad and somewhat desperate as he waves meekly from his position facing the reader/audience. In the very last panel when the curtain drops and "fin" appears on the page we also see a picture of a cockroach scurrying off stage. We could perhaps have a series of transforming images being presented: starting with the cartoonist as member of the media and cultural commentator, to Cuco Rocha, pissed off Chicano and cultural commentator, and lastly the cockroach, the culture and people. While the insect is roughly in the same position as was Cuco it is not clear whether we think there has been a kind of Kafkaesque metamorphosis taking place — possibly foreshadowed when we first see Cuco on the cartoonist's t-shirt and the author is holding up a copy of the aptly named *The Metamorphosis* by "Francisco Kafka" at the time (42) — or an image of the Latino masses surviving and getting on with their lives no matter the outcome of this narrative/performance. I posit that both are accurate as they support the text's continued insistence on the complicated and unsure role of history as well as the importance of the power of caricature, of image generally, and the process of imitations, allusions and interextuality in the creation of the real.

Latino USA is an excellent example of the methods of *mezclando*— of continually mixing contradictory meanings, image narratives and textual ones, high culture and low culture, truth and fiction, disciplinary structures, insider and outsider meanings and assumptions and many more — that are the hallmark of Chicano texts. These blended elements find even more emphasis in the imagetext as many more levels of meaning are layered. With the inclusion of the author and cartoonist as characters and narrators of their own book, they are presented as tools to be utilized which forces us to re-contextualize the whole idea of "author," "narrator," and "subject." They become reflections of the text's de-composition of meaning rather than composition of meaning they appear as instigators of perpetual mixture. Because we see the caricatured bodies of the author and cartoonist they inhabit very different spaces that lead to *mezclando* as a strategy for survival as it responds to hierarchies of power. Again the mestizo is more important here as the representative of the gap between, interpreted quite differently depending on from which side we are viewing it, *mezclando* is the mechanism that highlights this irrevocable and paradoxical position and more than that, insistently makes it possible. Consequently *Latino USA* as "mestizo" text demonstrates this conflict — this view from the gap — not just what the gap is and that it exists, but the process of embodying and disembodying perspectives from within.

Thus the cartoon, the caricature, is necessary and particularly evocative of a specific use of *mestizaje*: the author who identifies with the Hispanic is a "mestizo" from the Latin American perspective whereas the cartoonist is "mestizo" from the American landscape of race. They represent these differences as images themselves, and in their views, ideas and reactions that run through the text. The images serve to embody these contestations and through connection with language or through only silence present bodies which are defined through different national landscapes and can not be melded into one term or one history. Therefore, not just in its writing, but in its working through *mezclando*, it demonstrates the difficult terrain of Latino ideologies, of the borders, of the *mestizaje* of multiple "other" histories. The histories in *Latino USA* do not exist merely as dates on the page or even images of famous people or moments, but in the gap between ways of being, ways of operating, that while they are incredibly divergent and at cross purposes, still meet in the middle of a new territory, albeit temporarily.

Notes

1. See for example Gema Pérez-Sánchez's analysis of the development and use of the comics medium as a response to the Franco dictatorship in Spain in *Queer Transitions in Contemporary Spanish Culture: From Franco to La Movida*. 143–186.

2. Indeed, what's particularly inappropriate about Nericcio's appropriation of "mestizo" as a genre or analytical tool is his statement that's it's ironic that his first text is by Jaime Hernandez who actually is a mestizo, i.e., a Chicano from Southern California. The only irony here is that he goes on to divorce this linguistic, racial and cultural identity all together from his reading of the comics.

3. See McCloud for his inclusion of indigenous Mexican codices; see Fernando Benítez's "The Demons of José Guadalalupe Posada" for a fuller discussion about the artist's satirical use of the skeleton figure, or calavera.

4. Clearly here I disagree with Allatson's framework of defining *Latino USA* as "a comic that falls into the genre of history" after which he positions Stavans' author function as entirely sinister by using image as an "innocent" style in order to center all of Latino history and Latino Studies on himself to the point that he "reformulat[es] ... Latino history and discourse so they are unimaginable without him" (19).

5. I exclude here a detailed discussion of either the Calavera or Cantinflas as they primarily exist as individual characters on the page while I am focused here on analyzing the three paired characters. However, I will discuss here Stavans' character's association with Cantinflas in particular. It could be argued they supply the last pairing as they appear to gaze at each other from across the stage, each partially behind the opposite curtain. Indeed, Cantinflas smiles and seems to wave at Stavans (1). Quite simply Stavans is loosely paired with Cantinflas as both comedian and "word slinger" (n. pag.) as they seem to travel lightly through the text but both make powerful statements. Not quite a pairing I suggest the character of the author sees Cantinflas as his "partner in crime" if you will; as a humorously disruptive force.

6. Emphasis in original.

7. In an interesting turn by Alcaraz there are four major figures that also demonstrate this difference in historical representation — bandits to Americans, heroes to Mexicans — in the stories of Juan Cortina, Gregorio Cortez, Tiburcio Vázquez and Joaquin Murrieta. They are represented in Alcaraz's realistic style as just heads with no typical peasant costume (39). The page following does unpack the discrepancy in the legacy of Gregorio Cortez as both outlaw and hero that features him riding a horse in this very costume.

Works Cited

Alcaraz, Lalo. Email interview. 4–5 August 2008.

Allatson, Paul. "Ilan Stavans's *Latino USA: A Cartoon History* (of a Cosmopolitan Intellectual)." *Chasqui* 35.2 (2006): 21–41. Print.

Anzaldúa, Gloria. *Borderlands/La Frontera: The New Mestiza.* Spinster's/Aunt Lute: San Francisco: 1987. Print.

Benítez, Fernando. "The Demons of José Guadalupe Posada." *Images of Mexico: The Contribution of Mexico to 20th Century Art.* Ed Erika Billeter. Trans. Missie M. French. Dallas: Dallas Museum of Art, 1987. 88–90. Print.

Campbell, Duncan. "Los Angeles Muralists Look Beyond the Brick Wall." *The Guardian.* 14 February 2000. N. pag. Web. 10 June 2008.

Hatfield, Charles. *Alternative Comics: An Emerging Literature.* Jackson: University Press of Mississippi, 2005. Print.

"Lalo Alcaraz." Interview by Ana Merino. Excerpted from *The Comics Journal #270.* 17 August 2005. *The Comics Journal.* N. pag. Web. 15 July 2008.

McCloud, Scott. *Understanding Comics: The Invisible Art.* New York: Harper, 1993. Print.

Nericcio, William Anthony. "Artif[r]acture: Virulent Pictures, Graphic Narrative and the Ideology of the Visual." *Mosaic: A Journal for the Interdisciplinary Study of Literature* 28.4 (December 1995): 79–109. Print.

Noriega, Chon. "Introduction: Postmodernism or Why This Is Just Another Poster." *Just Another Poster? Chicano Graphic Arts in California.* Ed. Noriega. Santa Barbara: University of California Press, 2000. 19–21. Print.

Paredes, Americo. *"With a Pistol in His Hand": A Border Ballad and Its Hero.* Austin: University of Texas Press, 1958. Print.

Pérez-Sánchez, Gema. *Queer Transitions in Contemporary Spanish Culture: From Franco to La Movida.* SUNY ser. *In Latin American and Iberian Thought and Culture.* Jorge J.E. Gracia and Rosemary Feisdorfer Feal, eds. New York: State University of New York Press, 2007. Print.

Pérez-Torres, Rafael. *Mestizaje: Critical Uses of Race in Chicano Culture.* Critical American Studies ser. Minneaplis: Univeristy of Minnesota Press, 2006. Print.

Richardson, Lynda. "'The Czar of Latino Literature and Culture' Finds Himself Under Attack." *The New York Times,* 13 November 1999. B 13. Late Edition. ProQuest. Web. 20 May 2008.

Saldívar, Ramón. *Chicano Narrative: The Dialectics of Difference.* Madison: Wisconsin University Press, 1990. Print.

Stavans, Ilan. *Latino USA: A Cartoon History.* Illus. Lalo Alcaraz. New York: Basic, 2000.

_____. *The Riddle of Cantinflas: Essays on Hispanic Culture.* Albuquerque: University of New Mexico Press, 1998. Print.

_____, ed. *The Norton Anthology of Latino Literature.* New York: Norton, 2009. Print.

Stavans, Ilan, and Harold Augenbraum, eds. *Growing Up Latino.* New York: Mariner, 1993. Print.

Vargas, George. "A Historical Overview/Update on the State of Chicano Art." *Chicano Renaissance: Contemporary Cultural Trends.* Ed. David R. Maciel, Isidro D. Ortiz and María Herrera-Sobek. Tucson: Univeristy of Arizona Press, 2000. 191–231. Print.

PART III

READING THE HERO

9

"3X2(9YZ)4A": Stasis and Speed in Contemporary Superhero Comics

MARTYN PEDLER

In Scott McCloud's groundbreaking examination of what makes sequential art tick, *Understanding Comics,* he casts himself as a stand-up comedian, struggling to accurately define the medium. When an outraged member of the audience shouts out "What about Batman?! Shouldn't it have Batman in it?" he is quickly ejected, off-panel (9). McCloud's heckler is, of course, correct: Any discussion of comic books *should* have Batman in it — or, at the very least, an examination of superheroes and their adventures. McCloud, along with critics like Scott Bukatman, Douglas Wolk, and David Carrier, convincingly makes the case that while comic books may share some of their visual vocabulary with cinema, they must be carefully analysed as their own, specific form. Equally, superhero comics have their own techniques, conventions and obsessions that twist sequential art into its own hyperbolic language.[1]

Skin tight costumes and secret identities; brightly-coloured, spectacular adventures; battles between good and evil settled — at least until the following issue — through violence; and most of all, superhero stories feature a focus on action. Action is everything. It's why Superman's ability to fly is an integral part of the appeal of the character, tapping into the desire for unrestricted mobility that is part of "America's dreamwork" (Engle 337). It's no coincidence that Superman's unforgettable description involves speeding bullets, powerful locomotives, and leaping tall buildings. As recent blockbuster cinema brings more and more superheroes to the big screen, they inevitably star in action films, which share their interest in kinetic display. One of the strengths of the visual storytelling of comic books is that it seems to be so simple and self-evident to understand (Carrier 85). However, watch Douglas Wolk's struggle with the fog of semiotic confusion of *Showcase* #4 from 1956:

> Is this comic a showcase for art, as in a museum? A series of frozen representations of reality or representations of something so unreal that body moving at high speed leaves parallel lines

of ink behind? A movie that isn't really a movie, made out of individual images that the eye can see in or out of sequence or at the same time? Something that breaks destructively out of attempts to fix it in its place? (5)

The star of this issue is DC Comics' scarlet speedster, "The Fastest Man Alive": the super-hero known as the Flash. Whether Barry Allen or his successor, Wally West, the Flash is defined by his speed—and yet born into a medium that consists only of still images. Giving the Flash motion is a sophisticated set of techniques designed to express both movement and time, borrowing from cinema while also diverging wildly from it (Bukat-man, "Online Comics" 133).

> "Why can't he be more like the Flash? The Flash doesn't sit around—
> he does things!"—Iris West in *Flash* #113, 1959.

His schemes thwarted, the evil cult leader Kobra attempts final revenge on the Flash by firing a powerful laser at his beloved, Linda, in *Flash #99* (1995). With a last burst of speed, Flash outraces the laser and saves her—but his velocity means he is pulled into the mythical "speed force," never to return. As he becomes pure energy, the panels showing us the faces of his friends and enemies start to break down, falling apart on the page, shattering like panes of glass. With a final, vertical *KRA-KOW*, the Flash disappears in a burst of white light.

The above synopsis, presented in straight lines of sensible type, simply can't recreate the experience of following the Flash across those pages. For one, there's an alarming lack of exclamation points; also quotes that sit comfortably in word balloons can look prim or pathetic when excised from them. The most successful superhero novels are books that invent and twist their own heroes, like Michael Chabon's *The Amazing Adventures of Kavalier and Clay* (2001). Novels that adapt already existing comic book storylines are redundant curiosities; novels that present original stories of Batman, Spider-Man, and the rest are not considered part of the "real" continuity of their comic book adventures. Copyright difficulties with the heroes of Marvel and DC Comics, however, leave most academics who want to discuss more than a few pages with no choice but to translate those complicated panels into prose. Words are simply not adequate—lacking the colour, shape, and iconography to properly describe these superhuman characters.

In comic books, words aren't just words—they're pictures, too, lettered to create a visual onomatopoeia, crushing, zapping, whooshing, spelling out their power. Straight text, trapped in balloons or boxes, is kept to a minimum. Douglas Wolk estimates that it only takes 150 or so words on a six-panel page before it starts to seem cluttered (25). That's only slightly more words than contained in this paragraph you're reading now. While academic writing about superheroes might never pack the *KRA-KOW*s of comic books, this paragraph, and those above and below it, are best seen with imaginary thick, black rectangles around them—prose-panels, if you will. The white space between them is a Bizarro World version of the comic book "gutter"; the non-space that "plays host to much of the magic and mystery that are at the very heart of comics!" according to an excited Scott McCloud (66). Here, as in comic books, the real action takes place, invisibly, between the words.

The fact that comics legend Will Eisner described the word balloon as "a desperation device" (134) indicates how dialogue only seems to come into play when action somehow fails — or, better yet, left as pithy, tough-guy dialogue embroidered around the art. If superheroes can't seem to be successfully translated into prose, their "action comics" certainly share common ground with contemporary action cinema. Cinematic action heroes eschew verbal communication, choosing to let deeds do the talking; their heroic status marked by a "reticence with language" (71). The 1980s were particularly filled with "hard body" heroes, who would be captured in body-builder poses by the camera, letting them display their spectacular musculature — often at the cost of traditional narrative momentum (Tasker, *Spectacular Bodies* 76). Action cinema exhibits elements of so many different genres that it is best characterised not by plot, but by sequences of fights, chases, explosions, athletic feats, and cutting-edge special effects (71). Compared with regular humans, the adventures of these heroes prove them almost superhuman again and again.

If action stars are superheroic, it only takes some quick box-office math to see that superheroes are now action stars. The last ten years have been filled with adaptations of some of Marvel and DC's biggest characters, and their success shows the power of these superheroes as transmedia properties. In Sam Raimi's *Spider-Man* (2002), for example, a human Peter Parker often turns into a computer-generated Spider-Man — and as the primary showcase for special effects, the studios promote exactly how these inhuman characters are created (296). Free from the limitations of flesh, Spider-Man can now fight on the sides of skyscrapers, performing impossible midair stunt sequences. The superhero body is a site of freedom: from gravity, from inertia, from all human limitations over mobility (Bukatman, "Boys in the Hoods" 188). While action cinema is a slippery category, it always foregrounds "a visceral, even sensual, evocation of movement and violence" (Tasker, *Action and Adventure Cinema* 5); superheroes fit that definition as neatly as they do their spandex costumes.

Even on paper, a superhero's body remains a special effect: hypermuscled physiques that are bursting with energy, armoured against harm, ever fluid, transforming, and adolescent (Bukatman, "X-Bodies" 68). These qualities — combined with distinctive costumes, logos, and colour schemes — make bodies visually spectacular, and comic artists render them in loving detail. Rob Liefeld, from the style-obsessed Image Comics school of the '90s, is the patron saint of bodily obsession. He obsessively inks each muscle almost to the exclusion of all else, even if it means obscuring the ongoing storytelling in the sequence of panels. His comic books are left lurching from one dramatic full-page shot to the next (Wolk 34). Liefeld certainly pushes the envelope, but he is only exaggerating qualities typical of all superhero stories, where splash pages holding back story for the sake of display. These faux pin-ups can function similarly to lavish spectacles in Hollywood epics — slowing down the action to a crawl to be shown in fetishistic detail (84).

Any critical analysis of action cinema must deal with the long-standing supposed divide between spectacle and narrative (75). Seen through Tom Gunning's influential work on the theory of attractions, action cinema oscillates between traditional narrative progress and self-aware spectacles that interrupt the plot with blatant display. His description of the temporality of attractions is of particular interest to sequential art: that of an "intense form of the present tense" (Gunning 4,5). It's a good way to describe the process of reading a comic book, as each panel acts as a specific "'now,' a discrete image, waiting to be stitched together with the next. David Carrier, again comparing comics and cinema, compares the process to watching a movie with a jerky, out-of-sync projector (Carrier 51). A major difference? If fine art is meant to induce contemplation by holding the eye, comics constantly rush forward (Carrier 98). The reader has total control over how long to stare at any given panel, be it a double-page splash or barely an inch across, but is always carried forward. Even the monthly schedule of superhero comics means that one issue supplants the last, and, once read, is immediately waiting to be supplanted again by the next. As Scott Bukatman writes, "To be a superhero, you've got to be able to move" ("Boys in the Hoods" 189). The same can be said of their fans.

"Time's not frozen. It just looks that way to me — because I'm moving at near-light speed without the slightest effort!" — The Flash in *Flash* #91, 1994.

In *Flash* #114 (1960), "The Big Freeze," Captain Cold activates a device that sends "an impulse of absolute cold" throughout the city, freezing everyone and everything into stasis except for Iris West and himself. Dogs are snap-frozen in mid-chase, men in mid-stride. Apart from the expositional dialogue and some new, icy-blue colouring in the sky, however, there'd be no way to tell this from any other panel in the issue. It's why cold-based villains like Captain Cold and Mister Freeze tend to leave some helpful icicles on their victims — otherwise, how do we know it isn't just a typical comic book pose? Elastic temporality is a trademark of superhero stories, and of Flash comics specifically. When Barry Allen first gains his powers, it doesn't just manifest as hypervelocity — it's also that objects slow down, hanging motionless in the air. The next hero to take up the mantle of the Flash, Wally West, takes revenge on a super-fast enemy named Inertia by freezing him, barely mobile, and leaving him in the Flash Museum to be gawked at by tourists: "He's trapped for eternity in a frozen body ... forced to stare, with eyes that take a hundred years to blink" (*All-Flash* #1, 2007).

The most lyrical description of the Flash, courtesy of writer Alan Moore, evokes these same notions of temporality and mobility: "There is a man who moves so fast that his life is an endless gallery of statues" (*Swamp Thing* #24, 1984). Yet the Flash is *also* a statue on these pages. That's why we are always provided with visual cues to suggest his motion. Stopwatches and speedometers abound, in comics with titles like "Around the World in 80 Minutes!" (*Showcase* #13, 1958). When the Flash knocks a pot out of a bystander's hand during a superspeed battle through a marketplace on page four, he conquers the villain and returns to catch the pot before it hits the ground on page eight, handing it back to its owner, saying "Gotta run" (*JLA* #3). Even the way that Wally West's narration begins each issue by stating "I'm the fastest man alive" highlights the anxiety that perhaps we won't be able to tell by the images alone. In 1986, Alan Moore and Dave Gibbons' classic *Watchmen* called its superheroes by the collective noun of "masks," showing the obsession with identities, secret and public (Bukatman, "X-Bodies" 54); now, Marvel Comics use the term "capes" instead in their hero-versus-hero storyline *Civil War*

(2006). Capes foreground motion, rather than disguise, and are important visual accessories to help imply a flying hero is in motion.[2]

These cues exist within the panels, but most motion sits between them. Any two panels, side by side, make us notice what's changed and we fill in the motion required to make sense of those changes (Wolk 133). When done correctly, this closure results in a fluid reading process; done awkwardly, it's the "jerky projector" that Carrier mentions above. Most interesting is McCloud's preferred metaphor of mobility for this closure: readers flinging themselves from the first panel to be caught by the next moment, and the next. "Is it possible that closure can be so managed in some cases," he says, "that the reader might learn to fly?" (McCloud 90). Panels themselves might be frozen images, but there's endless movement between them. Superheroes also move beyond the edges of their panels, stretching their clean, clear boundaries with fists, capes, and energy blasts warping any attempt at a simple, geometric grid. Heroes might be supposed agents of order, but their adventures are visually much more like chaos (Bukatman, "Boys in the Hoods" 186). Superhero comics aren't just daunting for new readers because of their decade-long-running stories, but also because of the complicated visual landscape transmitting them.[3]

If the way panels are arranged on the page is confusing, then the temporality of a single panel is no less complicated. Despite the way that superhero stories are less verbal than other media, language plays an important role in the way a still image creates its own sense of passing time, by adding a temporal dimension—the time it takes these words to be read or spoken (Wolk 25). Dialogue is used to guide the reader around the page, too. For example, to show super-speed, *Flash* comics spread his dialogue thin—"often" "with" "one" "word" "per" "balloon"—to show how quickly he's covering distance throughout the panel. And the reverse-logic plays out in commonly impossible, midair, mid-battle speeches. Visually, it would appear that a panel is meant to contain a single moment—so should we read a paragraph long speech by Wolverine to imply that he's just hanging still in the air while he speaks? Even the "now" of a panel has a beginning, middle, and end. A panel without any words can, perversely, seem to last even longer, as its lack of timing makes it seem timeless (McCloud 102).[4]

The unification of words and pictures results in storytelling techniques that confound the traditional opposition between narrative and spectacle. Take Raimi's first *Spider-Man* movie (2002). We see Spider-Man kidnapped by his arch-nemesis, the Green Goblin, and taken to a rooftop for an exposition-filled chat. They sit and stand, mostly still, to exchange promises and threats; a scene to forward the narrative, before the movie happily swings back towards spectacle. This scene is particularly stilted and odd: not just because it's between two characters hiding their faces, but because there would be no need for it in a comic book. Instead, this conversation would take place during a fight scene, and the exposition would serve the dual purpose of also guiding the reader around action-packed panels. To defuse the narrative / spectacle split in cinema, critics have suggested a third term: "action" (Jancovich 85). It accounts for the fact that its spectacular moments actually do advance the plot, as visual conflicts have been narrativized (Higgins 76). In comic books, all conflict is rendered as spectacular; ideological battles are rendered just as visually as physical ones. You can witness the childlike green Hulk wrestle with the cunning gray Hulk over control of Bruce Banner's subconscious, for example, in *Hulk* #373 (1990). Combine that logic with comics' seemingly unique way of allowing twin streams of movement and exposition to take place at once, and it's a natural fit for action as a "third term" to best explain their ongoing narrative momentum.

> "I feel like an ant crossing the Sahara."
> — The Flash, waiting in a bank queue, in *Flash #71*, 1992.

In 1992, Superman was beaten to a much-hyped (but inevitably temporary) death by Doomsday, a new villain, all inhuman grunts and protruding bones. The crossover moves from using four panels per page in one issue, then three panels per page in the next, until culminating in *Superman #75* (1992). This issue is comprised entirely of splash pages — with Superman's death revealed on a special, third fold-out page. Panel size doesn't only relate to temporality in superhero comics. It's also about impact. Is there anything in action cinema that recreates the sense of actively unfolding that third page? Or tilting *Fantastic Four #252* (1983) on its side, as it is drawn in a "widescreen" aspect ratio? Or realising that Red Arrow and Vixen, buried amidst underground rubble, didn't know they were actually upside down — and having to turn the comic upside down to experience their realisation (via upside down lettering) in *JLA #11* (2007)? Like Gunning's cinematic attractions, this suggests a very different relationship to the viewer. These spectacles invoke the logic of exhibitionism in their displays, directly and actively addressing the spectator (5).

Contrast the above with the prestige project *Marvels* (1994). Retelling early events of Marvel Universe history through an everyman narrator and photographer, Phil Sheldon, the issues open and close with darkroom imagery, superheroes captured in developing film. The series is filled with these moments of mediation: superheroes in black and white newspaper pics, playing in movie newsreels, or caught by the reflection in a camera lens. Sheldon narrates:

> To follow the Marvels through their combat, as the Sub-Mariner bolted from landmark to landmark sowing destruction, the Torch a streak of fire on his tail — it must have seemed like a glorious aerial ballet. Dangerous, beautiful, and thrilling. And maybe it was. But not for us [*Marvels #1*, 1994].

Instead, Sheldon is trapped down on the street, far away, surrounded by the chaos and destruction left in the Marvels' wake. When he finally gets close enough to see the heroes — and be part of the action — he is struck down by debris and loses an eye. He wears a patch for the rest of the series, a constant reminder to watch from a respectful distance. *Marvels* is illustrated by Alex Ross, who has been called "the Norman Rockwell of comics" (*Alex Ross Mythology*, 2003). It differs from traditional comic art in that it is painted, and moreso, painted from real-life models. The attention to detail in this newly "realistic" artwork —filled with nostalgic trappings of the era — gives the images of the heroes a different kind of power (Bukatman, "X-Bodies" 71). When the series retells the world-shattering battle of the Silver Surfer and Galactus from *Fantastic Four #50* (1966), the fantastic alien beings leak out into the borders and gutters of the page, while the human drama is kept separate, contained in small panels. Since the publication of *Marvels*, Alex Ross has developed a huge following for his cover-shots of superheroes, posing for the camera, resolutely not in motion. The flying trapeze-act of interpretation and closure does not apply here — there is no impetus to find the moment both before and after the image to create an ongoing narrative (Carrier 50). Even his sequential art feels like beautiful, disconnected moments. McCloud points out that if you're going to paint a world full of motion, "then be prepared to paint motion!" (109). Ross's version of this is to synthesize a photographer's eye. When he paints a hero in motion, it's as Lois describes Superman in *Whatever Happened To The Man of Tomorrow?* (1986): "I was falling, and a violet comet was falling beside me. The reds and blues ran together, you see, so that's how he looked when he flew … a violet comet."

In the real world, objects don't have a clear black outline around them at all times. Amongst all the conceptual pyrotechnics of superhero comics, it's easy to forget a simple and all-important fact: they are usually drawn (Wolk 118). In *Flash* #95 (1994), the first part of a storyline called "Terminal Velocity," we find the Flash running through an impossible landscape of images and colours, somewhere in the timestream: "What is this effect?" he wonders. "Have I been processed by Industrial Light & Magic?" Yet despite this psychedelic backdrop, one element remains perfectly clear and focused, and that's the Flash himself. Occasionally we'll see him as a blur of speed, as do the bystanders of his stories, but the majority of the time we're there, keeping pace with him, even if he's travelling so quickly that everything else on the page has been reduced to abstract speed-lines. It's common wisdom — and undeniably true — that superhero stories are largely power fantasies for the powerless adolescent (Fingeroth 19). As with cinematic action heroes, the near-omnipotent abilities of the heroes better allow narcissistic identification to take place for the audience (Neale 11). Fantasies of mastery don't just come through bullet-proof skin and rippling muscles, however. Superman's mastery over Metropolis comes in part from his super-vision: watching from high above, X-raying all obstacles, seeing everything in perfect detail. As if granted by a radioactive spiderbite, superhero comics bestow a similar sense of visual mastery. Everything is legible through this "panoramic and panoptic" gaze of both the hero and the reader (Bukatman, "Boys in the Hoods" 194).

A glance back at some of the more complicated covers of superhero crossovers illustrates this visual logic. The first issue of DC's epic *Crisis on Infinite Earths* (1985) shows dozens of identical earths destroyed by crackling energy, surrounded by more than a dozen costumed beings hanging in space in various states of distress. Twenty years later, Marvel Comics' *Civil War* (2006) featured wraparound covers showing scores of superheroes mid-battle; the final issue showed them lying bleeding and unconscious instead. Every hero and villain is drawn in perfect focus. Unlike in action cinema, these scenes are not cut up across time and space by frantic editing. They're laid out for the reader, who "edits" them only in the time it takes for the eye to flick across the page to a new point of attention (McCloud 97).[5] It might be a mistake to compare these scenes to cinema at all. The heroes, like everything in comics, are a result of what Carrier calls the "aggressive caricature" of comic art; the automatic distortion that results from pencil and ink, instead of the supposed emotional neutrality of other forms (6). These barrel torsos, veined armed, and hypermuscled bodies — especially in the Rob Liefeldian era — are "autoreferential," only comparable to other bodies of other heroes (Bukatman, "X-Bodies" 59).

"Catch lightning in your hands sometime. Spend a month between the ticks
of a second and tell me what noise you hear when you crack the sound barrier."
— The Flash in *Flash* #80, 1993.

The super-sight allowed by comic art lets us see everything — even the impossible. We see Peter Parker's face symbolically half-covered by his iconic mask upon sign of trouble, or Bruce Wayne in street clothes somehow casting Batman's shadow behind him. We see the dotted outline of the Invisible Woman's forcefield and Wonder Woman's invisible jet. *Crisis on Infinite Earths* begins in deep space, showing the reader the big bang of the "multiverse"; as in Gunning's moments of attraction, no stand-in spectator is required inside the diegesis to justify it (5). When the cosmic gods Eclipso and the Spectre recently warred on earth, their battle was invisible to everyday inhabitants: "Their struggle, though gargantuan, goes unnoticed by humankind. There is only so much the human mind can accommodate, after all" (*Countdown to Mystery* #8, 2008). But not to us. We're not just bystanders like Phil Sheldon. We see it all, and the exhibitionist logic of display — of events being presented "just for us" — is often hammered home by comic-book narration that speaks right out of the page.

Superheroes are so used to achieving the impossible that it's only fitting the visually impossible is used to depict them. The Flash might not wear a cape, but the speed lines and lightning bolts that stretch from his speeding form serve the same purpose. Stranger still are moments when he appears multiple times within the one panel to show he's too fast to be captured in a single temporal moment. In Grant Morrison's arthouse comic series, *The Invisibles* (published by DC's adult imprint, Vertigo) this technique of rendering temporality is an avant-garde abstraction (Wolk 265); in superhero comics, it is just part of the regular vocabulary of the impossible.[6] Similarly, Morrison's deconstructionist epic *Animal Man* showed his characters actually breaking through the panel edge and into the guttering of the page. It's a moment of pure horror, haunted by shadows, saying: "spooned out my own eyes and still I see. We're not real." (*Animal Man* #24, 1990).[7] But a years later, when Animal Man encounters this same white non-space, it's described in superhero sci-fi lingo as "Space-B," and concerns that it will be more "existential isolation trauma" are quickly assuaged (*52: Week 49*, 2007).

The Flash has to deal with this kind of visual oddness all the time. Barry Allen runs so fast that he breaks the time barrier, first represented by the strange typography of digits just hanging in the air around him (*Showcase* #14, 1958). Wally West, moving faster than the speed of light, breaks free of the visuals around him and into the pure white of the gutter, sitting between the original scene and the "speed force": a wall of multicoloured light (*Flash* #137, 1998). This is "solid speed." It's time represented as space — just as it is in the spatiotemporal landscape of the comic page. As with spectacle-driven science fiction cinema, superhero comics regularly depict the infinite and the sublime, and both media exhibit this obsession in their titles alone (Bukatman, "The Artificial Infinite" 258 and

Wolk 56).[8] The endless space and time of the sublime is a place of hyperbole and excess, causing sensations of awe and astonishment; Bukatman holds that the special effects of science fiction create tamed versions of these infinities to allow the spectator a sense of mastery while viewing them ("The Artificial Infinite" 281). Comic books go one better. Marvel Comics even made infinity an anthropomorphised being — part of the five cosmic individuals alongside Eternity, Death, Oblivion, and Galactus — for superheroes to encounter. The Flash even briefly (and spectacularly) wore a crackling, golden costume made of pure speed-force, explaining that it was speed "condensed into three-dimensional space. I think" (*Flash* #132, 1997).

Giant, planet-devouring Galactus trails irony as well as destruction in his wake. When he seemed ready for his moment of transmedia glory, ready to appear on the big screen in the special-effects-laden *Fantastic Four 2: Rise of the Silver Surfer*, his comic book visual was unpalatable for the realism required by cinema. Instead, he was presented as a destructive space-cloud. In the Marvel Universe, however, it was revealed that Galactus doesn't *really* look as Jack Kirby draws him. Galactus simply can't be perceived by human senses: "Yes, you're big ... but humanoid ... nose, fingers, optic nerves, etcetera ... is how my brain registers you so it doesn't melt down. Truth is, you're so far beyond what I recognize that my piddling human senses are beneath you" (*Fantastic Four* #521, 2005). Galactus' visual, too fantastic for the cinema screen, is a watered-down version of his "real" form, which is too much for the comic page to contain. In the multi-dimensioned universe inhabited by superheroes, it's intriguing to imagine that "aggressive caricature" is actually protecting us from the unmediated sublime: a "spatiotemporal grandeur," as Bukatman puts it ("The Artificial Infinite" 286), that no technology can tame or represent — whether pencil and ink, or expensive CGI effects.

The Flash comics have a magic word, of sorts: "3X2(9YZ)4A." It's a mathematical formula that "describes a fourth-dimensional construct. It can't be realised in three-dimensional geometry" (*Flash* #78, 1993). Even comic book art — impossibly abstract as it often is — renders the equation as simple letters and numbers. Correctly imagining it, however, will bestow a burst of inhuman speed. How? Why? It's beyond explanation. The Flash is a man of action, too busy moving from present tense to present tense to let questions such as this bother him. When he skips between panels, through the white of the gutter, it's just to show exactly how fast he's moving. *The Flash* comic has a favourite trick of showing two panels, a millisecond apart, but between which the Flash is implied to have invisibly performed lengthy tasks; sometimes even within a single panel, as when he says "Be right back" and "Okay, I took a quick look" almost at once (*JLA* #20). This depiction of impossible movement, filling the space between each moment with huge distances of conceptual flight, is exactly the kind of superheroic technique that Bukatman suggests presents the dialectic between movement and stasis with such force ("On-Line Comics"133).

The Flash is held responsible for rejuvenating interest in superheroes, with DC Comics writer Geoff Jones even saying that "without Barry Allen, we'd still be reading comic books about cowboys" (*New York Daily News* 2008). As more and more heroes are claiming their own Hollywood blockbusters, it's been suggested that this big screen success — combined with dwindling audiences of superhero comics themselves — may mean that the future will hold only "screened" versions of these stories (Fingeroth170). The spectacles created specifically for the comic-book page require a specific, complicated, and often joyously impossible visual vocabulary for motion, and it is perhaps impossible to translate. Let's leave the final words for the Flash, who here could be talking about the sequential art contained in his monthly adventures:

> "When you do this trick right there's a point where ... momentum ... overcomes ... gravity."—The Flash in *Flash* #54, 1991.

Notes

1. Elements of this chapter are adapted from an earlier version of this essay published as "The Fastest Man Alive: Stasis and Speed in Contemporary Superhero Comics" in *Animation: An Interdisciplinary Journal* 4:3 (November 2009).

2. It's all very well for Brad Bird's animated superhero film *The Incredibles* to mock the ridiculousness of capes—"Stratogale! April 23rd, '57! Cape caught in a jet turbine!"—because it belongs to a medium that has the luxury of visible motion.

3. For further explanation of the tangled continuity of long-running superhero comics, see "The Tears of Doctor Doom" in *Overland* 191.

4. This is also why seemingly taciturn heroes often keep up a running, Philip Marlowe-style internal dialogue, epitomized by Frank Miller's *Batman* comics.

5. Temporality is further complicated by the fact that even when focusing on a particular panel, we remain aware of the rest of the page; we take in now, past and future at once (McCloud 104). The only superhero movie to attempt to recreate some of these sensations is Ang Lee's underappreciated art-block-buster, *Hulk* (2003). His shifting split screens act as panels, unstuck in time, and at one point he replaces traditional editing with pulling back, revealing a whole wall of frames, and then zooming in on another—much as the eye might on a page (Lichtenfeld 303).

6. In fact, these multiple images are a long-running feature of *Flash* comics, arising from representations of his own speed; the numerous super-fast characters who share his logo as part of the "Flash Legacy"; and villains like the Mirror Master, who can create duplicates of himself at will. When the cover of *Flash* #74 features multiple Flashes with the blurb "Too many speedsters!" it's not immediately obvious why this should be different from any other issue.

7. For more on Morrison's meta-take on superheroes, see "Morrison's Muscle Mystery versus Everyday Reality ... and Other Parallel Worlds!" in *The Contemporary Comic Book Superhero.*

8. Readers are so used to the procession of *Infinity Gauntlets* and *Infinite Crises* that their latest crossover attempts to generate drama using the opposite logic—calling itself the dangerously finite *Final Crisis* instead.

Works Cited

Bukatman, Scott. "The Artificial Infinite: On Special Effects and the Sublime." *Visual Display: Culture Beyond Appearances.* Ed. Lynne Cooke and Peter Wollen. New York: New, 1995. 254–289. Print.
_____. "The Boys in the Hoods: A Song of the Urban Superhero (2000)." *Matters of Gravity: Special Effects and Supermen in the 20th Century.* Durham: Duke University Press, 2003. 184–224. Print.
_____. "Online Comics and the Reframing of the Moving Image." *The New Media Book.* Ed. Dan Harries. London: BFI, 2002. 133–143. Print.
_____. "X-Bodies (The Torment of the Mutant Superhero) (1994)." *Matters of Gravity: Special Effects and Supermen in the 20th Century.* Durham: Duke University Press, 2003. 48–80. Print.
Carrier, David. *The Aesthetics of Comics.* University Park: Pennsylvania State University Press, 2000. Print.
Engle, Gary. "What Makes Superman So Darned American?" *Popular Culture: An Introductory Text.* Eds. Jack Nachbar and Kevin Lause. Bowling Green, OH: Bowling Green State University Popular Press, 1992. 314–343. Print.
Fingeroth, Danny. *Superman on the Couch: What Superheroes Really Tell Us About Ourselves and Our Society.* New York and London: Continuum, 2004. Print.

"The Flash Outruns the Reaper 23 Years after Saving Universe and Dying." *New York Daily News*, 30 April 2008. N. pag. Web. 5 May 2008.

Gunning, Tom. "'Now You See It, Now You Don't': The Temporality of the Cinema of Attractions." *The Velvet Light Trap* 32 (Fall 1993).

Higgins, Scott. 2008. "Suspenseful Situations: Melodramatic Narrative and the Contemporary Action Film." *Cinema Journal* 47.2 (Winter 2008): 74–96.

Jancovich, Mark. "Dwight Macdonald and the Historical Epic." *Action and Adventure Cinema*. New York and London: Routledge, 2004. 84–100. Print.

Lichtenfeld , Eric. *Action Speaks Louder: Violence, Spectacle, and the American Action Movie*. Middetown, CT: Wesleyan, 2007. Print.

McCloud, Scott. *Understanding Comics: The Invisible Art*. New York: HarperCollins, 1994. Print.

Neale, Steve. "Masculinity as Spectacle: Reflections on Men and Mainstream Cinema." *Screening the Male: Exploring Masculinities in the Hollywood Cinema*. Ed. Steven Cohan and Ina Rae Hark. London and New York: Routledge, 1993. 9–22. Print.

Pedler, Martyn. "Morrison's Muscle Mystery versus Everyday Reality ... and Other Parallel Worlds!" *The Contemporary Comic Book Superhero*. Ed. Angela Ndalianis. London and New York: Routledge, 2008. 250–269.

_____. "The Tears of Doctor Doom." *Overland* 191 (Winter 2008): 34–39.

Tasker, Yvonne. Introduction. *Action and Adventure Cinema*. New York and London: Routledge, 2004.

_____. *Spectacular Bodies: Gender, Genre, and Action Cinema*. London and New York: Routledge, 1993.

Wolk, Douglas. *Reading Comics: How Graphic Novels Work and What They Mean*. Cambridge, MA: Da Capo, 2007.

10

My Wonder Woman:
The "New Wonder Woman,"
Gloria Steinem, and the Appropriation
of Comic Book Iconography

ANDREW J. FRIEDENTHAL

Molded from the clay of isolated Paradise Island, with life breathed into her by the Greek gods, Wonder Woman, a.k.a. Princess Diana of Themyscira, a.k.a. Diana Prince, was born in 1941. While her mother may have been Hippolyte, queen of the Amazons, her father was a being of far more human proportions, a psychologist by the name of Dr. William Moulton Marston. Dr. Marston had been hired by All American Comics (sister company to DC Comics) as an advisor on the creation of comic books that would be suitable for impressionable youths (Daniels 20).[1] His biggest contribution to All American, and arguably to American culture itself,[2] was the creation of Wonder Woman, one of the first female superheroes, and certainly the longest lasting. Over the course of the ensuing six decades, Wonder Woman would pass through the hands of a multitude of writers, artists, and editors, each of whom created their own unique version of the character who would, at her best, resonate with the readers, and the America, of the time.[3] Each of these different visions of the character would impact upon certain creators and readers who would, within the contested terrain of the world of comic book iconography, think of that version as "*my* Wonder Woman."

The late 1960s Wonder Woman was envisioned within an America that was home to protests, radicalism, and an early second-wave feminism that, according to feminist historian/theorist Judith Evans, "emerged from the 1960s New Left, and that decade's movement for black Civil Rights," and which began, "with a claim of 'adequate similarity,' that is, of no differences that could justify discrimination on the grounds of sex" (13). As Evans further posits, "If feminism is a protest against women's oppression, there is no confining its story, by country, culture, or time" (13). Given her status as a super-powerful woman fighting for the rights of her "sisters" against equally powerful foes, Wonder Woman, as she was originally created in the 1940s, certainly fell under the purview of Evans' "story." The life of Gloria Steinem, the famous co-founder of *Ms.* magazine, also seems to follow the story. An outspoken writer/activist heavily associated with the feminist movement by the 1970s, Steinem was a lifelong Wonder Woman fan, having found as a child that, "Charles Moulton[4] ... had seen straight into my heart and understood the fears of violence and humiliation hidden there.... In short, [Wonder Woman] was wise, beautiful, brave, and explicitly out to change 'a world torn by the hatreds and wars of men.' She was Wonder Woman" (*Wonder Woman: Five Decades* 8–9).[5] Steinem was such a fan that, later in life, she tried to get the rights to Wonder Woman so she could write the superhero's story into a musical (Heilbrun 128–129), and also wrote a movie treatment for a live-action Wonder Woman film (Stern 345). Little did Steinem know just what an impact she would one day have on the future of her heroine, as they both faced the tumultuous days of early 1970s. Steinem's appropriation, during this era, of Wonder Woman as a feminist icon was a decisive act that points to the still-existent tension between comic book characters as commodities for the companies publishing them, and as important symbols and icons for the readers and fans who have grown up with, and still follow, the adventures, stories, and lives of those same characters. It is in this way that such seemingly innocuous superheroic characters as Wonder Woman become true political icons, invested with the ideologies of various contesting interest groups.

The State of Feminism and Comic Books in the Late 1960s

Second wave feminism of the kind advocated by Steinem was, as Jennifer Baumgardner and Amy Richards (both at one point editors at *Ms.*) put it, "trying to identify ... the huge hole that grows in a woman who is trying to be equal but has internalized society's low estimation of women" (135). As a part of this mission, *Ms.* was "a feminist forum that assumed women's full humanity and published the diverse voices of those who [were] trying to achieve it.... *Ms.*'s editorial mission expressly teased out the pro-woman angle on political issues" (113). In a tumultuous period defined by the Vietnam War overseas and the fight for civil rights for people of all races at home, the feminist movement of the late-60s/early-70s was yet another sign of change. Within the movement, "diverse voices" *were* fighting actively for the full equality and even "humanity" of women, during "a time when a few women were beginning to figure out that the gigantic lack of confidence in females wasn't all [their] individual faults." (Steinem *Outrageous Acts* 10). At its best, then, feminisms of this era were focused on creating a respected voice for women that was both unified, for strength and power, and yet at the same time individualized, for the expression of different racial and cultural issues. As Steinem herself describes her wakening to this feminist cause:

> If it weren't for the Women's Movement, I might still be dissembling away.... Once this feminist realization dawned, I reacted in what turned out to be predictable ways. First, I was amazed at the simplicity and obviousness of a realization that made sense, at last, of my life experience. Second, I realized, painfully, how far that new vision of life was from the

system around us, and how tough it would be to explain the feminist realization at all, much less to get people (especially, though not only, me) to accept so drastic a change [Steinem "Sisterhood" 5].

Indeed, during this era, attempts at drastic changes were being made everywhere, even in the four-color world of the comic books.

In the late 1960s, comic book super heroes were as subject to the turbulence of the time as any other American. Comic book writer and historian Louise Simonson explains:

> The 1960s through the early 1970s was a time of burgeoning sexual freedom, women's libera-tion, inexorable and compelling movement towards social justice and equality, and the con-fusion of a disputed war.... In 1968, Wonder Woman's writers and artists tried to create more realistic stories that would showcase a liberated woman who, like Batman, was powerful by her own choice [Simonson 27].[6]

Wonder Woman, of course, was not the only character drastically changed by writers and editors in response to the tumult of this era. According to comics historian Les Daniels, these alterations were partially a result of changing ownership and management at DC Comics: "In 1968, DC Comics was undergoing a whole series of artistic and eco-nomic upheavals, and even heroes as well known as Superman and Batman were about to be substantially revamped" (123). However, Daniels somewhat subjectively declares that, "no major character in comics before or since has ever experienced a metamorphosis to compare with Wonder Woman's, and the resulting controversy ... transformed the Amazon into a political symbol of national significance and exposed her to an ideological scrutiny that she has never entirely escaped" (123). The changes to Wonder Woman, both the character and the comic book, were radical, to say the least, and in many ways rep-resented an attempt on the part of DC Comics' writers and editors to respond to the "new woman" of the feminist movement.

Introducing the "New Wonder Woman"

Beginning in 1968 with Issue #178 of the regular *Wonder Woman* comic book, Wonder Woman underwent a saga in which she changed the style of her alter ego, Diana Prince, from a drab military secretary into a hip, modish figure that her longtime love interest, Steve Trevor, found more attractive. Immediately following (though seemingly unrelated to) this change, Queen Hippolyte and the Amazons remove themselves from the mortal world, giving Wonder Woman the option to come with them or to remain in "Man's World" without any of her old powers. Wonder Woman opts to stay, in order to save Steve Trevor's life, and finds herself now living life as powerless Diana Prince, who quickly gains a blind Asian mentor, named I-Ching, from whom she learns martial arts (Daniels 123). Nevertheless, Diana is unable to save Steve from the machinations of the evil Dr. Cyber, who, with "staccato bursts of machine-gun fire" (Fleischer 64) mortally wounds the love of Diana's life. Alone (save for I-Ching) and powerless, Diana Prince, the "New Wonder Woman," would move on to several years' worth of adventures as a superspy-like-figure, bearing more than a passing resemblance to Diana Rigg's character from the then-popular television series *The Avengers* (Daniels 128–129).

Author and self-proclaimed Wonder Woman expert Carol Strickland has carefully indexed and described the issues comprising the "New Wonder Woman," also known as the "Diana Prince era" (*The New Wonder Woman Index*). Her index of this era extends from *Wonder Woman* #178, where Diana Prince first gains her new "mod" look, through *Wonder Woman* #204, where a crazed sniper kills I-Ching and knocks Diana unconscious, giving her an amnesia that is cured by the Amazons, who, having no knowledge of the past year (in story time), end up erasing the memories of the "New Wonder Woman" era from Diana's mind.

What Strickland, who claims to have read these stories as they were being published, points out is that, despite its association with the superspy stories that were its most common trade-in-stock, the Diana Prince era featured an enormous array of story types within an approximately twenty-five issue run:

> This was the series that showed us that Wonder Woman is the most versatile superhero on the stands.... She faced opponents from the realms of faerie, from the streets, from mythology, from everyday life, from sword-and-sorcery fantasy — with a tad of gothic horror thrown into the mix. And she still kept a firm hold on the superheroic world. Has there EVER been another comics character to do the same? [*Truly, Modly, Deeply*].

Strickland's account, although created well after the fact, is a rare example of a female fan's response to this era of *Wonder Woman* adventures, as most of the letters published in the *Wonder Woman* comic books at this time were written by males.[7]

Since all the creators who were working on *Wonder Woman* were men, and most of the readers of the comic were men, an interesting dynamic was being created, in which males on both sides of the reader/creator dynamic were in conversation with one another on how to create a "new (Wonder) woman" for changing times. What was lacking from this debate, of course, was the voice of the women, themselves, the very people who were creating the "new woman" in the real world. In an unpublished dissertation that analyzes the history of Wonder Woman as an American female icon, Francinne D. Valcour notes how this conversation took place:

> From the letters sent into *Wonder Woman* during the Diana Prince era, it is difficult to determine the overall reception of the transformation, although the editors continually support the new character.... Through the letter column, [writer-editor Mike] Sekowsky hoped to decipher exactly what type of contemporary, independent woman readers desired.... Given Sekowsky's choice to alternate fantasy with realism and his outright questioning of the preference of their audience, he appears unsure of *Wonder Woman's* direction and how the readers received Wonder Woman's transformation to a mortal interacting in realistic situations [296–297].

Perhaps because of his own lack of confidence, DC Comics ended up replacing Sekowsky, who had co-created the whole Diana Prince era along with writer/activist Dennis O'Neil (the man responsible for a plethora of realistic, issues-based superhero stories throughout DC Comics which are still critically celebrated to this day), with a female editor, Dorothy Woolfolk, who produced several reprints of the earliest "New Wonder Woman" issues (Valcour 297). Woolfolk's time on *Wonder Woman* was short-lived, though, as within five issues she was replaced by O'Neil, who worked as editor, and usually writer, of the series until its changeover to Robert Kanigher, who had previously edited the series in the 1950s, with issue #204. As O'Neil himself has described this time, "I saw it as taking a woman and making her independent, and not dependent on super powers. I saw it as making her thoroughly human and then an achiever on top of that, which, according to my mind, was very much in keeping with the feminist agenda" (quoted in Daniels 126). In response to feminist complaints, though, O'Neil ultimately admitted, "I'm not ashamed of what we did, but I'm not sure I'd do it again" (Daniels 126). Woolfolk, it would seem, despite having the benefit of actually being a woman, was edged out of her editorial role by a bigger name in the world of comic books — and indeed *all* of the "bigger names" in comic books at this time were male names. Rather than giving over the "new Wonder Woman" to a female editor, DC allowed O'Neil to parlay his critical success of crafting stories around race, poverty, and drug abuse, in such comic books of the day as *Green Lantern/Green Arrow*, into a tenure of writer-editor on *Wonder Woman* where, though he tried his hardest, he could at best only create a *man's* vision of an independent, feminist, "new" woman. Needless to say, this was at odds with the feminist movement's most crucial goal, which was to create a voice for the voiceless women, and to never allow a man's vision to stand in for a woman's voice.

In general, then, the response to the Diana Prince era was rather mixed. Although editorial director Carmine Infantino, as well as Sekowsky (writing in the letter column), reported a large jump in sales, Valcour notes that, "according to comic scholar Robert Klein's analysis of Marvel and DC sales between 1969 and 1989, *Wonder Woman* sales failed to change remarkably during this time" (316). The fan response was mixed; the editorial staff was confused about what to do with the character; the publisher was mostly concerned with sales that rose only marginally, at best; and the character herself was barely recognizable from the classic version of Wonder Woman, clad in red and gold, deflecting bullets with her bracelets and tying up villains in her magical golden lasso. What Sekowsky, O'Neil, Infantino, and DC had failed to consider, however, was exactly what sort of a meaning the classic *image* of the superheroine held for American women, particularly those, like Steinem, who were major voices in the feminist movement of that time. It was at this historical moment that, as comics historian Maurice Horn has said, Wonder Woman was, "discovered as an early representative of the feminist movement in the comics" (116) and indeed as a representative, in 1972, of the feminist movement in America.

Enter Gloria Steinem

Exactly how Gloria Steinem first became aware of the Diana Prince era is unclear. According to science fiction writer Samuel R. Delany, who scripted several issues for O'Neil at the very end of his time as *Wonder Woman* editor:

> One day about six weeks after I had come on board, Gloria Steinem was being shown through the [DC] offices. Proudly they showed her the new Wonder Woman. Steinem hadn't looked at a *Wonder Woman* comic, however, since she was twelve. Immediately she exclaimed: "What happened to her costume? How come she isn't deflecting bullets with her magic gold bracelets anymore and tying people up with her magic lasso?" Steinem didn't get a chance to read the story of course. But she complained bitterly: "*Don't you realize how*

important the image of Wonder Woman was to young girls throughout the country?" She had a point, I admit. But, a day later, an edict came down from management to put Wonder Woman back in her American-flag falsies and blue bikini briefs and give her back all her super powers ["Author Q & A"].

As Steinem herself, recalls, though, it was not a chance comment that influenced DC, but rather a concerted effort on the part of herself and her fellow activists:

> It was in this sad state that I first rediscovered my Amazon superhero in 1972. *Ms.* magazine had just begun, and we were looking for a cover story for its first regular issue to appear in July. Since Joanne Edgar and other of its founding editors had also been rescued by Wonder Woman in their childhoods, we decided to rescue Wonder Woman in return. Though it wasn't easy to persuade her publishers to let us put her original image on the cover of a new and unknown feminist magazine, or to reprint her 1940s Golden Age episodes inside, we finally succeeded. Wonder Woman appeared on newsstands again in all her original glory, striding through city streets like a colossus, stopping planes and bombs with one hand and rescuing buildings with the other [*Wonder Woman: Five Decades* 15].

The differences between these two versions of Wonder Woman's switch back to a super-powered, flying heroine are seemingly minor, but they contain an absolutely crucial difference — in Delany's version, it is a "bitter complaint" from Steinem, said off the cuff, that influenced DC's editors to change Wonder Woman back, while in Steinem's account there was a full feminist movement of numerous women involved, rather than just one person's impulsive remarks.[8] Whereas Delany casts Steinem as a single, powerful individual, Steinem herself states that she worked as a part of an organized movement of women to pressure the already-vacillating DC Comics to give Wonder Woman back her classic look and powers.[9] For Steinem, this was a considered, activist project, one of "rescuing" Wonder Woman from the depowered state to which she had been relegated. It was, in fact, essential to Steinem's entire feminist project that she and other women, working as a collective, develop a strong self-esteem from work such as this: "Looking back at all those male-approved things I used to say, the basic hang-up seems clear: a lack of esteem for women ... and for myself.... And this lack of esteem that makes us put each other down is still the major enemy of sisterhood" (Steinem "Sisterhood" 8–9). This sense of esteem, then, was not just for the self, but for the sisterhood as well.

In fact, the article about Wonder Woman in *Ms.* was not even actually written by Steinem, but rather by Joanne Edgar, as Steinem was running late on a deadline (Thom 42). This was, after all, more than just an individual fetish for Steinem, but rather an important piece of voice-claiming for the entire movement she was involved in. Edgar, in the article, provided a history of the heroine, a description of her contemporary state in the comic books, and a declaration that the character and comic book would be, "reborn in the following year to reflect more of the independence and strength embodied in the Marston crafted superheroine" (Valcour 3080. This declaration was mirrored by Steinem in an introduction to a book of reprints of classic Marston *Wonder Woman* tales, published in 1972 as the second half of *Ms.*'s campaign to "rescue" Wonder Woman:

> Looking at [Wonder Woman's] most recent adventures is even more discouraging. By 1968, she had given up her magic lasso, her bracelets, her invisible plane, and all her superhuman Amazonian powers.... She was a female James Bond — but far more boring since she was

denied his sexual freedom. She had become a simpleminded "good girl." In 1973, Wonder Woman comics will be born again; I hope with the feminism and strength of the original Wonder Woman — *my* Wonder Woman — restored.... If we had all read more about Wonder Woman and less about Dick and Jane, the new wave of the feminist revolution might have happened less painfully and sooner [*Wonder Woman* 6].

Wonder Woman, then, was an important part of Steinem's life as a feminist, just as the iconography of the superheroine was important to the feminist ethos of *Ms.* As a result, when Wonder Woman was depowered, Steinem and her cohort felt betrayed: *her* Wonder Woman had been replaced by a superspy imposter. The original Wonder Woman needed to be rescued by a team of heroines putting together the nation's first feminist magazine, a task which the founders of *Ms.* felt more than up to, and, indeed, at which they soon succeeded.

Samuel Delany and "Women's Lib"

Before Wonder Woman would return to the realm of the magically powered super-heroes, however, one last controversial issue was still to be published, one of the issues that were guest-scripted by Samuel Delany. Issue #203 of *Wonder Woman* has come to be known as the "Special Women's Lib Issue," thanks to a cover blurb bearing that message. The issue featured a story wherein Wonder Woman attends a "women's lib" meeting after encountering a corrupt department store owner who underpays and mistreats his female employees. The story ends with Wonder Woman and her new "women's lib" friends shutting down the department store, leading to "the former Grandee employees confronting the women's group about their responsibility for 250 women being out of work" (Strickland *The New Wonder Woman Index*). During the course of the story, Wonder Woman utters perhaps the most controversial piece of dialogue of her career, stating that, "I'm for equal wages, too! But I'm not a joiner. I wouldn't fit with your group. In most cases, I don't even like women?" (Strickland *The New Wonder Woman Index*).

Karen M. Walowit, in an unpublished dissertation on Wonder Woman, argues that the issue, "represents the worst sort of threatened male fantasy of what might be involved in women's liberation" (220), as the "liberated" women were shown as doing nothing other than shutting down a department store run by a well-to-do male figure. Indeed, the storyline of the individual issue seems to only show an at-best surface level understanding of the feminist concerns of the day. The fact that Wonder Woman declares herself "not a joiner," for example, is completely out of keeping with the collectivist notions of 1970s feminists.[10] Even Carol Strickland, who was such a fan of the Diana Prince era, found the issue troublesome: "Of all people, WONDER WOMAN doesn't know anything about the women's movement? [...] She doesn't believe in changing society? WONDER WOMAN?!!! I can only shake my head at this preachy, preachy story and declare that for me at least, it was out of continuity. Never happened" (*Truly, Modly, Deeply*). Strickland had found "Diana Prince to be a symbol of Modern Womanhood without preaching" (*Truly, Modly, Deeply*), and yet she simply could not stand the "Special Women's

Lib. Issue" because of its extreme preaching and its lack of insight into actual feminist concerns, such as those with which Steinem was involved.

What is interesting about this issue, though, is that all of its critics — and there are many — refer to Delany as yet another male writer who has an inadequate knowledge of the actual feminist movement in the 1970s. However, he is perhaps given short-shrift by Strickland and others, as, due to DC Comics' decision to switch back to the more classic Wonder Woman, he only saw published the first of six issues that he had plotted out, all of which dealt with feminist concerns: "[M]y stories were abandoned, and I was dumped as a writer — and Wonder Woman never *did* get a chance to fight for the rights of a women's abortion clinic. It's a case of the world being over-determined — and over-determined in some destructive ways. But Steinem had no ideas of the stories her chance comments were used to scuttle" (quoted in Strickland *Truly, Modly, Deeply*). Again, the change to Wonder Woman was not necessarily due to Steinem's "chance comments," but they certainly did eliminate the direction that Delany was hoping to take Diana Prince in, where she would end up fighting "a gang of male thugs trying to squash an abortion clinic staffed by women surgeons" (Strickland *Truly, Modly, Deeply*).

Wonder Woman #203 is certainly by no means a strong example of actual "women's lib." However, to completely vilify Delany for the story is a bit of an extreme reaction. This was merely the first part of six in a continuing storyline that was to expand upon Diana Prince's feminist horizons, joining with other women to fight off real-world patriarchal "villains" who were subjugating women. Delany, as much as any of the other creators on *Wonder Woman*, was caught between telling a story in a serialized format in order to express his own ideas, and at the same time being responsible for a character who served as a huge commodity for DC Comics. Indeed, interviews with Delany — a gay man and one of the first African American writers of science fiction — show him to be a writer who is very interested in issues of identity and self-assertion, rather than merely a patronizing chauvinist:

> In a time when identity politics is sustaining a necessary and clarifying attack/analysis that will doubtless leave it forever changed into something more flexible and useful, more provisional and provisioned, I am interested in the "identities" (I use the term in its most informal manner of those who have fallen through the categorical cracks without having slipped wholly free of the nets of desire [Rowell and Delany 255].

Furthermore, Delany is also aware that whatever his authorial intention may be, the act of reception by readers will cause a multitude of different interpretations to come about: "The books themselves try to erect, in their small ways, internal road signs to guide the reader once within. But the reader who wants to ignore those signs and read against the grain is just as welcome ... as the reader who wants to let extant rhetorical expectations take her or him from sentence to sentence, page to page, chapter to chapter" (Rowell and Delany 254). Unfortunately for Delany, it was just as he came on board, and had only told one sixth of his intended story, that the decision was made to move the commodity of Wonder Woman in a different direction. Thus the individual issue that he saw published does, indeed, display some rhetoric that is opposed to the collectivist aspect of second-wave feminism, and there is no way for a reader to reevaluate that rhetoric in light of the "road signs" laid out across the entire intended six-issue arc.

Cover Story

It is not just the story of *Wonder Woman* #203 that has been criticized, however, but also the cover of that issue. As one online comic book commentator notes, "In hindsight, there might have been a *better* imagery to communicate the 'Women's Liberation' concept than a bound-and-gagged woman thrusting her chest forward" (*Cover to Cover*). Indeed, the covers of the Wonder Woman comic books have always been at odds with the messages portrayed therein. The covers are often filled with "numerous images of women in bondage, a concept that Marston claimed cut down on violence, but which he certainly knew was sexually stimulating to some people" (Daniels 59). This bondage theme, along with the over-sexualization of the female figure on the *Wonder Woman* covers, was controversial in Marston's day, and continues to be controversial today, in more contemporary covers created by the artist Adam Hughes, who unapologetically caps off his theory that "comic book covers [are] the last line in advertising, and the first line in storytelling" by proclaiming that there is, "One Undeniable Truth ... which there is no argument against, no subtle aspect of subjectivity to allow for the existence of any possible polar way of thought. And the Truth is: SEX SELLS" (13). In the Diana Prince era, with its internal and external pressures to present a more independent, feminist sort of Wonder Woman, these "SEX SELLS"-style covers are particularly troubling and contradictory to the message of the stories, as Valcour describes:

> While Diana Prince and Wonder Woman challenge sexism and discrimination within the pages of the comic book, the covers of these same issues often depict women as submissive, dominated and even tied up. The creators produced a rash of these covers between 1968 and 1975.... Though these covers differ, they hold striking similarities. All portray women scantily clad in white clothing that accentuates their chest. Each highlights women chained or bound and many portray an ominous and threatening figure who is not revealed to the audience. On each cover a woman appears submissive and helpless [324–326].

For Steinem and her fellow activists, a large part of the importance of Wonder Woman *was* the image on the cover, as many young girls would encounter those covers without ever seeing the stories and content therein. The icon of Wonder Woman was in the *image* of Wonder Woman, and the bondage-filled covers of powerless women, be they Diana Prince or somebody else, were harmful to a movement that based itself on the empowerment and equality of women. For this exact reason, the cover of the first regular issue of *Ms.* featured a fully powered Wonder Woman in all her star-spangled, superheroic glory.

The iconography on this *Ms.* cover was important to the feminist movement, showcasing a powerful woman engaged in feats of strength, both mental and physical, that represented female capability. On the cover, Wonder Woman is seen as a giant, striding across an average American street which is portrayed as adjacent to a war-torn battlefield, most likely in Vietnam. As Wonder Woman uses her golden lasso to safely hold aloft several American homes, a billboard on the street below proclaims "Peace and Justice in '72," while the magazine's banner, just above her head, reads, "Wonder Woman For President." Despite her colossal size here, Wonder Woman is seen in a protector's role, saving the houses cradled in her lasso while looking down on the battlefield with a worried expression. She is depicted as a powerful woman, rather than as a helpless and/or over-sexualized figure — for the creators of *Ms.*, the nature of Wonder Woman's femininity was in the fact that she was *powerful*, not that she was glamorous or sexy.[11]

This image is so crucial to the ethos and ideology of *Ms.* that the recent 35th Anniversary Issue features an homage to that cover, with the original itself re-printed in the table of contents ("Contents" 5). Interestingly, though, on the cover of this anniversary issue, the very obvious worried look on Diana's face is replaced with a more straight-forward smile.[12] The anniversary issue is a moment of celebration, as stated on the cover, while the original *Ms.* cover was a moment of concern, both for women in general and for the state of Wonder Woman at the time. This satisfied smile, however, is somewhat troubling; the cover of *Ms.*'s Anniversary issue is expressing a sort of progress narrative of having succeeded in creating a voice for women over the past thirty-five years. As Baumgardner and Richards express, "for anyone born after the early 1960s, the presence of feminism in our lives is taken for granted. For our generation, feminism is like fluoride. We scarcely notice that we have it — it's simply in the water" (17). However, they go on to point out that, "Third Wave [feminism]'s goals are derived from analyzing how every issue affects this generation of young women. [...] And we have modern problems of our own" (21). Scholar and theorist Marysia Zalewski explains this Second Wave / Third Wave divide (which she calls a divide between "modernist" and "postmodernist" feminisms) as one that must be grappled with in complex ways by contemporary feminists:

> There clearly *are* some significant differences between 1970s and 1990s feminisms, most obviously in the realm of theory, but I would argue that the differences do not have to imply dismissals of either group of feminisms by the other. How might we think of or use feminism — in theory and in practice — in the twenty-first century? ... [A]s we move through the twenty-first century and popular (best-selling) feminism turns its focus towards men as the "new victims of gender," then perhaps one crucial way to "recover" feminisms is to be found in recovering feminisms from the intolerances of other feminisms — as well as the more traditional "others" [142].

It seems problematic, then, for *Ms.* to take a congratulatory tone when Third Wave feminism, inherited by the daughters, both spiritual and literal, of Second Wave feminists like Steinem, is still struggling with so many complicated issues. For *Ms.*, though, perhaps seemingly achieving the Second Wave goal of finding a voice for women (as evidenced by, for example, the continued publication of *Ms.* itself for three-and-a-half decades) is, indeed, cause for a celebration.

Worried or celebratory, the image of Wonder Woman clearly holds importance to *Ms.* and, of course, to Steinem, herself. As Valcour has pointed out, it is no surprise

> that Steinem would choose *Wonder Woman* as the symbol for the front cover. In 1972 few female icons existed, and fewer still that demonstrated the strength, sisterhood and independence of Marston's Wonder Woman. By demanding that *Wonder Woman*, a comic book overwhelmingly crafted by men, change to what Steinem considered more representative of strong women, Steinem was appropriating power for women and the women's movement [314].

Wonder Woman has, indeed, become a tremendous symbol for the feminist movement. Her image is still consistently used by *Ms.*, and their web-site even features a store full of Wonder Woman merchandise, including a poster of that first cover (Ms. Magazine Web-Site). The figure of Wonder Woman, as the first and most powerful of all female superheroes, is certainly an unsurprising choice for the symbol of the feminist movement. She embodies strength, truth (when ensnared in her lasso, a person is unable to lie), wisdom, beauty, mythology, and love, all of which combine to form the image of femininity and womanhood in which followers of Steinem's brand of feminism believe. In this way, Wonder Woman does not just exist as an important figure and image for feminists, but becomes a full-fledged icon.

Iconography

Icons are classically associated with the Catholic Church's representation of holy figures and objects. In contemporary usage, however, icons are far more associated with popular culture, including, according to theorist Klaus Rieser, "fictional as well as historical characters..., locales, monuments, or typical natural elements..., and ... logos, isotropes, and computer icons.... Despite the large amount of icons populating the U.S. cultural and social landscape, any reader with more than rudimentary knowledge about the USA will recognize most of them immediately" (7). Advertising professors even advise their students to, in best case scenarios, create ads that "no longer need to just aim for attention," but that, "get customers to want more from *ads* in order to revere the *icons*" created by the advertisements (Springer xiii).

It is no surprise, then, that famous comic book characters such as Superman, Batman, and, yes, Wonder Woman have attained this iconic status. Louise Simonson, herself a writer of many comic book icons (particularly Superman), explains the relationship between fan/reader and character:

> Like any works of fiction, comics are an interaction between creators and readers. Some characters grow in the popular imagination until they almost seem to take on lives of their own.... It's almost as if, on some level, [the fans] believe these characters are real people — and the creators who write and draw their stories are simply chronicling the continuing adventures of living, breathing individuals who exist beyond their two-dimensional appearances on comic book pages.... The creation of comic books involves separate but interlocking universes — the publishing company, the creators, the fictional lives of the characters, and the fans' reaction to it all [33].

The relationship described by Simonson is certainly one that holds true between Steinem and Wonder Woman. For Steinem, Wonder Woman *did* exist beyond the pages of the comic book — she existed as an *icon*, both a personal one for Steinem's girlhood self-esteem and a public one for the feminist movement to latch onto and appropriate. The empowerment of this particular icon is further described by feminist comic book historian/analyst Lillian S. Robinson: "And why, finally, am I looking for Wonder Woman? What do I — do we — need from that myth, even in its fragile comic book avatar? Well, the word *empowerment* ... is an authentic need implicit in this particular discourse. The wonder of the woman warrior represents recognition of achievement at what is, in any event, exceptional for women" (19).

On one level, then, comic book iconicity is established by an interaction between a character and the fans of that character. However, the actual *portrayal* of the icon is determined by the creators — the writers, artists, editors, and others — who are in control of the character's fate at that particular moment in time. As scholar Marc Edward DiPaolo points out, "Whether Wonder Woman will succeed in inspiring young women today will partly depend on who gets to tell stories with the character, and on how her image is 'marketed' to the young" (170). It is the *creators* who are behind the stories that portray the icons, and they can craft a particularly feminist or a particularly misogynist Wonder Woman story that the readership can only respond to, but not directly affect until after the fact.

The confines that creators function within are, however, important to note. Wonder Woman, for example, is owned by DC Comics, who have a vested interest in the sales of her comic book and in the licensing and marketing of her image. The experience the publisher had with Steinem and *Ms.* in 1972 serves as a reminder of the importance of that image to a particular female market (and let it not be forgotten that the Wonder Woman merchandise sold by the *Ms.* magazine web-site is all licensed by DC), and they maintain strict control over how that image can be used, even by creators. *Wonder Woman* the comic book and Wonder Woman the character are commodities, serving the final purpose of making money for DC Comics and its parent corporations. Wonder Woman, the icon, has the same troubles of any other icon, as explained by Rieser:

> A particularly noteworthy aspect of icons — one which accounts for their lasting value in American culture — is that they are in an ambivalent, tension-fraught position between on the one hand a suturing function, as hegemonic tools of dominant groups to control the shifting identities and interest of the mass of people and, on the other hand, as democratic elements in the media age, as symbols of popular interests [8].

Jargon aside, what Rieser is saying is that icons are utilized by those with the power to control the icon — in this case, DC Comics — and those who "democratically" appropriate the icon, such as Gloria Steinem did in the 1970s.

This, indeed, is one of the key tensions inherent in the popularization of comic book super heroes. When a character such as Wonder Woman achieves a certain level of success, wherein somebody who has never read a comic book can recognize her, then she has, to a certain extent, escaped the grips of the company that owns the character. That is to say, although DC Comics still retains copyright over and legal possession of Wonder Woman, the *idea* of Wonder Woman has become so popular that she exists as an imagined figure beyond the confines of the comic book panels. It is precisely in this way that Wonder Woman becomes an icon. The continuing troublesome tension surrounding that iconography, though, is that she at the same time still remains a commodity for DC Comics, one to be exploited for economic motives.

Feminist Iconography

Although feminist activists may gain clearance to use Wonder Woman on the cover of *Ms.*, they can only take their use of the icon so far before the restricting confines of copyright law serve as a reminder of her ultimate commodification. Nevertheless, the appropriation of Wonder Woman by 1970s feminists was quite an important move towards representing to DC Comics that Wonder Woman's iconography is an important aspect of why readers and buyers are interested in putting their money towards her. It was this very reminder that led DC to change Wonder Woman back to her more familiar super-powered state.

The concept of iconographic appropriation is particularly important as regards the feminist movement of that time. For a group of women who were fighting against the powerlessness imposed upon them by a male-dominated society, the ability to, as Steinem phrased it, "rescue" Wonder Woman from her depowered state was quite literally a process of empowerment. As Steinem relates, she even found herself in a position where the creators of Wonder Woman deferred to her judgment: "One day some months after her rebirth, I got a phone call from one of Wonder Woman's tougher male writers. 'Okay,' he said, 'she's got all her Amazon powers back. She talks to Amazons on Paradise Island. She even has a Black Amazon sister named Nubia. Now will you leave me alone?' I said we would" (*Wonder Woman: Five Decades* 17).

The introduction of this "Black Amazon" was in fact crucial to the approach taken by Wonder Woman's editor, Robert Kanigher, following her re-empowerment. As Valcour explains:

> the issues that highlight Wonder Woman's return place an exaggerated emphasis on including women of color, first through Nubia then through Prince's job at the U.N. ... Previous to this new incarnation of the comic book, women of color enter *Wonder Woman* infrequently and play only insignificant roles.... By including aspects of both the classic Wonder Woman and feminist issues in the series, DC could simultaneously satisfy Steinem's disapproval and retain their theme of social relevance [320–321].

The fact that women of color had been ignored in *Wonder Woman* until now was, in and of itself, at odds with second wave feminism, which cast its net of sisterhood over all races. Steinem, for example, "knew that interest in the women's movement was widespread. Her speaking on college campuses and in communities across the country convinced her of that. She always came paired with an African-American woman speaker, a device designed to reach the widest possible audience" (Thom 7). Despite the addition of African American women to the continuing story of *Wonder Woman*, and despite the attempt to maintain a sense of relevance while allowing Wonder Woman to represent the iconic empowerment of women, illustrations of the character, particularly on the covers, remained as over-sexualized and sexist as ever. Lillian S. Robinson notes that the Kanigher Wonder Woman stories, "continue[d], for some time, to be illustrated so as to send the old, sexist message to anyone experiencing comic books chiefly on the level of the visual" (84).

Steinem and *Ms.*, however, had moved on. Once Wonder Woman was returned to her costume and her powers, engaged on the covers in superheroic feats (though of course still occasionally tied up and bound while doing so), there was no longer a concern about pressuring DC Comics to portray a feminist message within the book itself, something that (perhaps failingly) *was* a part of Dennis O'Neil's focus in the Diana Prince era, particularly as Samuel Delany came on board as writer. By focusing on the icon as image, rather than on the narrative within the comic book, Steinem was, herself, treating Wonder Woman as a commodity for the feminist movement to utilize imagistically. As Robinson explains:

> this uniquely uncritical approach — uniquely uncritical, that is, for feminism, which has rarely hesitated to question most other established institutions and verities — is due to the preference for a heroic icon over an understanding of how the representation of such an icon derives from and serves — as well as challenges — the dominant social forces. Perhaps it is fair to say that, in this case, at least, feminists behave as if they are unconvinced that cultural studies is a useful political weapon, whereas the value of the icon goes unquestioned [6–7].

By not following up on its victory, *Ms.* was at least partially responsible for recreating a more powerful iconic image at the expense of a more dynamically feminist character, as the writers and editors had been at least attempting to create in the Diana Prince era.

With *Wonder Woman* #212, new editor Julius Schwartz, in an effort to reinvigorate sales, brought in a series of guest stars who narrated the stories, in essence battling Wonder Woman for the role of protagonist in her own book. According to Schwartz:

> I never particularly cared for Wonder Woman, so I came up with the gimmick of having the Justice League [a team composed of the world's preeminent superheroes] spy on her, so to speak, to see how she handled her activity, and whether she was worthy of being readmitted [after having quit during the Diana Prince era]. It gave me the opportunity to do a series of issues in which I would have a guest star featured, and it did well in the sales department [Quoted in Daniels 134].

Inside the comic book, Wonder Woman was taking second billing. On the covers, however, she was still a fully powered superhero, and thus fully able to maintain her iconic feminist status.

Nostalgia, Cultural Memory, and Iconography

Steinem, in her appropriation, rescuing, and re-empowerment of Wonder Woman, was fully engaged in a nostalgic longing for the character of her childhood, of whom she used to read "under the covers with a flashlight, in the car while my parents told me I was ruining my eyes, in a tree or some other inaccessible spot; any place that provided sweet privacy and independence" (*Wonder Woman* 2). In her uncritical approach to the icon, however, she was willfully ignoring some of the less savory aspects of Marston's stories, such as the overemphasis on moments of bondage. She would, in her introduction to *Ms.*'s collection of early Marston Wonder Woman stories, admit to these flaws: "Of course, the Wonder Woman stories are not admirable in all ways. Many feminist principles are distorted and ignored" (*Wonder Woman* 4). However, she easily jettisons these problems, explaining that, "Compared to the other comic book characters of the period, however, Wonder Woman is still a relief" (*Wonder Woman* 5). Nevertheless, it is precisely this lack of engagement with the problematics of Wonder Woman's stories, as compared with her iconic image, that led to the character's stewardship under an editor who "never really cared for Wonder Woman," and who was free to tell stories with no feminist message or ethos so long as he put the iconic, classic image of the character on the cover.

Steinem is here engaging in a process described by theorist George Lipsitz, "in which collective memory and popular culture are peculiarly linked —... the infinitely renewable present of electronic mass media creates a crisis for collective memory, and ... collective memory decisively frames the production and reception of commercial culture" (Lipsitz vii).[13] Lipsitz theorizes that, in a contemporary society saturated by mass media, personal and historical memory is displaced by a "collective memory" of popular culture. American cultural touchstones, for example, are no longer historical events such as wars and presidential elections, but rather particular films, television shows, and comic books that serve as a collective history for people born in extremely different geographical locations and cultural milieus.

In this case, it is Steinem's memory of the comic book adventures and imagery of Wonder Woman, along with the similar collective memory of her fellow feminist-activists both at *Ms.* and in general, that frames the reception of the character as icon. This collective memory is "a crucial constituent of individual and group identity in the modern world" (Lipsitz viii), in this case of a particularly *feminist* identity in the modern world. For those attached to this particular branch of feminism, Wonder Woman served as an iconic symbol of fighting back against a cultural demand for submissiveness in women, and as a collective memory of that fight for power. This fight is one shared by all women in the movement of various backgrounds, with Wonder Woman serving as the touchstone around which to rally: "Instead of relating to the past through a shared sense of place or ancestry, consumers ... can experience a common heritage with people they have never seen; they can acquire memories of a past to which they have no geographic or biological connection" (Lipsitz 5). For those women who gathered to defend Wonder Woman's classical image and powers, that remembered past is one like Steinem's, in which Wonder Woman "rescued" them from the violent world of male superheroic battles which often ended in death. Nevertheless, by focusing that memory, and that rescue, solely on the iconic imagery of Wonder Woman, and not on the narratives involving her, they left Wonder Woman to over a decade's worth of mediocre, humdrum stories that hardly stood as paragons of female empowerment. Had they focused equally on empowering the *Wonder Woman* stories and not just the Wonder Woman iconography — perhaps by continuing to demand a female writer, or at least a female editor such as Woolfolk — then perhaps they could have powerfully invigorated those stories, as well.

Wonder Woman Today

Over the years since 1972, Wonder Woman has passed through many creative hands. In 1983, following an event in the DC Comics universe called the "Crisis on Infinite Earths," the unique opportunity was made available to recreate Wonder Woman from the ground up, a task assigned to writer-artist George Perez. As frustrating as it may have been for the recreation of *the* feminist icon to be handed to yet another male creator, Perez was at least honest about that flaw. His solution, however, was to make minimalist gestures to female points of view. According to Daniels (in his ever-celebratory tone):

He consulted not only with his wife, Carol, and his editor, Karen Berger, but also with DC President Jenette Kahn and with feminist Gloria Steinem, and ended up announcing that "the one thing I cannot help is my sex." ... Perez clearly felt an obligation to tread carefully around the comic book character who had somehow become an icon of a political movement. Yet the people who felt responsible for exerting a moral authority over the series did not really represent the average audience for super-hero comic books, and it is a tribute to Perez that he was often able to strike a balance with Wonder Woman [168–169].[14]

As Daniels here points out, the readership of *Ms.* and the readership of *Wonder Woman* do not, in fact, quite overlap, as is evidenced by the lack of complaint against Schwartz' tenure as editor. Although Wonder Woman is an icon to feminists, her continuing adventures are not necessarily of particular interest, which may explain why for over sixty-five years there was no regular female writer or artist on the monthly *Wonder Woman* comic book.

In early 2007, however, this changed, with a storyline in the third volume of *Wonder Woman* written by best-selling novelist Jodi Picoult. In the introduction to the collected volume of her storyline, Picoult explains that she accepted the offer to write *Wonder Woman* not only because she would "be only the second woman to write the comic book in its long history," but also because she, too, engaged in the collective memory of Wonder Woman as a feminist icon for girls: "I'd always been a fan of Wonder Woman (who hasn't?)" (5). It is noteworthy that Picoult admits to having always been a *fan* of Wonder Woman, but not necessarily a reader.[15]

Picoult's Wonder Woman story, however, lasted only five issues. Following three issues of fill-ins, the writing duties on *Wonder Woman* were taken over by Gail Simone, the most popular contemporary female comic book writer, and also a long-time fan *and* reader of the character. In a *New York Times* profile, which proudly declared that, "she is the first woman to serve as 'ongoing writer' (to use the industry's term) in the character's 66-year history," Simone is in fact described as an "avid [comic book] reader, her habit aided by unreliable television reception" (Gustines). Fittingly, her first storyline, beginning with November, 2007's *Wonder Woman* (volume 3) #14, involves a retelling of Wonder Woman's origin, focusing in part, as did Picoult's story, on the superheroine's relationship with her mother, while at the same time portraying Diana as a capable, heroic warrior out to squash a society of evil villains (Simone). Simone, through a multi-faceted portrayal of Wonder Woman as a fully realized, fully vocal character who is concerned with contemporary issues beyond simply her own status as empowered woman, seems intent on creating *Wonder Woman* stories, and not just Wonder Woman imagery, that embody notions of Third Wave feminism.[16]

As Simone explained to the *New York Times*, "We have the first year and the second year mapped.... I plan on being around as long as they'll have me" (Quoted in Gustines). Finally being portrayed by a concerned female writer, it would seem that Wonder Woman's future-in-feminism is assured for the next several years. However, at the same time as Picoult's *Wonder Woman* issues were being published in serial format, Suzan Colon and Jennifer Traig released a DC Comics-licensed book that offers a humorous take on female office politics using panels of art from the *Wonder Woman* comic books. Although the entire book is meant to be tongue-in-cheek, it includes painful lines — such as, "Even

Wonder Woman has to answer to Major Steve Trevor" (Colon and Traig 28) and, "You could become distracted by your [office] relationship and start forgetting about work" (Colon and Traig 109) — that are entirely out of keeping with both the character and with any sort of empowered feminist message.

This book serves as a reminder, perhaps, that despite Wonder Woman's iconic status, she still is ultimately a commodity controlled by DC Comics, who will license her out even if that licensed product is at odds with what the icon represents. The vested interest for the corporation is in the monetary capabilities of the character and the image, and not in the politically iconic status of that character. It is in response to moments like these — where the narrative content of a book, and not just the iconic image on the cover, conflicts with Wonder Woman's message of empowerment — that readers and fans should heed the words of Gloria Steinem: "You will see whether Wonder Woman carries her true Amazon spirit into the present. If not, let her publishers know. She belongs to you.... However simplified, that is Wonder Woman's message: Remember Our Power" (*Wonder Woman: Five Decades* 18–19).

Notes

1. Although Les Daniels' *Wonder Woman: The Complete History* is clearly authorized, and thus somewhat sanitized, by DC Comics — Daniels admits as much in his acknowledgments page — it remains the most comprehensive history of Wonder Woman available to date. Daniels, himself, is perhaps the world's preeminent comic book historian, with almost a dozen books to his name. His work, though, is mostly straightforward history, with little analysis, virtually no criticism, and a celebratory tone that comes from the fact that most of his books are authorized, if not commissioned, by the major comic book companies.

2. Marston was also, however, involved in the invention of the lie detector.

3. Circulation of DC Comics, and of *Wonder Woman* in particular, is certainly international, particularly in regards to Great Britain, but the corporate and editorial offices for the company are located in New York City, with the content in the comic books almost always geared toward American audiences.

4. "Charles Moulton" was Marston's pen name when writing the *Wonder Woman* stories.

5. This introduction, it should be noted, is a reworked and updated version of Steinem's introduction to the "*Ms.* Book" collection of early Wonder Woman stories, entitled simply *Wonder Woman*, published in 1972.

6. Like the Daniels history of Wonder Woman, Simonson's *DC Comics Covergirls* is heavily sponsored by, and indeed copyrighted to, DC Comics, and thus mainly celebratory in nature.

7. Most readers of mainstream superhero comic books, in the 1960s and 1970s and today, are in fact male.

8. It should be noted, however, that even though the feminist outcry probably had something to do with Wonder Woman gaining her powers back, many DC Comics titles were, as a general editorial push at this point, reverting to their early 1960s status quo, not just *Wonder Woman*. Additionally, *Ms.* was published by Warner Communications, which also published *Wonder Woman*, and Steinem had a personal relationship with owner Steve Ross. There is, then, the possibility that a personal intervention from Steinem *was* involved, as suggested by DC's then-publisher Carmine Infantino. See Thom 31–33 and Daniels 131.

9. I am indebted to my colleague Anne Gessler for helping me to more fully formulate this concept.

10. During the course of the story, Wonder Woman does ultimately join up with the "women's lib" advocates, but her statement still remains controversial in its indication that, until this particular moment in her life, Wonder Woman has had no knowledge of female power, voice, and sisterhood, all of which were, as Steinem would argue, integral parts of her initial creation.

11. The tension between feminist concerns and the notion of "sexiness" is certainly a pertinent issue here, but it is also a much larger debate than can be addressed in the current argument. For a relatively

recent, journalistic/sociological exploration of this tension, see Ariel Levy, *Female Chauvinist Pigs: Women and the Rise of Raunch Culture* (New York: Free, 2005).

12. This is, however, a bit hard to see, as this cover is made out of a composite of other *Ms.* covers, re-colored to help create the image of Wonder Woman.

13. Although Lipsitz's focus is obviously on *electronic* mass media, it can also be quite easily applied to comic books and comic book characters.

14. The treatment of Wonder Woman within the *Crisis on Infinite Earths* miniseries — wherein one parallel Earth version of her ascends to godhood while another is devolved into clay — surely bears closer attention, but is beyond the scope of the current discussion. Suffice it to say, at the end of that miniseries, Wonder Woman was made into a blank slate to be fully recreated by Perez, utilizing those aspects of various retellings of her origins that he particularly favored.

15. Picoult's portrayal of wonder Woman follows up on threads established by previous writer Allan Heinberg, who had actually re-invigorated the figure of superspy Diana Prince as an agent for the fictional Department of Metahuman Affairs, an active and empowering job for Wonder Woman's disguised alter ego (who is now her "secret identity," rather than the identity left behind by a process of depowering). The years 2007 and 2008, in fact, seem to be a sort of renaissance for certain aspects of the Diana Prince era. In addition to "Agent Diana Prince," 2007 saw the return of I-Ching, in a storyline playing out in the November and December 2007, issues of the Batman family of comic books. Perhaps most importantly — and maybe even most surprisingly, given the ultimate outcry over the era — in February 2008, DC Comics released a paperback collection (and only the first volume!) of the earliest Diana Prince era stories, under the title of *Diana Prince: Wonder Woman* vol. 1. See http://dccomics.com/comics/?cm=8755 (accessed 27 November 2007).

16. For a further explanation/exploration of Third Wave feminism, see Levy, note 11.

Works Cited

"Author Q & A: Samuel R. Delany on *Dhalgren*." N.p. n.d. Web. 26 November 2007.

Baumgardner, Jennifer, and Amy Richards. *ManifestA*. New York: Farrar, Straus and Giroux, 2000. Print.

Colon, Suzan, and Jennifer Traig. *What Would Wonder Woman Do?* San Francisco: Chronicle, 2007. Print.

"Contents." *Ms.* Fall 2007. Print.

Cover to Cover: I Am Woman, Hear Me Roar! N.p. n.d. Web. 17 October 2007.

Daniels, Les. *Wonder Woman: The Complete History*. San Francisco: Chronicle, 2000. Print.

DiPaolo, Marc Edward. "Wonder Woman as World War II Veteran, Camp Feminist Icon, and Male Sex Fantasy." *The Amazing Transforming Superhero! Essays on the Revision of Characters in Comic Books, Film and Television*. Ed. Terrence R. Wandtke. Jefferson, NC: McFarland, 2007. Print

Evans, Judith. *Feminist Theory Today: An Introduction to Second Wave Feminism*. London: SAGE, 1995. Print.

Fleischer, Michael L. *The Original Encyclopedia of Comic Book Heroes Volume Two Featuring Wonder Woman*. New York: DC Comics, 1976/2007. Print.

Gustines, George Gene. "Wonder Woman Gets a New Voice, and It's Female." *New York Times*, 27 November 2007. Print.

Heilbrun, Carolyn. *The Education of a Woman: The Life of Gloria Steinem*. New York: Dial, 1995. Print.

Horn, Maurice. *Women in the Comics: Volume 2*. Philadelphia: Chelsea House, 2001. Print.

Hughes, Adam. "Foreword." *Comics Covergirls*. Louise Simonson. New York: Universe, 2007. Print.

Lipsitz, George. *Time Passages: Collective Memory and American Popular Culture*. Minneapolis: University of Minnesota Press, 1990. Print.

Ms. Magazine Website. N.p. n.d. Web. 27 November 2007.

Picoult, Jodi. *Wonder Woman: Love and Murder*. New York: DC Comics, 2007. Print.

Rieser, Klaus. "Preface: Icons as a Discursive Practice." *U.S. Icons and Iconicity*. Ed. Walter W. Holbling, Klaus Rieser, and Susanne Rieser. Vienna: LIT, 2006. Print.

Robinson, Lillian S. *Wonder Women: Feminisms and Superheroes*. New York: Routledge, 2004. Print.

Rowell, Charles, and Samuel R. Delany. "An Interview with Samuel R. Delany." *Callaloo* 23 (Winter 2000): 247–267. Print.

Simone, Gail, writer. *Wonder Woman* 3.14. New York: DC Comics, 2007. Print.

Simonson, Louise. *DC Comics Covergirls*. New York: Universe, 2007. Print.

Springer, Paul. *Ads to Icons: How Advertising Succeeds in a Multimedia Age.* London: Kogan Page, 2007. Print.

Steinem, Gloria. Introduction. *Wonder Woman.* New York: Holt, Rinehart and Winston, 1972. Print.

_____. Introduction. *Wonder Woman: Featuring Over Five Decades of Great Covers.* New York: Abbeville, 1995. Print.

_____. *Outrageous Acts and Everyday Rebellions.* New York: Holt, Rinehart and Winston, 1983. Print.

_____. "Sisterhood." *The First Ms. Reader.* Ed. Francine Klagsburn. New York: Warner, 1973. Print.

Stern, Sydney Ladensoh. *Gloria Steinem: Her Passions, Politics, and Mystique.* Secaucus, NJ: Birch Lane, 1997. Print.

Strickland, Carol. *The New Wonder Woman Index.* N.p., n.d. Web. 17 October 2007.

_____. *Truly, Modly, Deeply: The Diana Prince Era.* N.p., n.d. Web. 17 October 2007.

Thom, Mary. *Inside Ms.: 25 Years of the Magazine and the Feminist Movement.* New York: Henry Holt, 1997. Print.

Valcour, Francinne D. *Manipulating the Messenger: Wonder Woman as an American Female Icon.* Ph.D. diss., Arizona State University, 2006. Print.

Walowit, Karen M. *Wonder Woman: Enigmatic Heroine of American Popular Culture.* Ph.D. diss., University of California, Berkeley, 1974. Print.

Zalewski, Marysia. *Feminism After Postmodernism: Theorizing Through Practice.* London: Routledge, 2000 Print.

11

Paneling Rage:
The Loss of Deliberate Sequence

MICHAEL P. MILLINGTON

Within the comics medium, trade paperbacks[1] have become an increasingly profitable and desirable mode of consumption, and the conversion from serialized comic books to the square-back form entails significant alterations to the text when the advertisements are dropped—panels and page placement shift to accommodate the resulting gaps. In some cases, the conversion amounts to a disruption of the intentional sequence of panels and pages, a move that nullifies the building of tension and undercuts the rising action in individual scenes. Brian K. Vaughan's *Y: The Last Man*,[2] in its transformation from comic book series to trade paperback, demonstrates how this disruption sometimes significantly alters the reader's experience of a text. Vaughan's 60-issue comic book series follows Yorick Brown on a journey across the globe in search of his girlfriend, Beth Deville, after a mysterious plague wipes out every creature with a Y chromosome except Yorick and his pet monkey Ampersand.

Yorick's father, an English professor, named the protagonist and his sister Hero after Sharkespeare's characters. Yorick bears particular weight because the association with Shakespeare's figure echoes the notion of death as ineluctable; Yorick as the last hope to repopulate Earth suffers constant threats of death and refuses to surrender himself sexually for the sake of breeding. Yorick is constantly on the verge of becoming just another skull in the graveyard among the rest of hu(man)ity. Hope that Beth survived the disaster drives Yorick to pursue her from continent to continent.

In the series, frequently shifting perspectives and jumps in space and time provide constant tension, often enhanced by dream sequences and unexpected turns. Several key scenes in the series employ deliberate sequences of panels and pages that incorporate full-page advertisements to establish delayed climaxes. The use of full-page breaks between sequential panels in the narrative extends the time required to read the string of images and allows anticipation to build. When the crossover is made from serialized issues of *Y:*

The Last Man to trade paperback compilations, the climactic panels in several sequences shift, and readers no longer have to turn a page to reach the pivotal images. The intentional breaks are removed, and with them, the necessary tension.

The growth in trade paperbacks, as opposed to graphic novels (which have no need for advertisements), brings disruptions to the form. As of yet, no methods have been developed and employed on a large enough scale to compensate for the significant relocations of panels within a deliberately designed sequence of pages. But market forces continue to drive publishers to churn out trade paperbacks as quickly as possible.

The Market Favors Conversion

The energy behind the comic industry, the economic force driving the trade paperback market, sets hurdles before writers and artists racing for a spot in the increasingly popular art form. Douglas Wolk, in *Reading Comics: How Graphic Novels Work and What They Mean*, writes that publishers "in the mid-'80s ... realized that once stories had been serialized in individual pamphlets, they could be collected in books with a reasonably high profit margin" (43). The trade paperback allows readers who start a series after several issues have already been printed — or after the series has ended — to read the breadth of the material without having to hunt down individual issues, which can be hard to find if the series grew in popularity but the print run remained comparatively small. The desire to accommodate readers involves much more than avoiding missing issues.

Current trends in the comics market reflect what the industry perceives as a consumer-friendly option for printing comics. The success of Art Spiegelman's *Maus*[3] (1986, 1991), the Pulitzer Prize winning story of survival during the Holocaust, and Alan Moore and Dave Gibbons's *Watchmen* (1987) "create[d] a demand for more self-contained, artistically satisfying volumes of comics on library and bookstore shelves" (Wolk 44). Both series were relatively short: *Maus* (collected into two slender volumes of 160 and 144 pages) and *Watchmen* (twelve issues: 416 pages). According to Wolk, the comics industry realized "that was where the money was, and within a few years the economic engine of the industry had made a major conversion: instead of trade paperbacks being a way to amortize the cost of producing the books of which they were components" (46). Attracting the largest audience possible was, and still is what really matters to big publishers.

To tap into the growing trade paperback market, major publishers made a conscious effort to explore the new terrain. Charles Brownstein, in an analysis of the current publishing trends in the comics industry, writes that in the '90s, "DC has increased its commitment to graphic novel publishing, first by aggressively repackaging successful periodical comics as graphic novels and by offering creators the opportunity to create original graphic novels" (17). This trend is seen in Vaughan's career as a comics writer. The success of serializations and trade paperbacks of *Y: The Last Man* opened the door for his series *Ex Machina*[4] and his first self-contained graphic novel, *Pride of Baghdad* (2007, Vertigo). Taking advantage of audience reading habits, Paul Levitz, president of DC Comics from 2002 to 2009, says, "The book formats allow us to attract a group of readers who can show up when they feel like it, and I think that potentially opens the door to a much wider range of customers" (quoted in Brownstein 17). To delve into a comic, readers no longer need to make weekly trips to the comic store or wait for new issues to arrive in the mail. The stories can be read in large chunks at the audience's convenience, but the structure of a comic does not always translate from one format to another; something is always/inevitably lost.

Advertisements play a significant role in the construction and publication of comics series, providing revenues to offset costs in exchange for full-page ads dispersed throughout individual issues. The relatively low cost for a single issue (usually a few dollars) exists because, as Phillip Thurtle notes, "in an average comic-book length of roughly thirty-four pages, more than eleven pages ... contained advertisements" (274). That amounts to one-third of the average issue being filled with advertisements that the writer, artist, and editors must then navigate. But because most comics still first appear "serialized in twenty- to forty-page installments, which are more or less economically foolproof" a comics series has "to build to some kind of climax every twenty-two pages" (Wolk 61, 48). Artists and writers are forced to construct story arcs made up of six twenty-page segments for the serialized format, which is then compiled into a larger but compact volume, "reaching out to adults who'd rather read projects like [writer Ed Brubaker and artist Sean Phillips's] *Criminal* or *Y: The Last Man* as squarebound paperbacks once or twice a year than pick up floppies once a month" (73). The transition from the 24-page floppy to the stiffer trade paperback involves page shifts to compensate for the loss of advertisement pages and cover material, the latter often collected in the back of each volume.

In the individual issues of *Y: The Last Man,* the advertisements are at times arranged in a manner that directly complements the narrative pace. The building of tension and delaying the reader from seeing subsequent panels prior to following the complete sequence are disrupted, muted, and even completely removed from the narrative when the series is converted from individual issues to trade paperback, disturbing the intended structure and form of the narrative, which, in turn, alters the reception of the work and blunts the provocation of desired emotions: in the case of *Y: The Last Man*, fear and desperation at key moments of revelation.

The Journey Begins

Vaughan's *Y: The Last Man* spanned sixty issues spread over six and a half years. Yorick and his pet monkey, Ampersand, are at first believed to be the only male mammals left on Earth after the plague strikes. It is later revealed that two astronauts in orbit over Earth at the time of the event and Doctor Matsumori, Dr. Mann's father, also survived the disaster. Throughout the series, Yorick fights to evade capture by renegade militias (the Daughters of the Amazons and the now-all-female Israeli army) and nearly every woman interested in hetero-sex or prolonging the human race. Yorick must also ward off accidental death or injury and keep from being turned into a sperm donor for every woman on Earth, the latter subverting the stereotypical male fantasy of wanting to be the only man in a world of women, the only choice and, therefore, the best choice for procreation. Yorick's hesitance to engage with any and every woman he comes across stems from devotion to his girlfriend, Beth, an anthropology student working in Australia at the time of the catastrophe and who was trying to tell him something important when communications satellites plummeted to Earth, having no one to control them because the over-whelming majority of workers were male. The circumstances of Yorick and Ampersand's survival remain mysterious for the most part throughout the series. Yorick's mother, Jennifer Brown, member of the U.S. House of Representatives and the highest-ranking woman in the U.S. government when promoted to Secretary of the Interior after the plague, assumes the top spot through presidential succession, giving her authority of military actions and international relations. President Brown[5] assigns Agent 355, a secret agent and member of the Culper Ring (a group of spies answering directly to the president and responsible for assassinations and preventing international incidents), as Yorick's protector. Together, 355 and Yorick travel with Dr. Allison Mann, a geneticist, in search of the plague's cause and a way to re-establish a male presence on Earth. However, Yorick's only goal is to find Beth and ask her to marry him. Further tension arises when President Brown suspects a rogue band of Culper Ring agents of trying to kidnap Yorick. The President contacts Alter Tse'elon, leader of the Israeli army, who then sets about tracking Yorick's group.

Y: The Last Man: Whys and Wherefores,[6] the final story arc, represents the emotional climax of the entire series, bringing together the sexual, emotional, and physical relationships of the three primary forces in the series: Yorick, the ever-sought-after male; Beth, Yorick's source of motivation; and 355, Yorick's bodyguard and his only stable relationship throughout the series. The pre-plague bond with Beth and ensuing separation from her create a displacement of emotion (love, hate, loneliness, a sense of belonging) that is cast on 355, a devout lesbian who starts a relationship with Dr. Mann. The search for Beth and the cause of the plague lead Yorick and 355 through encounter after encounter with death. Each issue, it seems, Yorick finds a new way to put himself directly in harm's way and force 355 to save him from dangerous circumstances, strengthening their emotional bond.

De(con)struction of Sequence

During a dream sequence while on a train ride through Russia in *Issue #55*, Yorick's emotional state reveals his continually more-complicated relationships with 355 and Beth. Entering 355's quarters on the train in search of his amulet — a token thought to be the reason Yorick and Ampersand survived the plague — Yorick sees her standing clad in dominatrix gear: low-rise pants with exposed thighs and buckles down the sides, long sleeve top with breasts exposed, all pleather, and a leather whip, in an aggressive stance with legs spread, an end of the whip in each hand, resting on her knees (15).[7] Yorick, always the naïve male, assumes he's intruding, but 355 tells him to enter and close the door, while she crawls towards him across the bed, saying "Nothing you haven't seen before, right?" (16). Yorick stands, dumbfounded. 355 says, "I'm your friend, aren't I? [...] Then I have to tell you you're making a terrible mistake." Yorick replies, "What does that mean?" "You already know" 355 says as the text bubble trails off to the right corner of the right-hand page, implying that Yorick's pursuit of Beth is "a mistake," producing a sense of eroticism made clear in Yorick's wide-eyed expression and slight smile. The page break prohibits what Will Eisner in *Comics and Sequential Art: Principles and Practices from the Legendary Cartoonist* (1985) identifies as a common human reaction to comics — the tendency to look at images out of sequence:

> The most important obstacle to surmount is the tendency of the reader's eye to wander. On any given page, for example, there is absolutely no way in which the artist can prevent the reading of the last panel before the first. The turning of the page does mechanically enforce some control [40].

The natural impulse is to look ahead to what is coming, more easily accomplished in comics than in other media. The break in the narrative, provided by the limitations of a page, prolongs the tension and eroticism. This pacing and page design functions within the larger narrative as what T.S. Eliot, in "Hamlet and His Problems," calls an objective correlative: "a set of objects, a chain of events which shall be the formula of that particular emotion; such that when the external facts, which must terminate in sensory experience, are given, the emotion is immediately evoked" (141). In comics, the use of the mechanical elements — closure, page design, panel shape, size, arrangement, and page placement — contribute to the pacing, thus evoking emotions. Tension and eroticism in Yorick's scene with 355 on the train are the product of similar situations dispersed throughout the series, each with similar mechanical structure and pacing, which rely on the proper placement of pages relative to one another, creating page breaks that directly contribute to developing the intended emotion.

The eroticism in the train sequence reflects, condenses, and modifies a similarly tense and expository scene. In the "Girl on Girl" story arc,[8] hetero- verses homo-sexuality plays a primary role, exposing the desires and frustrations between several characters. Aboard *The Whale*, a cruise ship turned heroin smuggling vessel, Yorick discovers the intimate relationship between Dr. Allison Mann and 355, a connection building from their first encounter in "Unmanned," the first story arc (116). The two women stand as the only lasting female presences during Yorick's life after the plague, remaining reliable, trustworthy, but unavailable sexually, rendering them as neither temptations to split him apart from Beth nor women seeking to enslave or kill him, marking themselves as clearly separate from the Amazons and other rogue groups. In *Issue #33*, after waking from a dream about being kicked out of class in grade school for joking about a girl who started menstruating — establishing Yorick as sexually conscious at a young and (im)mature age — Yorick starts to feel seasick, so he heads to Dr. Mann's cabin to ask for some Dramamine. The first page of the sequence consists of three horizontal panels that show Yorick asleep, a lamp falling from the nightstand and crashing on the floor, and Yorick with his hand over his mouth, saying "UK." The second page depicts the cruise ship in a horizontal panel across the top, Yorick retching over a railing in a square panel beside a square close-up of him with his wrist in front of his mouth. The coloring of the second page contains heavy blue tones, reflecting the cold wind blowing Yorick's blue cape and the choppy waves of the dark blue ocean. The bottom two panels depict Yorick walking into the wind, face concealed by the cape, then with his hood removed and opening the door to Dr. Mann's room apologetically: "Dr. Mann? Sorry to wake you, but I was wondering if you had any Dramamine or" ("Girl on Girl" 31–2). The coolness of the wind and the blue tones immediately shift on the next page to warmer purple as a large panel — more than two-thirds of the page — shows Yorick's back and the side of his face in the bottom left and 355 straddling Dr. Mann, both naked, on a bed on the right, and a word balloon coming from 355, which contains, "Yorick?" (33). 355 has her eyes open and head facing Yorick, while Dr. Mann's eyes remain tightly closed, and the bottom panel depicts Yorick with a quizzical facial expression, "…" in the text balloon. The following page includes three horizontal panels in which 355 dresses herself and two side-by-side panels across the bottom in which she exits the room. In the second panel, Yorick says, "This is officially the weirdest nightmare I've ever had" (34). Fundamental to the sequence and pacing is the placement of each page in relation to the advertisements.

To create suspense and lead into a shocking moment of revelation, the pages are arranged as follows in *Issue #33*: first page (Yorick asleep and waking up) on the right, second page (Yorick retching and opening the door) on the left of the next spread, full-page advertisement on the right, climax of the sequence on the left of the next spread, full-page ad on the right, and the concluding moment on the left of the next spread — a total of five pages. The placement of the first ad in the sequence establishes a clear pause in the succession of images, delaying what lies in the darkness beyond the door. The warmer tones in the image of Dr. Mann and 355 provide a clear juxtaposition with the cooler, calmer tones that precede the panel. The ad across from the page generates another pause, suspending the moment and allowing for the images to be digested multiple times. This is the first time 355's sexual relationship with a woman appears in visual form — her lesbian relationships have been the subject of many conversations with Yorick up until then — and it is also the first time Yorick has seen her with another woman. The shock to both the reader and Yorick — the visual depiction of her lesbianism has been thus far conveyed only in her stereotypically rugged clothing — is the first solid evidence of her sexual disconnect from Yorick, one alluded to but never actualized. Previously, as Lyndsay Brown writes in "Yorick, Don't Be A Hero: Productive Motion in *Y: The Last Man*,"

> 355 has always been coded as straight, and potentially interested in Yorick: the comic deals with both issues … by having 355 deny loving Yorick except in "the way a panther loves her helpless, annoying cub. As briefly as she has to" [Girl on Girl 24] [4].

The image of 355 engaging in sex with another woman casts the possibility of a relationship with Yorick into doubt, particularly when the woman is the third member of their tightly-knit group. The advertisement provides a breather while simultaneously prolonging the moment. Turning to the final page reveals the impact of Yorick's interruption: 355 dresses while saying, "This isn't what it looks like," conveying her remorse and embarrassment in front of the person she is supposed to be protecting. The remorse is later confirmed when 355 argues with Dr. Mann: 355 says, "It's done, Allison. Last night was a mistake. There's nothing else to —" (46). In dropping the advertisements in the conversion to trade paperback, the suspense and prolonged moments dissipate and readers can see the panels in the form of a two-page spread, instead of separate, disjointed spreads. In addition to revealing the disruption of the delayed sequence when switching formats, *Issue #33* also establishes a sequence of action that is later recycled for a very different purpose.

The use of similar sequences of events establishes a guide to allow readers to anticipate the narrative stream and create expectations when parallel situations appear later in the storyline. In addressing the aesthetic qualities of literature on which critics should focus, R.S. Crane writes that "we can similarly add new dimensions to the technical criticism of the drama or novel by fixing our attention not simply on the material character of the devices used but on the often striking formal modifications which the same devices undergo when they are employed for different poetic ends" (21).

Eliot's objective correlative reaffirms the notion of the deliberate pacing of a narrative as a function of art. Yorick's intrusion on Dr. Mann and 355 creates a momentary rift between him and 355 and leaves him in a vulnerable state, during which Kilina, captain of *The Whale*, passionately kisses him in her cabin. Yorick is "thereby unsettling his bond of monogamous heterosexual partnership with a moment of irrational desire" (Brown 3). The trauma of finally witnessing 355 having lesbian sex fractures his perception and leaves him open to being led astray by Kilina. The previously feared disruption of his relationship with Beth and the pain and desperation upon seeing 355 fuse in the scene from *Issue #55* analyzed previously in this study.

The circumstances of the cruise ship in *Issue #33* are adjusted in *Issue #55*, placing Yorick and 355 alone aboard a train. (Dr. Mann left the group in the "Kimono Dragons" story arc[9] after killing her father, who had made a number of clones of her, and entering a relationship with Rose, a woman stabbed by 355 after the sexual encounter in *Issue #33*, and for whom Dr. Mann sympathizes.) In the analyses already presented, the two scenes unfold in a similar manner: Yorick goes looking for something (Dramamine or the amulet) and bursts in on a hypersexual scene. *Issue #33* establishes Yorick as an intruder who disrupts and destroys a romantic moment, while *Issue #55* establishes Yorick as the reason for the moment, Dr. Mann having been removed from the group. Yorick stands in front of the dominatrix-clad 355, wondering what mistake she is referring to. In contrast to the pages preceding the moment between Dr. Mann and 355, the colors in the train sequence are much warmer red tones, conveying heat and excitement; clearly, both are read as sexual awareness ("Whys and Wherefores" 155–6). Instead of delaying the door opening until the third page, Yorick enters the room in the second of three panels on the first page (which appears on the right of a spread), exposing a partially nude 355 in the third and largest panel on the page. Sex is not the revelation in this sequence. Yorick has seen her in such a position before, with Dr. Mann. The sequence places him directly in the situation and prolongs the moment until the next page, which appears on the left of a spread across from a full-page advertisement, further prolonging the moment of revelation.

The act of turning the page of *Issue #55*, by readers eager to find out what "mistake" Yorick is making, reveals the decaying body of Beth reaching forward, skin melting from her bones, nose dripping a grotesque liquid that runs down and off her chin, shirt torn, clavicle poking through the rotting flesh, fingernails black, eyes glassed over, and maggots in her nose, mouth, and hair; a text balloon reads, "That you're gonna die if you come for me" ("Whys and Wherefores" 17). Yorick bursts out of the dream to find 355 sitting on a box beside him, watching while he sleeps. They sit and talk about Yorick's insecurities — whether he's going bald, whether he will still be attracted to Beth when he sees her after a five year separation. "That's longer than she and I dated," he says (20). After 355 says, "I've gotten fat as a house since the boys died," Yorick's attraction to her becomes apparent: He replies, "Oh, shut up. You're totally hotter now than when I first got saddled with you. You were all butch and scary back then. You're way more … *womanly* these days" (ellipsis, emphasis original 20). The image of a decaying Beth is quickly put out of Yorick's mind, as he and 355 wrestle around playfully in an obvious moment of sexual tension.

The act of turning the page from dominatrix 355 to the rotting mess that is Beth, prolonging the horrifying image, is destroyed in the trade paperback. When the advertisement is dropped from the page facing 355's erotic crawl toward Yorick, the full-page panel of decrepit Beth shifts forward, placing it on the same two-page spread. Noting Eisner's comment on the eye's tendency to wander, the moment of shock is obliterated before the reader can even read the sequence of panels on the preceding page. The eyes tend to linger in place when a page is turned, and, thus, the panel of 355 standing in the middle of the room, breasts exposed and holding a whip, shifts to reveal Beth's corpse. The build up to revealing the "mistake" is gone, and readers who only see the trade paperback (or read it first) experience an entirely different sequence of panels. The piercing yellows of Beth's skin and hair, much brighter than the black pleather and red tones of 355's room, immediately attract the eye, and the correlation to the scene in *Issue #33* can hardly be discerned; the placement of the ads is fundamental to establishing a pause and heightening tension. A crucial tool at the writer and artist's disposal is nullified in the conversion from 24-page floppy to squareback. The tool is essential to the objective correlative in each instance: panels are placed in deliberate sequence and must be revealed at a controlled pace. As Wolk writes, in the sequencing and placement of panels, a comic is "designed to read clearly and to provoke the strongest possible somatic response. You're supposed to react to it with your body before you think about it" (50). The immediate reaction to the image of Beth is one of disgust and repulsion. Without the delay advertisements provide—and in looking at these two sequences, it is apparent that neither is done accidentally—the immediate reaction circumvents the intended build up to the "somatic response." The growing medium of trade paperbacks kills much of the tension built into the structure of serialized comics; however, the future of the medium continues to trend away from the marketing and consumption of individual issues.

Comics as Future

Despite the lingering view of comics as a juvenile medium, the growing acceptance of the field as worthy of consideration continues to broaden the scope of acceptable literature in a seeming less literate culture. Michael Cart, in "A Graphic Novel Explosion," writes, "at a time when many observers are claiming that reading is on the wane, a literary art form that combines a tradition of excellent, carefully edited text with newly kinetic eye- and attention-grabbing visuals could be the salvation of young-adult reading" (1301). Cart correctly perceives the medium—rooted in the visual component of narrative—as exciting and able to attract the eye; and Cart also accurately claims that graphic novels "could, in fact, offer a new kind of interactive engagement between reader and book" (1301). The attachment to a particular comic series stems from the ability of the writer and artist to maintain interest. In "A Comic-Book World," Stephen E. Tabachnick notes that graphic novels offer all of the qualities expected from "good literary books," with the addition that comics "provid[e] the speed of apprehension and the excitingly scrambled, hybrid reading experience we get from watching, say, computer screens that are full of visuals as well as text" (25). Time is fundamental to comics, but not just in the sense that they can be read quickly or efficiently: as Eisner states, time is the

> dimension of human understanding that enables us to recognize and be empathetic to surprise, humor, terror and the whole range of human experience [and in] the manipulation of the elements of time to achieve a specific message or emotion, panels become a critical element [26].

Human perception is crucial to interpreting works of art, and, in this case, comics. The sequence of panels has a very critical and direct impact on the succession of events and images and how a reader responds to what is depicted.

To achieve maximum effect, the placement of specific events must be carefully selected. In tracing the objective correlatives in William Shakespeare's *King Lear*, Norman Maclean constructs his essay, "Episode, Scene, Speech, and Word: The Madness of Lear," in such a way that the elements of drama operate in a descending manner to produce in the audience/reader an awareness of Lear's madness. Maclean writes that, in establishing Lear's decline into madness as tragic, there must be "a moment everyone will recognize as 'the worst' and be willing to take as 'madness'" (600). As such, "Shakespeare uses actions, which are more discernible than emotions, to mark the descent into the pit" (600), and, thus, particularly because drama is the medium at hand, actions drive the narrative and "the protagonist becomes worthy of being a tragic hero" (601). The relationship between 355 relies on key moments of revelation — Yorick's acknowledgement of her (homo)sexuality, his acceptance of the subconscious fear rising up though his dreams, and, ultimately, 355's acknowledgement of her love for Yorick — to avoid becoming a simple, blasé "they love each other but just don't know it yet" tale.

When Yorick arrives in Paris to meet Beth and see her for the first time in five years, which for readers who began reading the series with the very first issue translates to six years and six months, the reunion lasts long enough for one more moment of revelation. After a four-page sex scene, Yorick and Beth stand naked in her room for seven more pages as they catch up on the past five years; however, the conversation reveals that each harbored false assumptions about the other: Yorick is shocked that Beth would be so conventional as to take his last name when they get married, the importance of finding out what really killed all (or most) of the men, and the nature of Yorick's nightmares: Yorick wants to believe it when he says, "My dreams were meaningless!" ("Whys and Wherefores" 57–61). The argument culminates in a two-page sequence. The first page features four horizontal panels, the first of which features Yorick consoling Beth, saying, "Are you ... are you crying? Seriously? Why the hell do I always do that?" to Beth, who has a hand over her face. In the second panel, Beth wipes tears from her eyes and says, "You *knew*. You knew all along," into the third panel with, "That's what your dreams were about. You *knew* what I was trying to tell you on the phone that day," concluding in the last panel: "You knew I was going to *break up* with you" (64). The next panel follows after a turn of the page and consists of a single panel of Yorick from the waist up, saying, "What?" And it is in that moment that Yorick realizes the futility of his search for Beth, and the loss he suffers. "What?" is the ultimate question, and the ultimate expression of despair. Within that single utterance, Yorick expresses anguish over the violence and brutality he confronted on his journey, the people he saw die, friendships severed, and love lost. But in that single word — "What?" — Yorick is simultaneously released from his attachment to Beth, free to find 355 and begin anew. And the delay for the utterance of "What?" — instead of positioned after the turn of the page — is miserably squandered when the advertisement gaps are filled in and the issue is placed in line and bound into a squareback. The question/answer appear to the reader before the moment has been prepared.

A Y in the Road

Douglas Wolk writes that because the medium is shifting, a new conversation needs to take place. Wolk says that, looking at the trend leading away from "24-page floppies" to trade paperback volumes, we need to decide "how to read and discuss comics now that they're very different from what they used to be" (11). The industry still maintains the serialize and then repackage into larger volumes way of publishing comics. But to engage in a new conversation about comics, we must accept two things: (1) David Carrier's assertion that "Comics are read like books, by one person, who by turning the pages determines how fast he or she moves through the narrative" (65), and (2) that we lose elements critical to the pacing and fundamental meaning of comics when the work is written for serialization and, later, the content is retained but the placement of the content is modified to fit the burgeoning mode of consumption: trade paperbacks.

Yorick's epiphany — his fear, desperation, freedom — hardly resonates unless we must turn the page.

Notes

1. Trade paperback refers to compilations of shorter comics, in the case of this essay a multi-issue comic book series collected into paperback volumes every six months, and later compiled into larger hardback volumes. Graphic novels differ in that they stand as deliberately constructed volumes, not a later reprint of multiple comic book issues or comic strips. Graphic novels include, for example, Brian K. Vaughan's *Pride of Baghdad* (2006).

2. Issues 1–55 of *Y: The Last Man* appeared on a monthly schedule, running from September 2002 to May 2007. Issues 56–60 appeared bimonthly from July 2007 to March 2008.

3. *Maus I: A Survivor's Tale: My Father Bleeds History* and *Maus II: A Survivor's Tale: And Here My Troubles Began*, portions of which appeared in Spiegelman's *RAW.*

4. August 2004 to August 2010, DC: Wildstorm.

5. President Jennifer Brown is later replaced after the United States holds a special election.

6. Issues 55–60.

7. All page numbers referring to the narrative apply to: Vaughan, Brian K. *Y: The Last Man: Whys and Wherefores.* New York: DC Comics, 2008, or other corresponding trade paperback forms of the series. Use of this source provides easy access to the panel sequences under discussion. However, juxtaposition of this source with the original serialized issues remains the crux of the argument. Using page

numbers from these sources promotes easy cross-referencing with the original issues, which lack pagination.

8. *Y: The Last Man*, issues 32–36.

9. Issues 43–48.

Works Cited

Brown, Lyndsay. "Yorick, Don't Be a Hero: Productive Motion in *Y: The Last Man*." *ImageTexT: Interdisciplinary Comics Studies* 3.1 (2006). Web. 8 March 2010.

Brownstein, Charles. "DC Pushes Graphic Novel, Backlist Growth." *Publishers Weekly* 248.31 (July 2001): 17. Print.

Carrier, David. *The Aesthetics of Comics*. University Park: Pennsylvania State University Press, 2001. Print.

Cart, Michael. "A Graphic-Novel Explosion." *Booklist* 99.14 (2003): 1301. Print.

Crane, R.S. Introduction. Crane 1–24.

_____, ed. *Critics and Criticism: Ancient and Modern*. Chicago: Chicago University Press, 1952. Print.

Eisner, Will. *Comics and Sequential Art: Principles and Practices from the Legendary Cartoonist*. Tamarac, FL: Poorhouse, 1985. Print.

Eliot, T.S. "Hamlet and His Problems." *Praising it New: The Best of the New Criticism*. Ed. Garrick Davis. 138–42. Print.

Maclean. Norman. "Episode, Scene, Speech, and Word: The Madness of Lear." Crane 595–615.

Tabachnick, Stephen E. "A Comic-Book World." *World Literature Today* 81.2 (2007): 24–8. Print.

Thurtle, Phillip. "The Acme Novelty Library: Comic Books, Repetition, and the Return of the New." *Configurations: A Journal of Literature, Science, and Technology* 15.3 (2007): 267–297. Print.

Vaughan, Brian K. writer, and Pia Guerra, penciller. *Y: The Last Man*. 10 vols. New York: DC Comics, 2003–2008. Print.

Wolk, Douglas. *Reading Comics: How Graphic Novels Work and What They Mean*. Cambridge, MA: Da Capo, 2007. Print.

About the Contributors

David **Bordelon** is an associate professor of English at Ocean County College in Toms River, New Jersey. His publications include essays on nineteenth-century transatlantic sensation, nineteenth-century popular fiction, and reading in Victorian America.

Rikke Platz **Cortsen** is a Ph.D. candidate at the University of Copenhagen working on a dissertation concerning time and space in comics. She has written articles and presented papers on various Scandinavian comics artists, *Arkham Asylum*, and time and space in the works of Alan Moore, the main subject of her master's thesis.

Luminita **Dragulescu** earned her Ph.D. from West Virginia University. Her research interests include American literature after World War II, African American literature, race theories, trauma studies, gender and sexuality studies, and life writing.

Andrew J. **Friedenthal** helped to co-found, and served as its resident dramaturge, the nonprofit theater company Odyssey Productions, based in New York City and Washington, D.C. With an M.A. in performance studies from New York University, he then moved to Austin, where he is a doctoral candidate in American studies at the University of Texas at Austin. His research interests focus on escapist entertainment.

Ellen M. **Gil-Gómez** is an associate professor of English at California State University, San Bernardino, where she teaches courses about Chicano/a literature and culture as well as women's studies and contemporary theory. She is the author of *Performing La Mestiza: Textual Representations of Lesbians of Color and the Negotiation of Identities* and numerous essays on identity and literature.

John Joseph **Hess** is a visiting assistant professor of American literature at the Harriet L. Wilkes Honors College of Florida Atlantic University. He earned his Ph.D. from the University of Notre Dame.

Jake **Jakaitis**, director of Undergraduate Studies in English at Indiana State University, has published work on Philip K. Dick, Don DeLillo, and Tim O'Brien. His articles and reviews have appeared in *Cultural Critique*, *Jump Cut*, *Science Fiction Studies*, and *African American Review*.

Michael P. **Millington** attends Indiana State University, pursuing an M.A. in postmodern American literature. His research explores the role of visual art in fiction and the discursive prose style of David Foster Wallace's fiction and nonfiction.

Martyn **Pedler** is a Ph.D. candidate at the University of Melbourne who is working on "X-Ray Vision," his interdisciplinary thesis on superhero narratives. His critical work on comic books has also been published in *Animation: An Interdisciplinary Journal, Overland,* and *The Contemporary Comic Book Superhero.*

Pamela J. **Rader** is an associate professor of English at Georgian Court University in New Jersey, where she teaches world, women's, and multi-ethnic literatures. She continues to publish on the works of Sandra Cisneros, Maryse Condé, Edwidge Danticat, Louise Erdrich, Marjane Satrapi, and other contemporary writers.

Julia **Round** lectures in the Media School at Bournemouth University, U.K., and edits the academic journal *Studies in Comics.* She has published on cross-media adaptation, television and discourse analysis, the application of literary terminology to comics, the graphic novel redefinition, and the presence of gothic and fantastic motifs and themes in this medium.

Daniel **Stein** holds a Ph.D. in American studies from the University of Göttingen, where he is an associate in the research unit Popular Seriality — Aesthetics and Practice. He is writing a book on authorship in American superhero comics. He has co-edited *American Studies as Media Studies* and *Comics: Zur Geschichte und Theorie eines populärkulturellen Mediums* and has published work on comics in the *International Journal of Comic Art* and *Studies in Comics.*

James F. **Wurtz** is an associate professor of English at Indiana State University, where he is also a faculty member in the Liberal Studies program. He has published articles on James Joyce, Virginia Woolf, Elizabeth Bowen, and British First World War narratology. He has also published a critical edition of the Irish writer J.S. Le Fanu's first novel, *The Cock and Anchor: Being a Chronicle of Old Dublin City.*

Index